NORTH AMERICAN INDIAN LIFE

Customs and Traditions
of 23 Tribes

EDITED BY
ELSIE CLEWS PARSONS

ILLUSTRATED BY
C. GRANT LA FARGE

DOVER PUBLICATIONS, INC.
New York

Published in Canada by General Publishing Company, Ltd., 30 Lesmill Road, Don Mills, Toronto, Ontario.

Published in the United Kingdom by Constable and Company, Ltd., 3 The Lanchesters, 162–164 Fulham Palace Road, London W6 9ER.

This Dover edition, first published in 1992, is an unabridged republication of the work originally published under the title *American Indian Life by Several of Its Students* by B. W. Huebsch, Inc., New York, in 1922. Those plates originally in color have been converted to black and white for the present edition.

Manufactured in the United States of America
Dover Publications, Inc., 31 East 2nd Street, Mineola, N.Y. 11501

Library of Congress Cataloging-in-Publication Data

North American Indian life : customs and traditions of 23 tribes / edited by Elsie Clews Parsons ; illustrated by C. Grant La Farge.
     p.   cm.
  Originally published: New York : B.W. Huebsch, 1922.
  ISBN 0-486-27377-6 (pbk.)
  1. Indians of North America—Social life and customs. 2. Indians of Mexico—Social life and customs. I. Parsons, Elsie Worthington Clews.
E98.S7N63   1992
972'.00497—dc20   92-22904
                                                 CIP

TABLE OF CONTENTS

PAGE

PREFACE I

INTRODUCTION 5
By A. L. Kroeber, Professor of Anthropology, University of California . .

PLAINS TRIBES:

TAKES-THE-PIPE, A CROW WARRIOR 17
By Robert H. Lowie, Associate Professor of Anthropology, University of California

A CROW WOMAN'S TALE 35
By Robert H. Lowie, Associate Professor of Anthropology, University of California

A TRIAL OF SHAMANS 41
By Robert H. Lowie, Associate Professor of Anthropology, University of California

SMOKING-STAR, A BLACKFOOT SHAMAN 45
By Clark Wissler, Curator of Anthropology, American Museum of Natural History

TRIBES OF THE MIDDLE WEST:

LITTLE-WOLF JOINS THE MEDICINE LODGE 63
By Alanson Skinner, Assistant Curator, Public Museum, Milwaukee

THUNDER-CLOUD, A WINNEBAGO SHAMAN, RELATES AND PRAYS 75
By Paul Radin, Late of the Department of Anthropology, University of California

HOW MESKWAKI CHILDREN SHOULD BE BROUGHT UP 81
By Truman Michelson, Ethnologist, Bureau of American Ethnology, Smithsonian Institution

EASTERN TRIBES:

IN MONTAGNAIS COUNTRY 87
By Frank G. Speck, Professor of Anthropology, University of Pennsylvania

HANGING-FLOWER, THE IROQUOIS 99
By Alexander A. Goldenweiser, Lecturer in Anthropology, New School of Social Research

Table of Contents

PAGE

THE THUNDER POWER OF RUMBLING-WINGS 107
By M. R. Harrington, Ethnologist, Museum of the American Indian, Heye
Foundation

TOKULKI OF TULSA 127
By John R. Swanton, Ethnologist, Bureau of American Ethnology, Smithsonian Institution

TRIBES OF THE SOUTH-WEST:

SLENDER-MAIDEN OF THE APACHE 147
By P. E. Goddard, Curator of Ethnology, American Museum of Natural
History

WHEN JOHN THE JEWELER WAS SICK 153
By A. M. Stephen, Sometime Resident Among the Hopi and Navaho

WAIYAUTITSA OF ZUÑI, NEW MEXICO 157
By Elsie Clews Parsons, Member of the Hopi Tribe

ZUÑI PICTURES 175
By Stewart Culin, Curator of Anthropology, Brooklyn Institute Museum

HAVASUPAI DAYS 179
By Leslie Spier of the Department of Sociology, University of Washington

EARTH-TONGUE, A MOHAVE 189
By A. L. Kroeber, Professor of Anthropology, University of California

MEXICAN TRIBES:

THE CHIEF SINGER OF THE TEPECANO 203
By J. Alden Mason, Assistant Curator in Anthropology, Field Museum of
Natural History

THE UNDERSTUDY OF TEZCATLIPOCA 237
By Herbert Spinden, Lecturer in Anthropology, Harvard University

HOW HOLON CHAN BECAME THE TRUE MAN OF HIS PEOPLE 251
By Sylvanus G. Morley, Associate, Carnegie Institution of Washington

THE TOLTEC ARCHITECT OF CHICHEN ITZA 265
By Alfred M. Tozzer, Professor of Anthropology, Harvard University, and
Curator Middle American Archaeology, Peabody Museum

PACIFIC COAST TRIBES:

WIXI OF THE SHELLMOUND PEOPLE 273
By N. C. Nelson, Associate Curator of North American Archæology,
American Museum of Natural History

ALL IS TROUBLE ALONG THE KLAMATH 289
By T. T. Waterman, Ethnologist, Museum of the American Indian, Heye
Foundation

Table of Contents

PAGE

SAYACH'APIS, A NOOTKA TRADER 297
By Edward Sapir, Head of Division of Anthropology, Geological Survey of Canada

NORTHERN ATHABASCAN TRIBES:

WINDIGO, A CHIPEWYAN STORY 325
By Robert H. Lowie, Associate Professor of Anthropology, University of California

CRIES-FOR-SALMON, A TEN'A WOMAN 337
By T. B. Reed and Elsie Clews Parsons. Mr. Reed is an Alaskan (Ten'a) student in Hampton Institute

ESKIMO:

AN ESKIMO WINTER 363
By Franz Boas, Professor of Anthropology, Columbia University

APPENDIX 381

NOTES ON THE VARIOUS TRIBES

ILLUSTRATOR'S NOTES

Preface

"SHE always says she will come, and sometimes she comes and sometimes she doesn't come. I was so surprised when I first came out here to find that Indians were like that," the wife of the Presbyterian Missionary in an Indian town in New Mexico was speaking, as you readily infer, on her servant question.

"Where did you get your impressions of Indians before you came here?"

"From Fenimore Cooper. I used to take his books out, one right after the other from the library at New Canaan, Connecticut, where I grew up."

At that time, during the youth of this New Englander past middle age, few anthropological monographs on Indian tribes had been written, but it is doubtful if such publications are to be found in New England village libraries even to-day, and it is more than doubtful that if they were in the libraries anybody would read them; anthropologists themselves have been known not to read them. Between these forbidding monographs and the legends of Fenimore Cooper, what is there then to read for a girl who is going to spend her life among Indians or, in fact, for anyone who just wants to know more about Indians?

From these considerations, among others, this book was conceived. The idea of writing about the life of the Indian for the General Reader is not novel, to be sure, to anthropologists. Appearances to the contrary, anthropologists have no wish to keep their science or any part of it esoteric. They are too well aware, for one thing, that facilities for the pursuit of anthropology are dependent more or less on popular interest, and that only too often tribal cultures have disappeared in America as elsewhere before people became interested enough in them to learn about them.

Nevertheless, the cost of becoming popular may appear excessive —not only to the student who begrudges the time and energy that must be drawn from scientific work, but to the scientist who is asked

1

to popularize his study in terms repugnant to his sense of truth or propriety. Hitherto, American publishers appear to have proposed only to bring Fenimore Cooper up to date, merely to add to the over-abundant lore of the white man about the Indian.

In this book the white man's traditions about Indians have been disregarded. That the writers have not read other traditions from their own culture into the culture they are describing is less certain. Try as we may, and it must be confessed that many of us do not try very hard, few, if any of us, succeed, in describing another culture, of ridding ourselves of our own cultural bias or habits of mind. Much of our anthropological work, to quote from a letter from Spinden, "is not so much definitive science as it is a cultural trait of ourselves."

For one thing we fail to see the foreign culture as a whole, noting only the aspects which happen to interest us. Commonly, the interesting aspects are those which differ markedly from our own culture or those in which we see relations to the other foreign cultures we have studied. Hence our classified data give the impression that the native life is one unbroken round, let us say, of curing or weather-control ceremonials, of prophylaxis against bad luck, of hunting, or of war. The commonplaces of behavior are overlooked, the amount of "common sense" is underrated, and the proportion of knowledge to credulity is greatly underestimated. In other words the impression we give of the daily life of the people may be quite misleading, somewhat as if we described our own society in terms of Christmas and the Fourth of July, of beliefs about the new moon or ground hogs in February, of city streets in blizzards and after, of strikes and battleships. Unfortunately, the necessarily impressionistic character of the following tales, together with their brevity, renders them, too, subject to the foregoing criticism. Of this, Dr. Kroeber in the Introduction will have more to say, as well as of his impression of how far we have succeeded in presenting the psychological aspects of Indian culture.

The problems presented by the culture, problems of historical reconstruction, Dr. Kroeber will also refer to, but discussion of the problems, of such subjects as culture areas, as the current phrase goes, as diffusion and acculturation, will not be presented in this book—it is a book of pictures. But if the reader wants to learn of how the problems are being followed up, he is directed to the bibliographical notes in the appendix. If the pictures remain pictures for him, well and good; if they lead him to the problems, good and better. Anthropology is short on students.

E. C. P.

Introduction

THE old ethnology, like every science in its beginnings, was speculative. The new ethnology is inductive. Fifty or sixty years ago the attempt was first made to read the riddle of human origins and substantiate the answer by facts. One student after another—Spencer, Tylor, Morgan, and others—thought out a formula that seemed a reasonable explanation of how some activity of human civilization—institutional, religious, or inventive—began, developed, and reached its present condition; and then ransacked the accounts of travelers, missionaries, and residents among primitive tribes for each bit of evidence favorable to his theory. Thus the origin of marriage was plausibly traced back to the matriarchate and ultimate promiscuity, of society to totemic clans, of the historic religions to a belief in souls and ghosts, of pottery to clay-lined basketry. Twenty-five years ago this theory fabrication was in full swing; and in many non-scientific quarters it still enjoys vogue and prestige.

It is plain that the method of these evolutionary explanations was deductive. One started with an intuition, a rationalization, a guess, then looked for corroborative facts. Inevitably, all contrary facts tended to be ignored or explained away. What was more, the evidence being adduced solely with reference to whether it fitted or failed to fit into the theory under examination, it was torn from its natural relations of time, space, and association. This was very much as if a selection of statements, made by an individual on a given topic, were strung together, without reference to the circumstances under which he uttered them and without the qualifications which he attached. By the use of this method of ignoring *context,* a pretty good case might be made out to show that the Kaiser was really a pacificist republican at heart, Huxley a devout if not quite regular Christian, and Anthony Comstock a tolerant personality. Roosevelt could be portrayed as either a daring radical or as a hide-bound reactionary. Just such contrary interpretations did emerge in the older ethnology. Totems, for instance, were held by one "authority" to have had their origin in magical rites concerned with food-supply, by another in a sort of nick-names, by a third in a primitive, mystic adumbration of the concept of society itself.

Gradually it began to be recognized by students that this method might be necessary in the law-courts, where each party advowedly contends for his own interests, but that in science it led to exciting wrangling rather more than to progress toward impartial truth. And so a new ethnology modestly grew up which held for its motto: "All possible facts first, then such inferences as are warranted." "All facts" means not only all items but also these items in their *natural* order: the sequence in which they occur, their geographical relation, the degree to which they are associated.

The anthropologist no longer compares marriage customs from all over the world as they come to hand. He realizes that marriage is likely to be a different rite as it is practiced respectively among peoples, with and without civil government, or among nations that have come under the influence of a world religion or remain in a status of tribal ceremony. The whole culture of the group must be more or less known before the history and meaning of an institution can become intelligible. Detached from its culture mass, a custom reveals as little of its functioning as an organ dissected out of the living body.

Equally important for the interpretation of ethnic facts, are their geographical associations, their distribution. Is a custom or invention peculiar to one people or is it shared by many distinct peoples occupying a continuous area? Such a question may seem trivial. But the answer usually bears heavy significance. A unique institution, or one found in various spots but in disconnected ones, is, other things equal, either of recent and independent origin in each locality, or it is a lingering survival of a custom that was once wide-spread. In short, it represents the beginning or end of a process of development.

On the other hand, where we find an art or institution possessed in common by dozens or hundreds of tribes situated without any gaps between them on the map, it would be far-fetched to assume that each of them independently evolved this identical phenomenon. Why presuppose a hundred parallel causes, each operating quite separately, when one will suffice, in view of the fact that human beings imitate each other's manners and borrow knowledge. We know that Christianity, gun-powder, the printing press, were originated but once. Even with history wiped out, we could infer as much, from their universality among the nations of Europe.

Now this is just the situation as regards primitive peoples. Their history *has* been wiped out—it was never preserved by themselves or their neighbors. But knowledge of the geographical occurrence of a custom or invention, usually affords rather reliable insight into its history, sometimes into its origin. When the available information shows that Indian corn was grown by all the tribes from Chile and Brazil to Arizona and Quebec, it is evident that the history of native American agriculture is as much of a unit, essentially, as the history of Christianity or of fire-arms. It is a story of *invention* only at its outset, of *diffusion* and amplification through its greater length. When pottery is further discovered to possess almost exactly the same aboriginal distribution as maize, it becomes likely that this art, too, was devised but once; and likely, further, that it was invented at about the same time as maize culture and diffused with it.

By evidence such as this, reënforced by the insight gained from the stratification of prehistoric objects preserved in caves and in the ground, native, American history is being reconstructed for some thousands of years past. The outline of this history runs about as follows.

Eight, ten, or twelve thousand years ago, contemporary with the last phase of the Old Stone Age of Europe or the opening there of the New Stone Age, man, for the first time, entered the New World. He came from Asia across Behring Strait, a narrow gap with an island stepping-stone in the middle, and probably frozen over solidly in mid-winter. In race he was Mongoloid—not Chinese, Japanese, or Mongol proper, but *proto-Mongoloid;* a straight-haired type, medium in complexion, jaw protrusion, nose-breadth, and inclining probably to round-headedness; an early type, in short, from which the Chinese, the Malay, and the Indian grew out, like so many limbs from a tree. This proto-Mongoloid stock must have been well established in Asia long before. This is morally certain from the fact that the proto-Negroids and proto-Caucasians were living at least ten to fifteen thousand years earlier, as attested by their discovered fossils, Grimaldi man and Cro-Magnon man.

Well, somewhere about 8000 B. C., then, bands of proto-Mongolians began to filter in through the easy, northwest gate of America. Others pushed them behind; before them, to the south, the country was ever more pleasantly tempting, and life easier. They multiplied, streamed down the Pacific coast, wandered across to the Atlantic, entered the tropics in fertile Mexico, defiled through Panama, and slowly overran South America. Separate groups of entrants into Alaska may have brought distinct languages with them; or, if they all came with one mother-tongue, their migrations to diverse environments and long, long separations provided ample opportunity for differentiation into dialects, languages, and families. The history of speech in the Old World covered by records, is but little more than three thousand years old, just a third of the ten thousand years with which we are dealing in America. Multiply by three the difference between twentieth-century English and ancient Sanskrit or one of its modern representatives such as Bengali, and there is just about the degree of speech distinctness that exists between the American language families, such as Siouan and Algonkin, Aztec and Maya.

So with the racial type. Fundamentally, one physical type stretches from Cape Horn to Alaska. Superficially, it is intricately variegated—here with round heads, there with long—with short faces or hooked noses or tall statures or wavy hair, in this or that group of tribes. In fact, it might seem that during ten thousand years the variety of climates and habitats might have succeeded in moulding the Indian into racial types of even greater distinctness than we encounter; until we remember that he found the two continents empty, and was never subjected to mixtures with white or black or dwarf races, to mixtures such as were experienced by many of the peoples of the eastern hemisphere.

What the first immigrants brought with them in culture was rudimentary. They kept dogs, but no other domesticated animal. They were not yet agricultural, and subsisted on what they wrested from nature. They knew something of weaving baskets and mats; clothed and housed themselves; probably had harpoons and possibly bows; made fire with the drill; cut with flint knives; and believed in magic, spirits, and the perpetuity of the soul.

In and about southern Mexico they prospered the fastest, became most numerous, acquired some leisure, began to organize themselves socially, and developed cults of increasing elaborateness. They "invented" maize-agriculture and pottery; architecture in stone; irrigation; cloth weaving and cotton growing; the smelting and casting of copper, silver, and gold; a priesthood, calendar system, picture-writing, pantheon of gods, and sacrifices; and accustomed themselves to town life.

Gradually these amplifications of culture spread: slowly to the north, more rapidly and completely to the south, into the similar environment of Colombia and Peru. Not all of the civilization devised in Yucatan and Guatemala, was carried into South America. Writing and time reckoning, for instance, never squeezed through the Isthmus, and the Incas got along with traditions and records of strings. On the other hand the South Americans, also growing populous and wealthy, added some culture elements of their own—bronze alloying, the hammock, the Pan's pipe, the balance scale, the surgical art of trephining the skull, the idea of a vast, compactly organized empire.

In Peru then, and in Mexico, two nearly parallel centers of civilization grew up during thousands of years; sprung from the same foundation, differentiated in their superstructures, that of Mexico evidently the earlier, and, at the time of discovery, slightly more advanced. The Peruvian civilization, if we include with it those of western Colombia and Bolivia, rayed itself out through the whole southern continent, becoming feebler and more abbreviated with increasing distance from its focus.

The South Mexican center similarly diffused its light through most of the northern continent. First its influences traveled to northern Mexico and the Southwest of the United States—Arizona and New Mexico, the seat of the Cliff-dwellers. There they took new root and then spread northward and eastward—altered, diluted, with much omitted. We may compare Mexico to a manufacturing district, where capital, inventiveness, resources and industry, flourish in mutual alliance; the Southwest to one of its outlets, a sort of distributing point or jobbing center, which imports, both for its own consumption and for re-export; the articles of trade in this case being elements of civilization—inventions, knowledge, arts.

Throughout, it was a flow of things of the mind, not a drift of the bodies of men; of culture, not of populations. And the radiation was ever northward, counter to the drift of the migrations which had begun thousands of years before, and which, in part, seem to have continued to crowd southward even during the period of northward spread of civilization. It was much as in Europe fifteen hundred years ago, when Goth and Vandal and Frank and Lombard pounded their way southward into the Roman empire, but the civilization of Rome—writing, learning, money, metallurgy, architecture, Christianity, laws—streamed ever against the human pressure, until the farthest barbarians of the North Sea had become, in some measure, humanized.

Thus the Southwest learned from Mexico to build in stone, to grow and weave cotton, to irrigate, to obey priests, and in some rude measure to organize the year into a calendar. None of these culture elements traveled farther. But the maize-beans-squash agriculture, pottery-making, the organization of cult societies, the division of the community into clans, reckoning descent from one parent only, some tendency toward town-life and the confederation of towns, all of which the Southwest had also acquired from Mexico, it passed on to its neighbors, notably to those of the Gulf States between Louisiana and Georgia. Here, these institutions were once more worked over and, in the main, reduced, and then some of them passed on northward, first to the Mound-builders of the Ohio valley, and then to the Iroquois of New York. From the Iroquois, in turn, some of their Algonkian neighbors and foes were just beginning to be ready to learn certain betterments, when the white man came and swept their cultures into memory.

We have thus, a series of culture centers—Mexico, Southwest, Southeast, Iroquois, Atlantic Algonkins—of descending order of advancement, and subsequent to one another in time. They constitute a ladder of culture development, and, although undated, represent a real sequence of history.

One area was but haltingly and sparsely infiltrated from the Southwest: the North Pacific Coast, centering in British Colombia. In this mild and rich environment a native culture grew up that, in the main, went its own way. It did not attain to the heights of Mexico, scarcely even equaled the Southwest. Pottery and agriculture failed to reach it. But out of its own resources, it developed, independently, a number of the arts and institutions which the remainder of North America drew from Mexico: clan organization and cult societies, for instance, the beginnings of a calendar and cloth weaving. And it added features, all its own: plank houses, totem poles, a remarkable style of decorative art, a society based on wealth. Here then we have a minor, but mainly independent culture center of the greatest interest.

In a still smaller way, and without as great a freedom from southern influences, the tribes of the treeless Plains, in the heart of the continent, developed a little civilization of their own. This was founded on what they had originally got from the Southwest and Southeast, was remodeled on the basis of an almost exclusive dependence on the buffalo, and underwent a brief and stirring efflorescence from the seventeenth to the nineteenth century, after the Plains tribes had got horses from the Spaniards. Here, then, grew up customs and appliances like the tepee, the travois, the camp-circle, warfare as a game with "coups" as counters.

Similarly in the far north, along the shores of the Arctic, where the Eskimo spread themselves. Here, almost nothing penetrated from Mexico, but stern necessity forced a special inventiveness on the mechanical side and the way was near for the entrance of influences from Asia, some few of which may have diffused beyond the Eskimo to the North Pacific Coast tribes.

Such, then, are the outlines of the history of the native, American race and civilization. It is a long and complexly rich story, only partly unraveled. Those who wish it in greater fullness will find it in Wissler's *The American Indian*. Only enough has been sketched here to show that modern anthropology is an inductive science with a minimum of speculation; that it aims at truly historical reconstructions and is beginning to achieve them; and that it lies in the nature of its tasks to distinguish and analyze the several native culture-areas or local types of Indians before proceeding to conclusions based on combinations.

Therefore it is, that many small items of ethnic knowledge acquire considerable importance. From the average man's point of view, it is of little moment that the Zuñi farm and the Yurok and Nootka do not, or that the former refuse to marry their dead wives' sisters and the latter insist on it. At best, such bits of facts have for the layman only the interest of idle curiosities, of antiquarian fragments. To the specialist, however, they become dependable means to a useful end, much as intimate knowledge of the position of arteries and nerves serves the surgeon.

But, just as the exact understanding of anatomy which modern medicine enjoys, bulks to infinitely more than any one anatomist could ever have discovered, so with ethnology. No one mind could ever observe or assemble and digest all the cultural facts that are needed. Many workers are busy, have been systematically busy for two or three generations. Though they may, now and then, enliven their toil by a scientific quarrel over this or that set of facts or interpretation, they are inherently coöperating, laboring cumulatively at a great joint enterprise. Sometimes, they divide their interests topically: one specializes on social customs, another on material arts, a third along lines of religion. But, in the main, the cultural context is so important that it has been found most productive for each investigator to try to learn everything possible about all the phases of culture of a single tribe, or, at most, of two or three tribes.

To do this, he "goes into the field." That is, he takes up his residence, for a continuous period or repeatedly for several years, among a tribe, on its reservation or habitat. He enters into as close relations as possible with its most intelligent or authoritative members. He acquires all he can of their language, reduces it to writing, perhaps compiles texts, a dictionary or grammar. Day after day he records notes from visual observation or the memory of the best informants available on the industries, beliefs, government, family life, ceremonies, wars, and daily occupations of his chosen people. And with all this, there flow in his personal experiences and reactions. The final outcome is a monograph—a bulky, detailed, often tedious, but fundamental volume, issued by the government or a scientific institution.

It is from intensive studies such as these, that the stories which form the present volume have sprung as a by-product. Have sprung as a sort of volunteer crop, it might be said, under the stimulus of the editorial suggestion of Dr. Parsons. The monographs have a way of sticking pretty closely to the objective facts recorded. The mental workings of the people whose customs are described, are subjective, and therefore much more charily put into print. The result is that every American anthropologist with field experience, holds in his memory many interpretations, many convictions as to how his Indians feel, why they act as they do in a given situation, what goes on inside of them. This psychology of the Indian is often expressed by the frontiersman, the missionary and trader, by the man of the city, even. But it has been very little formulated by the very men who know most, who have each given a large block of their lives to acquiring intensive and exact information about the Indian and his culture.

There is, thus, something new, something of the nature of an original contribution, in each of these stories; and they are reliable. To many of us, the writing of our tale has been a surprise and of value to ourselves. We had not realized how little we knew of the workings of the Indian mind on some sides, how much on others.

The fictional form of presentation devised by the editor has definite merit. It allows a freedom in depicting or suggesting the thoughts and feelings of the Indian, such as is impossible in a formal, scientific report. In fact, it incites to active psychological treatment, else the tale would lag. At the same time the customs depicted are never invented. Each author has adhered strictly to the social facts as he knew them. He has merely selected those that seemed most characteristic, and woven them into a plot around an imaginary Indian hero or heroine. The method is that of the historical novel, with emphasis on the history rather than the romance.

There is but one important precedent for this undertaking, [1] and that single-handed instead of collective, and therefore depictive of one people only, the Keresan Pueblos. This is *The Delight Makers* of Bandelier, archæologist, archivist, historian, and ethnologist of a generation ago; and this *novel* still renders a more comprehensive and coherent view of native Pueblo life than any scientific volume on the Southwest.

The present book, then, is a picture of native American life, in much the sense that a series of biographies of one statesman, poet, or common citizen from each country of Europe would yield a cross-

[1] In this connection Grinnell's recent story of the Cheyennes, "Where Buffalo Ran" should not be overlooked. Ed.

sectional aspect of the civilization of that continent. France and Russia, Serbia and Denmark, would each be represented with its national peculiarities; and yet the blended effect would be that of a super-national culture. So with our Indians. It is through the medium of the intensive and special coloring of each tribal civilization, that the common elements of Indian culture are brought out most truthfully, even though somewhat indirectly.

There are only a few points at which the composite photograph, produced by these twenty-seven stories, should be used with caution, and these disproportions or deficiencies are unavoidable at present. The first of them is religion. The book is likely to make the impression that some sixty per cent. of Indian life must have been concerned with religion. This imbalance is due to the fact that religion has become the best known aspect of Indian life. Ritual and ceremony follow exact forms which the native is able to relate with accuracy from memory, long after the practices have become defunct. Moreover, once his confidence is gained, he often delights in occupying his mind with the matters of belief and rite that put an emotional stamp on his youth. Social usages are much more plastic, more profoundly modified to suit each exigency as it arises, and therefore more difficult to learn and portray. The mechanical and industrial arts have a way of leaving but pallid recollections, once they have been abandoned for the white man's manufactures; and to get them recreated before one's eyes is usually very time-consuming. Thus, through a tacit coördination of Indians and ethnologists to exploit the vein of most vivid productivity, religion has become obtruded; and some excess must be discounted. Yet the overproportion is perhaps all for the best. For the Indian is, all in all, far more religious than we, and the popular idea errs on the side of ignoring this factor. The stories are substantially truthful in their effect, in that the average Indian did spend infinitely more time on affairs of religion than of war, for instance.

On the side of economics and government, the book is underdone. It is so, because ethnological knowledge on these topics is insufficient. It is difficult to say why. Possibly ethnologists have not become sufficiently interested or trained. But economic and political institutions are unquestionably difficult to learn about. They are the first to crumble on contact with Anglo-Saxon or Spanish civilization. So they lack the definiteness of ceremonialism, and their reconstruction from native memories is a bafflingly intricate task.

As regards daily life, personal relations, and the ambitions and ideals of the individual born into aboriginal society, in other words the social psychology of the Indian, we have done much better. In fact, collectively we have brought out much that is not to be found anywhere in the scientific monographs, much even that we had not realized could be formulated. This element seems to me to contain the greatest value of the book, and to be one that should be of permanent utility to historians and anthropologists, as well as to the public which is fortunately free from professional trammels. The exhibit of the workings of the Indian mind which these tales yield in the aggregate, impresses me as marked by a rather surprising degree of insight and careful accuracy.

Only at one point have we broken down completely: that of humor. One might conclude from this volume that humor was a factor absent from Indian life. Nothing would be more erroneous. Our testimony would be unanimous on this score. And yet we have been unable to introduce the element. The failure is inevitable. Humor is elusive because its understanding presupposes a feeling for the exact psychic situation of the individual involved, and this in turn implies thorough familiarity with the finest nuances of his cultural setting. We could have introduced Indian jokes, practical ones and witty ones, but they would have emerged deadly flat, and their laughs would have sounded made to order. An Indian himself, or shall we say, a contemporary of the ancients, may let his fancy play, and carry over to us something of his reaction: witness Aristophanes, Plautus, Horace. But the reconstructor, if he is wise, leaves the task unattempted. That prince of historical novelists, Walter Scott, for the most part collapses sadly when he tries to inject into his romances of the Middle Ages, the humor that marks his modern novels of Scotland; and so far as he salvages anything, it is by substituting the humor of his own day for the actual mediæval one. *Hypatia* is a superb picture of the break-down of Roman civilization; but how silly and boring are its humorous passages! A greater artist, in *Thaïs,* and another in *Salammbô,* have wisely evaded attempting the impossible, and, at most, touched the bounds of irony. Where the masters have succumbed or refrained, it is well that we scientists, novices in the domain of fiction, should hold off; though we all recognize both the existence and the importance of humor in Inddian life. This element, then, the reader must accept our bare word for—or supply from his own discrimination and intuition.

A. L. KROEBER

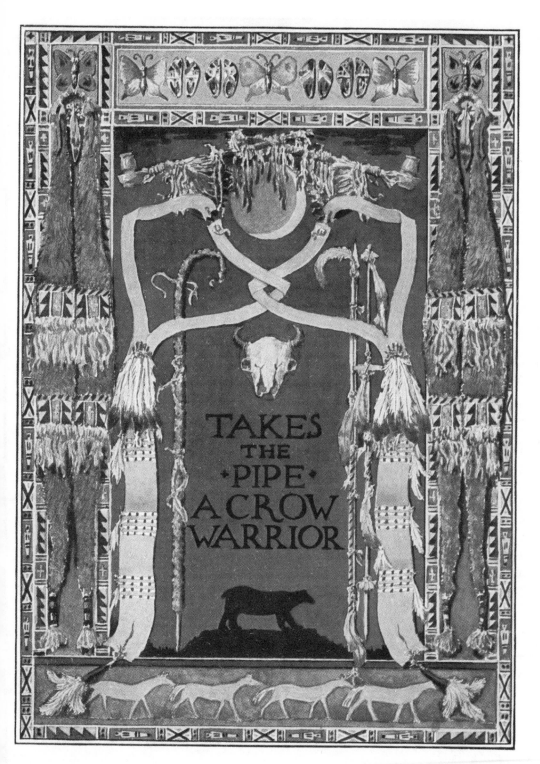

TAKES
THE
·PIPE·
A CROW
WARRIOR

Takes-the-pipe, a Crow Warrior

I

HORSES neighing, women scurrying to cover, the report of guns, his mother, Pretty-weasel, gashing her legs for mourning,—that was Takes-the-pipe's earliest memory. Later he learned that his own father, a famous warrior of the Whistling-water clan, had fallen in the fight and that his "father," Deaf-bull, was really a paternal uncle who had married the widow. No real father could have been kinder than Deaf-bull. If anything, he seemed to prefer his brother's son to his own children, always petting him and favoring him with the choicest morsels.

When Pretty-weasel needed help in dressing a hide or pitching a tent, her sisters and cousins of the Sore-lip clan came as visitors, often bringing moccasins and gewgaws for their little clansman, Takes-the-pipe. One of the sisters stood out more clearly than the rest, a lusty wench who would pull Deaf-bull by the ear and pour water on his face when he took an afternoon nap. He in turn would throw her on the ground and tickle her till she bawled for mercy. Another salient figure was the grandmother, old Muskrat, who used to croon the boy to sleep with a lullaby: "The dog has eaten, he is smoking. Haha, huhu! Haha, huhu!" Whenever she came to the refrain she raised a wrinkled, mutilated hand, and snapped what remained of her fingers in the child's face.

The people were always traveling back and forth in those days. Now Takes-the-pipe was throwing stones into the Little Bighorn, then with other boys he was chasing moths in the Wolf Mountains. When he caught one he rubbed it against his breast, for they said that was the way to become a swift runner. One fall, the Mountain Crow traveled to the mouth of the Yellowstone to visit their kin of the River band. All winter was spent there. It was fun coasting down-hill on a buffalo-rib toboggan and spinning tops on the smooth ice. Each boy tried to upset his neighbor's with his own, and when he succeeded he would cry, "I have knocked you out!" Takes-the-pipe was a good player, but once he came home inconsolable because his fine new top was stolen, and another time a bigger lad had cheated, "knocking him out" with a stone deftly substituted for the wooden toy. His mother comforted him saying, "That boy is crazy! His father is of the Bad-honors clan, that's why he acts that way!"

Takes-the-pipe was still a little fellow when Deaf-bull made him a bow and arrows, and taught him to shoot. Now he ran about, letting fly his darts against birds and rabbits. There was ample chance to gain skill in archery. The boys would tie together a bundle of grass and set it on a knoll, then all shot at this target, and the winner took all his competitors' arrows. Whenever Takes-the-pipe brought home a sheaf of darts, his father would encourage him, saying, "You'll be like Sharp-horn, who always brings down his buffalo with the first shot." And when his son had killed his first cottontail, Deaf-bull proudly called Sliding-beaver, a renowned Whistling-water, feasted him royally and had him walk through camp, leading Takes-the-pipe mounted on his horse and proclaiming his success in a laudatory chant.

One spring there was great excitement. The supply of meat was exhausted, yet the buffalo remained out of sight. Scouts were sent to scour the country in search of game, but in vain. At last Sharp-horn offered to lure the buffalo by magic. At the foot of a cliff he had the men build a corral. He summoned Deaf-bull to be his assistant. "Bring me an old unbroken buffalo chip," he said. Takes-the-pipe found one, and together he and his father brought it to the shaman. "Someone is trying to starve us; my medicine is stronger than his; we will eat," said Sharp-horn. He smoothed the earth in his lodge and marked buffalo tracks all over. He put the chip on one of the tracks and on the chip a rock shaped like a buffalo's head, which he wore as a neck ornament. This rock he smeared with grease. "The buffalo are coming, bid the men drive them here," he said.

Deaf-bull went out and issued the orders received from Sharp-horn. On the heights above the corral, old men, women and children strung out in two diverging lines for the distance of a mile or two. The young men rode far out till they sighted the herd, got behind it and chased the game between the two lines nearer and nearer to the declivity. They drove them down into the corral. Some were killed in leaping, others stunned so they could be easily dispatched. That was a great day for Takes-the-pipe. He rode double with his father, and Deaf-bull was a person of consequence. Had he not assisted Sharp-horn? Then, too, he was a member of the Big Dog Society, and the Big Dogs were the police for that season with power to whip every man, woman or child who dared disobey Sharp-horn's orders.

After the hunt, the meat-racks sagged with the weight of the buffalo ribs, and the people made up for past want by gorging themselves with fat and tongues. One evening the Big Dogs held a feast and dance, the next evening the Fox society, then the Lumpwoods, and so on. There were promiscuous gatherings, too, where the valiant warriors rose to tell the assembled multitude about their exploits, while the old men exhorted the callow youths to emulate the example of their fathers and the camp reëchoed the ancient warriors' songs:—

> Sky and earth are everlasting,
> Men must die.
> Old age is a thing of evil,
> Charge and die!

On one of these occasions Takes-the-pipe was proudly listening to Deaf-bull's record. He would have been a chief, had he ever wrested a gun from an enemy in a hand-to-hand encounter; in every other essential he more than passed muster. Three times he had crawled into a Piegan camp and stolen horses picketed to their owners' tents; six times he had "counted coup" on enemies, touching them with his lance or bare hand; twice he had carried the pipe and returned with blackened face as leader of a victorious expedition.

While Takes-the-pipe was listening spell-bound to his father's narrative, he felt a sudden pinch. He turned round to smite his tormentor only to face Cherry-necklace, a boy somewhat older than himself. He was Sliding-beaver's son and that put a different complexion on the matter, for Sliding-beaver, like Deaf-bull, was a Whistling-water, so their sons might take what liberties they chose with each other and enjoy complete immunity. At present, however, Cherry-necklace had more important business than playing a trick on Takes-the-pipe. "Magpie," he whispered, "they are playing magpie." Off both boys dashed to a creek nearby, where some twenty lads were already assembled round a big fire. They smeared their faces with charcoal till one could hardly recognize his neighbor. "Now, we'll be magpies," they said, "Takes-the-pipe is a swift runner, he shall lead." They scampered back to camp. The women, seeing them approach in their disguise, snatched their meat from the racks to hide it inside their tents. But Takes-the-pipe had already fixed his eye on some prime ribs, pounced upon them and carried off his prize, followed by the other boys, each vanishing with what booty he could safely capture.

It was a great gathering about the fireplace by the stream. One of the lads strutted up and down as a crier and announced, "Takes-the-pipe has stolen the best piece!" Then he and a few others who had won like delicacies were granted their choice of the spoils, whereupon all feasted. When they had done eating, the oldest boy declared, "We'll remain seated here. If anyone gets up, we'll rub our hands with this grease and smear it over his body." So they sat still for a long time. At last Cherry-necklace forgot about the warning and got up. In an instant they were upon him like a pack of wolves. Here was a fine chance for Takes-the-pipe to get even for that pinch; he daubed Cherry-necklace's face all over with the fat. Others followed suit and soon his body glistened with grease. He leaped into the creek to wash it off, but the water glided off the fat.

II

The people were moving along the Bighorn, with the long lodge poles dragging along the ground. Some dozen girls with toy tents were transporting them in imitation of their mothers. Takes-the-pipe was riding with the Hammers, a boys' club patterned on the men's societies. The members treated dogs or deer as enemies and practised counting coup on them. Takes-the-pipe as one of the daredevils carried one of the emblems of the organization, a long stick with a wooden hammer-head pivoted some two feet from its top. Suddenly an idea struck him. "Hammers," he cried, "let us offer a seat on our horses to the girls we like!" No sooner said than done. He himself had had his eye on Otter for some time, and presently the two were riding double.

In the evening when the women of the camp pitched their lodges, the Hammer boys' sweethearts set up theirs a little way off. They played at married life. Takes-the-pipe sneaked into his mother's lodge, purloined some meat, brought it near Otter's tent, and bade her fetch the food, which she then cooked for him. Other boys and girls did likewise. Thus they played every day while on the march. Once Takes-the-pipe killed a young wolf and brought a lock of its hair to the young folks' camp. He pretended that it was an enemy's scalp and set it on a pole and all the girls had to dance the scalp dance around it. There followed a recital of deeds; the boys who had struck wolves were allowed to claim coups against the Dakota, and those who had touched deer might boast of having stolen picketed horses.

It was a gay journey. But one evening when Takes-the-pipe had bragged of his mock exploits, Cherry-necklace suddenly appeared on the scene and taunted him before all his playmates, "You think you are a man, because you are as tall as Deaf-bull," he cried, "you are nothing but a child fit to play with little girls. Have you ever been on the war-path? *I* went with Long-horse and struck a Piegan." Takes-the-pipe hung his head. It was only too true. Cherry-necklace was not so much older, yet he had already distinguished himself and might recite his coup in any public assembly. Takes-the-pipe had no answer for he knew nothing to fling back in his "joking-relative's" teeth, but he resolved forthwith to join a war party at the earliest opportunity.

Not long after this Shinbone let it be known that he was setting out on a horse-raid against the Dakota. Now Takes-the-pipe had his chance. Well-provided with moccasins by his clanswomen, he joined a dozen young men starting afoot on the perilous adventure,—perilous because, though Shinbone was a brave man, this was his first attempt at leading a party and it remained to be seen whether "his medicine was good." They walked for four days. As Takes-the-pipe was the youngest of the company, he had to fetch water and firewood, and one morning when he slept too late they poured water all over him.

Warily the party advanced. On the fourth evening Shinbone ordered them to halt on a little knoll. "Yonder are the Dakota lodges," he said, "early to-morrow morning we will go there." He took his sacred bundle, unwrapping a weasel skin stuffed with deer hair, and pointed it toward the camp. "The Dakota are tired," he said, "they will sleep late." Before dawn he roused the party. He appointed two young men as scouts. They came back. "Well," he asked, "how is it?"

"Where you pointed, there are the Dakota lodges," they replied.

"It is well," he said. He chose four others to drive all the loose horses out of the camp. They left. They had not gone far when they were overtaken by Takes-the-pipe. "What are you doing? Go back. He did not send *you*."

"I am going to the camp to cut a horse or strike a coup."

"You are crazy! We are older than you and are still without honors. We are here to steal horses, not to score deeds. The one who is carrying our pipe is a new leader, he may not be very powerful and you will spoil his luck. Go back!"

But though they threatened to beat him, Takes-the-pipe would not return and so all five approached the camp. There were the lodges ranged in a circle. The inmates seemed plunged in sleep. Near the edge a herd of horses were peacefully grazing. The scouts quietly stole up to them and began to drive them off toward the rest of their party. In the meantime Takes-the-pipe was getting his bearings in the strange encampment. He cast about for a picketed horse, but there was none to be seen. Then of a sudden, chance favored him. Out of a little tent on the outskirts of the circle a wizened old man came hobbling on a staff. Takes-the-pipe stole up behind him and dealt him a stunning blow. "Hēha!" he cried, counting coup on the prostrate foe. Then he dashed towards his friends, who had watched him from a little distance. As yet there was no alarm, but no time was to be lost. They mounted and drove the horses before them. When they reached Shinbone, the rest of the party got on horseback. "Now we will run!" said the captain.

They had come and gone to the Dakota afoot and slowly enough; now they were mounted, and traveled at top speed, for they knew that before long the enemy would be in their wake. They rode on and on till they got to the brink of a rapid stream. Here, some of their stolen horses turned back, but the greatest number they saved, driving them through the ice-cold water, where they themselves felt as though they must die from the cold. They traveled that day and all through the night without stopping to eat. On the following morning they reached the Crow camp, sore and worn out, but with sixty head of horses. By rights they all belonged to Shinbone, but after the fashion of a good leader, he was generous to his followers and let them have nearly half of the herd. Takes-the-pipe won three horses.

His parents rejoiced when they heard of his coup and his booty. His mother and her sisters at once prepared a magnificent feast, to which all the Sore-lip women contributed. On such occasions it behooved a young man to give lavish entertainment to his father's kin, so that he might live to be an old man. So Deaf-bull invited all the eminent Whistling-water men, and Takes-the-pipe selected Sliding-beaver from among them, presenting him with a fine bay horse. Then Sliding-beaver trudged through camp, leading Takes-the-pipe's horse and singing the young man's praises.

III

He was rolling a hoop and another youth was hurling a dart at it when Shinbone clutched him by the arm. "Come, I'll make a man of you. You shall take the place of your elder brother." Takes-the-pipe knew what he meant: a cousin of his belonging to the Fox society had fallen in a skirmish with the Dakota, and his fellow-members had been casting about for a clubbable kinsman.

Now a new sort of life began for Takes-the-pipe. He no longer roamed about aimlessly or consorted with random companions. His fellow-members were now his constant associates. Spare time was whiled away in the lodges of eminent Foxes, beating the drum and singing the songs of the organization. Now and then the younger members took jaunts to the hills with their sweethearts. Again there was a philandering when the Foxes and their girls went berrying or up to the mountains to drag lodge poles to camp. Often enough a wealthy member had a herald invite all the Foxes to his lodges, where they were feasted, and held a dance. There, too, valiant men rose to expatiate on their prowess. The Foxes had done well that year. Shinbone had struck the first coup of the season, thus making his club take precedence of the rival Lumpwood society. By the rules of the game the Lumpwoods had lost the right to sing their own songs, and when they danced they were obliged to borrow those of the Big Dogs, exposing themselves to the mockery of the Foxes. That year Takes-the-pipe joined a number of war parties and succeeded in capturing an enemy's gun. Now he, too, would rise and tell about his martial experiences.

The following spring there were great doings. The Foxes were electing new officers in place of the last year's standard-bearers. Three or four of the elders had had a council and now they came to the club lodge where all the members were gathered. Two of the emblems of the society were straight staffs, two were hooked and wrapped with otterskin. Each was pointed at the bottom, for in sight of the enemy the bearer was obliged to plant it into the earth, and stand his ground regardless of danger or death, without budging an inch unless a companion plucked out the fatal lance. That was why the officers were called "men doomed to die." If they escaped unscathed by the end of the year, they retired with all the honors of distinguished service; if they died in battle, they were solemnly mourned by their fellow-members and other tribesmen; but if they failed in duty, they became the pariahs of the camp.

There were not many young men eager to undertake so arduous an office. The electors were passing round the circle, offering a pipe to likely candidates, for to smoke it meant acceptance. Some of the faint-hearted ones crouched behind others to escape notice and even some, who were forward enough on other occasions, shrank back. First the elders went to the tried warriors. No trouble was expected with Shinbone, and as a matter of fact he readily consented. Next they came to Lone-pine, Sliding-beaver's eldest son. He, too, smoked without sign of reluctance. But now the electors were beginning to cast about among the younger fellow-members, for they were coming towards Cherry-necklace. Cherry-necklace was no coward; he had shown his mettle in more than one encounter. Yet he was very fond of having a good time. Would he willingly accept appointment? No, he was squirming uneasily and refused the pipe. Rather, he would have refused it, but Lone-pine, his brother, seized him by the bang of his hair and forcibly made his lips touch the pipestem. Thus Cherry-necklace too was "doomed to die." And now the elders passed round once more in search of the last officer. Takes-the-pipe's heart began to beat. What if they asked him? It would be an honor for one so young, but did he wish to die? They were coming straight toward him. He seemed to hear the old song:

> Sky and earth are everlasting,
> Men must die.

Yes, if he died, what mattered it? He would yield without coaxing and shame Cherry-necklace. He eagerly clutched the pipe and became one of the bearers of a hooked-staff.

While the Foxes were holding their annual election, the Lumpwoods were going through a like procedure. A day or two later, a defiant call was heard from their lodge. They were ready for the annual indulgence in licensed wife-stealing. Only the Foxes and the Lumpwoods took part in this pastime, the other societies being mere spectators. If a Fox had ever had for his sweetheart a Lumpwood's wife, he was now privileged to kidnap her from her rightful husband, who would only make himself a laughing-stock if he interposed objections, let alone violence. Takes-the-pipe remembered that Otter was now married to a Lumpwood named Drags-the-wolf, so he went to the lodge and called her. Drags-the-wolf was game. He had the reputation of being very fond of his pretty, young wife, but he knew the proper way for a Crow to act. Instead of restraining her, he himself said, "He is calling you. Go!" Takes-the-pipe brought her to his parents' lodge. His mother and sisters gave her a beautiful elk-tooth dress and other Sore-lip women from all over the camp brought her moccasins and beaded pouches. Then the Foxes selected from their number an old man who had once rescued a wounded tribesman from certain death by dashing into the thick of the fray, and carrying him off on his horse. This man, for none other might venture, rode double with the kidnapped bride, all the other Foxes parading jubilantly behind and twitting their rivals with the capture of so handsome a Lumpwood woman.

IV

Shinbone had come home from a war party with blackened face and taken the rank of chief. No wonder, the people were saying. Had not the Thunderbird adopted him when as a young man he prayed and thirsted for a revelation? Men must undergo suffering if they wanted supernatural blessing so that they could become great men among their people. Of all the Crow chiefs, only Drags-the-wolf had been in luck: him the Moon visited as he was peacefully slumbering in his tent and granted him invulnerability and coups. The other distinguished warriors had had to mortify their flesh in order to gain favor.

That spring the herald proclaimed that Red-eye was going to hold a Sun Dance. He had lost a brother and was hungering for revenge. What surer way to attain it than to fast and dance before the sacred doll till it became alive and showed him a scalped Dakota in earnest of victory and vengeance? But Red-eye's announcement was a signal for all the ambitious youths to plan for a public mortification of their flesh at the same time in the hope of winning supernatural favor. So, while the pledger of the ceremony was dancing up and down with his gaze riveted on the holy image in the rear of the lodge, a dozen young men were undergoing torture for their own ends. Some were dragging through camp two buffalo skulls fastened to a stick thrust through holes cut in their backs. Others—and Takes-the-pipe among them—decided to swing from the lodge poles. So he begged Sharp-horn to pierce the flesh above his breasts, run skewers through the openings, and tie the rods to ropes hung from a pole. Thus attached he ran back and forth till he had torn out the skewers. Yet when he had fallen to the ground faint and blood-stained no vision came for all his pains.

He wanted to become a chief like Shinbone, so he went on a mountain peak to fast. Without clothes save his gee-string and a buffalo robe, he slept there overnight. He awoke early, the sun had just risen. He took a piece of wood and put on it his left forefinger. "Sun," he cried, "I am miserable. I am giving you this. Make me a chief!" With a huge knife he hacked off the first joint. The blood began to flow. He lost consciousness. When he came to, it was evening. His finger ached. He tried to sleep, but the pain and cold kept him awake. Of a sudden he heard a man clearing his throat and a horse's neighing came closer and closer. A voice behind him said, "The one whom you wanted to come has arrived." He turned about. He saw a man on a bay horse; his face was painted red and he wore a shirt with many discs cut out from its body, yet hanging from it as though by a thread. From the back of his head rose a chicken-hawk feather. The rider said, "You are miserable. I have been looking for you for a long time but could never quite reach you. I will adopt you as my child. Look! I am going to run." He began to gallop; the dust flew to the sky. Then the trees and shrubs all about turned into Piegans and began shooting at the horseman. Arrows came whizzing by him and bullets flew round him and the enemies were yelling after him, but he wheeled round unscathed. With his spear he knocked down one warrior and counted coup on him. He rode up to Takes-the-pipe: "Though you fight all the people of the world, dress as I do and you need have no fear of death before you are a chief. That man I struck is a Piegan; you have seen his country, go there, I give him to you. As I am, so shall you be; arrows will not hurt you, bullets you can laugh at. You shall be like a rock. But one thing you must not do: never eat of any animal's kidneys."

When Takes-the-pipe got back to his people, he was very glad. Two things remained to be done before he might call himself chief: one was to lead a victorious war party, the other to cut a picketed horse. His vision enabled him forthwith to play a captain's part. He shot a chicken-hawk and took one of its feathers to be worn at the back of his head on his expeditions. He prepared a shirt like the one he had seen and a spear that resembled exactly that borne by his patron. Then he gathered his war party. His sisters and other Sore-lip women made moccasins galore for him. He set out in the dead of night. For several days they traveled north and west. On the Missouri they ran into a few Piegans in a hunting-lodge. They killed them all and took their scalps. Thus they could return with blackened faces. One of the enemies had a thumbless hand, so the year was known ever after as "the winter when they killed the thumbless man."

V

He had been wounded in the knee. He could not understand it. He had been promised that his body would be like stone. He had worn his feather at the back of his head, as in every fight since the time of his vision, yet his kneecap had been shattered in a skirmish with the Dakota. And it was an ugly injury. Red-eye had salved it with bear root, but the cure-all had failed. Bullsnake, foremost of doctors, blessed by the buffalo, had waded into the river to wash his knee, but all in vain; he remained crippled. Then he knew that he had unwittingly broken his guardian spirit's rule; there had been a feast before the fatal battle and then he must have eaten of the forbidden food.

Soon there came surety. In a dream appeared the man on the bay horse and said: "I told you not to eat kidney, you have eaten it. You shall never be chief." Takes-the-pipe had now struck many coups and captured guns and carried the captain's pipe. His record surpassed that of any man of his age, but he lacked the honor of cutting a picketed horse. How could he ever gain it now? Horse-raiders started on foot, and he could only painfully limp across the camp.

Young women, drawn by his fame, often visited him in his tent, but their attentions soon palled on him. His mother tried to console him. "Of all the young men you are the best-off; you have struck more coups than the rest and own plenty of horses; the young women are crazy about you. You ought to be the happiest man in camp." But he would watch the bustle of preparations for new raids that he could not join; he would ride about of an evening and chance upon the foot-soldiers setting out from their trysting-place, and would look after them, wistful and envious and sick at heart.

Sharp-horn, the aged sage, advised him to go for another vision; possibly the guardian spirit would relent. So Takes-the-pipe started out on horseback and rode far away towards the mountain where he had prayed before. At the foot he hobbled his horse and painfully climbed to the summit. He lay down, with outstretched arms, facing the sky. "Father," he wailed, "I am miserable, take pity on me." He lay there during the night but at the first glimmer of dawn there was still no message from the mysterious powers. All day he stayed about the jagged bowlders without drink or a morsel to eat.

Long after nightfall a muffled tread became audible and as it came closer it was the tramp of a buffalo. Then a bull was standing over him, scenting his breath and caressing his naked breast with shaggy fur. At last he spoke in Crow. "I will adopt you my son. I have seen you suffering from afar. What other Indians have prayed for shall be yours. Look at the inside of my mouth." He looked and there was not a tooth to be seen. "So long as you have teeth, my son, you shall not die. You shall marry a fine, chaste, young woman and beget children and see your grandchildren about you. When you die you shall be so old that your skin will crack as you move from one corner of the lodge to another."

But Takes-the-pipe shook his head and said, "Father, it is not because I crave old age that I am thirsting; I want to be a chief like Shinbone."

"My son, what you ask is difficult. As I hurried to you from my home, I overtook another person traveling towards you; perhaps you will still be able to get what you desire." Takes-the-pipe sat up to ask further counsel, but the bull was gone and nothing but a bleached buffalo skull was gaping at him in the gloaming.

All next day he fasted and prayed on his peak, addressing now the Sun, then the Thunder, then again the Morningstar. His throat was parched when he lay down at dark in his old resting-place. He did not know how, but of a sudden the darkness was lifted and the hilltop shone with a gentle radiance. An old woman was standing at his feet, resting on a digging-stick; she wore a splendid robe with horsetracks marked on it in porcupine-quill embroidery. "My child," she said, "you have not called me, nevertheless I am here. I heard your groans and started towards you but another person passed me on the road. I am the Moon. When children fall sick, doctor them with this root; their parents will give you horses. I will make you the wealthiest of all the Crows."

But Takes-the-pipe shook his head and answered, "Grandmother, I am not suffering to gain wealth, I want to become a chief like Shinbone."

"My dear child, you are asking for something great. As I came hither, I saw another person starting to come here. Perhaps he has more power than I, and can grant your wish." He was eager to ask her more, but her form faded into nothing and only the sheen of the waning crescent remained visible.

Another day he fasted and drank no water. He was now very weak, so that he dragged himself about with the aid of a cane. Was there no power to help him in his distress? Night came as he lay wailing and peering into the darkness, when a handsome young man stood before him. "I was sleeping far away, you have roused me with your lamentations," he said. "I have come to help you. You shall be my son. Do you recognize me? I am the Tobacco your old people plant every year. So long as they harvest me, the Crow shall be a great tribe. They have forgotten the way to prepare the seed, their crops will be poor. I will show you how to mix it before planting. Then you will make your tribe great and teach others and receive all sorts of property in payment."

And Takes-the-pipe answered; "Father, I am not suffering in order to plant tobacco and gain property, I want to be a chief like Shinbone."

Then the man replied, "My son, everything else in the universe is easy for me, only what you ask for is hard. That one who used to be your father is very strong. 'Don't eat kidney,' he said. You have eaten it. I cannot make you chief. Listen, my son. All things in the world go by fours. Three of us have come to help you. We have been powerless. A fourth one is coming, perhaps he can do it."

The next day Takes-the-pipe could hardly crawl on all-fours. His head swam. He seized his knife and chopped off another finger joint on his left hand. Then holding aloft the bleeding stump he cried, "Fathers, I am giving you this. Make me a chief!"

Suddenly a huge figure came panting toward him, shaking a rattle and singing a song. "I am the last," said a big bear; "though I am heavy and slow, I have arrived."

Takes-the-pipe called out to him joyfully, "Father, I knew you were coming. Cure my knee so that I can go out to cut a picketed horse and become a chief."

"My son, the one who used to be your father is very strong. He does not want you to be a chief. Well, I too am strong. If you are a man, I can help you. If you are faint-hearted, I am powerless."

"Father," said Takes-the-pipe, "make me great; make me greater than other men, and if I die what matters it?"

"My son, there are many chiefs in camp; of *your* kind there shall be but one. Tell me, have you ever seen the whole world?" Without waiting for an answer, the bear lifted him up. Mountains and streams and prairies and camps came into his vision. The berries were ripe and the Crow camp loomed in sight and the Tobacco society were harvesting the precious seed. Far away were hostile lodges. Then the leaves were turning yellow and the enemy were setting out to raid Crow horses. One Crow all alone was riding towards them. "My son, do you see that horseman with trailing sashes? They were trying to hold him back, he has broken loose. He could not be a chief; he wants to die. He is a Crazy Dog. He speaks 'backward'; he cares little for the rules of the camp. Where there is danger, he is the foremost. Dress like him, act like him, and you shall be great. The people will speak of you so long as there are Crows living on this earth. This I will give you if your heart is strong."

"Thanks, father, thanks! What you have shown me is great; I will do it. I wanted to live and be a chief. It cannot be. There is no way for me to live; I shall die as a Crazy Dog."

Then the bear vanished.

VI

The people were gathered near the mouth of the Bighorn. There was merriment in camp after a successful hunt. Suddenly was heard the beating of a drum and the chanting of a strange song. All ran out of their lodges to see what was going on. Who is that man on the richly fitted-out horse? He approaches the center of the circle, shaking a rattle. Two sashes of deerskin, slipped over his head, descend to the ground. Sliding-beaver is leading the horse, halting from time to time, and beating a drum. At the fourth stop he cried aloud: "Young women, if you would be this man's sweethearts, you must hasten, he is about to die!" Then he beat his drum and addressed the rider: "Remain on horseback, do not dance!"

Forthwith Takes-the-pipe dismounted and danced in position. Then because he did the opposite of what he was told everyone knew him for a Crazy Dog pledged to court death. Straightway Pretty-weasel began to lament: "I begged him not to do it; he has done it!" But the other women cheered lustily, and Sliding-beaver sang his praises aloud as he slowly led him outside of the camp circle.

Then for a while he appeared every evening, dancing and shaking his rattle. He would ride through camp like a madman. When a few were gathered eating some meat, he would walk his horse into their very midst as if to run over them. Then they would cry out, "Trample on us." And the Crazy Dog would turn aside and let them eat in peace. At night the best-looking young women paid him visits; even married women went there and their husbands did not mind it. Sometimes two or three would come of a single night. Famous Whistling-waters came to tell him what a great thing he was doing. All the eminent warriors in camp, Drags-the-wolf, Red-eye, and Shinbone, were looking on him with envy.

The cherries had ripened and one day a woman offered him some. He said, "When I decided to do this, the grass was sprouting. I did not expect to live so long, yet to-day I am eating cherries. Well, I will see whether I can achieve what I wish." When they went hunting the next time, he got some buffalo blood and mixed it with badger blood and water. In the mixture he saw his image with blood streaming down his face. "Yes," he cried, "I have seen it. What I am longing for is coming true!"

The leaves were turning yellow when a tribesman caught sight of some Dakota raiders. The young men drove them off and the enemy took refuge in the dry bed of a stream. There, the Crow warriors were going to attack them. They were getting ready when Pretty-weasel rushed into their midst, crying, "Bind my son! Don't let him go!" They looked for him. He was not to be found. All alone he was dashing toward the enemy. They galloped after him. He was close to the coulée, shaking his rattle and singing his song:—

> Sky and earth are everlasting,
> Men must die.
> Old age is a thing of evil,
> Charge and die!

He rode straight up to the enemies' hiding-place. At the edge he dismounted. Several Dakotas were peeping out. "There is no way for me to live," he cried, "I must die!" He shot one foe and struck him with his rattle. Then another Dakota shot him in the left temple, and Takes-the-pipe fell dead.

The Crow warriors caught up, and killed every man in the raiding party. Pretty-weasel reached the spot and wiped the blood from her son's forehead. The men put him on a horse and brought him to camp. Wailing, they went home. There the Sore-lip women clipped their hair and gashed their legs. The Whistling-water men rode up and down singing the praises of the dead Crazy Dog. His fellow-Foxes propped up the corpse against a backrest, knelt before it and wailed. Their officers ran arrows through their flesh and jabbed their foreheads till the blood flowed in streams. Then they set up a scaffold on four posts, wrapped the body in a robe, and placed it on top. Beside the stage they planted a pole. From it was hung his drum, and his sashes swept down as streamers blowing in the wind. His rattle they put into his hand. Then the camp moved.

ROBERT H. LOWIE

A Crow Woman's Tale

"A STORY, grandmother, a story!"

"What, in the daytime, outdoors? And in the summer too? Don't you know that we tell tales only of a winter night?"

"Oh, grandmother, those old rules are gone. Do tell us a story to keep us awake on this hot day."

"Well, what shall it be? Shall I tell you how Old-woman's grandchild conquered the monsters that haunted the earth?"

"No, you've told us that one many times. Tell us a new one."

"Well, you shall hear one you have never heard before; a new story and yet a true one."

There was a young Crow maiden named Beaver-woman who was as good-looking as any girl the Crows had ever known. She was neither too tall nor too short, her waist was slim, and her nose was as straight as a nose can be. She made the finest moccasins in all the tribe and knew how to embroider them with the prettiest quill designs. Throughout the camp there was no one for whom she did not have a kind word. The young men respected her for they knew she would not romp with them as some girls did, and those older ones who had been on the war-path were eager to take her to wife. Yet though one suitor after another came to offer horses to her father, the beautiful girl refused them all. At length her parents grew impatient and scolded her. "What are you waiting for? Your brothers have need of horses. Do you expect Morningstar to come down from the sky and woo you?"

Then for the first time she spoke of her hopes. "One day when the grass was sprouting, I went to the creek to fetch some water. There my eldest brother's comrade, the one they call White-dog, spoke to me and courted me, then left with a war party. I have seen him in my dreams, returning with booty. He is bringing home horses; he will offer you more than all the other suitors together who have tried to buy me."

Then one of her brothers laughed in derision, and another good-naturedly, and still others kept their peace, while her mother mumbled, "Some dreams have come true and some only mock one. I liked the looks of the horses you refused."

But a few days later, when the cherries were ripe, White-dog came back with his party, driving eighty head of horses stolen from the Sioux. Many he allotted to his followers and many he gave away to his father's clansmen; but of the remainder he offered the twenty finest to Beaver-woman's parents. Then she was happy and said, "My dream has come true." Her parents, too, were very glad, and she went to live in her husband's lodge.

White-dog had an older wife named Turtle, whom he had inherited from a brother killed in battle. Turtle did not like the newcomer, but White-dog would not allow her to abuse Beaver-woman. He was very proud of his young and beautiful wife. When the people moved camp, it was Beaver-woman who bore his buffalo-hide shield; and when he came back from the enemy with spoils, she was the one to dance with his bow or spear while Turtle and other women looked on with envy. There was one thing he prized even higher than her good looks, and that was her virtue. Other men were having all sorts of trouble with their wives, but he was sure of his. When he heard of a married woman eloping with her lover, he would say proudly, "My wife will soon be the only one who shall dare chop down the tree for the Sun Dance lodge"; for only a wife who had never erred was allowed to take part in this sacred rite.

All went well until one spring soon after Beaver-woman had borne her first child. You young men have your dancing-clubs today, some of you are Hot Dancers and others belong to the Big-Ear-Holes. That's the way we Crows used to have it in the old days, only we had *real* societies, the Foxes and the Lumpwoods. They didn't just dance and feast; they tried to be brave in war and each society sought to outdo the other. But they fought in another way, too. Sometimes it happened that a Lumpwood or a Fox had once had a mistress who afterwards married into the other society. Then for a few days in the early spring he was allowed to kidnap her. No matter how badly he felt about it, her husband durst not protect her, it would have been a terrible disgrace. He must never take her back so long as he lived, or the whole camp would jeer at him for the rest of his days. Often a man might feel like fighting, but he would control himself and say, "She is nothing to me, take her." Then the people would praise him, saying, "That one has a strong heart."

Well, one day in the spring, a hooting was heard in camp. The Lumpwoods, headed by Red-eye, were ready to steal the Foxes' wives, and the Foxes had answered the call of challenge. White-dog was not greatly interested in these doings. He was lounging in his lodge, talking to his younger brother, Little-owl, while Beaver-woman was crooning a song over her baby. Of a sudden the tramping of feet was heard, the door-flap was rudely lifted, and Red-eye's head was thrust through the opening. Beaver-woman faced him calmly. "What's the matter?" she asked.

He answered with a song:

"My sweetheart is the one I love,
I am taking her away."

"Go away, you're crazy," she said, "I have never been your sweetheart!"

"What, don't you remember what happened at the spring?"

"Yes, you were going to hug me and I drenched you with water. Go away to your real sweetheart."

But now Red-eye had entered the lodge with two of his companions and was about to lay hands on her. Then she knew that it was no jest, that he was falsely claiming her as a one-time mistress and she screamed aloud at her husband.

"He is lying, you know he is lying! Help me!" All this time White-dog was sitting in the rear of the lodge, stiff and silent. He knew the charge against his wife was false, and hatred filled him against her wanton accuser. He also knew that unless he fought for her now she was lost forever. But it was not a man's part to show resentment at such times. Just because no one in camp would believe in Red-eye's tale, he, White-dog, would be all the greater for having shown a strong heart. So with stern face he turned to his wife and said, "They are calling you, go." But as they seized her, up sprang Little-owl, White-dog's younger brother, a gentle young man who loved Beaver-woman and had always shown respect for her instead of teasing her as most brothers-in-law do with their brothers' wives. He picked up a large butchering-knife from the ground and rushed at Red-eye crying, "You lie, you lie!" But now White-dog, too, leaped up and with his greater strength pinioned his brother's arms behind his back. He wanted no scuffle when his wife was being kidnapped; it would have been a disgrace. Thus Red-eye dragged Beaver-woman away without interference.

The Lumpwoods had a grand feast and a dress parade on horseback, and Beaver-woman had to ride double with the greatest warrior in the society. They had dressed her up in the finest elk-tooth dress and everyone admired her good looks, but she was sad and could not hold back her tears. All the Foxes stood round about to see the spectacle, and among them was White-dog, looking on as if nothing had happened. For he wanted to show what a strong heart he had.

When the celebration was over, Beaver-woman had to live as the wife of Red-eye, whom she hated. One night she stole to White-dog's lodge and begged him to take her back. But White-dog got angry and bade her depart. "Do you believe he was ever my lover?" she asked.

He answered, "I do not believe it, but he has made the charge and seized you. Go back. I do not want people to sing songs in mockery of me." And when she lingered he thrust her out and struck her a blow,—he who had never beaten her before. Then she mournfully retraced her steps towards her new home. But before she had gotten very far she felt a light tap on her shoulder. She turned about and faced not White-dog but his younger brother.

"The people here are bad," said Little-owl, "come, let us two flee. By the mouth of the Yellowstone there are Crows too, and down the Missouri are the villages of the Corn-eaters. I have relatives among both; let us go and live with them." So in the same night they packed some dried meat and other necessaries and they started northward down the Yellowstone without being detected in camp.

But on the second day's journey they were espied by a group of scouting Cheyenne. Little-owl fought bravely but was killed and scalped. Beaver-woman with her baby became a captive of the hostile tribe, and the leader of the party took her as his wife, when they got back to the Cheyenne camp. Her new husband was a great warrior and treated her kindly, but he was an elderly man and she could not love him as she had loved White-dog. She grieved, too, for gentle Little-owl who had died for love of her, and she longed to go back to her own people.

About a year later another Crow woman was brought to camp as a captive. That was a joyful day for Beaver-woman. Now she learned all the news about her own people. She heard that Red-eye was dead, killed by lightning, and all the Crows said it was because he had abducted an innocent woman. White-dog had not married again; he had even sent away Turtle, his elder wife. He was more famous as a brave than ever, for he had struck several enemies and stolen two picketed horses from the Sioux. The people talked about his recklessness and thought he would surely become a chief.

When Beaver-woman heard about her people, she was filled with a great longing to go back to them. "We are not far from our own people," she said, "let us run back there together. My husband is setting out against the Sioux; then we can escape." So they made their get-away and arrived in safety among their own tribe. Beaver-woman went straight to her first husband's lodge. She found him alone, smoothing an arrow-shaft. "They told me that other man was killed by lightning; I have come back," she said. But he hardly looked up.

"A man does not take back a kidnapped wife," he said, "go away." Then she saw that she had come in vain and, weeping, she went to her parents' home.

White-dog had always had a strong heart. But now the people were saying that he was positively foolhardy. When enemies were entrenched, he was the first to lead the attack; when a hostile camp was to be entered, he was the first to volunteer; he was always planning a raid against the Cheyenne or Sioux. But one time a Crow party returned wailing: White-dog had fallen in a reckless charge and they were bearing his corpse for burial among his people. His kinsfolk and the Foxes and all the tribe mourned his death, and the women in his family gashed themselves with knives to show their grief. But none grieved more, or inflicted more cruel wounds upon herself than Beaver-woman, and for a whole year she wore ragged clothes, and let her hair hang down disheveled. Then, because she was still good-looking, men came once more to woo her, and at length, because her brothers urged her, she married an oldish man and bore him children. And her children, as they grew up, married and had children too. But all her life she could not forget those early days when White-dog came and took her as his wife.

* * *

The old woman paused.

"Thanks, grandmother, yours is a good story and a new one, too. What times! Aren't we happy now to live in peace, without being disturbed by Sioux or Cheyenne and without the women being kidnapped by a society of our own?"

The old woman straightened up and looked at the youth with a disdainful glance. "You boys who go to school don't understand anything. The longer you stay there, the less sense you have. I once hoped to cut down the sacred tree in the Sun Dance! I bore White-dog's shield when the camp moved! I danced, holding his spear, with Turtle and all the other women looking on in envy! Little-owl died for love of me! White-dog threw away his life because he could not take me back!"

ROBERT H. LOWIE

A Trial of Shamans

BIG-DOG was troubled; he knew he should not sleep that night. White-hip, blind old White-hip, had passed him with a taunt. He did not mind the old fellow's gibes, yet. . . .

It all happened long ago. White-hip was stretched out in his lodge one night when a young kinsman named Shows-his-horse burst in upon him.

"They say you are a great medicine man, take pity on me, I am in distress."

"Well, what ails you?"

"As I approached my tent this evening, a man came out, wrapped in his robe. He has stolen my wife; I want revenge."

Then White-hip said, "You are my younger brother; I will help you. Who is it that has stolen your wife?"

Shows-his-horse replied, "It was Big-dog."

Then White-hip shrank back and asked, "Are you sure it was Big-dog? The night is dark, you may have made a mistake."

But the young man answered, "It was still light when I saw him,— a short, stocky man with the wolf-tails at his heels plainly visible dragging along the ground."

White-hip said, "My younger brother, it is wrong for a man to mind the loss of a woman. If your joking-relatives should hear of this, they will sing songs in mockery of you. This is dangerous business. The Thunder himself has adopted Big-dog as his child."

Then Shows-his-horse flared up. "They told me you were a great medicine man, that is why I came to you in my grief. I see you are afraid; your medicine is worthless."

Then for a long time White-hip spoke not a word. At length he said, "It will be very difficult, but my medicine is strong. Though the Thunder himself be his father, I will lay him low."

It happened that a few days later Big-dog set out on a war party against the Sioux. Then White-hip prayed to the sacred stone that was his medicine. And Big-dog's war party was met by a superior force of Sioux that killed one of his followers and scattered the rest. There was grief in the Crow camp and the people were wondering about Big-dog's first failure. But Shows-his-horse brought his three best horses as a gift to White-hip, and slowly the news leaked out that a trial of strength was on between the two great shamans of the tribe.

Soon after this event White-hip, too, wanted to go on the war-path, and the men who had been thwarted by Big-dog's failure were eager to join him. But the very night they set out, Big-dog prayed to the Thunder: "I do not want you to afflict my people; only he that leads them shall meet with disaster." And it rained and stormed in the war party's path, and a tree, felled by lightening, grazed the captain's shoulder. Then the braves were alarmed and insisted on turning back.

Thus, when either of the shamans had set out against the enemy, the other was sure to thwart him, till neither ventured on a war party, and the whole camp were wondering who should conquer in the end. At last Big-dog could contain himself no longer. Once more he addressed the Thunder: "These scars are from the flesh I cut as an offering to you, these finger-joints were chopped to make you a present. You made me your child. That one is mocking me and you. He thinks his is the greater medicine; smite him with blindness."

And before the cherries had ripened, White-hip had lost his sight. Then Big-dog triumphed and the Crows all said that he was the greatest shaman they had ever had and that his medicine was the most powerful of all; and White-hip was deserted by all but his next of kin, and became so poor that for a while a rope served him for a belt.

But the blind man still had faith in his medicine and one day he thus invoked it: "His father has made me blind and miserable. I do not care if you can make *him* miserable too. He has three sons. Kill them all and make him live till his skin cracks from old age and force him to beg his food from strangers."

Then on the next war party Big-dog's eldest son was slain by the Blackfoot; and people began to say that perhaps White-hip had not been conquered for good. And a year later his second eldest son died from sickness. Then the Crows all said it must be White-hip's work. And before the leaves had turned yellow, the shaman's last son was drowned in the Yellowstone. Then some said that, for all that, Big-dog had won, for he himself was well, while his enemy was blind. But others thought that White-hip, despite his blindness, had shown himself superior.

And as years passed, Big-dog grew infirm. He outlived his nearest kin and those more remote till no clansfolk remained. He would wander about from lodge to lodge, feasting on what strangers offered him in sheer compassion. He would hear mothers whispering to their children, "Big-dog was a great medicine man once and the whole tribe stood in awe of him, but White-hip had the greater medicine and laid him low."

And just now White-hip had passed him with a taunt. He did not mind the blind fellow's mockery, but one thought troubled and racked him and would not let him sleep at night: "Whose medicine was really the greater? Who had won?"

ROBERT H. LOWIE

SMOKING STAR
A BLACKFOOT
SHAMAN

Smoking-star, a Blackfoot Shaman

IT was one evening in summer, the time of the long day, when the twilight is equally long, that I sat before the tepee fire of my host, Smoking-star. According to his own belief, he had seen the snows of nine times around his hands, or ninety years, as we count it. He was regarded as by far the oldest living Blackfoot, but his eye was bright and his memory good. That evening as we smoked in silence, I mused on the cross-section of man's history this venerable life would reveal, if it could be read. I told him how I felt, and my pleasure if he would tell his story for me. He sat long and silently, as is the way of his people; then rose, and with great dignity, left the tepee. Presently he returned and when seated, said, "The Smoking-star, Mars, is high. He shines approvingly. I have long lived by his power. I believe He will not be offended if I tell you the story of my life."

So runs the tale of old Smoking-star as near as my memory can follow:

My father's name was Old-beaver, chief of the Small-robe band, to which band I still belong. My mother came from the Fat-roasting band, she was the younger wife of my father, her older sister being the first, or head-wife. A child always calls each of his father's women *mother* and also all the women married to father's and mother's brothers; just why this is we do not know, but it is our way. My father was very kind to me, but my older mother was cross.

I suppose I was born in a small tepee set up outside, for such is the custom. Also I suppose that for a time my mother laid aside all ornaments and affected carelessness of person. If anyone should gaze at her, she would say, "Don't. My child will look like you; you are ugly, etc." She was attended by women only, for men should not approach the birthplace. Even my father was not permitted to enter and it was many days before he saw me. In due time, I suppose, I was strapped to a cradle board. Later, a name was conferred upon me by my father, he being a chief.   Unless a man is great, he does not name his child, but calls some man possessing these qualifications.   Having once captured two guns from the Cree, my father told the story of that deed, or coup, and named me Two-guns.   It is the belief that the qualities of the namer and the name itself pass to the child; hence great importance is given to the name and the conferring of it is a solemn occasion.   The black-robe (priest) tells me it is much the same with your people.

Also, I suppose that when I got my first tooth, my grandmothers reminded my parents that it was time to do something.   So a feast was made, presents given, and prayers offered.   This was, no doubt, repeated when I took my first step and when I learned to speak. But I do remember having my ears pierced.   That is the first memory of childhood.   I can still see a terrible looking old grandmother standing up before me, holding up a bone awl.   I was never so frightened in my life.   You have seen how it is done at the sun dance, where some old woman cries out, "I quilled a robe, all with these hands.   So I have the power to do this."   Just like a warrior recounting a coup.

My real mother never reproved me, but when I began to run about, my older mother did not like to have me meddling with her things. Often she would make threats to me in a kind of song, as—"There is a coyote outside.   Come coyote, and eat up this naughty baby." Again, "Come old Crooked-back woman; bring your meat pounder; smash this baby's head."   The woman referred to was a crazy cripple who terrorized the children because some of them teased her.   I was very much afraid, so that usually all my older mother need say was, "Sh-h-h!" and mumble something about the coyote or the woman.   I have noticed that among your people, parents strike their children.   That is not our way.   If they will not listen to advice, an uncle may be called upon to exercise discipline and if necessary he will punish, but whipping is the way of the police societies.   Once I saw the police whip a chief because he broke the rules of the buffalo hunt.

Soon I began to play with the older boys; in winter we spun tops on the ice and in the snow, coasted the hills on toboggans made of buffalo ribs, or just stood up on a dry skin, holding up the end.   In summer there were all kinds of games: racing, follow-the-leader, arrow games, the wheel game, etc. I had a hobby-horse, made of a bent stick, with a saddle and bridle, upon which I played running buffalo and going to war. I even learned to play tricks upon old people. Sometimes we would be playing where old women came to gather firewood and when one of them had a great heap of wood on her pack line, she would squat with her back against the wood, the lines in her hands, and call for us to help raise the load; occasionally, we would assist until she reached her feet and then, with a quick push, send her sprawling with the wood on top. Then we would run away to escape a beating. Again, as water was carried in pails made of buffalo paunch, some boys would ambush the path and shoot an arrow into the pail, letting out the water. But usually we let older people alone, for, if caught, we were severely handled.

When about six years old one of my grandfathers made me a bow; he prayed for me and said if I killed anything I should bring in the scalp to prove it. He told me the story of Scar-face and the dangerous birds. Some time after this I killed a bird, my first, and my father made a feast, calling in many great men, who smoked many pipes, told of great deeds and predicted that I would be a great warrior. The skin of the bird was put into my grandfather's war bundle.

When we traveled my mother carried me on her saddle or put me on a travois, hitched to a dog or some trusty old mare. But when I was old enough to ride alone, my father went on the war path to the Assiniboin country and brought back six horses; one pony he gave to me. Before I learned to ride it well, it was stolen by the Cree. At the same time my older mother was killed and scalped while out picking berries. All this made a deep impression upon me and I resolved to prepare for the war-path and to take vengeance on the Cree, particularly for the loss of my pony. In the meantime my father gave me another pony.

One morning when I was about eleven years old, I was terribly frightened to find a man from a police society standing at the door, shouting for me to come out at once. It was cold and stormy, but he ordered me to the water for a plunge and when I stood on the bank whimpering, he threw me headlong into the icy current. The older boys were splashing about gaily, but it was hard for me. When I crept back to the tepee, shivering, my old grandmother began to sing a derisive song about a would-be warrior who turned to an old woman. After that I went daily to the bath and soon became hard and strong.

The next summer our people were camped on Milk River where buffalo were plenty. The berries were just turning. One day while herding the horses I fell to eating berries and that night became ill. The next day I was very sick and a doctor was sent for. Old One-ear came, a man all of us feared, sat by my bed, beat upon a drum, sang in a loud voice, then turned down the robes that covered me, held a tube of bone against my breast and sucked violently. Then he arose and spat out a grasshopper. Everyone said that I would soon be well, and I was. But while I was too weak to go out, my grandfather came in and told me tales of the war-path and occasionally of the Lost Children, the Woman-who-went-to-the-sky, Morningstar, Scar-face, Blood-clot, and other tales. I came to take a deep interest in these tales and to think more and more of going to war. When I could go out, my people were holding the sun dance and one evening I heard my father reciting his coups, putting on the fire a stick for each. At last when there was a great blaze from so much wood, the people all shouted. It was a proud moment for me and from then on I began to train for the war-path.

Before cold weather our people separated, as was their custom, and our band, with the Fat-roasters and the Many-medicines, made winter camp on the Two Medicine River. It was a cold winter, but buffalo were plenty and we did not mind. In the spring my father led a war party against the Crow. I knew nothing of it until they had gone, but even had I known, he would not have taken me. I felt very sad and spent most of the time sitting on a hill, meditating. One day, on coming to camp I heard the women and even old men wailing. I saw my mother before our door hacking her bare leg with her butchering knife. Then I knew what had happened. The camp crier began to shout out that a runner had come in from a distant camp to say that Old-beaver and all his party had been killed by the Crows. When I met my old grandmother, with blood streaming down her bare arms, the sight sickened me and I fled to the hilltop and meditated further. As I thought of how coup had been counted on my father, my anger grew and I vowed to take a Crow scalp at the first opportunity.

Our camp mourned long after this. It was also necessary to select a new chief. One Good-runner was well thought of and was our choice, but an evil-minded fellow named Crow-eye sought the place. Finding that he was in disfavor, Crow-eye secretly loaded a gun, entered the tepee of Good-runner and shot him down. Crow-eye's relatives put him on a horse and sent him away for a few days, while they made presents to the relatives of Good-runner. Well, in the end Crow-eye became chief, but it was a sorry time for us all.

As was the custom, my mother went to live with her people, or the Fat-roasting band. My mother's brother now took an interest in me. He gave me a gun. Guns were scarce in those days. My grandfather remembered when the first gun came to us and said that his father knew when the first horse came. I now spent much of my time with my uncle, though I still looked upon the Small-robes band as my band. He helped me to buy a place in the Pigeon Society and every spring and summer I danced with them and sometimes helped guard the camp at night when the great camp circle was formed.

It was during the summer following my father's death that I was taken on my first buffalo hunt. Sometimes boys were severely whipped by the police if found joining in running buffalo before they were old enough. But now my uncle took me with him. As guns were scarce, we kept them for war, and killed buffalo with arrows. When we rode at the herd, I took after a young cow. She was very fleet, but at last I drew alongside and sent an arrow into her. When she fell I stood by in awe. My relations praised me and my mother tanned the skin to make a robe for me. I was now a hunter and always joined in the killing unchallenged.

That autumn my mother ceased to mourn and married a man in the Lone-eaters band. After this I saw little of her, for they camped apart and I stayed with my uncle, but danced with my father's band, the Small-robes. About this time my uncle explained to me the ways of women and the duties of a man, so I began to look forward to having a woman of my own. I began to practice on the flageolet and to seek meetings with the girls of the camp on the path to the water hole; but I knew that though I had become a hunter, I had yet to go to war and to become a man. The opportunity soon came, for I was now about fourteen years old.

One day my uncle said, "Now it is time for you to go to war. When the moon is full, I shall lead a party to the Crow country. You can be the water boy." You know how it was with us, a boy might be taken to war to do errands. This is how he got his experience.

My uncle had a war bundle, or medicine, in which were a collar of coyote skin, a bird to tie in his hair, some tobacco, a pipe, paints, a whistle and a rattle. Every night we gathered in his tepee to sing the songs of his bundle and to work out the plan for our raid. At last, we were off, eight of us. Though still a boy, I was permitted to take my gun, my bow, and a knife. As we were leaving the tepee my old grandmother asked me not to go; she took my hand and began to wail, but I pulled away. At the edge of the camp stood my uncle's father-in-law. He pled for all to return. Said he, "I have many horses, more than you can get from the Crow. Take what you want and stay at home. I am old and have not long to be with you." But we marched by in silence.

Pranks are usually played upon a boy on his first war excursion. The first night one of the warriors said, "Take this pail and run down that path for water, it is far." I set out briskly only to step into a a deep pool of ill-smelling mud. About this I was teased, and all manner of jokes were made. Of course, the warriors knew the pool was there. They joked about my new paint, my new way of deceiving an enemy, my new perfume (love medicine), and so on. Finally one man in a very solemn manner conferred a new name upon me—Stinking-legs. From that time on, all of them called me by that name.

But by the next night we were in the open country and there was little hilarity. My uncle opened his bundle and performed the ritual for it, all of us singing in a low subdued tone. After this we traveled mostly by night and slept by day, though the warriors took turns scouting. On the fourth day, a scout reported the enemy.

"Now," said my uncle, "it is time to sing the 'tapping-the-stick.'" So we all sat in a circle and my uncle began singing very softly, keeping time by tapping lightly on the stock of his gun with the end of his pipe-stick. He sang about a love affair and at the end named the woman. So it went around the circle. The last man, next to me, sang, and then named a young girl I was very fond of. Instinctively, I grasped my knife, but then, Oh shame! I was not yet a war-rior, for here no one must resent.   So I desisted, but I lay awake the rest of the day struggling with my anger.   This was all very foolish, for the man was only teasing me; yet few men would venture to jest in such songs.

That night we stole out and found the Crow camp unguarded. So we took all the loose horses grazing outside and made off with them.   Not even a dog barked.   When at a safe distance my uncle told us to follow a warrior named Running-crane, that he and one man were going back to get scalps to pay for my father's death, that they would join us at the rendezvous later.   My uncle was accom-panied by the man who sang about my girl.   On the third day my uncle overtook us, but he was alone.   What became of his companion he knew not; he was never seen after they separated to steal into the Crow camp.   That was what came of jesting with medicine songs.   All holy things must be respected.   But my uncle had brought a scalp, a shield, and a gun.   So we were happy.

When we got home there was feasting and scalp dancing for all. Finally, my old grandmother drew me out into full view, harangued the crowd upon my greatness as a warrior and said, "Now you must have been given a new name.   What is it?"   I hung my head for shame, "Oh!" she said, "my grandson is modest."

Then my uncle came forward and told the story of the mud hole and called me, "Stinking-legs."   Then merriment broke loose and for a long time I was teased about it.

Two of the captured horses were allotted to me: one I gave to my grandfather.   Not long after my uncle told me it was time to seek power.   This meant that I must fast and sacrifice, seeking a vision. So I took my other Crow horse to old Medicine-bear, a shaman, offered him a pipe, and made my request.   My instruction took many weeks.   I was introduced to the sweat house and other ceremonies, learned how to make the pipe offering, to cry for power, and so forth. At last all was ready and old Medicine-bear left me alone on a high hill to fast, dance, and pray.   Each evening and morning he came and, standing afar off, exhorted me to greater efforts.   By the third day I was too exhausted to stand.   That night I lay on my back look-ing up at the sky.   Then I saw the Smoking-star.[1]   And as I gazed

[1] Meaning: "the star who smoked my pipe."

it came nearer and nearer. Then I heard a voice, "My son, why do you cry here?" Then I saw a fine warrior sitting on the ground before me, smoking my pipe. At last he said, "I will give you power. You are to take my name. You must never change it. Always pray to me and I will help you."

The next morning when old Medicine-bear came and stood afar off I said, "Something has been given me." Then he prayed and took me home. In due time he heard my story, composed a song for me, gave me a small medicine bundle and announced my new name. I was now a man of power. Many young men offered to go to war with me, so I soon began to lead out parties. Many *coups* I counted as the years passed, but all came by the power of the Smoking-star. Only once did this power seem to fail me on the war-path. I was alone and surrounded by the Cree. At last I called upon the Sun, offering to give him my little finger. Then I overcame my enemies. So at the next sun dance I chopped off this finger (the left) and offered it to the sun to fulfil my vow. But this belongs to the second period in my life, of which I shall speak later.

Shortly after I saw the Smoking-star, I took a woman. My uncle and my grandparents had often hinted of marriage. I was particularly fond of a girl in the Small-robe band, but could not court her openly because that was my band by right of my father, though I lived with the band of my mother, the Fat-roasters. It is not good for a man to marry in his own band where most of his relatives live, but he can freely marry a woman of his mother's band, if not too closely related to her. I could have joined my mother's band, as my uncle urged, and then married the girl, but that seemed to me like evading my duty to uphold the honor of my father and to take revenge for his untimely death. People would talk about it. So I courted a girl in my mother's band. As she was not closely related to me, there was no hindrance. Our courtship was secret, as is often the custom; when I led out my first war party she slyly passed me a pair of moccasins. I think no one knew of our attachment. You see my mother's people all looked upon me as one of their band, though they should not have done so, and so looked elsewhere for my future woman. Long afterward I learned that they had picked a woman for me from the Blood band, the widow of a young warrior, a good woman some ten years older than I, but it turned out otherwise.

The girl I courted was named Elk-woman.   She and I were nearing twenty and it was time for her to marry, past time in fact.   So her relatives arranged to give her to a man of the They-don't-laugh-band.   The relatives of both parties had feasted and talked over the affair and were about ready to exchange the first presents, when Elk-woman's relatives first suggested the marriage to her.   She asked for time to think it over.   That evening when I met her as usual in a secret place, she told me the story and cried.   Such a marriage was repugnant to her.   I knew the man and had already come to dislike him.   So that night we ran away.   I took my horse, gun, and bow. We rode double.   We went far up into the foothills of the mountains and made a secret camp.

Some two weeks later my uncle trailed us and we had a talk.   He said I had done a very foolish thing; that all of my woman's relatives were angry and that the prospective husband vowed vengeance. However, as he had himself made the man a present of a horse and smoked a pipe with him, his anger was waning.   He thought that since I had always adhered to my father's band I should go there to live.   Anyway my father's people would then protect me.   In due time presents could be made to my parents-in-law.   You see when a man takes a woman, he is required to give many presents to her parents; this is called paying for her.   So, I had stolen my woman because nothing had been paid.   This would always stand against me in the minds of the people.

The next day we went back to my father's band.   A poor old woman, an aunt of my father, one of my grandmothers, as we say, took us in as we had no tepee.   No one seemed to take notice of us. When I hunted I took some of the meat and left it by the door of my father-in-law, as was the custom.   Finally, my uncle's relatives got together and collected six horses, a few robes, a warrior's suit, and a great lot of dried meat.   In solemn procession they paraded over to the camp of my parents-in-law.   Then followed a feast and a reconciliation.

Not long after this I happened to meet my mother-in-law in a path.   No one must see the face of his mother-in-law; if he does he must make her a present to cover her shame.   This accident cost me my gun.   It was a grievous loss as we were still poor.   My woman had not so much as a travois-dog to bring wood.

At this point the narrator paused and began to fill his pipe. Presently he said, "The Smoking-star is still overhead. We have reached the fork of the first trail; the boy becomes a hunter, goes to war, has a vision, he joins the Pigeons, then marries and takes his place among the men of his band. So far he travels but one trail. Thenceforth it is different with us, some become warriors, some medicine men, some are chiefs. It is well that we rest here a little while, before I go on."

When the pipe was burned out the story began thus:—

Some time before I was married I bought into the Mosquito society when they sold out to the Pigeons. It was this way with us: There were nine societies for men, of different rank as follows; Mosquitoes, Braves, All-brave-dogs, Front-tails, Raven-bearers, Dogs, Kit-foxes, Catchers, and Bulls. Lower than all was a boy's society, the Pigeons. To enter these societies you first bought into the Pigeons; that is, you gave presents to an older member who in return transferred his membership to you. Every four years each of the nine men's societies sold to the next lower; so one might finally, if he lived to be an old man, become a member of the Bulls. These societies were spoken of as the All-comrades. Each had its own songs, dances, regalia, and ritual. When the whole tribe came together for the summer hunt and the sun dance, these societies were called upon to guard and police the camp. Their parades and dances through the camp were very impressive. As all the members of a society were near the same age, these organizations are often called age-societies by the white people.

In time I passed through all of the societies and became a Bull. When in the Raven-bearers we gave a dance at a trading post where Fort Benton now stands and two strange white men watched us. One of them drew a picture of us and afterwards the older man asked questions of me through an interpreter and wrote something in a book. I heard that he came from across the great water as did the first white people, but I never saw him again.[1]

---

[1] In 1832 a post was founded near the present site of Fort Benton, Montana, known as Fort Mackenzie. In 1833 it was visited by the famous German traveler, Maximilian, Prince of Wied, accompanied by the artist, Charles Bodmer. Maximilian gives us an interesting and detailed account of his travels in the Missouri country and is the first to give us good information as to the culture of the Blackfoot. See his *Travels in the Interior of North America*, translated by H. E. Lloyd, Cleveland, 1906.

When with my comrades in the Bulls we sold out to the Catchers, I became one of the old men to sit in council and advise the people. There are two leaders for each society. I was never a leader, because the leaders of one always sold to the leaders of the lower, and it so happened during my life that the same two men lived to reach the Bulls. So there was no chance for anyone else to lead. But we are now far ahead of my story, I must begin with my life as one of the young married men.

After I came back with my woman to live in my band, old Medicine-bear often sat in our tepee. (My woman soon tanned skins from my hunting and made a large fine tepee of our own.) He wished me to become a shaman like himself. You see I had experienced a real vision, few men who fasted received such power as came to me. I had the power to become a shaman, but I held to my vow to be a warrior. I was poor. So I led war parties against the Cree, Assiniboin, Snake, and Crow. Many horses and guns I took. Coups I counted and took three scalps from the Crow. But I meditated often upon the powers in the air, water, and earth. They are the great mysteries. Everything is done by them. About this time two things happened to me that turned my thoughts from war.

Our chief led a party against the Cree and invited me to go. The chief was jealous of me. As I told you, he was a bad man, but I could not refuse. Medicine-bear, the shaman, went with us to give us power. When we reached the Cree country I was ordered out as a scout. It was dark. As I went along I saw a tepee all by itself. I went up to it quietly and looked in. There was no one in the tepee except a man, his wife, and a little child. The little child could just walk and was amusing itself by dipping soup from the kettle with a small horn spoon. The man and his wife were busy talking and paid no attention to the child. Now the child looked up and saw me peeping through the hole, toddled over to the kettle, dipped up some soup in the spoon and held it to my lips. I drank and the child returned to the kettle for more. In this way the child fed me for many minutes. Then I went away. As I went along to my own party, I thought to myself, "I do not like to do this, but I must tell my party about this tepee. When they know of it, they will come and kill these people. This little child fed me even when

I was spying upon them, and I do not like to have it killed. Well, perhaps I can save the child; but then it would be too bad for it to lose its parents. No, I do not see how I can save them, yet I cannot bear to have them killed." I sat down and thought it over. After a while, I went back to the tepee, went in, and sat down. While my host was preparing the pipe, the child began to feed me again with the spoon. After we had smoked, I talked to the man in the sign-language, told him all about it, how I had come as a scout to spy upon them, how I was about to bring up my war party, but that they had been saved by the little child. Then I directed the man to go at once, leaving everything behind him in the tepee.

The man was very thankful and offered to give me a medicine bundle and a suit of clothes; but I refused, because I knew that my party would suspect me. Then the man suggested that he might place the bundle near the door, behind the bedding, so that when the war party came up and dashed upon the tepee, I would be the first to capture the bundle. (All the important property of the tepee is always kept at the back, opposite the door, and, when a war party rushes in, the swiftest runs to this place.)

Then I reported to my chief, telling him that I had discovered a camp of the enemy but that I had not been up to it or seen anyone. He started out at once, all of us following. When we had surrounded the tepee, we gave a whoop and rushed upon it. I kept behind and while the others were busy counting coup upon the things in the back of the tepee, I seized the bundle by the door. The chief was angry, but said nothing. When we were again in camp old Medicine-bear began to unwrap his war medicine-pipe to make a thank offering for our success. Then the chief faced me and denounced me as a traitor, accused me of warning the enemy and secreting the medicine bundle. My anger rose, I drew my knife, but at that moment old Medicine-bear sprang between us, holding the holy pipe in both hands. This is the custom, no one can fight over a holy pipe. The shaman made us each take the pipe and vow to put away our anger and hold our silence. So it was.

Never have I forgotten that little child. Some great power was guarding it. Its medicine was strong. Many times have I prayed to that power and sometimes it helped me, but I do not yet know what power it is. Yet somehow I took little interest in war, the child's medicine did that to me.

The next year I felt sad and gloomy. So I decided to go to war anyway. I led out a party of my own against the Crow. The fourth night I went out to scout. It was cloudy and rather dark. As I was stealing along a marshy place, a star rose out of the earth and stood before me. It was the Smoking-star. Something in me said, "Follow." Then the star led off slowly; gradually it took me to the back trail and then swiftly faded away, as it moved toward my woman's tepee at home. I sat down and prayed. In my mind the Smoking-star was telling me to go back.

When dawn came I returned to my party. I told my story. All agreed that we should go home for the signs were against us. When I got into our camp I saw many people standing about my woman's tepee and heard a doctor's drum. My son, my first born, was very ill. Three doctors had been called, one after the other. I gave them all my horses. As is their way, when they feared the sick one would die, they departed. At last, I went out to the top of a hill to cry to the Smoking-star. Surely, I thought, he would help me, but clouds overcast the sky and there was no answer to my appeal. That morning the boy died.

In the afternoon the body was wrapped in a robe and placed in a tree near our camp. As he died in the tepee, we could not use it again so we placed it at the foot of the tree. I cropped my hair and mourned many days. Now I was poor. All my horses went to the doctors. My woman's tepee was gone and once again we lived with our poor old grandmother in her little ragged tepee; but in a few days my woman's relatives gave her another tepee and after a time we again accumulated horses.

About this time Medicine-bear became a beaver bundle owner. My misfortunes turned my mind more and more to the mysteries of the powers around us and I began to learn the songs and the teachings of the beaver men. The ritual for the beaver bundle is long and difficult. There are more than three hundred songs to be learned before one can lead the ceremony of the beaver. In the bundle are the skins of beavers, otters, and many kinds of birds and water animals. With each of these there are songs, for each brought some power to the man who first saw it in a vision. My people did not plant corn, as did the Mud-houses (Mandan and Hidatsa), but the beaver men planted tobacco. At the planting and the gathering of the tobacco, the beaver bundle is opened and the ritual sung. The garden and the plants are sacred, for tobacco must be offered to all the powers of the earth, and of the water. A beaver man must keep count of the days, the moons, and the winters. For this he keeps a set of sticks like those sometimes found in a beaver's house. At all times he must be ready to tell the moon and the day; he must say when it is time to go on the spring hunt, to hold the sun dance, etc. Then he must watch the sun, moon, stars, winds, and clouds so that he may know what the weather will be. If he is holy and good, he will have visions and dreams of power and so become a shaman.

So after my son died I often sat with the beaver men. In time I learned many of the beaver songs and became chief assistant to Medicine-bear in the ceremonies. When I was an old man, Medicine-bear died; it was the year before I sold out of the Bull society (the year we saw the first steamboat). Then I became the leading beaver man, as I am still.

When I first began to study the beaver medicine, I spent hours on the hilltops and near the waters, meditating and watching the birds, animals, and the heavens. Yet such solemn thoughts did not occupy all my time as a young married man.

There was much sport in the winter camps. Many men played the wheel and arrow game and again the hand game. These were the favorite gambling games. The first was for two players, but the latter permitted team playing. Some men gambled away all their belongings and even their women. I never went so far. Once I remember two young men played the wheel game until one lost all his possessions except his moccasins and his breechcloth, finally losing these, to the great merriment of the whole camp.

My band had a great reputation for jokes. In this I was a leader. Once in the spring we fooled a man named Bow-string. This man had a favorite race horse which he guarded very carefully, picketing him outside his tepee. One day I dressed myself to look like a Crow, and while Bow-string was inside playing the hand game, untied his horse and led him off up the hills across the creek. Then a confederate gave the alarm. All ran out to see a Crow going off with the horse in broad day. Of course, everyone knew the trick, but Bow-string. Care had been taken to send all the other horses of the camp out to pasture with a herder. So Bow-string took a gun and set out with a pursuing party, afoot. Everybody in camp appeared to be greatly frightened, women screamed, and all the dogs began to bark. As the supposed Crow, I sprang upon the horse, waved a defiance and dashed over the hill.

Once out of sight I rode quickly around the hills and got back to camp after the pursuers had passed over the ridge. After a fruitless search for the trail, the party came back, Bow-string looking very sad. But there stood his horse tied as before! Then there was great uproar and jesting.

A favorite trick of mine was often played upon visiting strangers, especially upon dignified old men. I would invite the guest to my tepee to feast with a few of my friends. Then I would pretend to quarrel with my woman and we would fall to fighting. The others would try to separate us and so all begin to struggle, taking care to fall upon and thoroughly muss up the puzzled visitor.

Our people were fond of liquor, which could be had when we went to the trading posts in summer. At such times there was much fighting. We all wanted liquor because we believed that some mysterious power could be had in that way. Some men had visions while drunk, that made them shamans or doctors according to the powers that were given them. Sometimes I drank liquor too. Once when my woman was drunk also, we quarreled and I threatened to tomahawk her smallest child, but she snatched a burning stick from the fire and thrust the glowing end against my neck; you see the scar. After that I did not drink much. I was glad when the Great Father stopped the trading of liquor, it did us much harm.

Once a year in summer all the bands of our tribe camped together. A great circle of tepees was formed and the societies had charge of the camp. At this time the sun dance was held. It was very sacred and lasted many days. No man was wise enough to know how all parts of it were conducted, so many medicine men were needed for the different rituals. Some men would vow to torture themselves at this time. I once gave a finger to the sun, but that is not the real sacrifice. Those who made the vow have holes cut in the skin of their breasts and shoulders, through which sticks are thrust and cords attached. The ends of these cords are fastened to the center pole in the sun-dance lodge, where these devotees dance and cry for power until they tear themselves free or fall in a swoon: I never made this sacrifice. I was afraid, for it is very holy. Yet many times have I given bits of my skin to Natos (the sun) as the scars upon my body show. These were not given in the sun dance, but when I was fasting alone in the hills.

A good and virtuous woman may often save the lives of her relatives by making a vow to take the tongues at the sun dance. My woman did this in the year known as "Gambler-died-winter" (about 1845, according to most tribal counts). Her brother was about to die. So she went outside, looked up at the sun, and said, "I will take the tongue at the sun dance." Her brother got well. If she had not been a pure and good woman, he would have died. In due time old Medicine-bear, the beaver bundle man, was given a horse and called in to prepare her for the ordeal. During the spring a hundred buffalo tongues were sliced and dried. Only true women are permitted to slice them. If a woman cuts her finger or cuts a hole in her slice, she is turned out because she has not been true to her husband. At the proper time in the sun dance, as the sun is setting, the women who have vowed to take the tongues go forward and in turn, take up a piece of tongue and holding it up to the sun, declare their purity. It is the duty of any man, who knows the claim to be false to come forward with a challenge. My woman was not challenged. Everyone knew her to be pure and good.

Once she was the holy woman to give the sun dance. It was in the deep snow winter (about 1851) that she became ill. Many people were starving, for the buffalo had drifted far before the snowstorms. Then my woman addressed the sun, saying that she would give the sun dance, next year. Soon the people found buffalo and she got well.

A woman cannot give the sun dance alone, her man must also be good and brave. Both must fast four days and sit in the holy tepee. The holy natoas bundle must be opened and the woman wear its sacred headdress, with the prairie turnip and carry the digging-stick used by the Woman-who-married-a-star. That winter we were camped on the Missouri. The following summer we went to Yellow River to give the sun dance.

Now, it is our way, that the woman who vows to give the sun dance must buy a natoas bundle. The power and right to the ritual thus come to her. For this, many horses, robes, and dried meat must be given. When we came to bring our bundle all the people of our band and our relatives in other bands were called upon to help us by gifts. After the sun dance we kept the natoas bundle in our tepee and cared for it as the ritual required. My woman was now a medicine woman. She did not sell her bundle. In the Blood-fought-among-themselves winter she died (about 1858). I put the bundle in her robe, set up her tepee on a high hill and left her there. That is our custom.

She was a good and true woman. After that I went to live with my son, as you now see. I never took another woman because the Smoking-star appeared to me in a dream and forbade it.

In the course of time everyone came to look upon me as a shaman. No one will now walk before me as I sit in a tepee. In my presence all are dignified and orderly and avoid frivolous talk. Four times in my life the Smoking-Star has stood before me. All visions are sacred, as are some dreams, but when a vision appears the fourth time, it is very holy. Even a shaman may not speak of it freely. Many times have I gone to lonely places and cried out to the powers of the air, the earth, and the waters to help me understand their ways. Sometimes they have answered me, but all the truly great mysteries are beyond understanding.

In the year of the Camp-at-bad-waters-winter the Bull society sold out as I have said. That was the end of that society; there were but three of us left when we sold to the Catchers and those to whom we sold soon died. The ways of the white man were coming among us and many things were passing away. I was now an old man, fit only for sitting in council. I could no longer run buffalo, no longer go to war. So we have come to the last fork in the trail. I have smoked many pipes. I have sat in many councils, I have made many speeches to restrain our young men from rash and unjust actions. We are near the end. The Smoking-star will soon pass down in the west. Soon it will lead me to the sand hills where my spirit will wander about among the ghosts of buffalo, horses, and men. Your way is not our way, but you have loved us.   Perhaps your spirit also may return to wander with us among the sand hills of our fathers.   I pray that it may be so.   Now, it is finished.

Thoughtfully I left that fireside to find my blankets.   As I passed out through the night, I saw the "Smoking-star" sinking in the west. It shone to me with a new light.   The next winter my old friend passed into the beyond.   His body was laid on a tree scaffold near the favorite haunts of his band on Two Medicine River.

CLARK WISSLER

LITTLE WOLF JOINS THE MEDICINE LODGE

Little-wolf Joins the Medicine Lodge

I

IN THE LODGE OF THE MASTER

MATCIKINEU, Terrible-eagle, sat dozing in the dusk in his round, rush-mat wigwam. The fire smouldered, but random drafts, slipping in through the swinging mat that covered the door, encouraged little dancing flames to spring up, and these illumined the far interior of the lodge, so that it was possible to observe its furnishings down to the mustiest cranny.

Around the inner circumference of the wigwam, ran a broad rustic bench, supported by forked sticks and thickly strewn balsam boughs on which lay bearskin robes. The inner wall of the home was hung with woven reed mats, bearing designs in color, of angular figures and conventional floral motifs. Over Terrible-eagle's head, on smoke encrusted poles, swung several mat-covered, oval bundles, festooned with age-blackened gourd rattles, war clubs, and utensils and weapons of unusual portent. These were his sacred war and hunting bundles, packets of charms whose use and accompanying formulæ he had obtained personally from the Gods, while fasting, or purchased at a great price from others more fortunate than he. For Terrible-eagle was a renowned war leader, a hunter, and the greatest of all Mätc Mitäwûk, Masters of the Grand Medicine Society, a secret fraternal and medical organization, to which, in one form or another, nearly every Indian of influence in all the Great Lakes and Central Western region belonged.

The door covering was quietly thrust aside and Anäm, a wolf-like dog, trotted in to curl up by the fire, while after him, first dropping a load of faggots from her shoulders, stumbled Wábano-mitämu, Dawn-woman, wife of Terrible-eagle, who crouched down grumbling to enter the lodge, and turned on her time-gnarled knees to drag the kindlings in after her.

Roused by the noise, Terrible-eagle stretched and yawned, then reached over his head and took down a calabash-shell rattle, which he began to shake gently, while Dawn-woman shoved aside the birch-bark boxes that cluttered the floor, stirred up the fire in the round, shallow pit where it was glowing, and set among the hot embers a large, round, deep, pointed-bottomed kettle of brown earthen-ware, the base of which she screwed into the ashes by a quick, circular twist of the rim. Into this kettle she poured some water from a birch-bark pail; and, when it began to simmer, added a quantity of wild rice, smoked meat, and dried berries, which she stirred with an elaborate wooden-spoon paddle.

The random swish of Terrible-eagle's rattle now began to articulate itself in the form of a tune, the motif of which might have been borrowed from the night babblings and murmurings of a woodland brook. It rose like the prattle of water racing down stony riffles; it fell to the purring monotone of a little fall burbling into a deep pool.

Then, suddenly, Terrible-eagle raised his voice in song—a song without meaning to the uninitiated—yet a song potent with the powers of Manitous, and ancient as the pine forests.

"Ni mánituk, häwatûkuk, kê'nêäminûm."

"You, my gods, I am singing to you!"

"Look you, old fellow," cried Dawn-woman, squatting beside her cooking, "why do you sing that sacred song? There is no need to rehearse the chants of the Manitous when ice binds the rivers, and snow blankets the land! When new life dawns with the grass blades in the spring, then we will need to refresh our memories; not now, while the gods sleep like bears."

"Silence, old partner! You do not know everything! Even now there comes one seeking the knowledge of the path our brethren and fellows have trod before us. Listen!"

The lodge was hushed with the heavy silence of the Wisconsin forest in midwinter. Then came the crunch and squeak of approaching snowshoes slipping over the crusted drifts.

"N'hau, Dawn-woman! Prepare the guest place, spread robes behind the fire, dish out a bowl of soup! Some one of our people desires to enter!"

The noise ceased before the doorway, and Terrible-eagle, now hunched before the fire, paused before dropping a hot coal on the tobacco in his red stone pipe, to bid the guest to enter. "Yoh!" came the hearty response, and a tall, dark warrior, bareheaded save for a fillet of otter fur around his brows, ducked under the doorway and silently passed round the fire, on the left, to the guest place, where he seated himself, cross-legged, on a pile of robes. He was clad in a plain shirt of blue-dyed deerskin, deeply fringed on the seams, in flapping, leather leggings, high soft-soled moccasins, and a leather apron handsomely embroidered with colored porcupine quills wrought in delicate, flowered figures. He bore no weapon, and on his swarthy cheeks two round spots of red paint were seen in the firelight.

After the newcomer had eaten a bowl of steaming stew with the aid of a huge, wooden ladle, he lay back among the robes, puffing comfortably on a long-stemmed pipe with bowl of red stone, filled and lighted for him by the old man. As the cheerful odor of tobacco and kinnikinick permeated the lodge, the stranger began to speak. He informed the old people that his name was Muhwäsê, Little-wolf, of the Wave clan of the Menomini, that he had come all the way from Mätc Suamäko, the Great Sand Bar village on the Green Bay of Lake Michigan; that the young men had opened their war bundles, and danced preparatory to going to war against the Sauk, but that the Sauk had heard the news and fled southward. He ended with all the gossip and tittle-tattle of his band.

It was not until Dawn-woman slept, and the stars were visible in the winter sky through the smoke hole of the lodge, that Little-wolf went out abruptly, and returned bearing a huge bundle which he dumped on the floor at the feet of Terrible-eagle, and silently took his place on the lounge once more.

With trembling hands the old man undid the leathern thongs and unwrapped the bearskin with which the bundle was enclosed, and spread before him an array of articles that brought an avaricious sparkle to his red-rimmed eyes.

"Nimá, nékan! Well done, my colleague!" he exclaimed. "These are valuable gifts, and in the proper number. Four hatchets, four spears, and four knives of the sacred yellow rock (native copper), four belts of white wampum, and four garments of tanned deerskin, embroidered with quillwork, with much tobacco. Surely this gift has a meaning?"

"Grandfather! You to whom nothing is hard," replied the visitor. "It is true that I am nobody. I am poor—the enemy scarcely know my name. Yet I am desirous of eating the food of the Medicine Lodge, as all the brethren have done who have passed this way before me!"

"N'hau, my grandson! I shall call together the three other Pushwäwûk, or masters, fo their consent. What you have asked for, may seem as nothing to you—yet it is Life. These songs may appear to partake of the ways of children—yet they are powerful. I understand you well; you desire to imitate the ways of our own ancient Grand Master, Mä'näbus, who was slain and brought to life that we might gain life unending! Good! You have done well. In the morning I shall send invitation-sticks and tobacco to summon the leaders here, that your instruction may begin at once!"

II

THE INSTRUCTION

It was an hour after sunset. In the rear of the lodge sat Terrible-eagle and three other old men, with Little-wolf at their left. Before them lay the pile of valuable gifts, and, on the white-tanned skin of an unborn fawn, stood the sacred towaka or deep drum, hollowed by infinite labor from a short section of a basswood log, holding two fingers' depth of water to make its voice resonant, and covered with a dampened membrane of tanned, buck hide. Across its head was balanced a crooked drumstick, its striking end carved to represent a loon's beak. Before the drum, was placed a wooden bowl in the shape of a minature, log canoe heaped with tobacco, and four gourd rattles with wooden handles which shone from age and usage. A youth tended the fire and kept the air redolent with incense of burning sweet grass and cedar. Dawn-woman and Anäm, the dog, guarded the door.

Extending his hands over the sacred articles before them, Terrible-eagle began a prayer of invocation, calling on the mythical hero and founder of the Medicine Lodge, Mä'näbus, on the Great Spirit, the Sun, and the Thunderbirds; on the good-god Powers or Manitous of air and earth, and also upon the Evil Powers who dwell in and under the earth and water and hidden in the dismal places of the world, to appear in spirit and accept the tobacco offered them and to dedicate the fees presented to the instructors.

When the prayer was ended, all those gathered in the wigwam ejaculated "Hau," and three of the elders smoked and listened while Terrible-eagle began the instruction by relating the history of the origin of the Medicine Lodge. Taking the drumstick in his hand, Terrible-eagle gave four distinct strokes on the drum, and recited in a rhythmic and solemn tone, hushing his voice to a whisper when it became necessary to mention a great Power by name.

He told how Mätc Häwätûk, the Great Spirit, sat alone in the heavenly void above the ever extending sea, and willed that an island (the world) should appear there; how he further willed that there should spring up upon this island, an old woman who was known as "Our Grandmother, The Earth." He recited how the Earth Grandmother conceived, supernaturally, and gave birth to a daughter. How the Four winds, desiring to be born as men, entered the daughter's body and lay as twins in her womb, and how, when the hour of their birth came, so great was their power, they burst their mother, making women forever after liable to death in travail.

"Then," related Terrible-eagle, "our Earth Grandmother gathered up the shattered pieces of her daughter, and placed them under an inverted, wooden bowl, and prayed, and on the fourth day, through the pity of the Great Spirit, the fragments were changed into a little rabbit, who was named Mätc Wábus, or the Great Hare, since corrupted into 'Mä'näbus,' who was to prepare the world for human habitation.

"The rabbit grew, in human form, to man's estate, when he was given, as a companion and younger brother, a little wolf, but the Powers Below, being jealous, slew the wolf brother. Then, Mä'näbus in his wrath attacked the Powers below, and, as he was the child of the Great Spirit, they could not resist him. In fear the Evil Powers restored his younger brother to life, but, since he had been dead four days, the flesh dropped from his bones and he stank, and Mä'näbus, in sorrow, refused to receive him, and sent him to rule the dead in the After World, at the end of the Milky Way in the Western Heavens. Hence, human beings may not come back to life on the fourth day.

"At their wits' end to appease Mä'näbus, the Evil Ones called on the Powers Above who are of good portent. They erected a Medicine Lodge on the high hilltops, oblong, rectangular, facing east and west. The Power of the Winds roofed it with blue sky and white clouds. The pole framework was bound with living, hissing serpents instead of basswood strings, the food for feasting was seasoned with a pinch of the blue sky itself. Then the Powers entered. The gods of Evil took the north side where darkness and cold abide; the Good Powers Above sat on the south. Then they all stripped off the animal natures with which they were disguised, and hung them on the wall of the Lodge, and all appeared in their true forms, as aged persons.

"In council, guided by the admonitions of the Great Spirit, they decided to give to Mä'näbus the ritual of the Lodge, with its secret— long life and immortality for mankind—as a bribe to cease his molestation. But Mä'näbus refused to receive their message, until Otter volunteered to fetch him. Then Mä'näbus came, and was duly instructed and raised, by being slain and brought to life again, thus showing the great potency of the Powers who owned the Lodge.

"This very ceremony, just as it was given Mä'näbus, and later transferred to us, his uncles and aunts, with its rites, formulas, and medicines, is the same," concluded Terrible-eagle, "as we perform to-day, as all the brethren and fellows have done who have passed this way before us, since the Menomini came out of the ground, in the past." As he ended the old man struck the drum four times, crying, "My colleagues, my colleagues, my colleagues, my colleagues!"

When Terrible-eagle had concluded his part, there was a recess for refreshment and relaxation, which lasted until each had smoked, then another old pushwäo or master took up the work. He it was who related to the candidate the identity of the Powers Above and Below who had given the Medicine Lodge to mankind, through Mä'näbus. There were, he said, four groups of Evil Powers, who sat on the north side of the Lodge. First were the Otter, Mink, Marten, and Weasel; second the Bear, Panther, Wolf, and Horned Owl; third the Banded Rattlesnake, the little Prairie Rattlesnake, the Pine Snake, and the Hog-nosed Snake. The fourth group was composed of lesser birds and beasts. The Upper World which had not offended Mä'näbus, was not so well represented, and was composed of various predatory birds, such as the Red-shouldered Hawk and the Sparrow-hawks. These sat on the south side, and, in ancient days, human Lodge members had been seated according to the nature of their medicine bags.

The skins of any of these animals might be used as containers or sacks for the secret nostrums of the craft, but the Dog and Fox, which were formerly associated with the Wolf, had, by their cunning and their custom of eating filth and carrion, become too closely associated with witchcraft, and were now tabu.

The old master then told the candidates that each of these animals had donated some special power to aid mankind. Thus the Weasel gave cunning and ferocity in war and the chase, the Snapping-turtle, probably one of the vague fourth group of Evil Powers, had given his heart, which beats long after it is torn from his bosom, to grant long life. Each animal had four songs sung in his honor during the session of the Lodge, said the elder, and the third instructor would teach these to the candidate.

The old master informed his pupil that in his opinion the Medicine Lodge and its rites were found far to the east, in the country by the Great Sea Where the Dawn Rises, for he had once met a party of warriors, from the far off Nottoway or Iroquois, who spoke of a society and its ritual, given them by the animals, which had for its object long life and immortality for men.

Dawn-woman now fetched steaming rice and fat venison, marrow-bones and dried berries, and the little party feasted. The hour was very late, yet none thought of sleep. After the feast, the third elder did his part.

He selected a calabash rattle, and, sometimes rattling, sometimes drumming an accompaniment, taught the songs of the Lodge to Little Wolf. There were songs of opening and songs of closing, as well as the animal songs, each repeated four times, the sacred number, and each in groups of four. Each was made obscure and unintelligible to eavesdroppers by the addition of nonsense syllables. Some, indeed, were so ancient, and so clouded by vocables, that nothing but their general meaning was remembered even by the brethren. These passed for songs in a secret, magic language. Some chants were in other languages, particularly Ojibway, and all ended with the mystic phrase "we-ho-ho-ho-ho," which meant "so mote it be." The songs had titles, but these names too, were magic, and often gave no inkling of the meaning or wording of the song, and most of them avoided naming the animals or gods to which they referred, except by circumlocution, or by merely mentioning some prominent characteristic or attribute of the creature.

There were songs for the "shooting of the medicine"—an act which was so secret and mysterious that the candidate was as yet kept in the dark as to its meaning—and others for dancing, for thanksgiving and for dedication.

When the third elder had ended his synopsis of the songs, which the candidate had later to purchase and learn at leisure, the fourth and last past master took him in hand. His part, he said, was short, yet important. He showed the candidate certain articles which would be ceremonially given to the candidate at the proper time and place. Among these articles was the tanned skin of an otter, the nostrils of which were stuffed with tufts of red-dyed hawk-down, the under surfaces of the four feet and tail being adorned with fringed rectangles of blue-dyed doe leather, embroidered with conventional flower designs in colored porcupine hair and quills. This was to be the medicine bag of the new member. Through an opening, a slit in the chest of the otter, one could thrust a hand, and find in the little pouch made by the skin of the left forefoot of the animal, a small sea shell, called the konäpämîk, or medicine arrow, by which the essence of all the sacred objects contained in the bag was ceremonially "shot" or transferred to the bodies of the Lodge brethren during the performance of the ritual.

Three other medicines the otter skin contained. There were sacred, blue face-paint, the color of the sky; a mysterious brown powder holding a seed, wrapped in a packet with a fresh water clamshell; and another mixture of pounded roots called "Reviver," or Apisétchikun.

The clamshell was a sacred, ancient cup, in which the accompanying powder and seed were placed with a little water, and given to all candidates to drink. The mystic seed was supposed to be the badge of the Medicine Lodge, and was to remain in the candidate's breast, forever, even until he had followed the Pathway of the Dead along the Milky Way. The "Reviver" was a powerful drug for use at all times when life ebbed low, through sickness or magic.

"These then," said the last instructor, "are the ways and sacred things of Mä'näbus, given us Indians to have and use, as long as the world shall stand!"

So saying, he in turn retired, and the party rolled in their blankets to sleep before the sun could look in through the smoke hole of the wigwam.

III

THE INITIATION

It was the season when buds burst, and the young owls, hatched while the snow was yet on the ground, were already taking their prey. The discordant croaking of the frogs came as a roar from the marshlands. The arbutus was blooming.

Perched on the top of a warm, sunny knoll, was an oblong, dome-roofed structure of poles, covered with bark and rush mats. It was oriented east and west, and its length, a full hundred feet, contrasted oddly with its breadth of twenty.

It was the evening of the fourth day of the Mitäwiwin, or Medicine ceremony. The preceding three days and nights had been spent by the four masters, led by Terrible-eagle, in preparing Little-wolf within a room, formed by curtaining off one end of the lodge proper; in giving him his ceremonial sweat bath of purification; and in hanging the initiation fees, four sets of valuable goods—clothing, robes, weapons, copper utensils—on the ridgepole at the eastern end of the lodge; and in dedicating them.

As the sun set, the four old men and the candidate entered the lodge, followed by the men and women of the tribe who were already members of the society. Going in at the eastern door, the procession filed along the north side, and passing once regularly around, the people seated themselves on the right of the door, with the candidate on the west side of them, next to Terrible-eagle.

The night having largely passed in quiescence and instruction, towards dawn an officer of the lodge approached Little-wolf, and stood before him, facing the east. Thrusting his hand into his medicine bag he drew forth his sacred clamshell cup and the powder containing the seed, which he compounded into a drink, while he sang a song called "What Otter Keeps."

> "I am preparing the thing that was hung [the little seed],
> And that which was hung shall fall!"

When he had finished, and Little-wolf had swallowed the draft, this officer retired, and another came forward and took his place, singing. As he ended, he stooped over, coughed and retched violently until he cast forth a sea shell, which he held in the palm of his hand, and, chanting, displayed to the east, west, south, and north, after which he caused Little-wolf to swallow it, that it might remain in his body forever: the symbol of immortality, and the badge of a lodge member. When this had been accomplished the assistant gave place to a third, who sang his four songs and painted the candidate's face with the sacred, blue paint. Then a fourth and last assistant came before the candidate and the masters, bearing an otter-skin, medicine bag, which he laid at Little-wolf's feet, while he sang four songs concerning Otter, the most famous of which was entitled Yom Mitäwakeu, or "This Medicine Land," but which held no reference to otters whatever!

Now the old men conducted the candidate, four times regularly around the lodge, while they related to him somewhat of the story of the ancient Master Mä'nabus, whom he now represented. On the last circuit Terrible-eagle led him to a seat near the western end of the lodge, and there placed him, facing the east; remaining with the candidate standing behind, and holding his shoulders.

The men and women seated around the walls of the lodge sat tense. The silence was unbroken save for woodland sounds, for the great, dramatic moment had arrived.

The four assistant masters, who had just performed before Little-wolf, now assembled in the east, facing him, and the first, taking his medicine bag in his two hands, and holding it breast high before his body, sang, to the rapid beat of the drum, a song entitled "Shooting the New Member." At its end he gave the usual sacred cry "oh we ho ho ho ho!" blew on the head of the otter skin, and rushed forward as though to attack the candidate.

In front of the neophyte impersonator of the ancient hero the attacker paused, and jerked the head of his otter upward, crying savagely, "Ya ha ha ha ha!" The magical essence of the bag supposedly striking the candidate, he staggered slightly, but was steadied by a companion, only to meet the feigned attacks of the second and third assistants, at each of which he reeled once more. But the charge of the fourth fellow was so violent that the candidate fell flat on the ground. Stooping, the last man laid the medicine bag across the back of the apparently unconscious brother, to be his, thereafter. At a sign from Terrible-eagle, the four assistants approached the prostrate candidate, and raising him to his feet, shook him gently to remove their shots and restore him to life.

And now all was rejoicing. Steaming earthen kettles were carried in, filled with delicious stews and soups of bear and turtle flesh, partridges, and young ducks. Laughing, jesting, and good-natured banter filled the lodge until the last wooden bowl was scraped clean, when the utensils and scraps were carried out, and the drummer struck up a lively dancing tune. After the men and women had had each four sets of songs, a general dance took place, wherein the members circled the lodge, the new brother among them, shooting each other promiscuously with jollity, vying with each other to rise and point their bags or fall prone on the earth. All the time a loud and lively chant was sung:

I
"I pass through them! I pass through them! I pass through even the chief!"

II
"Ye Gods take part, invisible though ye be beneath us!"

When all was over, and Keso, the Sun, was almost noon high, the four assistants took down the invitation fees from the ridgepole, and distributed them to the four old Masters and the others who had taken prominent part in the ceremonial, and all the Indians filed out of the western door, singing:

"You, my brethren, I pass my hand over you. I thank you."

* * *

Muhwäse, Little-wolf, watched the last of his companions strike their camps; saw the coverings stripped from the lodge structure, saw the last party vanish in the brush.

He was a Mitäo! A member of a great fraternal organization, who might travel westward to the foothills of the Rockies, north to the Barren Lands, south to the countries of the Iowa and Oto, east to the land of the Iroquois, and find brethren who had traveled the same road, or at least one fundamentally similar. He had shown his fortitude and fidelity, those two great, cardinal virtues of the Medicine Lodge, and he had come through the sacred mysteries alive and in possession of the secret rites that had been handed down since the days when the Menomini first came out of the ground.

ALANSON SKINNER

THUNDER~CLOUD
A WINNEBAGO SHAMAN
RELATES AND PRAYS

Thunder-cloud, a Winnebago Shaman, Relates and Prays

I CAME from above and I am holy. This is my second life on earth. Long ago I lived on earth, long ago when this earth was full of wars. I used to be a warrior then and I was a brave man.

Long ago in battle I was killed. As I went along I thought I had stumbled and fallen on the ground. Then I got up again and went on my way. To my home I went. When I got home my wife and my children were there, but they would not look at me, they would not notice me. So I spoke to my wife, but she did not show in any way that she was aware of my presence. She did not show any signs that she was aware of anyone speaking to her. There I stood. I could not converse with them and they never looked at me. "What can be the matter?" I thought. At last it occurred to me that I was probably dead, so I immediately started out for the battlefield and there, surely enough, I saw my body lying. Then, for the first time, I knew that I was dead.

After that I tried for a long time to return to my original home; for four years I tried, but I failed, so I stayed on earth.

At one time I was a fish and I lived with them. Their life is much more wretched than ours, for they are often in lack of food. Yet they are happy beings for they have dances very often.

At another time I lived as a little bird. Now that is a wonderful existence when the weather is good, but when it is cold, life is a hardship. Often birds are in lack of food and suffer from cold. It was my custom to go to the camp of certain people who lived near and to stay there in the daytime. These people were hunting at the time and from their meat-racks I used to steal a little food.

A little boy was staying with them and we were always terribly afraid of him, for he had an object that was fear-inspiring. With this he would shoot and make so great a noise that we would fly away. At night we used to go home, to a hollow tree. Whenever I got there first, the others, coming after me in great numbers, would almost squeeze me to death and yet, on those occasions when I waited till all the others had entered, I almost froze to death.

On another occasion I became a buffalo and lived as a buffalo lives. Lack of food and cold weather did not bother us much, but we had to be on the alert all the time against hunters.

Then from that place I went home, to my spirit-home up above, the place I had originally come from. Now in the sky, up above, there is a doctors' home; that is the place I have come from.

After a while I wanted to leave my home and go to the earth again. The person in charge of that home is my grandfather. He at first objected to my going, but I asked him again and again. The fourth time I asked him, he consented. He said to me: "Well, grandson, if you really wish to go to the earth, you may go. Before you go, you had better fast, for if any of the spirits have compassion upon you, then you will be able to live in peace on earth."

I fasted for four years, and the spirits above, even as far as the fourth heaven, all approved of my going. They blessed me. Ten days I fasted and after that I fasted twenty days; and again I fasted thirty days. All the spirits blessed me, even those under the earth.

Then when I was ready to go to the earth, all the spirits gathered around me and they had a council. In the center of the world, there, they had a council. There they were to advise me. All the spirits were present. They told me that I would not fail in anything I attempted. There they tested my powers. The first thing they did was to place a spirit grizzly bear at the end of the dancing lodge. This bear, it was said, could not be hurt in any manner.

The lodge was full of spirits. Then they started to sing the songs that I was to use when on earth. After that, I walked around the fireplace, and taking a live coal, I held it in the palm of my hand and danced around the fireplace again. Then I shouted "wahi!" and struck the hand containing the live coal with the other hand. The bear, the invulnerable bear, shot forward and fell to the ground, flat on his stomach. A black substance oozed from his mouth.

Then the spirits said to me, "You have killed him. Powerful as he was, you have killed him. Clearly never will anything evil succeed in crossing your path." That I would fail in nothing they told me. Then they took the one that I had killed and taking a red knife they cut him into pieces and piled him in the center of the lodge.

There they covered him with a dark covering and said. "Now! Again you must try your strength." So I asked for the objects that I was to use on earth, a flute and a gourd. Those were the objects that I used.

Then I made myself holy. Those that had blessed me were present. Then I walked around the one who had been cut into pieces and I breathed upon him. Then for the second time I walked around the object and I breathed upon him, and the rest within the lodge, breathed with me. Four times I breathed upon him, and then he arose and walked away, a human being.

"Hoho, it is good," they said, "he has restored him to life. Surely, most surely, he is holy." Thus they spoke to me. "Well, grandson, you will ever be thus. Whatever exists you will be able to destroy and then to restore to life again. Most surely have you been blessed." Thus they spoke to me.

Then they placed a black stone in the doctors' lodge above, there where I was blessed and again they put me to a test of strength. Four times I breathed upon that stone and finally I made a hole right through the stone by the force of my breathing. So now, whoever has a pain, if he permits me to blow upon him, then I can blow his pain away for him. It makes no difference what kind of pain it is, for my breath has been made holy. They, the spirits, made my breath holy and strong.

Then the spirits presiding over the earth and those living under the earth, they also gave me a trial. A rotten log was placed before me. I breathed upon it, I spat water upon it, and the log rose up, a living man. He walked away. This power of spitting upon people, of squirting water upon people, I received from an eel; from an eel that was the chief of all the eels, an eel that lives in the center of the ocean, in the very deepest part of the ocean. He is perfectly white. He it is, who blessed me. Therefore it is that I can use water and that the water I possess is inexhaustible. This is what he told me.

Then I came to the people of the earth. Before I came, they all had a council meeting about me. When I came, I entered a lodge and there I was born again. I thought that I had entered a lodge, but it was really my mother's womb that I had entered. Not even then, at my birth, did I lose consciousness. As I grew up I fasted again, and then again all those who had blessed me before sent their

blessings to me once more.   It is for that reason that I am the dic-
tator over all these spirits.   Whatever I say will be so.

Now the tobacco you offered me is really not for myself, but for
the spirits, because I have really been sent here by the spirits to get
tobacco for them.   Here, there is a sick person and you have offered
me tobacco.   That is what I am on earth for: to accept this offering.
I tell you that this patient will live.

You will live, patient, so help yourself as much as you can and
make yourself strong.   Now as I offer tobacco to the spirits, you must
listen, and if you feel that I am telling the truth, then you will gain
strength thereby.

Here is tobacco for you, O Fire!   I offer tobacco to you.   You
promised me that if I offered tobacco to you, you would grant me my
request.   That you promised, if I placed tobacco upon your head.
Did you not say that to me after I had fasted for four days and you
had blessed me?   Now here there comes a plea from a human being,
from one who wishes to live.   Here, the tobacco is yours and I ask
that within four days, he be restored to his usual health.   I ask that
he regain his former health and be even as the rest of us.   I offer
tobacco to you, grandfather.   Here it is.

May you, O Buffalo, also add your strength, add your power.
Six days I fasted and then you sent your spirit upon me.   I entered
your lodge, your lodge that is in the center of this earth.   You Buffalo, you who are pure white in color, you blessed me.   So likewise
did the buffaloes with the four different colors.   Those blessings
that you bestowed upon me, those I now want.   The gift of being
able to breathe upon man, you gave me.   You told me I would not
fail.   Now that is what I desire.   Therefore it is that I ask that you
add your strength as you promised, for they, the people, have given
me plenty of tobacco.

Now you, O Grizzly Bear, here is tobacco.   At a place called
Pointed-hill there is a spirit in charge of a dancing lodge.   Now
all those in that lodge blessed me and said that I would be able to
kill anything that confronted me; that I would also be able to restore
to life whatever I wished.   Here I have opportunity of giving life
to a man.   I want him to live.   They have given me tobacco.   Here
it is.   When I was a ghost you took me to your home, and after I
had fasted for ten days you blessed me.   Those things with which

you blessed me, those are the things that I now want. The people are offering you tobacco, grandfathers,—here it is.

Now you, chief eel in the center of the ocean, you too blessed me after I had fasted for eight days. With your power of breath did you bless me, with your inexhaustible wealth of water. You gave me the gift of using it whenever I treated a patient. That is what you told me. All the water in the ocean you told me I could use. You blessed me with all the objects that exist in the ocean. Now here is a man desiring life, and I too wish him to live. It is for that reason that I speak to you in this way. As I now squirt water upon him, may it be as though it were your power. O grandfather, I offer you tobacco. Here it is. Here is tobacco for you.

Now you who are above, Turtle, you who are in charge of a doctors' lodge, you blessed me after I had fasted seven days and you carried me, in spirit, to your home. There in your home I found all the birds who have sharp claws and you all blessed me and you told me that however bad the pain was, you would be able to extract it. Therefore it was that you named me the extractor of pain. Now here comes a man with an intense pain inside of him. I am the one to remove it for him, for I am the one you blessed and whom you taught that in nothing would he fail. I am going to heal this man. Here is the tobacco.

You of the snake home, you the perfectly white one, Rattlesnake! Did you not bless me after I had fasted for four days? You said that on an occasion like this, you would help me. You blessed me with your rattles that I was to use as gourds. You blessed me and told me that I would accomplish all that I attempted, by the use of the rattle. I offer you tobacco therefore, that I may make this sick person live when I shake my gourd. That life would be opened before him, that is what you told me, grandfather.

Ho, you Night Spirits! You too blessed me after I had fasted nine days. You took me to your village, situated in the east. There you told me that your plants were sacred and you blessed me with them. Now that is what I want. You made my flute sacred. That I am speaking the truth, you well know. Now to me the people have come bringing a sick person, for whom they desire life. I too want him to live. That is why I am speaking to you. You promised always to accept my tobacco and here it is, grandfathers.

Ho, here is tobacco for you, Disease-giver! After I had fasted for two days, you caused me to know that you were the one that bestowed diseases, that if I desired to heal one who is sick, that it would not be difficult. To you, therefore, Disease-giver, I offer tobacco. I offer you tobacco that this person, who is sick, may become well again. That is what you promised me in your blessing.

Ho, you Thunderbirds! I offer you tobacco. When you blessed me, you said you would help me if I needed you. Now here I have someone who desires life. I, too, want him to live, and that is why I remind you of your promise. I ask your help, grandfather, as you promised it to me. Here is the tobacco.

Ho, I offer you tobacco, Sun. Here it is. You blessed me after I had fasted for five days and you said that you would come to my relief whenever I had a difficult object to accomplish. Now here is a man who desires life. He comes with offerings of tobacco to you. Since you have blessed me, the people have brought their offerings of tobacco to me.

Ho, grandmother, Moon! You too blessed me, Moon. You said that you would also add your power. Here is a man who desires life and I call on you to add your power, as you promised me, so that he may live. Grandmother, here is tobacco.

Ho, grandmother, Earth! To you I also offer tobacco. You blessed me and promised always to help me. You promised that I could use all the herbs belonging to you, all the best ones, and that then I would not fail in that which I attempted. Now that is what I ask on this occasion, and that you keep the promise you made to me and help me. I ask you to do for this sick man what these people are asking me to do for him. Make my medicine powerful, grandmother.

Ho, you the chief of all the spirits! You too have blessed me and you too said that you would help me. Therefore I offer you tobacco so that this person may live. If his spirit is about to wander, I ask that you keep away from him, that you do not seize him. This is what I ask of you and why I offer you tobacco.

Ho-o-o, to all of you spirits I offer tobacco, to all of you who have blessed me.

PAUL RADIN

HOW MESKWAKI CHILDREN
SHOULD BE BROUGHT UP

How Meskwaki Children Should Be Brought Up

Harry Lincoln, of the Meskwaki, has dictated the following free rendition
of a Meskwaki text written out in the current syllabary.

WHEN a boy becomes old enough to be intelligent, his parents begin
to teach him how to take care of himself and act righteously. They
usually tell him not to do a good many things. Children are taught
not to be naughty. They are told that if they are naughty, people
will have nothing to do with them. They are told that if they are
naughty, people will talk about them. And children are told not
to steal anything from their neighbors. Moreover, children are
taught not to talk to people. If they see any one going by their
place, they should hold their tongues, nor should they laugh.

And they also tell children not to visit other people too often.
"Every time they see you going anywhere they would say that you
are looking for something good to eat, if you go visiting too often,"
is what children are told. So children do not often visit too much.

They likewise tell children not to gamble. They tell them that
they might be lucky and win, but that it would not benefit them. And
they tell them that it is just as bad to lose. They caution them in
this way: "If you win, people will see your winnings and will try
to get you to gamble. And if you do, you will surely lose all that
you have won. And yet it is not right to be over-quiet. If you are
quiet and well off, that is not quite right either. If you have a lot
of horses, people will be jealous of you. Some one might want some
of your property, and you would not give it to him. That is how
it will be.

"The best way is to be kindly to every one, to speak kind words,
to treat your friends nicely, to keep your heart clean, and not to talk
meanly. If you do this, you will have a number of friends. And
when you are a young boy, do not fight with other boys. If any one
speaks badly to you, do not answer him. Let it go. This is one of
the best things you can do. And if you see some one doing something, you must hold your peace; do not be the one to start the news.

Do not tell what you saw him or her do. If you spread the report they will hate you. They will become your enemies."

And there is another thing which boys are told. Boys are told not to tattle to any one. They are told not to be too intimate with girls. It is not a right thing for a boy to do. They are warned: "If you do that, people will be jealous of you."

And there is another thing they are warned. "When there are many people, when something is going on, don't go over there, and try to show off. That will not benefit you. You may go to the crowd and see what is going on, but behave yourself. And if any one asks you a question, you are to tell the person that you know nothing about it. That is the best way to keep out of trouble."

And there is another thing which young men are told, which is: "If some one asks you to do a favor, you must always do it for him. Some time in the near future they will come around again and ask another favor of you. If you refuse, you straightway will begin to have trouble. But you should always do a favor for any one, so as to please them."

And another thing, young men are told, not to fear ashes: "By fasting and painting your face with ashes, you may get a blessing from the Manitou. If you do the right thing, you will surely be blessed. If you are afraid, the Manitou will know it. People claim that fasting and blackening one's face with ashes is one of the best things that they can do. In the early days it was said that if one fasted long to obtain a blessing from the Manitou, he often went on the war-path successfully; or he killed people by fasting so long. Such was the blessing the person obtained. And you can go and kill game easily. You may become a leader in anything. If there is a war you may become a leader. And you will always bring your men back safe and sound. They will not be killed by the enemy. You will surely be blessed by the Manitou if you take an interest in fasting, and are not afraid of doing so. After you have fasted long enough, if you desire anything, you will obtain it. So fasting is the right thing to do. And if you do this, you must get up early—before our grandfather, the Sun, rises. If anything happens to people where you are, after a few years, nothing will happen to you: you will not be destroyed. This is the only way you can live again. All the people will be benefited by you. This is the best life there is." And this is why children are taught to fast.

Boys are told that if they see an animal they must not destroy it. For if they destroy animals, they themselves will not live very long.   Boys are also taught to be good hunters.

Boys are taught nearly everything so that they can get along nicely with their wives after they are married.   They are told that if they are hustlers many girls will wish to marry them.

Of course this is after they have grown to be young men.   Up to that time they are merely made to fast.   And by fasting, is how they reach old age.   Also children are made to fast when any one dies. And they also tell children not to make a noise when some one dies; and not to play where the body is.   And they tell boys not to refuse if they are asked to do something.   "If you do what people who have lost their relatives ask you, they will be well satisfied with you. And some day you will exchange positions.   If you ask them a favor at that time, they will willingly do it," is what boys are told.

And this is what boys are told when they are growing up: "If you are asked to be a ceremonial attendant at clan festivals, you must do it.   By doing them the favor of waiting on them, you will benefit your own life.   And any time you are asked to do anything you must always do it, so as to please the people."

And after they grow up, they are told not to bother too much with girls, especially if they have sisters of their own.   They are told, "Sometime you may be desired as a son-in-law.   But if you bother with many girls, while going with one, they will think you are a no-body."   And they tell boys not to be intimate with girls unless they plan to marry them.   They are told, "You must not say anything evil to women: if you do, you will be talking evilly to your own sisters.

"And if you are going with a girl, if you are engaged to her, you must marry her, and treat her rightly.   You must go home with her and stay with your father-in-law and your mother-in-law.   You must treat them as nicely as you can.   And you should hunt for your mother-in-law and your father-in-law.   If you treat your wife meanly, every one will talk about you.   And that will make it bad for you.   At all gatherings people will talk about you, saying how badly you treat your wife.   The people will say many things about you, though you may not know it.   They will say you are jealous. And in that way people will always refuse you favors.   You will be treating your wife badly, if you pay no attention to the old people.

"You must obey your parents.   It is the right thing to obey one's parents.   And boys who do not obey their parents are the worst boys to-day.

"If you know any one has something of his own, you must not ask him for it, nor must you steal it.   It is not right to steal.   If you steal or ask for the thing you want, all the people will be afraid of you.   You are nothing but a beggar.   Every one will say that to you. They will call you a beggar."

Now when boys are beginning to be grown up, they are told: "You must not turn against your friends; you must be kind-hearted.   And you must not bother with any woman or girl who is married to another man.   You should not try to 'cut him out.'   It is dangerous to do that."   This is one of the most important things they try to get boys to understand.   By doing what is forbidden they might get into trouble; and they might end their lives.   Many boys end their lives before they are middle-aged by not listening to their parents.

And girls are taught a little differently from boys.   Of course they tell girls, in the beginning, the same thing, that is, how to take care of themselves.   They teach girls that if they obey the rules they will have an easier life as they grow older.   After they are old enough they teach them how to do things.   And they also make them fast.   They are asked to fast so that adversity shall not strike them when they grow up.   They make girls fast for four days.   They make them fast all winter, especially when they are beginning to be young ladies.   The reason why they make them fast is that they are supposed to dream of something that will take them through their life.   That is why they do not take regular meals like others, to prepare for a long life.

And they teach them to do something for themselves, especially when they grow up.   They teach them work, suitable for women. They teach them to learn to make mattings and how to make sacks. They also teach them how to make moccasins and beadwork.   Girls are told that they can get along nicely if they learn these things before they are married.   They are told, "You will be benefited by doing this for your husband.   Your relatives will be benefited by you."

And girls are told: "If you are a moral girl, your father-in-law and mother-in-law will treat you as nicely as they can.   And they will love you.   If you are quiet and well-behaved, you will be much better off than those girls who do not mind.   Men do not care for girls who do not mind and who are immoral.   If you do not mind and are immoral, no man will have you for his wife." That is why girls are taught to be good.

After they learn to make things, they are taught to cook meals. Girls are told that by doing so, they are leading themselves the right way. "By so doing you are leading yourself an easy way. Sometime you may grow up and make your own home." That is why girls are told to be willing workers.

And girls are told not to go off and live with other people. Of course people would like a girl to live with them a few days. But a few days later they might turn her out, especially if she were lazy. People do not wish to support a lazy person. This is why girls are taught to cook.

And after they are married, girls are especially told not to say anything about other persons, and not to feel unfriendly towards them. And they are told not to have any quarrels with other people, for that is not a right thing to do. They are told to be kind towards the people and not to have quarrels with any one. "This is the best way, to be friendly with every one. By so doing, the people will feel kindly towards you. They will always say a good word for you. People do not think anything of a mean person. If you are mean, some day some one will turn against you. Some persons are dangerous. They have secret ways to kill people." This is why girls are told not to be mean, or say mean things to other persons. And some girls hate their parents for telling them this. But it is a rule that children should be taught. The reason parents tell girls this, is because they love them so well. They are teaching them so they can attain an old age. Girls who were not taught, do anything they please. They do not care what they do. They spoil themselves.

Girls are supposed to be taught till they are married. After a girl is married, she has full control of herself, and may do whatever she thinks best. But it is best to follow the rules forever, to be kind to one's husband and the people. It is pretty hard to lead a righteous life.

When girls begin to have children they are told to be kind to their children and love them, and not to do anything bad to them. And they are taught that if they live quietly to an old age, they themselves will be the only relations they have.

And before children are well grown, they dare not go any place by themselves. Of course boys are different: they can go any place they please. And girls dare not do so, unless they have a good reason for it. They are taught to always be at home and do the work. They are told: "If you grow to be a young lady, if you walk around and do not do any work, people will not think anything of you. They will always talk about you. They will say that all you are good for, is to walk from place to place. They will say you are looking for a place to get your meals. They will say that you are looking for a place where you can get the finest food. They will say many things about you. They will even say that you are worse than a man. Every time you are on the road they will say, 'There goes a woman who goes about looking for good meals for herself.'" That is the reason why they desire a girl to be able to do things so that she can support herself after she is grown. That is why they tell girls to obey their parents. Their parents have had good experience and know what they are talking about.

And when girls arrive at puberty, they are told not to marry a divorced man. They are told to marry a young man. In the early days, people used to say to each other when girls married divorced men: "It is not natural for a girl to marry a divorced man, nor for a young man to marry a divorced woman." They told girls that if they married young men, that they would be benefited by getting horses, and so on. And a girl is told to look around and get the right kind of a boy. In the early days, they liked boys who killed game, trapped, sold furs, and so got money; but nowadays they tell girls to look around for boys that have horses, homes, everything they want. They say, "That's the right kind of a young man to marry— one that can support you."

Girls are also told: "When you are staying with your father-in-law and with your mother-in-law, you are supposed to help them in their work. When your mother-in-law begins doing anything, you must ask her if you may do it." A girl is taught this so that she can get along nicely after she is married. Girls are told: "If you don't do these things, people will talk about you, and say how lazy you are. And people will not like you." This is the reason why a girl is taught all manner of work.

And all girls are taught the same things. And in this way, they lead themselves the right way.

Truman Michelson

IN MONTAGNAIS COUNTRY

In Montagnais Country

ON the shores of a great lake were clustered the buildings of the old Hudson's Bay Company's Post, where the People of the Interior came every spring with their cargoes of pelts to trade for the articles which the white man made for them. Through the long, cold winters, the factor and his crew passed the time as comfortably as they could, with little to break the monotony of the days, while powerful blasts of cold, often bringing several feet of drifted snow in their wake, beat upon the buildings. In the summer, however, the time went quickly. From the vast, forested hills northward came the returning bands of trappers, bringing the results of their winter's hunt. From the regions nearer, the People of the Lake, by shorter stages, came in, too, with their peltry. So, with the two bands of nomads camped along the beach and on the grassy terrace between the lake and the forest of the upland, the scene was enlivened each spring by the presence of several hundred hunters, with their families, gaudily dressed and garrulous.

By day, in the heat of the sun, which makes these northern places blossom in acres of green and showy flowers, the newcomers wandered from tent to tent, exchanging gossip, talking, singing, gaming and planning for the coming of winter; and all the time gradually enlarging the store of their annual necessities by an irregular trade with the factor behind his long counter in the Post shop. By night among the tents, grouped in twos and threes, the twinkling lights illuminated scenes of quiet domestic life, where some were asleep on piles of tent litter and furs, while others were engaged in plying the busy needle or in the low conversation which made the early evenings such pleasant times for visiting between those who had not seen each other for many months.

The People of the Interior always came to the Post two or three weeks later than those whose hunting grounds were around the lake. Some of the families from the interior came six hundred miles, driving dogs which dragged their laden sleds, the canoes forming part of the loads, until, coming south to where the snow was giving way to the advance of the spring, they left the sleds and loaded the canoes, finishing their journey by drifting in them with the swollen current down to the great lake. The trading completed, the People of the Interior returned as they had come, by canoe and sled, leaving the Post two or three weeks sooner than the People of the Lake. This had been the procedure for innumerable generations.

The People of the Lake never envied their friends from the interior. Their nearness to the Post they considered a great advantage. They could even make a short journey to the Post in midwinter to enjoy the festivities of Christmas with the factor and his employees, while their friends in the interior were perhaps freezing or starving if the game had failed them.

The People of the Lake had begun to feel themselves wiser and more important than their simple forest neighbors. Often one of them would come back from the metropolis with new and smart-cut clothes, plenty of gin, and some household finery with which to decorate the shelves and tables of the board houses which they had erected on the lake shore, but above all, with glowing accounts of the great and busy city where everything could be had that a Montagnais might covet in his most prodigal dreams. To the People of the Interior, these tales sounded marvelous, yet, much as they loved to hear them told, there was a lingering suspicion in their minds that all was not as fine and grand as it was painted, judging by the strong breath, the fagged condition and the depleted pocketbooks of those who had experienced these transitory contacts with the outside world.

A product of the conditions which made the People of the Lake so satisfied with themselves was young Antoine, a stalwart youth, whose knowledge of French and the astute principles of business in general, made him invaluable to the independent fur traders who regularly came to the lake to drive bargains with the returning hunters. Antoine's clothes showed his advance in the social scale. Peg-top trousers, narrow-waisted jacket, suède-topped, patent leather shoes, blue celluloid collar, ready-made cravat, and a green woolen golf cap marked him at once as a denizen of the back streets of Montreal as much as his brown skin, oblique eyes, and sleek hair proclaimed his origin from the People of the North. In broken French, even in broken English, Antoine could swear in competition with the French-Canadian employees of the honorable Hudson's Bay Company's Post, and those of Revillon Brothers of Montreal who sought to compete with the great company. Antoine had actually cultivated an urbane swagger, he consumed innumerable packages of paper cigarettes and perfumed his system attentively with draughts of gin and brandy. At times, even, Antoine forgot that he was a Montagnais. It was only when reminded by his own people that it was unbecoming for him to prey upon them to the advantage of the traders, that his vanity was lowered to a point which made him agreeable to the other young men. To the girls he was more attractive, and among the People of the Lake there were few girls he had not sampled. At times his vain heart yearned to extend his conquests to the simple maids who came patiently with their parents on the toilsome journey from the hills and forests of the north.

The head man of the People of the Interior, old Shekapeo, whose name meant "Going Backwards," was a stern and practical hunter whose annual catch could generally be depended upon to contain the finest and rarest furs. While he was alive to the defects of character which made Antoine in figure and reputation so conspicuous about the Post, he often wondered if a matrimonial attachment between Antoine and his daughter would not be of considerable advantage. With his own opportunities of production and Antoine's far-reaching business experience and associations, he had more than once pictured the advantage, while puffing his pipe before the fire. And yet he could not make up his mind to discourage the growing intimacy between his daughter and a young man of his own band, whom he had always admired for his quiet energy and productive trapping. The girl herself, if left to her own judgment, would have had little to say. Born by the side of a remote lake on a beautiful still morning, when the heat of noontime was lifting a mirage to the north across the glassy waters, her mother had called her Ilitwashteu, Mirage, from the first phenomenon seen after the birth of her child. Mirage, like her father, felt the contrast between Good-ground and Antoine. But the mystery of Antoine was making him an object of growing interest in her mind. She had dared to raise her eyes from her moccasins and look directly at him once, when he had come to the tent to talk with her father on business.

Then, when her father's back was turned, Antoine spoke to her, but she did not go so far as to answer him.

It was winter. Shekapeo had returned to his hunting grounds in the region of the Lake of Steep Shores. Near him, this year, was camped the family of young Good-ground who was at this season trapping in that section of his hereditary hunting grounds for marten. The territories of the two families adjoined each other, though for several years each had been operating on the more distant tracts, with the idea of allowing the intervening zone to become replenished with the fur-bearing animals. Old Shekapeo and young Good-ground knew perfectly well where their respective bounds lay. During the winter they occasionally visited one another and sometimes planned to exchange privileges in each other's grounds. When, for instance, one year bear had been abundant in Shekapeo's district, owing to a forest fire in the month of flowers which had left in its wake an exceptional abundance of berries, the same winter on young Good-ground's territory, caribou had wandered in unusual numbers. Then they had allowed each other to cross the landmarks. Good-ground took toll on many of Shekapeo's bears, and Shekapeo took what he needed of Good-ground's caribou.

It happened late in the winter in the month of great cold that several members of Good-ground's family were taken sick with coughs and aching limbs. Sickness added to Good-ground's duties, and often he was prevented from following his line of traps properly, by the necessity of remaining at camp himself. One trip when he started to visit his ten traps, which were strung at a distance of about two miles apart along the banks of the River of Poplars, he found himself at the ninth trap by the end of the second day. So bad had been the conditions of travel, and his own feelings so oppressed, that, late this afternoon, he made himself a little fire where he had scraped away the snow with one of his snowshoes, and boiled himself a pot of tea. Near the fire lay his good dogs Ntohum and Kawabshet, "My Hunter" and "Whitey," names descended through many generations of canines. They were worn out and tired, from pulling the toboggan through the soft, deep snowdrifts. The nine traps had yielded a few furs, yet most of them were empty. The promise of bad weather added to the trouble. To the northeast a heavy bank of lead-colored sky appeared above the pointed tops of the vast spruce forest. Fitful blasts of wind came occasionally from the same quarter, growing more frequent during the afternoon and causing Good-ground many times to turn his head about and look behind, then urge the dogs with a few sharp words to greater exertions.

Now, smoking his pipe of stone, which several times he refilled with dry tobacco obtained from the Post so far away, his eyes rested first upon his fagged dogs, then upon the slowly spreading pall of gray, northward above the hills. The question of the tenth trap was resting heavily upon Good-ground's mind. Might there be anything held fast in its iron jaws, or would the machine be empty before his disheartened gaze, should he gather his forces together and press on against the rising wind for another three hours? The price to pay in risk to himself and his animals for whatever might be caught there, would be, indeed, the highest. With depleted provisions through another afternoon of struggle against the blizzard which was surely coming, a question arose in his experienced mind as to the actual possibility of its accomplishment. Should he turn about now and go down with the wind to the little shelter camp where he could spend the night, back on Round Lake, he would then be within a short day's voyage of his home camp. There his sick family, brothers, sisters and mother, were comfortably and snugly housed in their warm tent, roofed tightly with birch-bark and lined with caribou skins, making it warm as the inside of his fur-lined mitten. But what if trap number ten should contain an animal, perhaps a sable or even a black fox, whose pelt would bring the profit he so badly needed?

Having filled his pipe several times, and cleaned it with the blade of bone which he carried tied to his tobacco bag, it seemed as if Good-ground could not decide. Finally, with a motion of determination, he plunged his hand into the bag, which contained the carcass of a hare reserved for his supper. With a few cuts of his knife he got out the shoulder blade of the animal, and he removed the clinging flesh by tearing it off with his teeth till the bone was clean and brown; then upon the end of a split stick he held the hare's shoulder bone before the heat of his fire, and raised his voice in a low melody which came from between slightly opened lips. "Ka na ka na aa ka na he." While he sang, the bone, affected by the heat, grew black toward the center; finally a segment with a little crack split from the center and ran toward the edge, breaking through the bone and causing it to

burn away on one of its outer sides. The divination was complete.
The spirit of the hare had told him that his voyage would be unsuccessful.

Now, with a few deft and decided motions, Good-ground cleaned
out his pipe, replaced several articles which he had removed from
his bag, adjusted his snowshoes by kicking his feet into the stiffened
loops, and squared about toward the south, pulling the sled around
on its runners till it, too, pointed backwards along the trail over
which he had, thirty minutes ago, tramped down the snow to make a
path for his dogs. The animals needed no human urging to tighten
their traces and drag the sled forward in a trail, which even now was
being blown over with drifting snow coming slant-wise through the
forest on a furious wind. Kiwedin, the north wind, was now going
to rule the world of the people of the north. Whatever thought
Good-ground had a while ago as to what the tenth trap might have
yielded him had he gone to it, faded from his mind with the satisfaction that he was obeying his dream animal, and that probably he
would reach his home camp in time to escape the suffering which he
knew he would have met had he gone on to learn what trap number
ten contained. His forebodings were not without ground. It was
with difficulty that he reached his little camp station that night,
helped along by the wind at his back. His out-trail was now completely covered, but it had been possible for him to run ahead of his
dogs and break the snow for them with his snowshoes. That night at
his station he tried again his "mutnshawan" and the bone broke in
the same way as before. This time the crack in the surface of the
shoulder blade zig-zagged off in the direction of the home camp, a
sure indication that this was to be the direction of travel next day.

By the time the late northern dawn had lighted up the trail
sufficiently for him to follow it, Good-ground had fed his dogs and
himself on the remaining carcasses of the few beasts that he had taken,
in coming up to his line of traps. By dark, forcing his way through
growing drifts with the wind still at his back, he silently wound into
the cleared space, near the center of which stood the three bark tents
with their wisps of smoke driven horizontally from the poles, that
for almost nine months of the year he called home. Several little
fox-bred mongrel dogs limped out on the beaten footpaths from one
of the tents, and with wheezy coughs announced the return of the son

and brother to the females within the enclosure. They were building up the fire and preparing a stew of hare and smoked caribou meat. Good-ground lifted the skin hanging before the door, bent under its low arch, and stepped toward the fire, laying his game bag on the boughs near the knees of his oldest sister. The glances at his face and his return glance showed that all was well, they felt, while all were still alive. And smiles lighted their faces as the girl brought the contents of one of the packs from the sled and opened it before their eyes, though it contained only medium pelts and carcasses only large enough to go into the stew-pot for to-morrow's dinner.

The blizzard raged, the weak and sick ones got worse before they got better, and several weeks passed before Good-ground could muster the strength, and afford the time to harness his dogs again and move along the trap line. Smoked caribou flakes, hare carcasses, and a small portion of flour had carried them through the short period of famine.

Finally with the return of good weather and the subsidence of the wind, Good-ground was able to make his round of traps, baiting and resetting those which had been torn down by the force of the wind, the snow and the beating branches of the undergrowth. Arriving at the location of trap number ten, he scraped away the snow to find there the chewed and devoured remains of a splendid black fox! The loss, Good-ground realized as he stood there regarding the remaining patch of silky ink-black fur no larger than the span of his hands, would amount to $2500 at least. Had he visited trap number ten that terrible day, weeks ago, he might have secured the pelt.

On his return home Good-ground was to have another surprise. He found his neighbor old Shekapeo visiting his family, having ventured a day's struggle through the soft and deep snowdrifts, from a sympathetic desire to see whether all had gone well with the family whose lives depended upon the support of one young man.

Shekapeo heard the story of Good-ground's lost prize with impassive expression. But on his way home the next day, tramping ahead of his dogs he had time to think over the bad luck attaching to Good-ground. Shekapeo's thoughts then turned to the coming trading season at the Post, and in particular to the financial ascendancy of Antoine.

During that spring season at the Post, among the tales which cir-

culated was that about Good-ground and trap number ten. The
story of the adventure did not turn out to his credit, especially after
Antoine took occasion to say to Shekapeo, in the presence of the
family, including Mirage, that Good-ground was a fool to have
turned back at a time when a catch worth several thousand dollars
was waiting his enterprise.

To account for Good-ground's lack of success, Antoine even
remarked that Good-ground's dream spirit would not have lied to him
that day when he turned back, unless he had been a liar himself.

With the advent of the moon when the birds begin to fly, which
the white people at the Post called August, the People of the Interior
having finished their trading, repaired their canoes, and satisfied
their craving for society, bade adieu to their friends of the lake and
started on their return to the northern wilderness.   In the coming
voyage of ascent, Good-ground's three canoe loads of provisions
and supplies, in large part advanced to him in credit by the factor,
which were to last him through the winter on his hunting
grounds, would have to be carried over thirty-two portages.   If the
weather continued good he expected to make the return trip in forty
days.   The largest lake that he had to cross would be nine miles
wide, but if the wind blew hard he would have to make double that
distance by working around the shore line.   His load consisted of
about two thousand pounds in all, fifteen bags of flour, two hundred
pounds of pork, ten of tobacco, one hundred of flour, one hundred
of grease, twenty-five of tea, forty of salt, twenty boxes of baking
powder, twenty-five bars of soap, two boxes of candles, twelve boxes
of shells, four boxes of rifle cartridges, three hundred traps, from
beaver size down, and ten bear traps,—all this in three canoes.   With
the help of mother, sisters, and younger brothers, these canoes had to
be paddled in smooth water, while on the portages and in water that
was too shallow for paddling, they had to be relayed in loads on the
back.

Finally, their toilsome journey ended, Good-ground and the others
reached their distant hunt-grounds and reopened their home camps,
where, all summer during their absence, the porcupines and other
rodents had made havoc among the greasy furnishings; where even an
occasional passing bear had left his marks.   More than once the
caribou and moose had poked their noses well within the clearing

and among the deserted tents, as though they knew that the men, who in the winter time were so eager for their lives, were now far away killing fish to live on, and eating the white men's food put up in tin cans.

So another winter was passed by the People of the Interior, busy in killing the wild animals of the forest and busy, too, in reviving the spirits of the slain animals, as they believed, by constant resource to drumming, singing, praying, and other shamanistic performances.

This winter at the Post, for Antoine, at least, was also a season of great activity. Antoine's astute employer, an independent French trader, had conceived a scheme to secure the trade of the People of the Interior when they should come out from the forests in the spring. The scheme was nothing less than to have a score of cases of the strongest fire water sent to the lake, at great expense, hidden from the eyes of the revenue officers en route. The whole was to cost about all that the independent French company could afford to put into the venture, and incidentally, as his employer finally made clear to him, to absorb the whole of Antoine's available estate in the shape of over a thousand dollars ready cash. Antoine and his employer gloated together over the scoop that would be made when the People of the Interior were told that the old company factor had died and the Post was closed, and learned that the new company had gone to the trouble of providing for them their beloved liquor so that there should be at least something for which to trade their furs. It was planned that Antoine should ascend the river Where-Moose-Abound, down which the People of the Interior generally came, a several days' journey, and there intercept them and put through the hoax.

With considerable care, seven sturdy canoe men were engaged, with Antoine as their foreman, to transfer the disguised cases from the lake to a convenient point up the river where the People of the Interior, with their precious cargoes of fur, would be sure to pass by in their descent. On the great day, the flotilla with its spirituous cargo made an early morning start. The men, with occasional levies upon the contents of their load to refresh themselves, finally reached the destined point and unloaded the boxes, setting up their camp to wait for the arrival of the descending hunters. Antoine's expectations ran high. He pictured to himself the consternation with which the People of the Interior would receive the surprising news that he had to impart, and then the eagerness with which they would fall upon his stores of liquor. With their potations well begun, he expected that they would not stop until they had traded the best of their peltries for the last flask of his fire water. His visions were hourly more stimulated by draughts upon his stock.

That evening, when the voyagers had settled down about their leaping fire, nothing would have aroused the suspicion of the observer as to what was about to take place. The seven canoe men, who were from among the People of the Lake, had decided upon an action which, to their minds, seemed advantageous to themselves, as well as in accordance with the excise laws of the Dominion, but which was prompted above all by fidelity to their friends among the People of the Interior. These men of the People of the Lake had known from former years' experience what it would mean for their friends of the forest to be turned back to their distant hunting grounds with nothing but the remains of a drunken orgy to meet their requirements for the coming winter. Therefore had they decided, with great moral satisfaction, in the interests of self, of government, and of mankind exactly what their correct course should be.

Before the evening had worn away, Antoine felt himself enjoying the best of spirits. He did not notice, when one of the men asked him to pass the matches, that two of the others behind him were fumbling among some tangled thongs and ropes. He did not notice, until too late, a quick movement by which he was thrown on his back and quickly bound hand and foot, his hands behind his back. Attempts to reach his sheath-knife, frantic yells, squirmings, and attempts to bite the binding thongs were lost in a roar of laughter which greeted him when he was tumbled to one side of the camp like a strangled bear, to curse in French, and threaten them with every dreadful thing that the northern Indian has learned to fear. They only laughed at him as his store clothes became grimy and his urbane veneer disappeared. They laughed all the more, these merry Men of the Lake, when the boxes had been broken open with their keen axes and the corks pulled from a score of flat bottles, whose limpid contents disappeared down their throats between gurgles of liquid and gurgles of laughter and jokes.

Now for two days this merry camp of Bacchus made the forests echo with songs and cries, some from the throats of the Men of the

Lake, growing louder each hour, others growing feebler each hour from the throat of Antoine. Had the People of the Interior been within hearing distance, they might have thought that a band of marauding enemies had engaged one another in warfare on their peaceful river. And no doubt they would have gone into concealment until some of their scouts could have learned the cause of it. But it so happened that they were delayed many miles up the river at one of the portages; several invalids had required attention. When all were able to resume their journey they descended by easy stages to favor the condition of their patients.

It was not until the second day after the demolition of the boxes and their contents in Antoine's bivouac, that the flotilla carrying the People of the Interior swung around a point of the river, and came down upon the camp, where by this time all the merrymakers were strewn about in a profound sleep. Cautiously and reverently stepping ashore, the foremost men in the canoes of the People of the Interior believed that they had come upon a camp of the dead, although, as they afterward remarked, the odor pervading the air was not exactly of a funereal taint. It took but a few moments for them to connect the circumstances. It took but a few more for them to connect with a dozen of the flat bottles whose contents had either been reserved for this special occasion by the thoughtful Men of the Lake, or had been overlooked in the surge of feeling which had followed their first attack upon the load. It now became the turn of the People of the Interior to show solicitude for those men of the People of the Lake, who had so sacrificed their loyalty to their employer for the sake of their kinsmen. Even Antoine was stripped of his thongs and stood upon his feet. But two days of fasting and exposure in the damp moss in his wet store clothes, with nothing to eat or drink, had about exhausted his constitution. His companions were the first to resuscitate, and it was from their lips that the story of the event was learned by the bewildered People of the Interior.

A day or so later, refreshed with sleep, fresh fish, and cold water, the whole company pushed off from the shore. The People of the Interior continued their journey to the Post, but among some of them a change had taken place which was to affect in particular the relationship of two individuals. These two were Good-ground and Mirage.   FRANK G. SPECK

HANGING FLOWER
THE IROQUOIS

Hanging-flower, the Iroquois

I

SHE was born in a bark house. Her mother, Rising-sun, was surprised as she looked at the little face, for she felt that once before, long ago, she had seen that face, and presently the assurance came to her that the child was the image of her great-grandmother, Rising-sun's mother's mother, whom she had often seen when she herself was a little girl. Hanging-flower had been a great medicine woman in her day, and the fame of her art had spread far and wide; on one occasion, it was claimed, she had even cured a woman of insanity. Rising-sun could not hesitate long: she wished to name the baby Hanging-flower.

Soon after this, when Rising-sun had regained her health and vigor, she called on Clear-as-a-brook, the Keeper of names of the Bear clan, to which Rising-sun belonged. From her the mother learned that Hanging-flower, a remote relative of Rising-sun, of whom she remembered having heard, had recently died and that her name had been "put away in a box." The mother knew now that nothing stood in the way of the realization of her desire: Hanging-flower was to be the name of her little girl.

When the fall came, Rising-sun began to get ready for the great Green Corn Festival, and on the second day of the festivities she carried little Hanging-flower to the Long House where her name was ceremonially bestowed upon her, in the presence of all the people.

II

The first summers of Hanging-flower's life passed uneventfully. Rising-sun was a kind mother; for hours she talked to little Hanging-flower in soft, soothing tones, and at night she sang her to sleep with her doleful, monotonous lullabies. When harvesting time came and Rising-sun was busy in the cornfields with the other women, Hanging-flower was wrapped and tied securely to her carrying-board, which was then hung on a branch of an elm tree; there, gently swayed by the wind, Hanging-flower slept, while her mother was hard at work.

III

The summers passed, and Hanging-flower was a baby no longer. Her mother taught her the art of cooking; she also began to help when the corn was pounded in large, wooden mortars. Soon she learned how to embroider. And as her fingers grew nimble and her eyes fond of the colored beads and wampum shells, she began to feel that the world of buds and flowers and leaves was her own, hers and her mother's and of the other women;—the men knew nothing of such things.

Once, when Rising-sun's brother was staying for a visit, Hanging-flower overtook him at work on a small False Face; for a long time she watched him unobserved, and when he was gone, she practiced carving on bits of wood and bark until she felt that she was as good at it as any man. But of this she never spoke nor did she show her work to any one, as she had been taught that carving was not woman's work.

IV

The summers passed and Hanging-flower became a maiden. Her eyes were large, black and deep, and her hair which she wore in two large braids, fell heavily from her shoulders. As she passed along the road, some boys looked intently at her while others turned their eyes away and hurried their steps. But, one and all, she passed them by. Hanging-flower had become a great dancer, and many a flattering comment was heard among the older men and women as they watched her dance with the others at the Strawberry and Raspberry Festivals.

V

At the next berrying season Hanging-flower joined a group of young men and girls and together they went off to the woods. Old Ringing-voice, the great story-teller, was with them.

Every night, when the day's work was done and the boys and girls returned to camp with their baskets heaped full of red, juicy berries, they would all sit around the fire, while Quick-of-hand and She-works-in-the-house, who were reputed for their skill in cooking, prepared a delicious soup of corn meal, after which, berries in great quantities were eaten. Then Ringing-voice would light his pipe and leaning his back against a tree stump, the legs drawn up so that the knees almost touched his chin, he would begin to talk, in slow and measured phrases. It is here that Hanging-flower first learned of the language of the animals and of the great warrior who had been so kind to the beasts and birds of the woods and the fields, and who was brought to life by their efforts after he had succumbed to the arrows of the Sioux. She learned of the great medicine, ga'-nŏ-da, which the animals made of parts of their own bodies and gave to the warrior to be used as a cure for all sickness. She was thrilled as she listened to the story of Pale-face, the pure youth, who started out alone and, wandering through the woods, met the pygmies and learned from them the Pygmy or Dark Dance, which, her mother had told her, she would herself one day perform. And for many evenings in succession, the boys and girls were spellbound as Ringing-voice recounted the great story of the foundation of the League, of Deganawïda and Hayenhwáhtha, the great chiefs, who organized the League and prescribed the Law and established the Great Peace.

One night, as they were sitting around the fire, and Ringing-voice was absorbed in his tale, Hanging-flower suddenly became aware that some one was looking at her. She turned her head and saw Straight-as-an-arrow, the tall, slim youth, who was staring at her with large wondering eyes. She looked away, and not once during the long evening did she turn her head again.

Evening after evening, while listening to the stories, Hanging-flower felt his gaze fixed upon her. She never turned, she was afraid even to move, but she knew that his eyes were fixed upon her.

One night, when the moon was not shining and all was quiet in the camp, he came upon her like the wind. Seized with terror, Hanging-flower wanted to scream. Her lips parted, but no sound came; her heart was beating fast and she lay there in the wet grass, hot and trembling.

When next spring came a baby was born to Hanging-flower. It made no sound when it came, for it was dead. On the evening of that day, two forms, wrapped in blankets, slipped out of the bark house; one was carrying a small bundle in her arms. Quietly as shadows they glided along the road, until they reached the cemetery of the Bear clan. And there the two women buried the little, nameless thing that had come unasked for and unwelcome. No one had seen them, no one knew; and after a while, Hanging-flower herself forgot what had happened.

VI

Some time later Rising-sun paid a visit to her sister's village. It so happened that the Bean Feast was being held at that time. Rising-sun went to the Long House with her sister and her people. There she saw Fleet-of-foot, the great runner, and so charmed was she with his form, graceful as that of a deer, that she could not take her eyes off him. After the feast, Rising-sun spoke to Fleet-of-foot's mother. She asked Corn-planter to visit her at the home village.

VII

In a little while, Corn-planter came to visit Rising-sun. With her hostess she went to the fields where the corn was ripe and the women were busy harvesting it. She saw the long rows of bent backs, and the green and yellow cobs which would show for an instant over the left shoulders of the women, presently to disappear into the large baskets on their backs.

"That young girl in the third row," exclaimed Corn-planter, "seems to do work for two. Look how her hands fly through the corn!"

"It is Hanging-flower," answered Rising-sun, "my daughter. And a good wife she would make for Fleet-of-foot, the runner."

"Let her cook a basket of corn bread," said Corn-planter, "Fleet-of-foot will be ready."

VIII

That night Rising-sun told Hanging-flower that the time had come for her to be married, and that Fleet-of-foot, the great runner, was ready to accept her basket of corn bread. Saying not a word, Hanging-flower got busy with the corn meal and before morning the basket of bread was ready. Hanging-flower started on her way early, and by noon she had reached Corn-planter's village. The boys were running races when she arrived. With wide open eyes she stood, as Fleet-of-foot rushed by her, as if carried by the wind. Hanging-flower shut her eyes . . . and it seemed to her that she heard the rustling of the pines; she felt herself lying in the wet grass, hot and trembling; and through the mist she saw two shapes wrapped in blankets, bending over a nameless thing which they buried in the ground. . . .

When the races were over Hanging-flower saw Fleet-of-foot resting on a stump of wood in front of his mother's house. Then she stepped forward and placed the basket of corn bread before him on the ground. Fleet-of-foot rose and said nothing. He only looked at Hanging-flower with a sharp, piercing look and, taking the basket, entered the house. In a while Corn-planter appeared in the doorway. She invited Hanging-flower to step inside, and Hanging-flower had her meal with Corn-planter and her people. The sun was still high when she started on her way back and before nightfall she reached her village.

When Hanging-flower fell asleep that night she saw some deer running among the trees. One of the deer was larger and fleeter than the others. Hanging-flower was trying to catch it. Again and again she felt herself flying through the air, in pursuit, but just as she was about to seize it, it eluded her.

In the morning of the following day Fleet-of-foot arrived before the house where Hanging-flower lived with her people. As she saw him enter, she rose to her feet. In his hand he held a necklace of blue and white wampum beads. Presently he took them in both hands and placed them about her neck. Then Hanging-flower knew that she had a husband.

The Long House in which Hanging-flower had lived with her mother and several other families had been crowded for some time, and Fleet-of-foot decided that they had to start a new home for themselves. Many men and women, most of them relatives of Hanging-flower, helped the young couple to build a small bark house, and before many moons had passed the house was ready and Hanging-flower and Fleet-of-foot began to live there.

As the summers passed, other couples came to live in the house, and extensions were built to it, to accommodate the ever-growing numbers. This continued for some time, until the house became a Long House, like the others.

IX

When the next berrying season came, a son was born to Hanging-flower; and having consulted Spring-blossoms, her mother's mother, Hanging-flower gave him the name Glad-tidings. As Hanging-flower was lying on her bed and her blood was hot in her, she heard the sound of rattles outside and she saw her brother take his turtle rattle and join the False Faces, who were passing through the village. Hanging-flower knew that Glad-tidings was one day to become a chief, and that night she carved a little False Face and hid it in her bag, for she had heard the rattles and she knew that some day her son was to be a leader of the False Faces. Hanging-flower was very beautiful, as she lay there on her bed. Her large black eyes were even larger and deeper than usual; she had looked into the future.

X

Many summers passed and Glad-tidings had become a strong and handsome youth. He was very young, but the older men thought him wise and cool-headed. The women were wild over him, but he had no eyes for them. He would rather sit with the older men, always inquiring about ancient things and eager to learn the laws and traditions of his people.

One day, while Hanging-flower was pounding corn back of her house, a piercing sound was heard on the road, gwā-á! gwā-á! gwā-á! Hanging-flower shuddered, for she knew that a chief was dead. Soon the news came that Power-of-thunder, her brother, had been killed by a stray arrow during an encounter with the Sioux.

Spring-blossoms and Rising-sun were dead and Hanging-flower was the matron of her family now. When she heard the mournful news, she began to think of Glad-tidings. He was young, but wise and strong, and there was no other man in the family who might be made chief in his stead.

In a few days a Council of the family was called by Hanging-flower. There were some men at the Council, but mostly women, and although some other Bear people were there, most of those present belonged to Hanging-flower's family. When they were all assembled, Hanging-flower began to speak and as she spoke, all were silent. She spoke of Glad-tidings' youth, but recalled the many indications of wisdom and character which he had given, and before closing, she nominated her son to be chief in place of Power-of-thunder, her brother.

For many days after this, Hanging-flower was busy calling on the other chiefs of her tribe. First she called on those who belonged to the brother clans and then on those who were of the cousin clans, and when her nominee was ratified by all these chiefs, she brought his name before the Great Council of the chiefs of the League, who also approved of her choice.

And so it came that before the corn was gathered in that fall, Glad-tidings was made chief in place of his mother's brother.

XI

Some summers passed and strange rumors began to reach Hanging-flower. First came Full-moon, and in many words told the mother that Glad-tidings was suspected of having made a dishonorable agreement with the Sioux. He had promised, she averred, to exercise his influence with the warriors of his people so that they would not attack the Sioux while the latter were fighting the Algonquin. Then Crossing-of-the-roads came, Fleet-of-foot's brother, and he spoke in grave tones about the dishonor that Glad-tidings' act had brought upon his people. Day after day, men and women came and spoke earnestly and vehemently to Hanging-flower, and the tenor of the news they brought was always the same.

XII

Hanging-flower was pale and haggard now, and from day to day she was losing weight. But one day she felt that she was mother no longer, but the matron of her family. She called on Glad-tidings, the chief, and standing before him, admonished him in ceremonial terms to desist from his shameful ways, which were bringing dishonor upon his people. But should he persist, such were her parting words, she would call on him again, and then once more, accompanied by the Chief Warrior, and then she would depose him and he would be chief no longer.

The days passed and the rumors persisted. Hanging-flower called on Glad-tidings for the second time; and when she had spoken, he said nothing. In a little while, she called on him for the third time, accompanied by the Chief Warrior. As both of them stood facing Glad-tidings, the Chief Warrior said: "I will now admonish you for the last time, and if you continue to resist acceding to and obeying our request, then your duties as chief of our family and clan will cease, and I shall take the deer's horns from off your head, and with a broad strong-edged ax I shall cut the tree down." Having spoken thus, the Chief Warrior "took the deer's horns off Glad-tidings' head," and handed them to Hanging-flower, for from now on Glad-tidings was chief no longer.

Hanging-flower then went to the Council house and informed the other chiefs, in person, that Glad-tidings had been deposed. As she spoke, her heart broke, for she knew that "the coals had gone out on the fire" of her family, and the chieftainship was lost.

A few days after this, Full-moon called on Hanging-flower and informed her in many words that Feathered-arrow, Full-moon's son, was to be chief in Glad-tidings' place and that the chiefs of the League had transferred the chieftainship to her family.

In the evening of that day Hanging-flower, wrapped in a blanket, went outside of the village. For a long time she stood there, on the hill above the cornfields. Her thoughts turned to the past and for a long time she was lost in memories. . . . But of the future she did not care to think.

ALEXANDER A. GOLDENWEISER

THE THUNDER POWER OF RUMBLING WINGS

The Thunder Power of Rumbling-wings

THE strange events of which I write, took place in the summer of 1840, when I, then a man in the full vigor of my early forties, chanced to be in charge of a museum expedition sent to explore an ancient Lenape burial site situated on a hilltop in the northwestern part of the State of New Jersey.

On the tenth day of June we encountered an unusually deep grave of circular form, some six feet in diameter, in which, at a distance from the surface of perhaps seven feet, we encountered a number of slabs of stone piled up in the form of a cairn.

Removing these with care, we found beneath them a skeleton, which, when carefully uncovered and brushed off, proved to be of a full-grown man, lying on his right side, with his knees drawn up at right angles to his body and his hands near his face. Beside his crumbling breastbone lay a tiny mask of stone, bearing two little perforations which showed the wear of a suspending cord, and near it a knife blade of purple argillite and a small pipe of baked clay, bearing a very neat pattern, drawn into its surface with a sharp point while the material was still soft. At each side of the skull were the chalky remains of some shell beads, rather larger and coarser than wampum, but similar in form; while near the feet a little pile of neatly-made flint arrow points told of the one-time presence of a sheaf or quiver of arrows.

What archæologist has not sat upon the brink of a newly un-covered, ancient grave and wished that the fleshless jaws before him could speak and tell their story? Or wished that he himself could be transported backward in time for a brief space to learn something of the life of a bygone day? So I sat and so I wished; and then we photographed our find as it lay, and removed the specimens for safe keeping.

As the hour was late, we did not touch the bones, however, intending to remove them upon the morrow, and so we left them for the night, still surrounded by some of the stone slabs.

After dark I bethought myself that I had forgotten to bring in my notebook, and recalled that I had left it on the pile of dirt beside the grave, and so, guiding my steps by the flickering flashes of lightning from an approaching thunder-shower, I made my way thither. I remember that I had found the book and had just turned back toward the camp, holding out my hand to feel the first splashes of rain, when a blinding flash and a violent concussion sent me reeling, reeling, down,—into darkness. . . .

When I came to myself I could see nothing, but I knew it was raining steadily; I could hear the drops patter on the leaves; I could feel them on my body.

On my body? I must be naked! I felt my chest, it was bare and wet, my arms likewise. What had become of my clothes? I felt at my waist; it was belted, and in front hung something like a little apron, wet and slimy. My legs? I felt, and found them encased in long stockings of some sort, reaching nearly to the hips, and I could feel that some sort of supporters ran from them to the belt. My feet seemed covered with the same soft stockings which, like the apron, felt wet and slimy to the touch.

As I bent over to feel of my feet, something brushed against my cheek, something hard and cold, yet light and almost clinging. I put up my hand and felt; it seemed to be a string or rather loop of little beads.

Then I followed up with my fingers and found that the loop, with a number of other loops were, somehow or other, firmly attached to my ear in several different places from the lobe upward. I felt around and discovered there were so many of them that the top of the ear was bent over by their weight, and the lobe was somewhat stretched. I felt of each separate loop; each was firmly attached; and the other ear was in similar shape. I shook my head and could feel the swinging weight of them.

Puzzled, I started to run my fingers through my hair—a favorite habit of mine, and found that I had none! That is none to speak of—it was very short indeed, almost as if shaven, except for a bristly crest like a mule's mane, which ran from front to back over the top of my head, and ended in a little pigtail or queue in the back.

Something moving against my breast as I moved, I felt it and found a little hard, cold, oval object slung from a string about my neck; near it on another string hung a wet and slimy bag, and what felt like a small knife in a sheath.

I was puzzled indeed—I could not make out what had happened to me. As I sat thinking, I must have dropped off into a doze in spite of the rain, for when I opened my eyes again it was daylight.

I looked about me; it was still raining and a brisk wind stirred the tree tops; but I seemed to be in a strange, wild country for, although to my left I could look off over a valley, my eye met no houses, roads, or clearings, just a waste of tossing tree tops, in fact no sign of man except a distant blur of smoke, rising apparently from among the trees. I looked behind me; there stood a great tree, its wood showing white, its bark practically stripped off, while broken branches littered the ground. It had been struck by lightning.

I looked at my hands; they were lean, and tawny in color instead of fat and freckled as I knew them; I looked at my legs; they were encased in soiled and worn buckskin leggings; upon my feet were moccasins puckered to a single seam down the front, near which were traces of colored patterns now nearly worn away—and still I did not understand.

I pulled the queue around and looked at it; the hair was black and neatly braided, whereas my own, in those days, was red; I pulled around the beads attached to my ears; they were white and apparently made of shell, but were too close to my eyes to see plainly.

Then I investigated the things hung about my neck, and noted, with a start, that the oval, hard object was the little stone mask we had found in the grave. I pulled the knife from its sheath; it was of stone—argillite—not purple from age, but black, fresh-looking, sharp. And when I looked in the bag, I found what I had come to expect, the little, decorated pipe of clay, and with it some damp, shriveled leaves which must have been some sort of tobacco.

I could not avoid the conclusion; I was somehow transported back into prehistoric times, and had assumed the body and belongings of the Indian whose skeleton we had unearthed.

If this were true, I must have some weapons, I thought, and soon I found them—a five-foot, straight bow, lying beneath the broken branches that had fallen from the lightning-blasted tree, and a buckskin quiver. I pulled out the arrows; their points were of flint. I noticed that the sinew filaments that fastened them to the shafts were loosening from the dampness, and I found myself instinctively twirling each one between my fingers until the sinew was tight again.

The carcass of a deer lay also among the fallen branches, evidently a victim of the bow.

I noticed that I was feeling hungry so I slung my quiver, picked up my bow, and then, after a moment's hesitation, shouldered the deer and started down the hill toward the smoke.

After a while I found a trail leading in the right direction; this I followed until I reached the brink of a bluff from which I could plainly see the roofs of a number of bark houses above which rose the naked limbs of dead trees, making a strong contrast to the living, green forest all about them.

As I looked, I heard voices of people ascending the hill. I slipped into the bushes with my burden, out of sight but where I could peer out. The voices belonged to a number of men, apparently setting forth upon the hunt, armed with bows like mine. I noticed most of them wore leggings and moccasins of more or less the same shape as my own; that their hair with a few exceptions was cut like mine, and that they wore in their ears either strings of beads like mine, or tufts of downy feathers. And I noticed with surprise that I could understand, perfectly, their language.

From all this I judged that they must belong to the same tribe as myself and that it must be safe to proceed, so, after they had passed, I stepped from my hiding-place and went on down the hill and into the village.

The first thing to strike my eye was a big, rectangular, barn-like wigwam which stood near the middle of a large open square or plaza, the roof made of sheets of bark held in place with poles, and pinned at the ridge with two smoke holes. The sides were of logs; the door, which occupied the middle of the end facing me, was closed with some sort of curtain.

About the plaza stood fifteen or twenty smaller houses of similar form, but from a half to a quarter the size; these had but one smoke hole in the roof; and the sides, like the roofs, were of bark.

Some of these roofs were extended forward to form a sort of porch in front of the wigwam; in other cases a separate little shed stood in front, provided with a bark roof of its own, but open on all sides. From these sheds and porches rose a haze of blue smoke wafting a savory smell.

Beside me, at the edge of the plaza, stood one of the dead trees, the bark of which had been girdled round; and I could see blackened stumps where others had stood; while many such dead trees rose stark and naked from the garden patches about the village. I found out later that, in clearing land for village or garden, the custom was to chop the bark around the trees so that they died, to let them stand until thoroughly dry, then to fell them with the aid of fire and, splitting them up with wedges, use them for wood as needed.

Seeing some women standing beneath a shed from which came a hollow, thumping sound I made my way thither. Suddenly one of the group darted out from under the shed and came running toward me with a glad cry. "Oh Flying-wolf! So you have come back safe to me after all!" she exclaimed, grasping me affectionately by the arm and leading me toward one of the wigwams. "So the Mengwe did not get you after all! I am so happy!"

Thinking that this must be the wife of the man whose body I had taken, and that I must say something, I remarked, "Yes, I have really come."

"Ah!" she said with concern, looking up into my face, "how hungry you must be! I cooked your favorite stew against your return last night, but you did not appear, and the boy and I never touched it; I can warm it for you in just a little while. Hang the deer on the tree in the old place and go to your bed and rest until I have it ready; you must be tired. Or wait," she added, "I will spread a fresh mat I finished yesterday."

She passed into the wigwam and I followed, to find myself in a dwelling, the most noticeable feature of which was a pair of wide platforms or benches, one along the wall on each side, raised some two or three feet above the floor and covered with mats. Back of these benches or bunks, the wall was lined with colored mats; and the space beneath them was filled with assorted bags, baskets and bundles, while from the roof hung other bags and bundles, and a string or two of corn, the ears braided together by the husk. Behind the poles supporting the roof, was thrust a half-finished bow; near it hung a bundle of sprouts intended, probably, for arrows.

The woman spread a fresh mat on one of the platforms. "Lie here," she said, "I will build the fire inside here instead of out in the shed; our house feels damp after the rain."

I watched her as she went out, and saw her taking down some large object from a shelf in the shed, and by the time I had stretched myself on the mat she returned with a large, egg-shaped, earthen pot, and set its pointed end between three stones placed for the purpose in the fireplace in the center of the wigwam, and began to stir the ashes with a long stick.   Finally she uncovered some live coals, left from the night before, and gathering them in a heap with her stick, she placed some fibrous stuff, which looked like shredded cedar bark, upon them and began to blow into it.   Soon she had a lively blaze, which she fed with small sticks until it was well started.

Pulling the fire about the base of the pot, she soon had it bubbling, and, before long, set before me a wooden bowl of steaming, savory stew of meat, corn and beans.   Beside the first bowl she placed another, containing flat dumplings, which proved to be made of crushed, hulled corn flavored with berries, rather heavy but delicious.

On the edge of the stew bowl hung a short, wide, wooden spoon. As I ate, she sat on the edge of the bench just opposite me and chatted happily of this and that, rarely pausing for an answer—for which I was thankful.

Between mouthfuls, I looked her over.   She was a comely young woman of twenty-five or thirty, ever showing her even, white teeth in a smile, her kindly face as yet but little weather-beaten.   Her black hair was neatly parted in the middle and brought back and fastened at the nape of her neck with a sort of long, cylindrical knot which was wrapped in beads; several short loops of beads hung from the rims of her ears where there were evidently, as in my own case, a number of small perforations, while each lobe showed a hole perhaps a quarter of an inch in diameter.   About her neck were many strings of beads of different sorts; some looked to be of dried berries or seeds; others of bone, while some were certainly of shell, and one string looked like copper.

The upper part of her plump body was naked but for these beads; from her waist hung a skirt of buckskin reaching below the knees, neatly fringed and bearing a wide, embroidered border with an intricate design in colors; it was evidently a flat, robe-like piece wrapped about her waist, belted taut, and the top edge folded down over the belt.   Her legs were covered by leggings, her little feet in moccasins, both leggings and moccasins being of deerskin and embroidered with what I afterwards found to be dyed deer hair and porcupine quills.   Both wrists were wound with strings of beads.

As I ate, she talked on: "Your mother was over yesterday from

the Pulling-corn village.   She says she is making you a fine robe of
four soft, dressed deerskins, and is decorating the back with a large
picture of your Guardian Spirit, the mask being done in the little
shells she bought from those southern tribesmen who came up the
river in that big canoe—you remember.   She gave them in exchange
her whole stock of healing herbs, and had to work like a beaver to
dig another lot of the little roots before winter set in.

"She says she is going to sew each little shell on separately—you
know each has a little hole rubbed into it—so that even if one breaks
loose the others will not come off.   Talking of trading, when are
you going to get me that pair of Cherokee shell ear-pins you promised
me?   That old Shawnee woman in Possum-ground village has some
and there is not another pair in Lenape land.   See, I have stretched
the holes in my ears on purpose for them.

"And speaking of making things, when are you going to finish
that big, wooden bowl for me?   You brought the maple burl home
long ago, yet you only have it partly burned out, and there it lies
beneath the sleeping birch, and right by it is a whole basket full of
little slabs and pieces of sandstone for grinding it smooth.

"I know you have no flint scrapers, but don't you remember you
buried a lot of half-finished arrow points and little blocks of flint
to keep them fresh, just outside one corner of the shed?   They
ought to be moist enough to work easily and you could make all the
scrapers you want in a little while.

"The reason I need it now is because our son took the big old
feast bowl out to play canoe with, the other day when I was not
looking.   It was all right until three or four other little boys tried
to stand in it, too, all at the same time, then it split and is ruined.
It made me feel sad because that was the bowl that grandfather made
for mother when she and father built their first wigwam.   I shall
have to borrow another bowl for to-night."

During all this I had said as little as possible, for I did not want
to show my ignorance of all these things.   I could not bear to spoil
her happiness and let her discover that I was not really her husband.
Now, however, I ventured to inquire, "What is going to happen to-
night?"

"I forgot to tell you," she replied, "last night when you were away,
our war chief came to see you with a number of the elders from
here, and other villages.   They are going to get up a big war party

to punish the Mengwe who, you know, are getting too bold. You remember how one of their scalping parties killed my poor brother last year when they caught him alone out hunting; and how they killed your friend Breaker but a few moons ago. Last night when you did not come home I feared they had got you.

"The war chief says you know more about those trails to the north than any other Lenape—that is of our Unami tribe—and they want you to lead the party. Everybody said they had full confidence in your judgment and your bravery.

"I hate to have you go because it is so dangerous, and our son and I need our hunter yet a while, yet," she smiled sadly, "I am proud of my warrior too; the tribe needs you, and the ghost of my poor brother cries for vengeance.

"I told them to come again to-night and so they will be here I suppose. They spoke of bringing our tribal head chief, too. I was looking for women to help me cook for them, among that party pounding corn in that arbor, when you came into the village."

As she finished, I realized that the crisis had come; I could keep my secret no longer. I had not enough knowledge of tribal affairs to talk with the delegation, let alone lead a war party. I must tell her the truth, or at least that part of it I felt she could understand.

So I said to her. "Listen, my mate. You have been so glad to see me come home that I have hated to spoil your joy. But something happened to me last night—I know not what—and when I awoke this morning I found I had forgotten everything I ever knew. I did not even recognize my own clothing and body; I did not know myself to be Flying-wolf until you named me. I found my way to this village by accident, and know you to be my wife only by your actions; and at this minute I do not remember your name. Of our life I remember only the language; as for leading a war party, making a wooden bowl, or even hunting meat for you, all are equally impossible. I could no more do these things than a blind puppy, not because I do not want to do them, but because I have forgotten how."

She slid off the bench and coming straight across the wigwam grasped me by the shoulders with her two hands and looked full into my eyes. "Is this true, Flying-wolf?" she asked.

"Yes," I choked.

She stepped to the door and looked out for a while in silence; when she turned to me again her cheeks were wet. "Perhaps," she said, "if you should see your son whom you always loved so, your memory would come back."

She went out. Shortly she returned with a bright-looking little lad about eight years old, his long, black hair hanging loose, his lithe body naked except for a little string about his neck where hung some little bones which my experienced eye recognized as those of a turtle.

"Father," he cried, "why did you send mother after me? I was having such a good time down at the creek with the boys—we were playing Thunder-Beings hunting for horned water-serpents."

I laid my hand on his head and said, "All right, son, then run right back there and play." I met his mother's questioning eyes, and shook my head.

After sitting in a miserable silence a while, she asked: "Where did you awake this morning?"

"On that hill over yonder," I replied, pointing, "under a tree. I would know the place again because the wood of that tree shows naked and white, half the bark has been torn off by lightning. It must have been struck lately because the broken limbs lying about it are still green."

"Now I know what the matter is," she cried, springing to her feet. "You have been struck by one of the Thunder's arrows. And I know who can help you." She darted out.

She returned with a fine-looking elderly man whose long, iron-gray hair hung loose upon his shoulders, except for one little braid at the back, to which were tied several fine, large, eagle feathers, white with black tips. From the outer corner of each eye a blue line, apparently tattooed, ran zigzag down across his cheeks to his chin; on his naked breast was tattooed a rude but striking figure of a bird with wings spread, surrounded by many other zigzag lines. Here hung suspended from a string that passed around his neck, a tiny model of a war club, its ball-like head painted red.

"This is Rumbling-wings," said my wife. "If any one can help you, he can." And so I told him my story as I had told it to her.

He pondered for a while, then turned to my wife. "Run down to the spring, Whispering-leaves," he said, "and get us some fresh water." When she had disappeared with the bark bucket, he said,

"I think I understand what the matter is. Flying-wolf, whose body you occupy, must have been killed or stunned by the Thunder arrow, and your spirit, which must have been floating near, took possession of his body. Where you come from I know not, but you must have been thinking of us and our time, when your spirit was driven from its body by another Thunder arrow. Whispering-leaves must not know this—that her real husband may be dead.

"What can you do? You can either make up your mind to live out your life among us and learn to be what she expects of her husband, or you can go to that same hilltop with me some day, and I will call back the Thunders to set you free again. Then maybe, if your own body has not been destroyed, you may return to it, and, perhaps, Flying-wolf's spirit, if it has not already gone to the Land of Ghosts, will come back to this body. It is all a chance. To-night when the elders and chiefs come, lie in your bed here as if sick in body and say nothing; I will explain to them. As to what you want to do, think about it as long as you wish and when you decide, let me know. In the meantime learn all you can and take care of your mate and the boy."

Just then Whispering-leaves (I was glad to learn her name!) came in with the water, and the old man dipped a gourdful for me, then drank himself. "Thanks, daughter," he said to her, "your husband has been struck by lightning and his memory is very sick. Be good to him, and little by little it will come back. But do not expect too much of him at first. If you run short of food let my wife know. And you, Flying-wolf," said he, "whenever you want to learn something come to my house. I am alone every night." He went out.

I looked at Whispering-leaves and she at me; hope shone in her face, she smiled. The more I looked at her, the better I liked her.

The first night I visited Rumbling-wings, his wife, after spreading a mat for me, withdrew, murmuring something about visiting a neighbor for the evening. I had learned by this time the Lenape amenities, and so I did not start boldly off with my questions, but chatted quietly of this and that for a while, finally winding up with, "Why did my wife go to you when she heard I had been struck by a Thunder arrow? Why do you think you can call the Thunders to set my spirit free?"

"You are asking a hard question, my friend," said Rumbling-wings after a moment's cogitation, "and one which a Lenape does not like to discuss with another. But I realize that you have been cut off from the years of early training that most of our boys go through, and the only way I can make you understand is to tell you outright, and I feel that my Guardian Spirit will forgive me.

"In the first place, you know what the Thunder-Beings are—powerful spirits, helpers of the Great Spirit—in form at the same time man-like and bird-like. They bring the rain to water our crops and refresh the earth. You have often heard the rumbling of their wings in the storm, and have seen their arrows of flame shoot toward the earth as they hunt the great horned serpents and other man-destroying monsters which form their daily food. And it was one of those very arrows which, as you know, started you in life as a Lenape.

"Well, I suppose I must tell you, one of these Thunder-Beings is my Guardian Spirit and that is why people say that I am in league with the Thunder, and have Thunder power, and why they call on me in cases like yours.

"The Thunders must have picked me out for their favor even before I was born, as you will realize when you hear how I come by my name of Rumbling-wings.

"It appears that my mother confided to her brother, my uncle, that she was expecting me, and according to our custom she asked him to take particular notice of any dream he might have, in hopes of finding out the child's name. Not long after, he was overtaken at night, far from his village; it was black and stormy and he took refuge beneath an overhanging rock. He found a spot fairly dry, but rough and uncomfortable, and he fell into a troubled sleep. Sometime in the night he was awakened by something, he knew not what, and found himself sitting up, listening. He heard a distant rumbling of thunder among the mountains which seemed at last to take the form of words: 'Rumbling-wings is coming, Rumbling-wings is coming.' . . . All this he told my mother, and I was born shortly after.

"When the time came for our great autumn ceremony in the Big House—that large wigwam in the square you passed, coming here to-night, is one of them—my uncle took me in his arms and, standing before the centre post with its great, carved face of 'Mising' looking down upon me, he announced to the people that my name was Rumbling-wings. Even as he spoke there was a crash of thunder, late as it was in the moon-of-falling-leaves, and a wind sighed through the trees about the Big House, and they heard drops of rain patter upon the bark roof or fall hissing through the smoke holes into the two great fires below.

"Perhaps Whispering-leaves has told you how our people believe that after the birth of a child, its navel string has much to do with its disposition; so, if a girl, they take that string and bury it under the house or in the garden to make her fond of home duties; or, if a boy, they hide it out in the woods so he will like the hunt. Well, my father, so he told me, took mine to the wood, and hid it in a hollow tree. He had hardly done this when a thunder-shower came up and drove him to shelter; coming back on his way home he found the tree, where he had hidden my navel string, burning. It had been struck by a Thunder arrow.

"As a boy I knew nothing of the Thunder power except that when the great, black clouds fringed with yellow, began to pile up in the west, and others, young and old, looked upon them with dread, I alone of the village felt no fear. In fact I used to go out naked into every storm; the crash of thunder was as music to me, the bright flashes were beautiful, the pelting rain refreshed me. And, in truth, I do this yet, always stretching out my arms to my Guardian to thank him for having helped me thus far along the trail.

"But I did not know who my Guardian Spirit actually was until I had seen some twelve or fourteen snows. About this time my parents began to act strangely and to speak crossly to me. I did not understand why I deserved such a change in their feelings, and many a time I felt alone in the world. They even gave me the poorest part of the meat they had to eat, and scraps and leavings of corn bread, and stew that had begun to smell sour.

"One morning I was awakened before dawn by some one punching me in the ribs with a stick—well I remember how it hurt—and I heard my father say, 'We must drive this wretched boy away from here, I can not stand him any longer. Get up from there, dog-like!' and he punched me again. My mother who had always until lately taken my part in any dispute, took no notice, but bent over the fireplace, and soon a little fire began to flicker and finally filled our wigwam with light. She went to the water jar just inside the door, and I saw her dip into it our oldest, blackest, greasiest gourd cup. Then she turned to me and her face, usually so kind, seemed hard as flint. 'Drink, boy,' she ordered, handing me that cup, and I wonderingly obeyed.

"Then my father spoke, handing me a burnt and shriveled shred of meat no larger than his little finger—a piece full of dirt and grit where it had fallen to the floor. 'Eat this, miserable brat,' he cried, 'and get away out of my sight.'

"A sudden anger overcame me and I flung the morsel full in his face and darted for the door. 'Wait,' I heard him say, 'aren't you going to blacken your face? And besides I was going to tell you the rest of it, that you must not come back until you bring with you something great, but you started out too quick!' Did I see a fleeting smile on his stern face? Surely his eyes were twinkling!

"Then it dawned upon me what the matter was; I was expected to fast for power, and all this seeming abuse was nothing but a sham to make Those-above-us take pity on me as an outcast, suffering child, and grant me a vision from which I would gain a Guardian Spirit that would be my protector through life. Often had I heard older boys speaking of such things, but I had never realized that I, Rumbling-wings, was expected to go through the ordeal.

"Then said my father, 'It seems to me I have heard that some boys who were driven away from home, had to go up on Wolf mountain to the east end where there is a little cave that was nice to lie in while they prayed, because they could look out over the tops of the trees to the river and the hills beyond. Besides,' he added, 'I expect to go hunting up that way early to-morrow morning and I shall look into that cave to see if any one is hidden away there.'

"Then indeed I understood, and so under his direction, with my mother looking on, I rubbed my face with charcoal and, throwing about my shoulders the oldest and raggedest robe I could find—the one the dog had been using for a bed beneath the sleeping bench— I set out.

"All day I lay hungry in that little cave while mosquitoes and deer-flies from the woods, and fleas from the dog's robe bit me unmercifully. Yet I looked out over the valley as calmly as I could, praying to Those-above-us to take pity on me; yet nothing happened, except that when the day was nearly spent, a cloud came up behind me over Wolf mountain and overspread the sky, then went away grumbling without letting fall a drop of rain. That night, still hungry, I slept a troubled sleep and next morning, before sun up, in came my father with a little scrap of meat and a small gourd of water. As I drew out the cob stopper and drank, he asked me, 'Have you found anything yet?' When I replied 'No,' he took the bottle and departed.

"The same things happened on the two following days, and I got weaker and weaker from hunger, yet saw nothing but the black cloud every afternoon.

"But on the afternoon of the fourth day when the cloud came again it brought rain, and heavy thunder, and this, strange as it may seem, lulled me to sleep. And in my sleep I dreamed that I stood naked and alone on the bare sand-hills by the Great-water-where-daylight-appears, with nothing but a wooden war club, with its round head painted red, in my hand. And as I stood arrows came flying through the air from every direction and whispering past my head, struck quivering into the ground about me. But not one touched me, and my heart was unafraid.

"At this point I was awakened by an unusually loud crash of thunder and I opened my eyes to see the shower moving off across the valley, carrying with it a bow of beautiful colors and followed by the rays of a lowering sun.

"Somehow I felt satisfied then that I should go home; it was useless to linger longer in the cave. And so I started, staggering from weakness among the wet bushes on the mountain side.

"Weak as I was I nearly lost my footing, crossing the swollen creek, but at last I reached our village. The people looked curiously at me as I entered and made my way toward our wigwam.

"My father was sitting in front, scraping the charcoal from the inside of a wooden bowl he had been burning out; some one called to him, or perhaps he heard my step, and he looked up.

" 'Have you brought it with you, son?' he asked. On my reply that I had a dream he seemed very well satisfied and called to my mother who was looking out of our door. 'Wife, sweep and fix a place for our son to sit—he is bringing it with him!' Mother bustled about then and swept, and smiling, spread a fresh mat for me; I was surprised at her air of deference. Down I sat, and after the sun had gone beneath the edge of the world, she brought me a great bowl of stew, steaming and delicious, and a new, clean gourd of fresh water.

"That evening they really treated me as a guest. Father even filled a pipe for me, and then, when my mother's deep breathing from her place on the sleeping-bench told us that she slumbered, he asked me outright, 'What animal spirit or other Manitou has offered himself to be your helper?' 'I do not know,' I answered, and then I told him my dream, fearing in my heart that he would think it meant nothing.

" 'Son', he said when I had finished, 'you have done better than I dared to hope, you have indeed gained a powerful friend among Those-above-us, no less a personage than one of the Thunders!' And when I asked him how he knew, he replied, 'The wooden war club with a round head painted red is the emblem of the Thunder-Beings, and represents the fearful blows they strike. The fact that, while you held this club in your hand, the arrows did not wound you, means that your Guardian Spirit, the Thunder, will protect you. Don't you understand?'

"All that night in my dreams I was struggling and fighting, with whom I know not, but through it all I heard myself singing,

> In my trouble
> In my trouble
> I call upon my Helper
> And his answer
> Out of a dark sky
> It comes rumbling,
> It comes rumbling!

"And this ever since has been my war song, and the song I sing at our great autumn ceremony in the Big House, where all who have been so blessed sing of their visions." . . .

"So that," I said, as Rumbling-wings finished, "is why you wear that little, red, war club hanging about your neck! Now tell me why I carry a little stone face in the same way. I have tried to take it off several times, but Whispering-leaves will not let me."

"That," replied the old man, "represents Misinghalikun, the living Mask-Being, and a powerful Manitou he is, for the Great Spirit has given him control of all the wild animals of the forest. He is the Guardian Spirit of Flying-wolf, whose body you occupy, but I cannot tell you the story of his vision. No one could tell you that story but Flying-wolf himself. And where is he? You occupy his body, but I doubt if Misinghalikun will help you as he did him. I believe Flying-wolf won his great fame as a hunter through the power of this Guardian Spirit, and without that, you may have a hard time to live up to his reputation." And, I must say, so I found it.

Another evening I asked Rumbling-wings if his Guardian Spirit ever helped him in later years.

"Many times, and I will tell you some instances. When I had seen about twenty snows, I went with some of our kinsfolk to visit the Minsi, our allies living above us on Lenape River and in the mountains to the north and east of us here. You may have heard that, although their language is quite a little different from our Unami tongue, they too call themselves Lenape and their customs are almost the same as ours. From there we went with some of these people eastward across the mountains to see the Great River of the Mahicans of which we had often heard. Arriving at the river, we wished to cross to visit a Mahican village just opposite, but, although we made a signal smoke, no one dared put out from the village with a canoe to get us because there was a high north wind and the wide river was very rough. So I burned tobacco and prayed to my helper, the Thunder, and soon thunder-clouds arose in the west, and a west wind sprung up which killed the north wind and left the river smooth; and then the Mahican canoes came for us. We spent many pleasant days in their village, feasting and dancing, and visiting from one wigwam to another. Their language is very much like the Minsi, and enough like ours so that we could understand almost everything.

"Another time a war party of us Lenape set forth against the Susquehannocks, a tribe like the Mengwe. They lived on Muddy River in a big village circled about with a great stockade of sharpened logs, twice as high as a man, set on end almost touching one another. Time and time again we attacked them, but could not break through this stockade. nor could we pile fire against it to destroy it, so well did their bowmen defend it.

"At last we withdrew a little way to counsel and our war chiefs said to me, 'We must depend on you, Rumbling-wings, to help us overthrow this people who have harassed us so long. Call on your Guardian Spirit; help us to take this village!'

"And so, as there were no thunder-clouds in sight, I drew from my medicine bag a few scales of the Great Horned Serpent and laid them on a rock beside a little creek. You know how the Thunders hate these great snakes, and always begin to gather, the instant one of them shows any part of himself above the water. Well even these scales seem to attract them; I always use these scales to call the Thunders when I need them.

"Immediately the sky began to darken in the west—so I built a little fire, threw an offering of tobacco upon it, and prayed to my Guardian.

"Blacker and blacker grew the sky, nearly as dark as night. We could hardly see the yellow scud flying overhead beneath the mass of cloud. The air near the earth seemed hot, choking. All at once a few great drops of rain splattered down, and then we heard the roar of a mighty rain approaching across the forest. Soon it was pouring down about us like a water-fall.

"How long this downpour lasted I know not, but it stopped as suddenly as it began, and a few large hailstones fell, so large that we could hear them rattle on the bark roofs of the village. Then came a deeper roar out of the southwest, louder and louder, nearer and nearer. Suddenly a great thing rushed past us in a cloud of flying leaves and broken branches, and struck the village with a crash, full in the middle, and in a moment was gone. As it passed on we saw it; it looked like a great, twisting strand of long hair hanging from the clouds and dragging along the earth, sweeping before it the trees and the wigwams.

"The instant it passed, we saw that the log stockade was down and most of the houses of the village, but just then came another blinding flood of rain which held us back, and when we finally reached our goal we found a number of the Susquehannocks lying dead amid the ruins of their houses; and of those who were left alive and able to run, all were in flight somewhere in that rain-swept forest.

"As to the wounded, we dispatched those too badly hurt to take with us, and seized the rest as captives, and then, with all the weapons, pipes, beautiful clothing and ornaments we could carry, we made our way homeward. Thus the Thunder, my Guardian Spirit, helped me, and helped me to raise my name to what it is to-day.

"What finally became of the captives, do you ask? A few we

killed by torture, in revenge for what their people had done to us; some died; some we let go free after a year or two; others finally intermarried with our people and cast their lot with us. You know Traveling-everywhere's wife? She was one of those captives, given as a servant to his parents. She was but a young girl, and Traveling-everywhere, himself but little older, took pleasure in teaching her to speak our Lenape language. They got to liking each other so well that they finally built a wigwam of their own. Now you could hardly tell her from one of us."

I found it much easier to assimilate these beliefs and stories than to learn the every-day, practical side of Lenape life, at which I proved a tragic failure. Although I studied the methods of experienced hunters I never could master the knack of effective shooting with the bow and arrow. And I tried my best. Seldom could I bring down a deer. The neighbors grew tired of providing meat for me and my family.

Whispering-leaves did her part to perfection; everything she made or produced was of the very best, which made me feel my shortcomings all the more. And she would not let me touch the garden—the only thing I knew anything about. "Garden work is not manly," she would say. "I will not endure hearing the neighbors talk about my mate doing woman's work. How would you feel if you saw me going out of the village with a long bow on my shoulder? Or burning out a log for a canoe? Would you not feel shame to see your mate do an unwomanly thing? In our life, the man and woman must do each his or her part and neither is harder than the other. Surely to hunt all day and every day, good weather and bad, is fully as hard as wielding the hoe! How would you like to hear the neighbors say, 'Whispering-leaves ought to give Flying-wolf the skirt, and she put on his long leggings and breechclout?'"

I was even a failure at finishing her wooden bowl, although I had watched a number of men making such things and thought I had learned their method. I heaped hot coals on that maple burl, blew them until they burned deep, and scraped out the charcoal with shells and bits of flint again and again, until I thought I had it hollowed deep enough. Then I ground it patiently with bits of gritty sandstone. When I had finished, I thought I had accomplished a very good piece of work for a beginner. But Whispering-leaves, although she smiled and said sweet words when I laid it finished before her, and pretended to think it perfect, tucked it away after a few days, and when we had visitors and a big bowl was needed, she borrowed another bowl from the neighbors.

What hurt me worst was seeing her treasured finery disappear bit by bit, doubtless traded for meat and for skins to make our moccasins and every-day garments. First it was the seed beads, then those of bone, then one string of shell beads after another until only the copper beads were left. Finally they too were missing when I came home one night. One day I had occasion to search beneath the sleeping-benches for something and had to pull out the square basket in which she kept her treasures, her prettiest embroidered, festival attire. The basket felt so light that I looked into it—and found it empty.

Often the boy came in crying and said that his little companions would not let him play with them because, they said, his father was "no good."

And one night Rumbling-wings told me that he had seen the spirit of Flying-wolf in a dream the night before, and that he said he was living in a strange land and wanted to come back to his home.

But the crisis came when I returned one night, tired out from my fifteenth successive fruitless day's hunting, and found my Whispering-leaves crying bitterly. Although I begged her to tell me what the trouble was she refused, but at last she broke down. "My dear mate," she sobbed, "there is nothing to eat in this house, and there is no hope for anything, unless I sell that robe your mother made for you. All my pretty things are gone long ago, and all yours except that."

I caught her to me and held her tight in my arms for a moment, then dashed out into the night straight to Rumbling-wings' wigwam. "I am ready," I said. . . .

When I came to myself I was lying beneath the lightning-riven tree.

It did not take me long to find my place again in the modern world; but always to this day, when the clouds pile up and the thunder begins to mutter in the west, I think sadly of my lost Whispering-leaves and of my friend Rumbling-wings and his Thunder power.

M. R. HARRINGTON

TOKULKI
OF TULSA

Tokulki of Tulsa

TOKULKI was born in the Muskogee town of Tulsa, in the central part of what is now Alabama. Like all other Indian babies of that region he first saw the light in a brush shelter some distance back from his mother's home; for were he to be born in the latter it was thought misfortune might fall upon all its occupants. His name belonged to the Wind clan of Tulsa, and means two persons running. When the first bearer of the name was born, his father was absent on a war expedition during which he frightened two of his enemies who were on scout duty, so thoroughly that they ran off in haste, leaving their weapons in his hands. It was in commemoration of this event that the new-born babe received his name.

Tokulki's mother was waited upon during her period of seclusion by her own mother and another old woman of the clan, reputed most skillful in midwifery. Although it was late in the autumn this old woman took the infant immediately to the bank of the river and plunged him into it, after which he was strapped securely into a cradle, made of canes, by means of bark cords about the shoulders and thighs. Here Tokulki spent the next few months of his life, sometimes carried on his mother's back, sometimes propped up against the wall of the house while his mother was engaged in her household duties. But whenever he was so placed, the cradle was allowed to rest upon a panther skin, for his father and his uncles had all been famous warriors and it was expected that he would follow in their footsteps. Therefore he must have that about him which would communicate a warlike essence and make him fierce and bold.

Tokulki passed through the period when his principal experience of life was that there was something in it that gave him food and warmth, which was "mother," and when there was something light in which dark objects moved, or something dark in which light objects moved. There was one particular light object that he gazed upon continually, and which resolved itself into the house door, and another, red and hot, which he saw when he awoke at night and which resolved itself into the house fire.

The home into which he gradually came to consciousness was the winter house of his family. The framework was of hickory poles, set in a circle of perhaps twenty-five feet in diameter, with their slender ends gathered together at the top and supported by a central element of four wooden columns. Interwoven with this were thin, flexible pieces of wood plastered thickly with mud mixed with dry grass, and the whole covered inside and out with mats. The floor was excavated a couple of feet below the general level of the ground, and a shallow trench dug about it a little farther back, so that water would be carried off without entering. The doorway which had so early attracted Tokulki's attention was to the east where the first rays of the sun could steal into it, but it was seldom that it found any one but very young babies to awaken, for the duties of the day were assumed early and ended soon, except in times of merry-making or the great ceremonials. There was no vent for the escape of smoke which sometimes accumulated to an extent which would render the inside unendurable to a white man; but this was partly provided against by the judicious selection of wood,—old sticks of oak and hickory which would fall apart with little smoke, and leave a glowing bed of coals to radiate heat during much of the night. Around the walls of the house was a continuous seat made of matting, raised a foot and a half to two feet from the floor and covered with bearskins upon which most of the household slept.

The household consisted of Tokulki's father and mother, a brother and sister, his mother's mother, a married sister of his mother, her husband and two children, a younger brother of his mother, and an old man of the Wind clan, not closely connected with the family but making this his temporary home. More important in Tokulki's life than most of these, was an old man, living a short distance away, but a frequent visitor in the cabin, a man whom we should call "maternal uncle" in English; yet he was "uncle" not only to Tokulki and Tokulki's brother and sister and the children of his mother's sister, but to a large number of other boys and girls—boys and girls whom we should not consider related in the least. Tokulki, however, as he grew older, learned to call them "elder brothers," "younger brothers," and "sisters," and he learned that most of these were called "Wind people," like himself, but that some were called "Skunk people," and some "Fish people."

While still on his mother's back, Tokulki was taken down to the river every morning, and his mother dashed water over him and over herself even when the weather was bitterly cold. One of his earliest memories was of this cold douche after his warm night's rest. All of the inhabitants of the village except a few of the sick and decrepit, took this morning bath, the men and boys plunging in, the women and children contenting themselves in cold weather with a little splashing.

And it was the "uncle" of each band who saw to it that none evaded this regulation. He was always present, encouraging the smaller boys, scolding the timorous, and sometimes correcting the unruly by means of a stout stick. As he did so he poured good advice into their ears, and Tokulki soon learned that his "uncle" was the man to whom he must appeal in time of trouble, whose approbation he must win, and whose displeasure he must be careful to shun. Often, on winter evenings the uncle would gather his "nephews" and "nieces" together and instruct them, and he would tell them in particular of the deeds of their ancestors, sometimes assisting his memory by means of little strings of beads, or by referring to notches cut in sticks.

But when the old people were talking with one another, Tokulki's mother would by no means allow him to go near them, and sometimes, when his curiosity had gotten the better of him, she would box his ears soundly. In after life Tokulki learned that this was not because such behavior was considered disrespectful of the old people or annoying to them, but because old people have uncanny powers and may bewitch a child who hangs about them too closely. There was not much temptation to do this except in winter, for during the rest of the year the elders would be working or talking apart by themselves, or the old men would be in the square.

This "square" loomed larger in Tokulki's life the older he grew. It was only a short distance from his home. He was not allowed to play there, but he could walk all around the edge, marked by a ridge of earth which had been piled up by successive scrapings of its surface in preparation for the ceremonials. Near its western end were four long, narrow buildings plastered with mud and outlining a hollow square with entrances at the corners. They were open in front, and each was divided into three equal sections by transverse walls, which did not, however, reach to the roof. The middle section of the western cabin was slightly different, in that the back part was separated by another wall parallel to the walls of the building, and, closely shut up in the room thus formed, Tokulki knew that the ceremonial pots, rattles, drums, the dried medicines, and all of the most sacred possessions of the tribes were kept. In front the town chief or miko and his principal councilors had their seats. On the northwestern edge of the grounds loomed the tshokofa, the indoors council house, constructed precisely like a winter house except that it was very much larger. To the eastward extended a wide, open space kept bare of grass by intermittent hoeing and the pressure of many feet. In the middle of it rose a ball post, and at the farther corners stood two shorter posts where captives taken in war were burned. Almost every morning Tokulki could watch the leading men of his town assemble in this square, and between the buildings catch glimpses of the medicine-bearers carrying asi (an infusion of ilex vomitoria) in conch shells to regale the councilors. All that they had in their stomachs they forthwith ejected, that they and their minds might both be clear for the matters about to be discussed.

Frequently Tokulki accompanied his mother when she went in quest of firewood, or he would sit on the edge of the garden patch while his mother, his grandmother, and the other women of the household were at work, and sometimes he was given the temporarily congenial task of driving off crows. This garden was planted principally with pumpkins and beans, but most of the corn was in the great town garden farther off from the village, and thither all of the people marched in the spring, headed by their miko, with hoes made of hickory limbs over their shoulders, to prepare the ground for planting. Each household had its own patch separated from the rest by a narrow strip of grass, but the work was in common: first so-and-so's strip, next some-one-else's until all was completed. After that it was largely the duty of the women and children to keep weeds down and drive away birds, and there were little watch-houses on the edges of the fields for the accommodation of the guardians. The days when all worked were as much holidays as days of labor. The participants began early but worked only until shortly after noon. Then they partook of their principal meal in common, and after that there was usually a ball game followed by a dance around a big fire in the square, the light of which was reinforced by cane torches.

The ball game was usually played about a single post, though not the one in the square-ground, and it was indulged in by both men and women, who played against each other, the women throwing the ball with their hands, the men with their ball sticks. Single tallies were made by striking the pole above a certain mark, but five points were counted if the carved bird which surmounted it was touched. Sometimes, however, the men played their own game, a game similar to lacrosse except that two small ball sticks took the place of the one large one. Each side strove to bring the ball home to its own goal, marked by two straight poles set up a couple of feet apart, and twenty points constituted a game, ten sticks being stuck into the ground by the scorer of each side and then drawn out again. In dividing up, the Wind, Bear, Bird, Beaver, and some other clans, called collectively "Whites," played against the Raccoon, Fox, Potato, Alligator, Deer, and certain others who were known as "People-of-a-different-speech." But these games were only practice games, or make believe games. The regular games were always between certain towns, and they were very serious matters conducted with the deliberation and ritualism of a war expedition. Each game was preceded by careful negotiations: the players fasted and were scratched with gar teeth, they enlisted the aid of the supernatural by employing a medicine man, they marched to the appointed place as if to meet an enemy, wagered quantities of property on the result, and conducted it so energetically that serious injuries were sometimes inflicted.

In winter Tokulki's mother and the other women busied themselves making baskets and mats, twisting bison hair into garters for the leggings, and weaving cloaks—worn only by women—out of the inner bark of the mulberry. In the summer they made pottery and dressed skins, and the preparation of food kept them busy, of course, at all seasons. They must prepare their own flour by pounding the corn in a wooden mortar, at which they sometimes worked two and two. Sometimes they would relax their labors long enough to play a sort of dice game in which sections of cane took the place of our bits of bone. The men spent most of their winters seemingly to less advantage, much of it in smoking and recounting to one another tales of their hunting or war excursions, humorous sketches frequently revolving about the Rabbit, and sometimes myths of a more serious and sacred character. However, they devoted many hours in the aggregate to the repair of their hunting and fishing outfits, and to the manufacture of axes, arrow points, and other articles of utility, material for which had been laid aside during the preceding fall.

When Tokulki was able to run about freely by himself, his uncle made him a blowgun out of a long, hollow cane which he provided also with cane arrows with their butt ends wrapped in thistledown. He sent him out to try his skill upon the birds and smaller game animals, and more than once Tokulki came home proudly with birds, squirrels, and even an occasional rabbit. A little later they made him a bow and arrows, with which he attacked rabbits, and wild turkeys, and upon one happy occasion, he succeeded in creeping near enough to a young deer to dispatch it. He came home in triumph to his mother, telling her where the animal was to be found, and listened to the praises of his entire household, particularly those of his uncle, with flushing cheeks.

Upon this Tokulki's father and uncle began to instruct him in the arts of woodcraft. They took the head of a deer and placed splints inside of it so as to restore it as nearly as might be to its original shape, and showed him how to use it in stalking the living animal. They taught him how to make traps for the smaller animals, and where game was to be found. They also taught him that a piece of flesh must be cut out of every deer that was killed, and thrown away so that the deer might not be offended and leave the country. They taught him that he must not cast bones of game animals far off, when they fed them to their dogs, lest the animals afterward become shy. He was told that a sprig of old man's tobacco must be put under every fire made by the hunting party so that malevolent spirits would not follow them. Still later he was to learn about certain medicines and formulæ to insure success in the chase.

As soon as spring came, hunting of a somewhat desultory character began, but the families did not move far from town until after the annual ceremonies were over and the corn had been harvested, unless driven to it by famine, or drawn to certain points on the rivers by runs of fish. During this time Tokulki accompanied a hunting party to the bear preserve, a section of forest not far from Tulsa where bears were numerous and which was the common property of all the citizens. When the party approached a tree in which a bear had been located, Tokulki stood at one side to watch the method of procedure. He saw that one man climbed into a tree not far from that containing the animal they sought, and was given blazing slivers of pitch pine which he threw successively into the tree den. When its occupant was driven out, he was quickly dispatched by the hunters disposed below. The meat was distributed throughout the town for immediate consumption, but the fat was tried out and poured into bags made of whole deerskins which were then packed away for the winter season. Meanwhile, the women were hunting through the forests for roots, particularly groundnuts and the roots of a smilax which they called kunti. They also collected the seeds of a pond lily; a little later a profusion of berries enables them to vary their diet.

In April the miko called his leading men together and shortly afterwards was held the first ceremony of the season accompanied by fasting and the drinking of the red willow and button-snake root. At the time of the corresponding full moons in May and June, similar ceremonies took place, but these were merely in preparation for the great Fast (poskita), the culmination of the Southeastern religious season. And so it was that about the middle of July a messenger appeared at Tokulki's home, and delivered to the house chief a little bundle of sticks tied with deer sinew. Before handing it over, he drew one stick from the bundle and threw it away. Every morning thereafter the house chief did the same until but one stick remained and on that day the ceremony began. Similar bundles were carried to every household of Tulsa Indians far or near, all of whom synchronized their movements in such a way as to converge on the square-ground at the time appointed. Failure to come in then was both impiety and treason, and it was severely punished by the warrior class known as tastanagalgi, who would handle the absentee severely, and destroy or confiscate his property.

The poskita was the type of all the ceremonials of the tribes of the Southeast. The active participants were those men who had been on war expeditions and had received new names in consequence, names usually ending hadjo, fiksiko, imala, tastanagi, or yahola, and containing often the names of the clan animals, the towns of the Creek confederacy, or even foreign tribes. Generally speaking, the miko and the members of his clan sat in the west cabin, the "second men," or henehalgi, who were devoted to peace, in the south cabin, the higher classes of warriers on the north, and the common warriors on the east. Each cabin or "bed" contained from two to four "honored men," retired warriors who constituted the inner council in charge of the ceremony. This poskita was distinctly a peace ceremony when old enmities were forgotten, all but the most heinous crimes pardoned, and new resolutions made for the ensuing year.

At least one day was devoted to feasting, but after that a rigid fast was observed by all the active participants. Then those who had performed brave actions received new names and new war honors, while novitiates were shut up in the tshokofa and a strict fast was imposed upon them preparatory to their admission into the class of warriors and induction into adult life. During this ceremony, too, all of the fires, which were supposed to have become corrupt from contamination with worldly things during the year, were extinguished, and a new fire was lighted by the "Medicine Maker," the high-priest of the town, in the most impressive manner by means of the common fire drill. This new fire was first used to replace the fires in the square-ground and the tshokofa, and afterwards it was taken to one side of the square where the women stood ready to receive it and carry it to their several homes. The rituals extended over eight days, and on the last, just at sunset, the men marched in single file to the river, led by one of the Fish clan bearing a feather wand, and all plunged into its waters. They returned in the same order, the miko made a short farewell address, and the ceremony was over.

From this time until the harvest had been gathered in, Tokulki's people, and most of the others, did not stray far from town. In October was a sacred ceremony called the "Polecat dance," and afterward the people began to scatter rapidly for their fall hunting. Some proceeded to their camps overland, the women serving as beasts of burden; but the greater number, including Tokulki's family, had their hunting lodges near the rivers and reached them by means of canoes made of single trees, fire-felled and fire-excavated. Some parties went as many as seventy-five or a hundred miles from home, especially when they desired to hunt the woodland bison. This season was devoted especially to the preparation of quantities of dried venison against the coming of winter.

When game was plentiful, a series of merry-makings were indulged in. This usually began with the presentation of a ball, made of buckskin, to one of the men by his sister-in-law, who at the same time intimated that she desired venison, bear meat, or occasionally squirrels. Upon receiving this challenge, the man communicated the intelligence to all of the other men in camp and they set out on a grand deer, bear, or squirrel hunt as the case might be. Meantime the women busied themselves pounding corn, or perhaps kunti roots, into flour and preparing various sorts of dishes. When the men returned they also took the meat in hand and a great feast followed, with a ball game of the single pole type, and a dance to close the day. They would light a great fire and two men would station themselves near it, one with a drum made by stretching a deerskin over an earthen pot or cypress knee, the other with a gourd rattle, while the dancers went around the fire, usually sinistrally, in single file or two-and-two, under the charge of one or two leaders. The dances were usually named after animals, real or imaginary, and the steps and other motions were supposed to be in imitation of them. The men did most of the singing.

After a few days there would be another presentation of a ball and the same feasting, ball playing, and dancing would follow, and this was frequently kept up until the weather was very cold.

Sometimes sickness came upon a member of Tokulki's camp, and then Tokulki's mother's younger brother, who was doctor of the band, and at the same time Medicine Maker of the town, would be called in. Before prescribing, such a doctor often consulted the kila, or "knower," who seems to have combined the functions of prophet and diagnostician, but Tokulki's uncle never did this because he united the two functions in himself. Having determined the nature of the disease, he would go in quest of various herbs, or sometimes send members of the household after them. These he put into a great pot, poured water over them, and placed the pot over the fire. After the contents were sufficiently heated, he gave it potency by breathing into it through a hollow cane, while repeating a magical formula. This was done four times, the doctor meantime facing east. Sometimes, however, he prescribed sweat bathing in a lodge made of blankets thrown over poles, and containing heated rocks on which water was poured, and sometimes he declared the trouble was caused by witchcraft which he proceeded to cure by sucking the witching object out of the affected part by means of a bison horn.

If, in spite of all his efforts, death supervened, all of the people in that house and in the neighboring settlements began shouting and making loud noises so that the soul of the deceased would not stay about the dwelling but start upon its journey to the country of spirits. They removed the body to the house in town, wrapped in dressed deerskins and, after wailing over it, buried it in an oblong trench about four feet deep, excavated beneath the floor, lined with cypress bark, and covered with sticks upon which a thick layer of mud was plastered. The face of the deceased was painted red, he was seated facing the east, his most important implements, such as his bow and arrows, his war club, his paints, his pipe and tobacco pouch, were buried with him, and for four days the women of his family bewailed his death with loud howlings. The faces of all the mourners were painted black. The hair of a widow was unbound for four years, she discarded all ornaments, and was compelled to absent herself from all merry-makings. At the fourth poskita she was formally released by her husband's sister and either provided with a new husband from the same clan,—or clan connection,—or set free to marry whomever she chose. For a widower the period of mourning was only four months.

The medical practices of his uncle possessed a fascination for Tokulki who was present whenever he was tolerated. He had seen similar performances in the square-ground at the time of the annual ceremonies, and his mind, which had a mystical bent, eagerly fed upon them.

At intervals during all this time Tokulki had seen bands of warriors, including sometimes his father and uncles, march out against their enemies, and in particular there was an enemy to the westward, not large in numbers but led by a chief of rare size, strength, and sagacity, whose activities were constantly more threatening, and who was aided and abetted by a much more numerous people beyond him called Long Hairs. At last, raids from this quarter became so numerous and so many injuries were suffered that a great council was held in Tulsa and it was determined to draw their settlements closer together and erect a strong stockade about them. Tokulki, although still too young for the heavier work, was called upon to render such assistance as he could in the completion of the structure. While the older men marked out the course of the wall and planted in the ground good-sized tree trunks a few feet apart, Tokulki and the other young men brought together numbers of long, flexible branches or young trees which they wove from one post to another, covering the whole with a plastering of mud. About a hundred feet apart little watchtowers were raised above the top of the wall, projecting forward slightly in order to defend the intervening spaces against attempts of an enemy to scale or burn them. On the river side there was but one row of palisades, but elsewhere it was doubled. Toward the river, too, was the only opening, made by allowing the walls slightly to overlap. To approach this an enemy must creep along a narrow path between wall and water, exposed to certain death should he be discovered.

About two years after this fort was completed, Tokulki went upon his first war expedition. The "uncle" of his group was to be one of the party, and took this occasion to initiate his nephew into the cardinal tribal institution, man-killing, the one great avenue for the attainment of personal glory and social standing. The leader of the party was to be none other than the tastanagi lako, the head warrior of the town, and therefore when he sent out to drum up volunteers there was a great outpouring of the ambitious youth of the nation. For four days they remained shut up in the tshokofa, fasting, taking war medicine, dancing, and singing war songs to lash themselves up to the proper degree of martial fury. Each was provided with a war club, a bow, and a quiver of arrows, a shield of cane or bison-hide, and a sack containing fire sticks, paints, and a slender ration of parched corn meal. The ceremonies completed, they set out quietly in single file very early in the morning. With them they carried a sacred box made of splints which was usually borne on the back of the chief's assistant, and at every camp was placed upon a log, or hung upon a tree or post. Among other things it contained some of the painted bones of an enormous panther which the ancestors of this people had slain on their way from the far western country, and a part of one of the horns of an aquatic horned serpent. On occasion it was believed that this box gave forth oracular utterances, informing the party in what direction to proceed, or warning them of an attack.

On this occasion the spirit guardian appears to have been favorable, for they surprised four outlying camps of their enemies, took a dozen scalps, and carried off fifteen women and children as captives besides two grown men whom they subjected to the death penalty by fire. During this action Tokulki had the good fortune to save the life of the war chief's servant by engaging an enemy, about to strike him from behind. Therefore, after the triumphant return, he received the much coveted feather headdress, his first war name, and a seat in the eastern cabin of the square.

He had stepped upon the first rung of the social ladder and could attend all but the most secret and important meetings to decide the actions of the nation. It was not long before he received another name and left the cabin of the tasikaias for that of the imalas at the east end of the north cabin. Later deeds entitled him to the rank of tastanagi, the highest war grade, but being by birth a member of the white Wind clan he was assigned instead to a seat of honor in the peace cabin on the other side.

In spite of his prowess, however, Tokulki took less pleasure in warfare than most of his companions. He had, as we have noted, a mystical type of mind. The great ceremonies had a powerful influence over him, and the practices of his uncle, the Medicine Maker, proved a constant fascination. Blessed with a retentive memory, he rapidly picked up a fund of tribal lore which presently attracted the attention of the old men,—the custodians of the sacred legends and the keepers of the rituals. They talked earnestly about him with the Medicine Maker, as of one to whom his people might look for spiritual leadership in future days, and at his uncle's suggestion he and three other of the most promising youths of the Wind connection agreed to undertake the young men's poskita, "the first degree in medicine" if we may so term it.

Calling these youths into his house the Medicine Maker talked to them earnestly and then made an appointment to meet them at a remote spot in the forest, on the bank of a small stream away from the frequented trails. At the time and place agreed upon, he presented himself before them and directed them to make a sweat lodge by the bank of the rivulet. Then he began his instructions, going over as much of his more elementary knowledge as he thought they could grasp at one time, and, when he returned to his house, telling them to memorize all he had said carefully, until the fourth day, after when he would visit them once more. He repeated his visits and instructions at similar intervals for the better part of a month when he was satisfied with their progress and told them to go back to their homes. "Now," he said, "you understand how to heal wounds made by arrows and are entitled to wear buzzard feathers in your hair."

This degree was taken by Tokulki shortly after his first war expedition, but for some time other events interposed to prevent the continuation of his initiation. In the first place his family had decided that it was time for him to take a wife and assume a position in the tribe as the responsible head of a household of his own. He fell in with this arrangement as part of the natural order of things, and consequently his mother, accompanied by two or three of her clanswomen, visited the "uncle" of the Raccoon clan to which the chosen girl belonged. The recipient of the visit was not unaware of the offer about to be made and had called to his house some of the other leading men of his clan, the mother of the girl, and, as a matter of courtesy, her father. A few days thereafter the Raccoon people returned the visit and formally announced that the suit was accepted. The wedding might have been consummated then and there, by conducting the groom to his betrothed's house and holding a feast and dance, but Tokulki and his parents were ambitious to have him reach a high position in the tribe as soon as possible, and accordingly they delayed the ceremony until he could erect a house, garner a crop of corn, and lay by a supply of venison.

Word was sent to all of the male members of the Wind clan residing in that town to go into the forest and bring together a supply of poles, bark, bark rope, and other articles sufficient for the proposed house. The planting season was beginning, and when the town field was laid out, an extra plot was sowed for the new household. When this was ready to harvest, a corncrib raised on posts was put up near the site of the projected dwelling, and filled from Tokulki's new plot. The harvest being over, and the days cool enough for comfortable work out-of-doors, the men of the Wind clan came together again and appointed a day upon which the new house was to be raised. This work was carried out much like an old New England husking bee. It was placed under the direction of the one considered most skilled in such matters who assigned the various processes to all the rest. They worked with such a good will that it was practically complete by the middle of the afternoon. Afterward a common meal was served followed by a game of ball and the usual dance after dark. Sofkee, prepared like our "hulled corn," stood ready in pots at the service of any of those present.

A little later Tokulki went hunting and brought back dried venison to add to his winter's stores. It was only then that he and his bride were brought to their new home, where a final feast was partaken of by all together, speeches exchanged by the leading men of the Wind and Raccoon clans, and the new couple left in possession.

During this period Tokulki was too busily occupied to think of his earlier ambitions, but after his first child was born and the routine of his new life had become well established, they began to recur to him. He communicated his thoughts to the three young men with whom he had been associated before, and he found that they too were prepared to continue in their course. They approached the Medicine Maker again, and again submitted to the fasts, the sweat baths, and the repeated instructions, more rigorous now than before. This time they learned among other things the treatment proper for snake bite, and how, as they believed, to detect objects clearly on the darkest nights.

Tokulki was still unsatisfied. Every fresh revelation awakened new ambitions. His companions, however, were content with what they had acquired and with the prestige they had attained, and were wearied with the long and exhausting fasts. Therefore when Tokulki presented himself as a candidate for the third degree he went entirely alone. In fact, so rigorous was the ordeal to which he was at this time subjected, that he debated within himself whether he should not stop there. As it was, he had penetrated farther into the mysteries than all except ten or a dozen men in the fifty allied Muskogee towns.

He allowed two years to slip away before making up his mind to undertake the fourth and crowning ordeal. Finally, however, he set himself to the task, and he came triumphantly through, though the periods of fasting were doubled, and the memorizing more severe than any which he had before experienced. He returned to his house a mere shadow of a man, with hollow cheeks, sunken eyes, and almost fleshless bones, but with a position and influence in the Nation shared by none except the Medicine Makers of a few of the leading towns.

With the Medicine Maker of Tulsa, his instructor and uncle, Tokulki now came to be on the most friendly terms. It was natural that a man of such advanced mentality as Tokulki and such steadfastness of purpose should excite interest in his superior. It became evident that when the Medicine Maker died or gave up his spiritual headship his position would fall to Tokulki. Many were the talks which the two men had together, talks in which the older man unfolded whatever knowledge his long life of physical activity and spiritual contemplation had given him. Some was not new to Tokulki, some had been suggested to him by the other learned men, but much was novel and strange.

The world envisaged by the Tulsa sage was about like this: The middle earth which mankind knows, is flat and square and lies afloat upon "the wide white waters." There is a world above it and a world below it, and these are inhabited by beings like ourselves. Below are those left behind when the races now on earth found their way to its surface; above, those who had lived on earth but, having undergone the experience called death, had traveled westward, crossed a narrow point in the ocean stream, upon a foot log, and either remained with the malevolent spirits in that quarter or ascended to the fortunate region directly overhead, presided over by Hisakita-imisi, "the breath holder." The white streak in the sky which we call "the milky way" was said to be the very road which they traversed. Unavenged souls of those who had been killed in wars, however, were unwilling to begin their journey until scalps from the offending tribe were brought in, and meanwhile they remained about the eaves of the houses, moaning. Some said that bad spirits were reincarnated into beasts, but about this men differed. However, they were agreed that human beings might acquire such malevolent power as to become witches and assume the forms of animals while still living on earth. Their evil dispositions were attributed to lizards who had taken up their abode inside of the witch, but might be expelled by the proper medical rites.

The stars were thought to be attached to the under surface of the solid vault above, along which the sun and moon traveled each day. An eclipse of the sun was usually attributed to a great toad who might be frightened off by hostile demonstrations on the part of human beings.   To an eclipse of the moon people paid little attention.   The moon was inhabited by a man and a dog.   The rainbow was a big, celestial snake which had power over rain.

The world and all that it contained were the products of mind and bore everywhere the marks of mind.   Matter was not something which had given birth to mind, but something which had formerly been mind, something from which mind had withdrawn, was quiescent, and out of which it might again be roused.   This mind was visibly manifested in the so-called "living things," as plants, and, still more, animals.   Nevertheless, latent within inorganic substance no less than in plants and animals, was mind in its highest form, i. e., human mind.   This might come to the surface at any time but it did so particularly to the fasting warrior, the "knower," and the doctor. Indeed, the importance of these two last lay in their ability to penetrate to the human life within the mineral, plant, and animal life of nature, and bring back from that experience knowledge of value in ordering the lives of their fellow beings.   Not that mind was attributed to one individuality, but that it was recognized as everywhere of the same nature.

Its manifestations were not in all cases equally powerful.   Its manifestation in the panther, bear, and bison was more powerful than its manifestation in the raccoon, the rabbit, and the squirrel.   Some "inorganic" powers,—as, for instance, the wind, the rivers, and the sea,—were, however, even more powerful.   Peculiarly powerful were the thunder and the lightning, which were produced by two sets of animals.   The dangerous kind, the kind that "struck," was made by huge birds from whose eyes flashed fire, and this they flashed down at the other fire-producing creatures, enormous, horned serpents, who in turn shot the blue, harmless lightning upward.   Bones of these earth serpents were sometimes found after a rainstorm. Besides there were long serpents who lived in the waters and who, rearing their huge lengths straight upward at intervals, would allow themselves to fall over with a gigantic splash.   There were the sharp-breasted snakes, suggested to native imagination by the tracks of lightning, snakes supposed to run straight along the surface of the ground, cutting through roots and bushes as they went. There were bodiless snakes which rose whirling into the air on still mornings. There were creatures like bison which went by fours, each resting for a minute in the tracks of its predecessor. There were very little people who sometimes deprived travelers of their senses, and very big people who ate them.

Besides the embodied power in nature there was power not altogether differentiated from it, which was unembodied, or indistinctly conceived as embodied. This power could be invoked by the use of charms and the repetition of certain formulæ. "By a word" wonderful things could be accomplished; "by a word" the entire world could be compressed into such a small space that the medicine man who was master of the word could encircle it in four steps. It was power of this kind which was imparted to medicines, yet the source of this power was after all the anthropomorphic powers, which, at the very beginning of things, declared what the diseases were to be and also appointed the remedies to be employed in curing them. But when the doctor had prepared these remedies and placed them in a pot in front of him, they were not efficacious until he had repeated the prescribed formulæ, or prayers, four times, while breathing into the medicine through a hollow cane. In this way the spirit that made the medicine powerful passed into it through the breath of life in the doctor.

From this conception it came about that the supreme being of the Creeks, a kind of sky god, was known as Hisakita-imisi, "the breath holder." While he did not necessarily interfere actively in the relations between the lesser powers and mankind, his primacy was recognized, and they were spoken of as his servants; he was their miko.

What took place for the individual in time of sickness happened for the entire tribe annually at the time of the poskita. It had been given to men by Hisakita-imisi for their health and for the annual renewal of the life of the tribe, as well as the individual lives of those composing it. The square-ground fire was but a detached fragment of the sun, the sky fire, and both of these meant life, for both were necessary to the lives of men. The renewal of the fire was the renewal of life, an act by means of which, the connection between human lives and the life of the universe was restored, and the corruption, which had accumulated about the fire obtained the previous year, gotten rid of. Similarly the participants were cleansed internally by means of the poskita medicines, one of which was to make good the defects of the system and heal its diseases, the other to insure the enjoyment of positive benefits. Hence it was that a little of each was carried home by every household and hung up by the door, some of it being used occasionally in medicines until the next annual ceremony.

As to the origin of things, the Muskogee had obscure traditions. They believed that the solid land had come from the expansion of a bit of earth brought from the edges of the world or from the bottom of the ocean. They also told of a flood, but their story of human origins did not concern any tribes except their own and a few believed to be related closely to theirs. They thought that after their ascent from the world beneath at the point in the far west called "the navel of the world," they had traveled toward the southeast for a long time, led by their Medicine Maker, who, in turn, was guided by a staff, stuck upright in the ground every night and found inclining in the direction to be taken every morning. In the meantime, four "light beings" from the corners of the world had brought the knowledge of the poskita to them and had lighted their first poskita fire. During this period, ties of friendship sprang up between the several Muskogee tribes, and some that were not Muskogee. Two of the leading tribes, the Kasihta and Coweta, formed an agreement by which they were to play ball with each other at intervals, but were never to fight and as other towns or tribes became allied with these, they also became allied in the ball games until there came to be two classes of towns with about twenty-five on a side. Those headed by Kasihta were dedicated to peace and those headed by Coweta to war. . . .

One day—it was toward the end of summer—Tokulki and the Medicine Maker strayed some distance eastward of the town and sat down upon the side of a hill, where the older man reviewed the more important particulars of his teaching more impressively than ever before. After a time he paused, and then he said: "I have told you all that I know; this is what the Medicine Maker who was before me, and all of the knowers and the doctors have told me. It must be so. I believe it. Yet perhaps it is not all the truth. I think we are not to understand some of the things that they tell just as they sound; they have another meaning. Sometimes we can see what this other meaning is; sometimes we can not. Perhaps, too, like the poskita fire, it has become fouled by much contact with common things, by much repeating. Perhaps Hisakita-imisi did not tell our grandfathers all that he had in mind to tell. But much of it is good, and it is for the good of our people. So use what seems to you good! And the rest you need not use. And if Hisa-kita-imisi seems to tell you something that is better, if you think it is better for your people, use it! It is what he must have intended from the beginning. I tell you this because I feel that your times will not be like my times. The plant dies. In the spring the plant comes up again. It is the same plant, and yet it is not the same plant. It is like, but it is unlike.

"Have you not heard of the people who come across the wide, white water in canoes with wings? Even now I hear that a great number of them are marching through our country and that they are coming in this direction. Maybe the old things are to pass away." He stopped, and just then out of the east came a low noise, a noise strange to that country until then, but one which a white man of the time would have recognized as the discharge of a harquebus. It was a harquebus in the army of De Soto.

JOHN R. SWANTON

SLENDER MAIDEN OF THE APACHE

Slender-maiden of the Apache

SLENDER-MAIDEN was to have her dance in twelve days. The acorns were now ripening along Ash Creek; the stags, their horns fully grown, were taking on fat; thunder-showers were now falling, and the year was at its best. During the preceding spring, Slender-maiden's mother had noted her daughter's approach to womanhood. The winter before, Slender-maiden's father had gone to the mountains beyond Black River and hunted for half a month. The best of the deerskins had been carefully tanned and put away. On Cibicu Creek, a day to the west, lived a man noted for the fine buckskin suits he could make. Slender-maiden's father took four of these dressed deerskins and two of his best horses to this skilled man. The horses were given him for his work on the skins. Slender-maiden's father was told to come for the garments about the time corn showed its tassels.

Slender-maiden's mother and Slender-maiden herself were Wormwood clan. Many women of this clan lived in the neighborhood and they gladly agreed to help gather food for the feast. Slender-maiden's father was of the Adobe clan. His brothers promised to join him before the dance, in a hunt which should provide venison for the feast. There was, fortunately, a large number of horses belonging to the family with which those who sang the songs and directed the ceremony might be paid.

Slender-maiden's father rode up the creek to the marsh where he cut a supply of reeds. Of these he made tubes, which he filled with tobacco and tied at right angles, making crosses. These were sent by Slender-maiden's cousin, a young man but recently with a beard to pluck, to the medicine man living on Eastfork who knew the songs of Naiyenezgani, used for the dance of adolescent girls. When the young man arrived at the home of the singer he placed the cross on his toe. As the old man reached for the token he asked the young man from whence he came.

"I am Wormwood clan and I come from the valley of dancehouse. Slender-maiden's father, my uncle, asks that on the twelfth day you

147

sing for his daughter under the cotton-woods on Ash Creek. He sends you this deerskin, these beads of turquoise, of jet, of white stone, and of red coral. Besides he gives you a horse, and a saddle from Old Mexico."

"Sit, my grandchild," said the singer to the young man. The old man then filled his pipe and passed his buckskin bag of tobacco to the young man. "Call my brothers," he said to his wife before they began smoking. When they had gathered and the pipes were burning, the singer told the young man's errand and that their aid was required in the ceremony. Food was now brought and the young man was served.

A similar invitation was sent to a medicine man on Turkey Creek who knew the dance of the Gans.

A few days later the women of Slender-maiden's clan and those living in her camp loaded their burros and horses with the food for the feast and the necessary utensils. The sun was well up when they were ready to start, and by sundown the party camped when they reached a stream where oaks grew in profusion, about two-thirds of the way to Ash Creek. By noon the next day, camp was made under the cotton-woods in the valley of the creek.

The day before the dance was to be held a sweat lodge was built near the stream. In this dome-shaped lodge, parties of six and eight men went repeatedly for baths. The songs of Naiyenezgani were sung and the men were purified by the steam and heat. At midday, food was served to all those who had gathered in the vicinity.

Just before the sun rose the next morning, four blankets were spread, one above the other, and a cane, bent at the top, was stood up just east of this bed. Near the cane was placed a basket of shelled corn.

The singer from Eastfork with his chorus of young men formed a line just back of the western end of the bed. Slender-maiden now appeared and took her place in front of the singers, facing the rising sun. As the songs were sung in proper order Slender-maiden danced, swaying her body from side to side. When the proper song was reached, she knelt and moved from side to side on alternate knees with her face always toward the rising sun. Soon she lay prone on the bed and was molded to a form of beauty by her matronly attendant. Finally she was prayed for by all the assembled spectators who passed in line behind her and put pollen on the crown of her head. When the sun was about halfway to the middle of the sky she ran the appointed race and the morning ceremony was completed.

Every one was soon served with meat and soup.

That evening at about sunset a man without clothes, except a breechcloth, his body painted white with black stripes, appeared at the dance-ground and by signs inquired if a dance were in progress. On being told that was the case he ran away to a secluded spot. Soon peculiar noises were heard and the sound of rattles. Four men came in single file followed by a painted clown. The four wore moccasins and kilts below the waist but were painted black above with symbolic designs in white. Their faces were covered and on the tops of their heads were fan-shaped forms of wood covered with painted designs. After making a circuit of the dance-ground, these masked men danced for some time and then withdrew.

After nightfall a great fire was kindled and the masked men returned. Slender-maiden, bearing her cane, danced near the fire. With her were other maidens who occasionally invited young men to dance with them. While the masked men were dancing, the singer from Turkey Creek led the songs of the Gans, immortals who join with men in the celebration of attaining adolescence. The time of the songs was marked by the singers beating on a stretched skin.

> When the earth was made,
> When the sky was made,
> Where the head of the black earth lies,
> Where the head of the black sky lies,
> Where the heads of them meet,
> Black Thunder, Black Gan, facing each other with life stepped out.
> Black Gan with his dance spoke four times.

About midnight the singer from Eastfork and his assistants took their places within a house consisting of four poles only. A fire was kindled here, back of which, facing the east, stood Slender-maiden accompanied by a girl of her own age, and two youths. At intervals until dawn the songs of Naiyenezgani were sung while the young people danced.

> Estsunnadlehe
> From her house of white cloud
> Living white shell, her chief,

It echoes with me.
Estsunnadlehe
Long and fortunate life, her chief,
It echoes with me.

After breakfast more songs were sung and then the masked men appeared and assisted, first in painting Slender-maiden with white earth and later in marking with symbols the cheeks and hands of all the spectators. The ceremony was now complete and the assembly soon dispersed, some people to the gathering of acorns and some to their camps in order to tend their crops.

Among those who had been at the ceremony at Ash Creek was a young man named Red-boy. His home was on San Pedro Creek, one hundred miles south and west, not far from the country of the Pima. He had come to visit relatives in the White Mountain country for his mother was of the Adobe clan and her brothers and sisters were living on the White River.

Red-boy was much interested in Slender-maiden and resolved to seek her for a wife. His request was listened to, and his presents of horses were accepted. Slender-maiden herself was pleased, for the stranger was tall, and generous with his presents to her. The couple soon moved to a camp on Black River, where Slender-maiden was left behind while her husband joined a small party which was going to Mexico on a raid. Ten days later the party returned without loss and with a large number of horses. Red-boy had taken ten which he gave Slender-maiden's parents.

The next spring Red-boy and Slender-maiden went to the village on San Pedro and planted the land that had belonged to Red-boy's mother. Here they lived for five years, raising good crops and having plenty of deer from the surrounding mountains.

One day in August Slender-maiden and her sister-in-law were making baskets under the cotton-woods by the creek. Slender-maiden's five-year old daughter was sleeping under a willow nearer the stream where the breeze was cooler. Suddenly a roar was heard and a wall of water, mud, and torn-up trees rushed out of the canyon. The women jumped up, but before they could reach the sleeping child the water had rolled over in a brown flood. The women themselves were able to escape by climbing into the cotton-woods.

Saddened by this loss and disconcerted by the washing over of the farm by the waters of a thunder-shower, Slender-maiden and her husband moved to the White Mountain country and settled on Cedar Creek near her people. Here they lived for ten years. There were now five children, the youngest of which was a girl.

One day a messenger came from White River asking that Slender-maiden's husband come to treat a sick man. Red-boy knew the songs and ritual of a healing ceremony. He went with his wife, and camped by the man who had been suddenly taken ill. He was burning with fever and covered with an eruption. The songs were of no avail for before dawn the man was dead. The body was almost immediately placed in a cleft of the rocks in a nearby canyon and covered with sticks and stones.

That afternoon Slender-maiden and her husband moved down White River and a few days later to Black River in which she and her husband bathed. That night her head ached and she begged her husband to leave, lest he too contract the disease. When twelve days later the fever left her, she saw her husband sitting by, tired and worn with watching over her.

"Why did you not leave me?" she asked.

"Because I have loved you for many years," he replied.

In a few days he too was ill and then Slender-maiden, still weak, watched him until he was taken to the canyon for burial. When the plague had passed, Slender-maiden's children and near relatives were all dead except the youngest girl who had been left with an aunt on Cedar Creek.

Slender-maiden cut her hair, of course, and wore only a skirt and a poncho of cloth. Even when the year was up she did not allow her hair to grow. Her husband's clansmen, noting her disinclination to marry again, respected her wishes and did not assign her a husband. She continued the cultivation of her small farm and the care of her daughter.

The requests of her adolescence ceremony for long life were answered. So old is she that she must walk with a cane. Her hair is white, not with the symbolic white earth but with age. Her daughter, in middle age, unmarried, highly respected, but much sought for herself and her considerable herds, attends to her physical needs. For the remainder, Slender-maiden lives with her memories of a happy youth. P. E. GODDARD

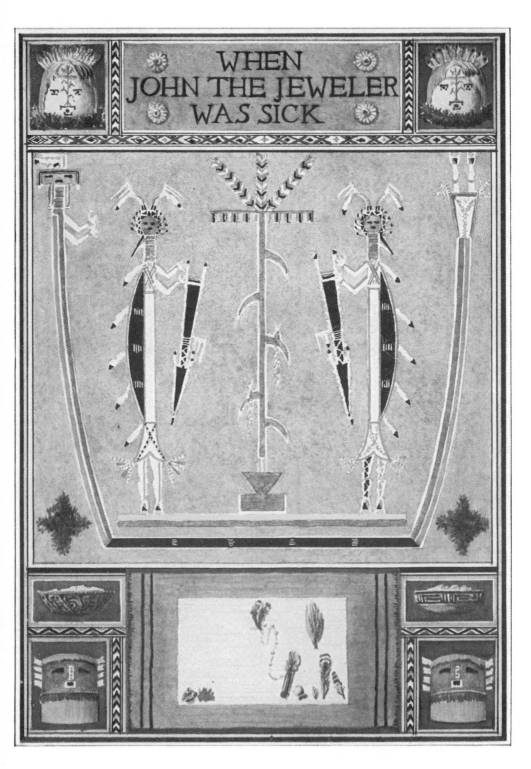

WHEN
JOHN THE JEWELER
WAS SICK

When John the Jeweler was Sick [1]

Told at St. Michaels, Arizona, by one of the Franciscan Fathers

YOU may remember having met here a Navaho friend of ours, one of the silver-smiths, whom we familiarly called "John the Jeweler." Early this year he went over to the Kohonino Cañon and stayed there four days. The day after leaving the Cañon he was taken with ague, and every day for twenty days he had a chill followed by fever and delirium. The strangeness of the disease had an extraordinarily depressing effect on him and during these twenty days he was in a state of utter collapse.

John the Jeweler is a medicine man, a minor priest, of considerable repute, and numbers of his friends came to see him, but none of them knew anything about his disease. The priests and the patient were inclined to attribute it to "a bad smell emanating from the Kohonino," but as there was also a band of wandering Paiutes there during the time of the patient's visit, they were not sure but that the bad smell may have originated with the Paiutes.

It was concluded in this emergency to call in the best mediciners of the region. The first to officiate was Ojkai yośna. His rites and song-prayers were directed to the Yè who dwells at the mouth of the pit through which all people came up to this world, and through which the spirits of the dead return to the lower world.

This pit is in the summit of that mountain in the north called Tjoliï. Between the patient and the mouth of the pit the priest made a fire with certain woods, and beside this fire he sang prayers to the Yè who sits on "this side" the mouth of the pit. He beseeched the Yè not to call the patient to descend the ladder leading to the regions of the dead. He rubbed the ashes and pulverized charcoal of his medicine-fire all over the body of the patient, first having rubbed him with a mixture obtained by melting the fat of the bison, mountain sheep, elk and deer, with a small portion of the fat of the domestic sheep. This grease was to make stick to the skin the charcoal and

---

[1] Manuscript contributed by Mr. Stewart Culin.

ashes of the medicine-fire. After the anointment the songs were sung again beside the patient.

The rites of Ojkai yośna lasted two days and nights and his fee was one horse, say fifty dollars.

The next shaman was Kuma byge. In the sick man's hut, a little hollow mound of clay was made, and within the hollow three stones were set; on these were laid splinters of piñon and cedar which were set afire. When they had burned to embers, the shaman shook his rattle and sang to the Yès of his father. He then laid upon the embers five herbs. The patient was laid naked upon the sand, close to the fireplace, and a blanket was spread over the fireplace, and the patient thus inhaled the fumes of the herbs, while the shaman sat alongside, shaking his rattle and continuing his song.

The treatment was performed at sunrise and sunset, and should last four days, with songs, dances and other ceremonies at night. But in this instance, at the close of the second day, an embarrassing circumstance occurred: the patient's wife's menstrual flow began. This at once put a stop to all further treatment. Kuma byge's fee was one horse, say fifty dollars.

After the wife got well, Etsĭdi bĭkĭs was summoned. To the leader of the four winds sang the shaman, the white wind of the East, the blue wind of the South, the yellow wind of the West, and the black wind of the North. Before the people emerged from the lower world the winds were taken up the pit at Tjoliĭ by the "Leader" and their directions assigned them. He caused them to blow upon the muddy surface of the earth while this upper surface was yet new and damp, until the world became dry enough for habitation. The winds expelled the evil influence of the bad Yès, and the new world became beautiful. So it was to this Leader that Etsĭdi bĭkĭs sang, asking him to bring the winds together, and expel the evil influence that threatened the patient.

The ceremonies lasted four days and nights and consisted of songprayers, exhibiting fetiches, shaking the rattle, blowing the whistle, and swinging the tsin boosni (which is like swinging the Thunder prayer stick of the Hopi). The fee of Etsĭdi bĭkĭs was a large horse, say sixty dollars.

The next shaman was called Hostin bĭkân. He administered herb roots, both raw and in infusions. The raw root of the Jamestown weed was given the patient at sunrise, noon and sunset. Each dose was something less than half an ounce of the recently dry root. This was chewed and swallowed. Closely following each of these doses, he was given a piece of the stalk of the Golden Alexander, about six inches long and as thick as the thumb. This he chewed, swallowing the saliva, but not the fiber. Between the songs, during the day and night, infusions were given the patient to drink, in quantities never to exceed half a pint at once. There were separate infusions of herbs known as: aze klohĭ, laughing medicine, aze bĭni, bad or dreaded talk medicine, thajuhuĭtso, great chief of water medicines, that is of medicinal herbs growing in marshes, all, I surmise, species of nightshade. Hostin bĭkân's ceremonies lasted a day and a night. His fee was a horse, say fifty dollars.

The last and most potent of the shamans was Kuma. He is chief of the clan to which the patient belongs. He lives about thirty miles southwest from our Cañon.

Kuma's prayers were directed to Hosdjoqun (the Killer) and Hos-(dje) Yelti (the Talker), guardian deities of Tjoliĭ. But all these prayers were more immediately addressed to the Yès who dwell in the Half-white-house, asking their mediation, that the "Killer" might withhold his hand, that the "Talker" might withhold the word of death. I presume you know that there is a mythic region in the north. It extends from nadir to zenith and has no horizon. It is a land of vertical strata of various colors, each stratum reaching from The Below to The Above. At each stratification is the house of a Yè, half in one stratum, half in the next. [1]

A sweat house is decorated on the outside with a rainbow in colored sands; a singing-house is built for the occasion; sand pictures (altars) are made on the floor of the singing-house; and there are dances of the masked participants.

Kuma's ceremonies lasted five days and nights. Every morning at sunrise, the patient was placed in the sweat house for about twenty minutes, say ten minutes in each. Nothing of special significance was done during the day, but from sunset to dawn the maskers danced before the singing-house, while within the singing-house, the

---

[1] I am under the impression that the ceremonies Dr. Washington Matthews observed several years ago at Fort Defiance were addressed to the Yès of the Half-red-house, but the motive in those ceremonies and in these of the Yès of the Half-white-house is the same, and the rites and songs very similar.

priests sang their prayers, made their sand pictures, and placed the proper fetiches before and upon them.   For a fee, Kuma received a fine horse and colt, worth one hundred dollars.

Aside from all these fees, sheep were killed to provide mutton, and other provisions were purchased to feed the shamans and their assistants, the dancers, and the numerous spectators who flock around when any of these religious ceremonies are in progress.   In these expenses the patient was assisted by all his relatives.

In these ceremonies, three weeks went by, with every day an ague. At the end of that time, the patient said that he was "looking down the descending ladder."

His friends then cinched him upon a saddle, and brought him here, muffled in a blanket, just like a bag of bones.   We had him dumped in the wool room.   This was four days ago.   We had no calomel, so we gave him a generous dose of blue mass, about thirty grains.   On the following morning we administered a liberal draught of castor oil, and then we gave him about thirty grains of quinine, in four doses, daily.   Two days ago his ague left him.   This morning he and his friends left for home.   Just as he was leaving, John the Jeweler told me he was feeling so well, he thought that by to-morrow night he could resume the performance of his marital duties.

A. M. STEPHEN

WAIYAUTITSA of ZUÑI

Waiyautitsa of Zuñi, New Mexico

"Isn't it hard to believe that life should be so intricate and complex among those meek, adobe houses on that low hill?"

We were on the last mile or so of the forty-mile drive through the red sandstone above and below, and the green cedar and spruce and sagebrush from Gallup to Zuñi; behind us to the southeast was the great mesa to which three centuries ago the people had escaped for a while from Spanish arrogance, the mesa where one day we were to seek for the shrines of the War Leaders and the Song Youth and the Earth Woman as we ostensibly hunted rabbits; and before us, barely in sight, so quietly does an Indian pueblo fit into the landscape, were the rectangular blocks of the many-storied Zuñi houses whose flat roofs make broken lines, mesa-like, against the sky. At the highest point, a three-storied house, the town crier was probably at that very moment calling out to the townspeople the orders of the governor and council for the following day; but we were still too far away to hear, quiet as was the air, and our unarrested eyes turned westward to the flaming spectacle of a sunset the like of which is not to be seen outside the sweeping valley plain of Zuñi.

Now and again, as you walk between those "meek, adobe houses," dodging a snouting pig, or assuming indifference to the dogs that dash out from every corner to snarl or yelp; now and again as you see the villagers going about their daily affairs, men driving in from the fields, or taking the horses in or out of the corrals, women fetching water from the well or bound on a visit to a neighbor, little boys chasing one another and babies playing about in the dirt, now and again that first impression of material simplicity returns and with it the feeling that the round of life must be simple, too. But the feeling never lasts long, never holds its own with the crowding impressions of ceremonial rain dance or pilgrimage or domiciliary visitation, of baffling sacerdotal organization and still more baffling sacerdotal feuds, of elaborate pantheon, of innumerable myths and tales, of associations in story or cult with every hill and rock and spring, of kinship ramifications and matrimonial histories, of irksome relationships with Mexicans and "Americans," and of village gossip which is made up so comprehensively of the secular and the sacred as to pass far beyond the range of even a New England church social.

It is not surprising that accounts of Zuñi are often bewildering. In our own complex culture biography may be a clarifying form of description. Might it not avail at Zuñi? I venture this biography of Waiyautitsa.[1]

Waiyautitsa is a girl's name; sex generally appears in Zuñi personal names. Sex appears somewhat in speech too. Waiyautitsa in learning to talk will make use of expressions, particularly exclamations, peculiar to women. In a recent list of the first words used by a Zuñi child, a boy, there was noted a comparatively large number of kinship terms in his vocabulary. The kinship terms of little Waiyautitsa would be somewhat different from a boy's. He calls a younger sister ikina; a younger brother, suwe; she calls either hani, meaning merely the younger. And, as the Zuñi system of kinship terms is what is called classificatory, cousins having the same terms as brother and sister, Waiyautitsa has even fewer words than her brother to express cousinship.

When Waiyautitsa is three or four years old she may be recognized as a girl not merely from her speech, but from her dress, from her cotton slip; at this age little boys wear trousers. But not for another three or four years, perhaps longer, will Waiyautitsa wear over her cotton slip the characteristic Pueblo woman's dress,—the black blanket dress fastened on the left shoulder and under the right arm and hence called in Zuñi, watone, meaning "across," the broad belt woven of white, green and red cotton, the store-bought kerchief or square of silk (pitone) which, fastened in front, hangs across shoulders and back, and the small foot, thick leg moccasins which cover ankle and calf in an envelope of fold upon fold of buckskin. Before Waiyautitsa is eight or even six she may, however, when she goes out, cover her head and body with a black blanket or with the gay colored "shawl" similarly worn. And I have seen very little girls indeed wearing moccasins or the footless black stockings Zuñi women also wear, or "dressing up" in a pitone, that purely ornamental article of

(1) It was this biography, published originally in "The Scientific Monthly" (Nov. 1919) and now revised, which suggested to us the comprehensive biographic plan of this book. Ed.

dress without which no Zuñi woman would venture outdoors. Without her pitone she would feel naked, she says, and any man would be at liberty to speak disrespectfully to her. When Waiyautitsa is about five, her hair, before this worn, like the boys, in a short cut, is let grow into a little tail on the nape of her neck. In course of time her pigtail will be turned up and tied with a "hair belt" of white, green and red cloth. From ear to ear her front hair will be banged to the end of her nose, the bang drawn sidewise above the forehead except at such times in ceremonials when it is let fall forward to conceal the upper part of the face.

This hair arrangement serves in ceremonials as a kind of mask, as you may see in the frontispiece picture of the headdress worn in the Thlahawe, a woman's corn dance. A mask proper, that quasi fetich which has so important a place in Pueblo ceremonialism, Waiyautitsa will in all probability never wear. Unlike her brother, Waiyautitsa will not be initiated in childhood into the Kachina society, and consequently she will not join one of the six sacred clubhouses or estufas which supply personators for the Kachinas or masked dancers. Not that female personages do not figure in these ceremonials, but as was the rule on the Elizabethan stage, women are impersonated by men.

To this exclusion of girls from the Kachina society and from participating in the masked dances there are a few exceptions. To-day three women belong to the Kachina society. They were taken into it not in childhood, but in later life and, it is said, for one of the same reasons women as well as men are taken into the other societies of Zuñi. Cured by ceremonial whipping of the bad effects of nightmare or of some other ailment, they were "given" to the estufa credited through one of its members with the cure. Of the three women members only one is said to dance, and she is accounted mannish, katsotse, girl-man, a tomboy.

Waiyautitsa will likely not be initiated into the kotikyane, but she is quite likely to be initiated into another society,—into the Great-fire-brand or Little fire-brand, or Bedbug or Ant or Wood society, into any one of the thirteen Zuñi societies except three, the bow priesthood or society of warriors, of warriors who have taken a scalp, or the Hunter society or the Cactus society, a society that cures arrow or gun-shot wounds. As women do not hunt or go to war, from membership in these groups they are excluded or, better say, precluded. As we shall see later, affiliation by sex is, in ceremonial affairs, along the lines of customary occupation.

If Waiyautitsa falls sick and is cured by a medicine man of the medicine order of a society she must be "given" either to the family of the medicine man or to his society. Initiated she may not be, however, for a long time afterwards, perhaps for years. Initiations take place in the winter when school is in session, the school either of the Indian Bureau or of the Dutch Reformed Church, and for that reason, it is said, initiations may be postponed until past school age. Despite the schools, I may say, I have met but two Zuñi women who speak English with any fluency. One woman is a member of the Snake-medicine society, into which she was initiated after convalescence from measles, a decimating disease at Zuñi, to be accounted for only through witchcraft. The other woman was accounted the solitary convert of the Dutch Reformed Church Mission in Zuñi until six or seven years ago she joined the Wood society because as a child she had been cured by them of smallpox.

After initiation, the women, like the men of a society, offer prayer sticks each moon, observing continence for four days thereafter, and they join in the four-day retreat in the ceremonial house of the society preliminary to an initiation. Unlike the men, however, the women do not spend the entire night, only the evening, in the society house, and, while there, they are listeners rather than narrators of the inexhaustible folk tales that are wont to be told at society gatherings. Men are the custodians of the lore, secular as well as esoteric, of the tribe, just as men and not women are the musicians. The men are devoted singers, singing as they dance or singing as a choir for dancers, and singing as they go to or from work in the fields, or as they drive their horses to water in the river or to the corrals on the edges of the town. Even grinding songs are sung on ceremonial occasions by men.

In the public appearances of the society, the women members figure but little. Societies supply choirs and drummers and ceremonial road openers or leaders to the masked dancers and, during the great koko awia (Kachina coming) or shalako ceremonial, to various groups of sacred personages. I have seen several dances in Zuñi and one celebration of koko awia, and I have seen but one woman officiate in public. As a daughter of the house which was entertaining the koyemshi or sacred clowns she was in attendance upon that group in the koko awia or Advent, so to speak, of 1915.

If Waiyautitsa belongs to a society, she will offer or plant the befeathered prayer sticks, which are so conspicuous a feature of Pueblo religion, but, being a woman, Waiyautitsa will not cut or dress the sticks. She will only grind the pigments and, perhaps, paint the sticks. Nor as a woman would she offer the sticks on certain other ceremonial occasions when the men offer them. Once a year, however, at the winter solstice ceremonial on which so much of Zuñi ritualism pivots, Waiyautitsa will be expected, even in infancy, to plant, planting for the "old ones," i. e., the ancestors and for the Moon, but not, like the men, for the Sun or, unless a member of the Kachina society, for the ancestral beings, the Kachina.

At the conclusion of the winter solstice ceremonial, when certain sacred figures called kwelele go from house to house, the women carry embers around the walls of the house and throw them out on the kwelele. It is the rite of shuwaha, cleansing, exorcism. There are a number of other little rites peculiar to the women in Zuñi ceremonialism. Through them, and through a number of rites they share with the men, through provisions for supplying food in the estufa to the sacred personators or for entertaining them at home or making them presents, women have an integral part in Zuñi ceremonialism. In what we may call the ceremonial management, however, they appear to have little or no part.

Even when women are initiated into the Kachina society, or are associated with the ashiwanni or rain priests, their functions seem to be primarily of an economic or housekeeping order. The women members of the rain priesthoods have to offer food every day to the fetiches of these sacerdotal groups—to stones carved and uncarved, and to cotton-wrapped lengths of cane filled with "the seeds the people live by." For the seed fetiches to be in any way disturbed in the houses to which they are attached, involves great danger to the people, and on a woman in the house, the woman member of the priesthood, falls the responsibility of guardianship or shelter. But even these positions of trust are no longer held by women—there are only six women ashiwanni among the fifteen priesthoods. The woman's position among the paramount priesthood, the rain priesthood of the North, has been vacant now for many years—no suitable woman being willing, they say, to run the risks or be under the tabus of office. Aside from this position of woman shiwanni, women count for little or nothing in the theocracy of Zuñi. They were and are associated with the men priests to do the work pertinent to women. In the case of the Zuñi pantheon or its masked impersonations, the association is needed to satisfy or carry out, so to speak, Zuñi standards or concepts of conjugality. The couple rather than the individual is the Zuñi unit. Sometimes, in ceremony or in myth, the couple may consist of two males.

There is one masked couple I have noted in particular at Zuñi, the atoshle. Two or three times during the winter our little Waiyau-titsa, together with other girls and very little boys, may expect to be frightened by the atoshle, the disciplinary masks who serve as buga-boos to children as well as a kind of sergeant-at-arms, the male atoshle at least, for adults. If the children meet the old man and his old woman in the street, they run away helter-skelter. If the dreadful couple visits a child indoors, sent for perhaps by a parent, the child is indeed badly frightened. I suppose that Waiyautitsa is six or seven years old when one day, as an incident of some dance, the atoshle "come out" and come to her house. The old woman atoshle carries a deep basket on her back in which to carry off naughty chil-dren and in her hand a crook to catch them by the ankle. With the crook she pulls Waiyautitsa over to the grinding stones in the corner of the room, telling her that now she is getting old enough to help her mother about the house, to look after the baby and, before so very long, to grind. She must mind her mother and be a good girl. I once saw a little girl so terrified by such admonition that she began to whimper, hiding her head in her mother's lap until the atoshle was sprinkled with the sacred meal and left the house to perform else-where his rôle of parent's assistant.

Whether from fear, from supernatural fear or fear of being talked about as any Zuñi woman who rests or idles is talked about, or whether from example, more from the latter no doubt than from the former, Waiyautitsa is certainly a "good girl," a gentle little creature, and very docile. Sometimes she plays lively games with her "sisters" next door like the game of bear at the spring. A spiral is traced on the ground and at the center is placed a bowl of water to represent a spring. The girls follow the spiral to get water for their little turkeys which, they sing, are dying of thirst. Then the "bear" rushes out from the spring and gives chase. But for the most part the little girls play quietly at house. In this way and in imitating at home her industrious mother or aunt, or her even more industrious grandmother or great-aunt, Waiyautitsa learns to do all the household tasks of women. She learns to grind the corn on the stone metate— that back-hardening labor of the Pueblo woman—and to prepare and cook the meal in a number of ways in an outside oven or on the American stove or on the flat slab on which hewe or wafer bread is spread. For the ever cheery family meal she sets out the coffee-pot, the hewe or tortilla, and the bowls of chile and of mutton stew on the earthen floor she is forever sweeping up with her little homemade brush or with an American broom. (A Zuñi house is kept very clean and amazingly neat and orderly.)

And Waiyautitsa becomes very thrifty—not only naturally but super-naturally. She will not sell corn out of the house without keeping back a few grains in order that the corn may return—in Zuñi thought the whole follows a part. And she will keep a lump of salt in the corn storeroom and another in the bread bowl—when salt is dug out, the hole soon refills, and this virtue of replacing itself the salt is expected to impart to the corn. There are other respects, too, in which Waiyautitsa will learn how to facilitate the economy. She will sprinkle the melon seeds for planting, with sweetened water —melons should be sweet. Seed wheat she will sprinkle with a white clay to make the crop white, and with a plant called k'owa so that wheat dough will pull well. Seed corn will be sprinkled with water that the crop may be well rained on.

From some kinswoman who is a specially good potter, Waiyautitsa may have learned to coil and paint and fire the bowls as well as the cook pots and water jars the household needs. She fetches in wood from the woodpile and now and again she may be seen chopping the pine or cedar logs the men of the household have brought in on donkey or in wagon. She fetches water from one of the modern wells of the town, carrying it in a jar on her head and walking in the slow and springless gait always characteristic of Pueblo women.

Perhaps that gait, so ponderous and so different from the gait of the men, is the result of incessant industry, a kind of unconscious self-protective device against "speeding up."

Waiyautitsa will learn to work outdoors as well as in. She will help her mother in keeping one of the small vegetable gardens near the town—the men cultivate the outlying fields of corn and wheat (and the men and boys herd the sheep which make the Zuñi prosperous), and Waiyautitsa will help her household thresh their wheat crop, in the morning preparing dinner for the workers, for relatives from other households as well as from her own, in the afternoon joining the threshers as the men drive horses or mules around the circular threshing floor and the women and girls pitchfork the wheat and brush away the chaff and winnow the grain in baskets. Waiyautitsa will also learn to make adobe blocks and to plaster with her bare hand or with a rabbit-skin glove the adobe walls of her mother's house, inside and out. Pueblo men are the carpenters of a house, but the women are always the plasterers, and Waiyautitsa will have to be a very old woman indeed to think she is too old to plaster. On my last visit to Zuñi I saw a woman seventy, or not much under, spending part of an afternoon on her knees plastering the chinks of a door newly cut between two rooms.

The house she plasters belongs, or will in time belong, to Waiyautitsa. Zuñi women own their houses and their gardens or, perhaps it is better to say, gardens and houses belong to the family through the women. At marriage a girl does not leave home; her husband joins her household. He stays in it, too—only as long as he is welcome. If he is lazy, if he fails to bring in wood, if he fails to contribute the produce of his fields, or if some one else for some other reason is preferred, his wife expects him to leave her household. He does not wait to be told twice. "The Zuñi separate whenever they quarrel or get tired of each other," a critical Acoma moralist once said to me. The monogamy of Zuñi is, to be sure, rather brittle. In separation the children stay with the mother.

Children belong to their mother's clan. They have affiliations, however, as we shall see, with the clan of their father. If the mother of Waiyautitsa is a Badger, let us say, and her father a Turkey, Waiyautitsa will be a Badger and "the child of the Turkey." She can not marry a Turkey clansman nor, of course, a Badger. Did she show any partiality for a clansman, an almost incredible thing, she would be told she was just like a dog or a burro.

These exogamous restrictions aside, and the like restrictions that may arise in special ways between the household of Waiyautitsa and other households, Waiyautitsa would be given freedom of choice in marrying. Even if her household did not like her man, and her parents had told her not "to talk to" him, Zuñi for courting, she and he could go to live with some kinswoman. No one, related or unrelated, would refuse to take them in. Nobody may be turned from the door. Nor would a girl whose child was the offspring of a chance encounter be turned out by her people or slighted. The illegitimate child is not discriminated against at Zuñi.

Casual relationships occur at Zuñi, but they are not commercialized, there is no prostitution. Nor is there any lifelong celibacy. As for courtship, very little of it can there be—at least before intimacy either in the more transient or more permanent forms of mating,—the separation outside of the household of boys and girls of various ages is so thorough. "But what if a little girl wanted to play with boys?" I once asked. "They would laugh at her and say she was too crazy about boys." "Crazy" at Zuñi, as quite generally among Indians, means passionate. (Girls at Zuñi are warned away from ceremonial trespass by the threat of becoming "crazy.")

The young men and girls do, to be sure, have non-ceremonial dances together, and in preparing for them there are opportunities for personal acquaintance. I saw one of these dances not long ago. It was a Comanche dance. There were a choir of about a dozen youths including the drummer, four girl dancers heavily be-ringed and be-necklaced, the pattern of whose dance, two by two or in line, was very regular, and a youth who executed in front of them or around them an animated and very beautiful pas seul. After dancing outside in the plaza, they all went into the "saint's house" to dance for her "because they like her"—a survival no doubt of the custom of dancing in the Catholic church observed by the Indians in Mexico and not long since quite generally in New Mexico.

But it is on the twilight trip to the well, the conventional Zuñi hour of courtship, that Waiyautitsa will be approached by suitors. Muffled in his black blanket the youth may step out from the corner where he has been lurking and put his hand on the girl's arm. If she will have none of him, she may avert her head and hasten on to overtake the woman in front, but if she fancies the fellow, she will pause, if but for a moment or two, to talk.   It is a brief encounter and, with somebody in front and perhaps another girl coming up behind, it is far from private; still after Waiyautitsa has had a few such meetings, "two or four," she is likely to invite the young man to join her household.   At first, for a few days, he will stay in the common room, in the room where all sleep (sleeping and dressing, let me say, with the utmost modesty), he will stay only at night, leav-ing before dawn, "staying still" his shyness is called.   Then he will begin to eat his meals with the household.   There is, you see, no wedding ceremonial and a man slips as easily as he can into the life of his wife's household.

Waiyautitsa will pay a formal visit on her bridegroom's people, taking his mother a basket of corn meal.   To Waiyautitsa herself her young man will have given a present of cloth for a dress, or a buckskin for the moccasins he will make for her.   Hides are a product of the chase, of cattle raising (cowhide is used to sole moc-casins), or of trade, men's occupations, and so moccasins of both women and men are made by men.   Women make their own dresses, although, formerly, before weaving went out of fashion at Zuñi, it is likely that men were the weavers, just as they are to-day among the Hopi from whom the men of Zuñi get cloth for their ceremonial kilts and blankets, and for the dresses of the women.   Even to-day at Zuñi men may make up their own garments from store-bought goods and it is not unusual to see a man sitting to a sewing machine.

A man may use cloth or thread for other than economic reasons. In case a girl jilts him he will catch her out some night and take a bit from her belt to fasten to a tree on a windy mesa top.   As the wind wears away the thread, the woman will sicken and perhaps in two or three years die.   A woman who is deserted may take soil from the man's footprints and put it where she sleeps.   At night he will think of her and come back—"even if the other woman is better looking."   Apprehensive of desertion a woman may put a lock of hair from the man in her house wall or, the better to attach him to her, she may wear it over her heart.   Women and men alike may buy love charms from the ne'wekwe, a curing society, potent in magic, black or white.   There is a song, too, which men and women may sing "in their heart" to charm the opposite sex. And there is a song which a girl may sing to the corn as she rubs the yellow meal on her face before going out. "Help me," is the substance of it, "I am going to the plaza. Make me look pretty." Rarely do our girls pray, I suppose, when they powder their noses.

Courtship past for the time being, courtship by magic or otherwise, Waiyautitsa is now, let us say, an expectant mother. Her household duties continue to be about the same, but certain precautions, if she inclines to be very circumspect, she does take. She will not test the heat of her oven by sprinkling it in the usual way with bran, for if she does, her child, she has heard, may be born with a skin eruption. Nor will she look at a corpse or help dress a dead animal lest her child be born dead or disfigured. She has heard that, even as a little girl if she ate the whitish leaf of the corn husk, her child would be an albino. If her husband eats this during the pregnancy, the result would be the same. On her husband fall a number of other pregnancy tabus, perhaps as many as fall on her, if not more. If he hunts and maims an animal, the child will be similarly maimed—deformed or perhaps blind. If he joins in a masked dance, the child may have some mask-suggested misshape or some eruption like the paint on the mask. If he sings a great deal, the child will be a cry-baby. The habit of thinking in terms of sympathetic magic or of reasoning by analogy which is even more conspicuous at Zuñi than, let us say, at New York, is particularly evident in pregnancy or birth practises or tabus.

Perhaps Waiyautitsa has wished to determine the sex of the child. In that case she may have made a pilgrimage with a rain priest to Corn Mesa to plant a prayer stick which has to be cut and painted in one way for a boy, in another way for a girl. (Throughout the Southwest blue or turquoise is associated with maleness, and yellow with femaleness.) Wanting a girl—and girls are wanted in Zuñi quite as much as boys, if not more—Waiyautitsa need not make the trip to the mesa, instead her husband may bring her to wear in her belt scrapings from a stone in a phallic shrine near the mesa. When labor sets in and the pains are slight, indicating, women think, a girl, Waiyautitsa may be told by her mother, "Don't sleep, or you will have a boy." A nap during labor effects a change of sex. When the child is about to be born, Waiyautitsa is careful, too, if she wants a girl, to see that the custom of sending the men out of the house at this time is strictly observed.

After the birth, Waiyautitsa will lie in for several days, four, eight, ten or twelve, according to the custom of her family. Whatever the custom, if she does not observe it, she runs the risk of "drying up" and dying. She lies on a bed of sand heated by hot stones, and upon her abdomen is placed a hot stone. Thus is she "cooked," people say, and creatures whose mothers are not thus treated are called uncooked, raw—they are the animals, the gods, Whites. To be "cooked" seems to be tantamount in Zuñi to being human.

It is the duty of Waiyautitsa's mother-in-law, the child's paternal grandmother, to look after mother and child during the confinement, and at its close to carry the child outdoors at dawn and present him or her to the Sun. Had Waiyautitsa lost children, she might have invited a propitious friend, some woman who had had many children and lost none, to attend the birth and be the first to pick up the child and blow into his mouth. In these circumstances the woman's husband would become the initiator of the child, if a boy, when the child was to be taken into the Kachina society. Generally the child's father chooses some man from the house of his own kuku or paternal aunt to be the initiator or godfather, so to speak, of the child. Ceremonial rites usually fall to the paternal relatives.

But the infant will receive attentions of a ritual or magical nature, likewise from his mother and her household. He is placed on a cradle board in which, near the position of his heart, a bit of turquoise is inlaid to preclude the cradle bringing any harm to its tenant. Left alone, a baby runs great risk—some family ghost may come and hold him, causing him to die within four days. And so a quasi-fetichistic ear of corn, a double ear thought of as mother and child, is left alongside the baby as a protector. That the baby may teethe promptly, his gums may be rubbed by one who has been bitten by a snake—"snakes want to bite." To make the child's hair grow long and thick, his grandfather or uncle may puff the smoke of native tobacco on his head. That the child may not be afraid in the dark, water-soaked embers are rubbed over his heart the first time he is taken out at night—judging from what I have seen of Zuñi children and adults a quite ineffectual method. That the child may keep well and walk early, hairs from a deer are burned, and the child held over the smoke—deer are never sick, and rapid is their gait. Their hearing, too, is acute, so discharge from a deer's ear will be put into the baby's ear. That the child may talk well and with tongues, the tongue of a snared mocking bird may be cut out and held to the baby to lick. The bird will then be released in order that, as it regains its tongue and "talks," the child will talk. A youth who speaks in addition to his native tongue Keresan, English and Spanish, has been pointed out to me as one who had licked mocking bird tongue.

Waiyautitsa will give birth to three or four children, probably not more, and then, as she approaches middle age, we may suppose that she falls sick, and after being doctored unsuccessfully first by her old father who happens to be a well-known medicine man of the Great Fire-brand society, and then by a medicine man from the ne'wekwe society whose practice is just the opposite, Waiyautitsa dies. Within a few hours elderly kinswomen of her father's will come in and wash her hair and body, and at dawn sprinkle her face, first with water and then with meal. The deceased will be well dressed, and in a blanket donated by her father's people she will be carried to the cemetery lying in front of the old church, a ruin from the days of the Catholic establishment in Zuñi. There to the north of the central wooden cross, i. e., on the north side of the cemetery, Waiyautitsa will be buried. Women are buried on the north side and men on the south.

Waiyautitsa will be carried out and buried by her father and other men in the household. No women will go to the burial, nor will the widower. The widower, as soon as the corpse is taken outdoors, will be fetched by his women relatives to live at their house. There they straightway wash his hair—a performance inseparable in Zuñi, as at other pueblos, from every time of crisis or ceremony. The hair of all the other members of Waiyautitsa's household will be washed at the end of four days by women relatives of her father. During this time, since the spirit of Waiyautitsa is thought to linger about the home, the house door will be left open for her at night. The bowl used in washing her hair, and the implements used in digging her grave will also be left outdoors. Her smaller and peculiarly personal possessions have been buried with her, and bulky things like bedding have been burned or taken to a special place down the river to be buried.   The river flows to the lake sixty miles or so west of Zuñi, where Waiyautitsa's spirit is also supposed to take its journey.   There under the lake it abides, except when with other spirits it returns in the clouds to pour down upon Zuñi fields the beneficent rain.   People will say to a child, when they see a heavy cloud, "There goes your grandmother"; or they will quite seriously say to one another, "Our grandfathers are coming."

Waiyautitsa's children may go on living at home with their grand-mother, Waiyautitsa's mother, or it may be that one of them is adopted by a maternal aunt or great-aunt or cousin.   Zuñi children, cherished possessions as they are, are always being adopted—even in the lifetime of their mother.   Adopted, a child—or an adult—will fit thoroughly into the ways of his adoptive household.   It is the household as well as the clan which differentiates the Zuñi family group from our individualistic type of family.   The household changes quite readily, but, whatever its composition, it is an exceedingly integrated and responsible group.

However the children are distributed, it will be the older woman or women in the household who will control them.   This household system is one that gives position and considerable authority to the elder women—until the women are too old, people say, to be of any use.   (In spite of this irony, I have heard of but one old woman who was neglected by her household.)   An older woman who is the female head of the household is greatly respected by her daughters and sons-in-law and grandchildren, as well as by the sons or brothers who continually visit the household and often, as temporary celibates, return to live in it.

The older woman is highly esteemed, but she is by no means the head of the household—unless she is widowed.   Wherever the household contributes to the ceremonial public life, her husband is paramount.   In the non-ceremonial, economic life, too, he has equal, if not greater, authority.   And in the general economy he more or less expects his wife to serve him and wait on him.   This conjugal subordination is not apparent to any extent among the younger people; the younger husband and wife are too much drawn into the corporate household life.   But as time passes and they in turn become the heads of the household, the man appears to be more given to staying at home, and more and more he takes control.

From this brief survey of the life of a woman at Zuñi, in so far as it can be distinguished from the general life, we get the impression that the differentiation of the sexes follows lines of least resistance which start from a fairly fundamental division of labor. From being hunters and trappers men become herders of the domestic animals, drivers or riders. Trade journeys and trips for wood or for the collecting of other natural resources are associated with men, and work on the things acquired is men's work—men, for example, are wood cutters, and bead makers, whether the objects are for secular or sacerdotal use. Analogously all work upon skins or feathers is work for men whether it leads to the manufacture of clothing or to communication with the supernaturals. Again, as farmers, men are associated with that system of supernatural instrumentalism for fertility and weather control which constitutes in large part Zuñi religion. In other words, the bulk of the ceremonial life, a system for the most part of rain rituals, is in the hands of the men. So is government. The secular officers are merely representatives of the priests. Zuñi government is a theocracy in which women have little part. The house and housekeeping are associated with women. Clay is the flesh of a female supernatural, and clay processes, brickmaking or laying or plastering, and pottery making are women's work. There are indications in sacerdotal circles that painting is, or was thought of as, a feminine activity. Corn, like clay, is the flesh of female supernaturals, and the corn is associated with women. Even men corn growers are in duty bound to bring their product to their wife or mother. Women or women impersonations figure in corn rituals. It is tempting to speculate that formerly, centuries since, women themselves were the corn growers. To-day, at any rate, the preparation of corn, as of other food, is women's work. Wherever food and its distribution figure in ceremonials, and there is a constant offering of food to the supernaturals, women figure. Fetiches are attached to houses and in so far as providing for these fetiches is household work, it is women's work and leads to the holding of sacerdotal office by women. The household rather than ties of blood is the basis of family life. The children of the household are more closely attached to the women than to the men. One expression of this attachment is seen in reckoning clan membership through the mother.

Household work at Zuñi as elsewhere is continuous. The women are always on the move. The work of the men, on the other hand, is intermittent. Hunting, herding and farming are more or less seasonal activities and are more or less readily fitted into ceremonial pursuits, or rather, in their less urgent periods, take on ceremonial aspects. In the ceremonial life the arts find expression, and the men and not the women are, by and large, the artists of the tribe.

Attached to the ceremonial life are the games of chance and the races that are played or run at certain seasons. Here again the intermittent habit of work of the men, together with their comparative mobility, qualifies them as gamesters and runners to the exclusion more or less of the women. Formerly, to be sure, the women played a pole and hoop game, and, given ceremonial exigency as among the Hopi, the women no doubt would run races.

Household work is confining. Hunting, herding, trading lead to a comparatively mobile habit, a habit of mind or spirit which in the Southwest, at least, is adapted to ceremonial pursuit; for Pueblo Indian ceremonialism thrives on foreign accretions, whether of myth or song or dance or design of mask or costume, or, within certain limits of assimilation, of psychological patterns of purpose or gratification.

To the point of view that the differentiation of the sexes at Zuñi proceeds on the whole from the division of labor, the native custom of allowing a boy or man to become, as far as ways of living go, a girl or woman, gives color. Towards adolescence, and sometimes in later life, it is permissible for a boy culturally to change sex. He puts on women's dress, speaks like a woman, and behaves like a woman. This alteration is due to the fact that one takes readily to women's work, one prefers it to men's work. Of one or another of the three men-women now at Zuñi or of the men-women in other pueblos I have always been told that the person in question made the change because he wanted to work like a woman or because his household was short of women and needed a woman worker.

And yet among the Hopi, where the economy is practically identical with the Zuñi, there are no men-women; in this tribe the institution, it is said, was never established. This, like other customs, is not merely a matter of economic adjustment; economic or psychologic propriety or consistency or predisposition may count, but of great importance also are the survival of traits from an earlier culture, and the acquiring of traits from the culture of neighboring peoples. Were we to understand the interplay of all these factors in the life, shall we say, of Waiyautitsa, we might be a long way towards understanding the principles of society, even other than that of Zuñi.

ELSIE CLEWS PARSONS

ZUÑI PICTURES

Zuñi Pictures

If there was any one thing in the wide world I wanted to do more than another, it was to visit the New Mexican pueblo where my friend Tenatsali [1] spent so many years of his strange career. He had discovered it and made it his own and before his death he turned over to me his title to its romance and mystery. This was all he possessed in it, for even the stone house he built with money earned by literary work had dropped from his lavish hands. It happened one winter while crossing the continent I heard there was to be a dance at the pueblo. The news decided me. I stopped off on the railroad, hired a team from the sheriff and had him drive me down to the town. It was winter; snow covered the heights and we were both chilled through when we reached Tenatsali's big stone house, then a trading store. The farmer-agent, a jovial man, who had been the trader in Tenatsali's day, lived in the other end of the building. He welcomed me as an old friend and told me stories of Tenatsali until late into the night, as we sat before his fire.

It was in his house Tenatsali had remained concealed in the long interval from the time he rode out so debonairly on the war-path to take a scalp, and the arrival of a scalp from Washington. He was obliged to perform a scalp-taking feat before he could be admitted to membership among the Priests of the Bow. As he would not secure a scalp in the orthodox way, he had to get one as best he could. It was a very old scalp, one from the National Museum collected by Lewis H. Morgan many years before.

I slept soundly after the long ride, but, rising betimes, sought a guide that I might go to the village, which is like an ant hill, across the little river, and then climb to the summit of that mesa to the East which overlooks the great valley. The two possible interpreters, youths who had been reared by the trader, were both sequestered in the village as they were to take part in the dance. And so it was decided I could do no better than engage a schoolboy who, while he spoke little or no English, could at least show me the trail up the

[1] Frank Hamilton Cushing. Tenatsali, one of the medicine plants, was his Zuñi name.

mesa. In spite of the snow the boy was barefoot, and his single garment was scanty protection from the cold. We crossed the wide stretch of plain, rounded the mesa and took the steep trail on the farther side. It was half obliterated by the snowdrifts, but the boy ran lightly ahead, up and up, stretching me a hand at the steep places until we reached the broad, table top. There in an open shrine stood the image of the war god, Ahaiyuta, his plumes bedraggled and blown about by the wind. We passed the ruins covered with spiny cactus and I waited while the boy, nimble as a goat, descended the trail beside the pinnacled rock to visit the old images of the war gods ranged in a row in their immemorial cave. There too he saw, I suppose, the painted jars that held the old masks of Sayatasha. When he came back we visited the other war-god shrine and descended the mesa to return across the plain to the store, tired and hungry after our seven-miles' round.

Here we found people from far and near who had come to see the dance. There was Jesus, the Mexican, and French Dan, Falstaffian and dissolute. There was the Missionary whom later I was to know better and the Field Matron, a wraith of a woman who went silently among the Indians and gave them some drug she had discovered through an advertisement in the "boiler plate" of her home paper. There were the Indians who fraternize with the whites, like the Albino and the old Mormon, or to give him his full name, Ten Cent Mormon, because he had been baptized by the Mormons in the early days and received ten cents to bind the bargain.

The conversation at the dinner table where we had a hearty, steaming meal was all about the dance, and even the sheriff was moved to express himself. It was the first time this particular dance had been performed for years. The Arrow-Swallowing society had given public exhibitions, but on this occasion there was to be tree-swallowing as well. It was plain enough that the agent and the sheriff really believed that the Indians had supernatural powers.

The agent accompanied me to the village that afternoon and guided me to a place in the large, central court where I could see the dance to advantage. A red blanket was spread for us to sit upon, and we took our places with the expectant crowd. Every living soul in the pueblo, dressed in their best and gayest clothes, lined the roofs of the terraced houses.

Few plays are staged more effectively than these performances. The adobe walls of the houses furnish a perfect background. The court seems entirely inclosed and the processions of dancers enter and return by passageways set at right angles on either side. In the centre of the plaza was a long, white, wooden box painted in colors with cloud-terrace and rain symbols which the musicians used as a resonator for their notched-stick rattles. While we talked, the agent pointed out familiar faces like Niña, the pretty granddaughter of old Nayuchi the war chief, and Lusalu, the fat governor. The small children played on the edges of the crowd and mud-bedaubed clowns lolled around the painted box. Two old men dressed in gala attire, with white smocks and gay bandas and sashes, took up the notched instruments and began scraping them in a rhythmic motion with plectra made of sheep bone. There are few more mysterious and disturbing sounds than this same scraping. The time is perfect, the rhythm inexorable. Something was about to happen.

Two long processions advanced slowly into the plaza. In single file, keeping perfect time, their turtle-shell, leg rattles in absolute unison, dressed all alike in kilts and armlets, with faces and bodies painted white, the dancers approached each other from opposite sides, and wonderful to behold, each dancer with head thrown back supported a tall spruce tree erect in his mouth. Below were the bodies of the white-painted figures, robust and vigorous, and above a moving forest. The processions continued to advance, and curved round the plaza until they displayed their entire length, halted with a loud faronfare of gourd rattles,—and then became still and silent. There were women among them—and one wearing a white, cylinder-shaped mask. Some children, neophytes, followed, and on one side a tiny boy with a miniature spruce brought up the rear. The dancers rested, withdrew the trees from their mouths and held them, butts upward with the top boughs resting on the ground. Then it was that the full significance of the performance was revealed. The butts, rudely chopped to a tapering point eight or more inches in length, had been entirely swallowed.

Again the strident notes of the rattles sounded. The dancers took up their trees, elevated and adjusted them in their mouths and danced as before. There was the same volume of coördinated sounds, of gourd rattles, of resonant shells and the swish, swish of the garments. Again the white mask danced on. . . . It grew dark and I left the plaza, in a daze. What did it all mean—the painted box, the swallowed trees, the white mask?

STEWART CULIN

HAVASUPAI
DAYS

Havasupai Days

I

LANSO is a hedonist of seven. Day dawns late down in Cataract Canyon, but even spring nights in Arizona are chill, and one's own soft-woven bedding, cedar-bark mat and rabbit-skin blanket, suffuse a warmth one would not willingly forego. But,—"Lanso," whispers grandfather Sinyella, "up and run toward the daylight. Run, that you grow straight and lusty. And heed me; take your torch and touch it to your elbows and your wrists that you may never be rheumatic as I, your relative. Oh yes, and as you turn back, fling the torch behind you, turn once again and snatch it up, that your memory may be strong too, that you may remember quickly a forgotten deer charm when you go to hunt."

Lanso leaves his creekside home, worms his way among the slender cotton-woods, and emerging on the race course, drops into a dogged trot through the deep sand. The race course—but that is a place for a mad, scrambling dash; perched with brothers, and sisters too, on the bare back of father's horse. What need to run afoot: foot races come at dance time, and that will have to wait until the harvest is in. Dance time—Lanso hums the songs. "Yes, I know them all; next time I, too, will dance. . . ."

It is lighter when Lanso turns back: all the Havasupai are astir. Acrid smoke begins to drift over the willow thickets; ethereal strata that rest in the still air against the towering rock walls; walls that stretch to the winter home high on the plateau above. There in the clearing is his home; the willow-thatched dome for rainy days, the branch-covered, dirt-roofed, box-like shade for refuge from the midday sun, and Hat's sand-drifted hut merging in the swell of the creek bank.

Lanso scents breakfast in the bubbling clay pot, the inexhaustible pot that stands day-long with open-mouthed hospitality extended to all comers. But even a cold-whetted appetite will not tempt him to a sidelong foray on the mess; no, there was bravery needed for the sharp reproach and unbearable ridicule meted out to unmannerly pilferers. Better to wait until Round-one, Hat's wife, should call the family, Lanso, her nephew, not last among them, to the stew of ground corn and big-horn meat, little loaves of corn meal tied in the husks and baked in the embers, sweet mescal juice, and salt from the cave far down the canyon. Then he would creep up to the elders grouped on the ground around the pots and baskets, and from the side of Fox, his favorite uncle, beg for tasty bits fished out with sharpened twigs, and to take his turn at the brimming, horn ladles.

"Now," said old Sinyella, "the brush is burned and our fields are cleared: to-day we will plant." So, off the whole family trooped; men and children on horses, the women, their babies strapped to the cradle-board in their arms, trudging along beside them. Lanso, clutching hard at his grandfather's back, rocked to the easy canter of their horse. Here was business afoot he understood: next to the victims that fell before his arrows—very small creatures, indeed— this would be his chief contribution to the family larder. Yesterday he had watched them playing shinney, gambling for the future crops, and he had guessed they would begin to-day.

Down through the broad fields they rode, noting here the dam that spread a somewhat broken wing to scoop the creek to the level of the fields, there an irrigation ditch that needed mending, until they reached the family fields. These were Sinyella's and had been Sinyella's father's and grandfather's, and one day would go to Lanso.

Turning out the horses to graze at the foot of the rocky slope, they climbed to the storage houses set high above the reach of devastating floods, plastered like swallows' nests in a crevice at the base of the cliff. The seed corn secured, Sinyella knelt in the field and scratched a hole with his pointed digging-stick. Then he prayed, "Grow good, corn; when your stalk grows, grow tall; grow like the ancient corn up there," and dropping some kernels in the hole, he chewed another and blew it toward the "corn," two white rocks high on the canyon wall. Then two short steps forward and he knelt to dig again. Lanso watched, and then followed; first a few kernels, a deft sweep to fill the hole, and then the next hill. Row after row they planted together under the white morning sun that rose to flood the canyon with its light and heat. . . .

Back in the deep shade of the huge cotton-wood he saw his grandfather playing with his little brother—a toddling fellow not yet worthy of a name. Now he was searching for his mislaid arrows for he heard a twittering from a nearby bush. "Yes," Sinyella teased the baby, "that bird is calling to you, 'You are not a boy; you have no arrow to kill me; you are a girl.'" Grandfather knew everything: he made fine bows and arrows, and he told long stories in the winter evenings. "Next winter," Lanso thought, "I will track rabbits in the snow when it lies in the cedar glades where our other home is; now I must hunt down here. . . ."

The bushes spawned boys, Lanso among them. There were birds to be shot, dogs to be worried, deadfalls to be looked to, horses to be watered, sprawled over, and raced. They all ran down the canyon to Coyote's, where there was that curious Navaho visitor to watch. Mornings are short when there are cliffs to scale, tanning to watch, flat cactus to roll for arrow-marks, food to beg from some friend—and relatives lived everywhere; Wooden-leg to listen to as he told of his trip to the Walapai people to fetch a bride, mock ambushes in the willows, and the creek, with its cooling embrace as it closes overhead. . . .

II

Panamida drove his horses down the creek bank in a cloud of dust. Standing belly deep, they sluiced the cool water through their outstretched throats. Panamida let it swirl around his dangling ankles; here was relief from the afternoon heat. Bending low he could look up-stream beneath the vaulting willows where the women were filling their water-baskets. "Fox," one called to him. "Fox," indeed! Who was this who did not know that they had begun to call him Panamida since his marriage. Couldn't she see that these three were Left-hand's horses: Left-hand, to whom he had given a big blanket, a black Hopi shirt, and much dried meat, all for Gathawinga when he had first gone to live at her father's and work for him. "When I have a son, I will build my own house on my family fields; Sinyella will give me a place," he thought. He knew he was to have a son: only yesterday Hat's girl had made a string-figure that resembled a boy.

Shrill laughter came from the dance-ground beyond the screening thicket: the women were playing hiding games and tossing dice over there. He laughed abruptly; Swollen-wrist's voice came bellowing the song,

"My tally sticks;
I want them to come back;
I am nearly dead."

"That fellow never does win the stakes," thought Panamida. "Well, those women should cook now for the dance to-night: later I will join them for the racing."

Panamida turned the horses out and sauntered down the creek side to Two-wives' sweat lodge, where a dozen breechclouted men were lounging about in the sand. One could usually find them here, gossiping through the midday heat. While they waited a turn to enter, old Corn-thief droned recollections of his youth: " . . . We found a flock of mountain sheep, with several rams among them. I shot a very big one, the others all ran off. The wounded ram jumped down the cliff, and ran along a very narrow ledge. I and Hat's father slid down from rock to rock, and followed him along that ledge until he stopped abruptly at its end. Suddenly he turned and dashed back at us, his head held down sideways. I flattened myself against the wall, Hat's father beside me; there was hardly room. The ram struck Hat's father, throwing him off the ledge: it is very high there. The ram stood quite still; those above me shot at him; when he was hit, he too tumbled headlong. Next day we tramped down the trail and found the body in the canyon. We carried it away, and dug a hole to bury it; we didn't have time to burn it. . . ." Panamida tried to recall Hat's father's name: no one said it now that he was dead.

Some one carried freshly heated stones into the little dome-shaped lodge. Panamida followed the next three to enter; there should be four at each of their four "sweats." He crouched down close to them on the carpet of leaves. It was blinding dark inside the tightly blanketed lodge. It was hot; whatever he touched burned. Sweat began to pour into his eyes and down his back. His hair felt dry and burning at the roots; each breath was a gulp of liquid fire that seared his nostril-edges and his throat. It was intensely still. Suddenly his neighbor commenced a song; he joined; that was better. Now there was a sharp hiss as the leader threw a handful of water on the rocks: he gasped, the steam was choking and the heat suddenly unbearable. He bowed his head close to the ground between his feet to suck in the cooler air there; then he raised himself slowly. Sweat still streamed from him; every muscle was relaxed; every ache was gone; he felt pure and renewed. Struggling out beneath the door flap, he stood up in the sunlight, poised on the creek bank, and plunged into the stream. He gasped; his breath was sharply driven out; but his skin tingled, his muscles quivered, he felt exhilarated.

Many races had been run when Panamida reached the dance-ground. He would not ride, though he had sung over his colt to make him fleet. Fragment-of-rock, his youngest brother, should ride, and he would bet. He would be chief when his father died: he must be dignified now. He sat beside Gathawinga and her mother, She-chews-men, who were weaving baskets. "The Navaho have come," he whispered to Gathawinga, "I have given one a basket of shelled corn for his big blanket for you: I have his horse too, for two big buckskins and a little corn." He went toward the visitors: "Well, you have only one knot in your string now; tonight we dance. Ten sleeps ago when you went to tell your chief to share our harvest bounty there were eleven. It is nearly sundown; the dance-boss has spread the meat and bread on a bed of willow leaves; guests must eat everything."

He drew back with his relatives that the Navaho and Hopi might eat first. Though they had not brought their women, these strangers could be trusted here, especially the Hopi, who lived so well and knew all manner of strange things, yet it was laughable to see them trotting by afoot when a man should ride.

But the enemy, those Yavapai; Panamida knew them too. He recalled the previous autumn when the owls were warning, "Some one comes from the south: hoo hu." And they had come climbing down into the canyon in the early dawn. He recalled the alarm; the women and children scrambling up to hide on the cliffs; the day-long pursuit up the canyon, the skirmish, and the enemy fleeing again. Then the Yavapai, tiring, had taken refuge on a little hill. "Good," Chief Manakadja had said. "We are hungry now: some of you ride back and fetch us food." After they had eaten they felt braver. Two took thick buckskins, which they hung from their bows before them. Panamida, crouching with arrow set, had followed in this shelter with the others. Boldly they marched up the hill, Yavapai arrows raining harmlessly on the flapping skins. Suddenly the carriers dipped their shields and the hidden archers let fly. They had nearly reached the summit, when Wasakwivama, who held a skin, was hit. "My arm is getting weak; I can't hold it up much longer; we had better go back." A second time they tried: the Yavapai arrows were exhausted, they were rolling rocks. Panamida chuckled at the recollection of his foolhardy spring, the sudden jerk that sent an unwary enemy sprawling down the slope to be pounced on and dispatched. Well, another feat like that and they might call him a chief even before his father died. The Yavapai had fled in the night, but they would return. "Yes," he ruefully reflected, "they like to come; they always kill so many. . . ."

Moonlight spread across the clearing as they danced: the eastern cliffs stood sharply black against the sky. The song ended, and the group around the pole melted away. Sinyella rose in his place among the watching families. "My own land, hear me. Let all of us remain alive always. I want to live well always. Ground, hear me." He prayed to the rocks, the ground, the creek: he told the young men to work hard, to dance well, not to be quarrelsome, as chiefs always spoke in the lull between the dances. Paiya, the best singer, again took up his place, facing the pole; Panamida, with the drum, stepped beside him; quickly others formed the circle with them. Shoulder to shoulder they stood; fingers intertwined. Paiya began to sing to the drum beats:

> "A fresh wind in that country,
> Girls dance circling."

He had dreamed that he had gone to that far land where he had seen them dancing. The others caught up the refrain: they stood singing for some minutes. Then when they sang in unison Paiya signaled and all began circling to the left with a short, sidewise shuffling step. Slowly the circle swung, fifty men in their gala dress, girls with their jingling ornaments; over and over they sang the song, to bring it to an end when the leader reached his starting point. They stood hardly a minute: none dropped out. "Nidjanwi," several prompted; so Paiya began the favorite:

"Nidjanwi, I do it;
I am the man who names himself;
Maidens stand alongside."

Soon all were chanting, and the circle moved again. Excitement was high; the old people called out encouraging compliments; girls shouldered their way beside partners of their choice; reluctant Navaho were laughingly forced into the throng. Panamida felt some one pushing against his thigh; there was little Lanso, his older brother's boy: "Yes, come in," as he made space. Another song, and they stopped to rest. Navaho paid a trifle to their partners for release. Now a grotesque figure dashed from the obscurity of the night; white mask, cross-barred body, yucca leaf switches in hand, he sprang about, whipping the laggards to the dance; adults were laughing, children scampering in fright, dogs barking. The dance commenced again. Panamida was hoarse, it was far from dawn, and this was only the first of three nights' dance.

III

Sinyella is half a skeptic. He sat back in the lodge and watched Sack, the medicine man, in the firelight beside his sister's sick grandson. Let the other relatives shout to make the shaman strong: he would wait, if the boy died, he would kill the incompetent. The shaman knelt over the boy, swaying as he sang, his head to one side, his left knuckles clenched over his closed eyes, his clashing rattle in the other hand. Once he stopped rigid with open mouth, so that his familiar spirit might leave his chest to search for sickening ghosts outside the house. Then he rose and went out into the dark. Sinyella heard his spirit halloing and whistling as it returned to him out there. The shaman reëntered and resumed his singing. He put his lips to the boy's forehead that the spirit might go in search of the sickness. He sucked the spirit back with a gulp, spat into his palm, and triumphantly exhibited its contents, some little white thread-like worms. "That was hard for me, but I have taken out all the sickness; there is no more there now." Well, the boy's father would give Sack a big blanket, but Sinyella decided that he, at any rate, would wait.

Musing as he waded through the crusted snow to his own lodge set snugly in the cedar thickets, he thought: Sack is young, he may not be much good, perhaps his spirit is weak. But I don't know much about these things: there's that star up there, Pagioga, the man-snatcher, and sometimes there are ghosts. I pray too: "Sun, my relative," I say, "do something for me. You make me work so I can do anything: make good things for us: keep me always as I am now." . . . Of late his ears had been frequently ringing; ghosts were whispering to him. Suddenly he shouted, "Huuuu; no, though you talk that way, I am not going to die."

It was well that they had collected a good store of pine nuts and wild seeds in the autumn after they left the canyon; the snow was thigh deep this winter. It was bitter cold; men and birds would freeze; the firewood on the ground was covered. But deep snow soon exhausted hunted deer and antelope, and there would be no lack of drinking water here on the plateau. The laden trees brought back to him that long past day when his father found the Navaho woman lost in the snow and took her to wife. He remembered other Navaho; those he had fought, those whose horses he had carried off, those who had despoiled him on a trading trip to the Hopi. There had been many a trip eastward to the Hopi villages, where the Navaho, quondam enemies, came to trade too. Presents exchanged, friendships renewed in night-long talks, buckskins and horn ladles traded for blankets, he would turn his packed horses back for the fortnight's journey across the arid wastes toward his canyon home. There he would wait the coming of the Walapai, his blood brothers, from the west. Or, if they did not come, he would carry the Hopi woven stuffs to trade in their country. Once he had even penetrated beyond their range to the Mohave in the low land of the Colorado River, where, astounded at his effrontery, they had permitted him to stay and peaceably trade.

In all countries they knew him well: that was why people called him chief. He made himself a chief. True, his grandfather had been chief, like his fathers before him. But his own father was never chief; no one would call him that; he was a good-for-nothing. Now when I die, he thought, my two oldest sons will share it, as they will my fields. I have taught them both to talk like chiefs.

As, stooping, he lifted the doorflap of his dome-shaped house he sensed to the full the flood of warmth and light. This was his own, these his people, and it was always good to be at home. The group reclining about the central fire broke off their cheerful chatter to greet him: back under the dark eaves he could hear the children, nominally asleep, giggling over some fine mischief. "The Walapai have come to ask our young men to join them next spring in a raid on the Paiute across the Grand Canyon; Panamida wants to go," they told him.

"Panamida will fight them soon enough, let him but stay at home."

"Panamida, younger brother, some nice Walapai girl will say to you, 'Here's a roasted lizard,'" said Grediva, mocking the gruff Walapai speech, amid the laughter of her relatives at the thought of eating lizard.

Sinyella smiled drowsily at the firelit faces: yes, all his own people. At his side he heard Lanso, "Grandfather, tell us just one story. Don't refuse this time; the snakes will not bother now, it is winter." Sinyella sat back where the children were listening, lying in the darkness. "Wolf and Coyote lived far to the west close to the ocean. Wolf said to Coyote, 'This country holds no game, no deer, no antelope. All we eat is rats; that's all we kill; that's the only meat we have. I think I want you to go right down in the water, way down to the bottom of the ocean.' Many elk lived under the water. Coyote tried: he went close to the water and put his head down, but he felt afraid. 'I'm afraid to go down: I want you to go.' Wolf said, 'All right, I will go down and hunt. I will hunt a big elk and drive it right out. I will come out again after four sleeps.'" . . .

LESLIE SPIER

EARTH-TONGUE
A MOHAVE

Earth-tongue, a Mohave

EARTH-TONGUE'S earliest recollection was of the dim, cool house, where he picked bits of charcoal out of the soft sand and crumbled it against his hand. Once a cricket appeared on the wattled wall, suddenly went back in when he thrust at it, and only a stream of dry soil sifted forth. And then there was the terrifying time when voices burst loudly into his sleep, people crowded in but stood helplessly awkward, while his father's brother shot insults of stolid hate into the ceaseless flood of his wife's vituperation. As the woman turned to beat a girl lurking in the corner and the man interposed and flung her off, Earth-tongue burst into bawling and clung to his mother. He saw the angry woman stamp on pot after pot, tear open her coils of shredded bark and strew them into the fire, and then, suddenly silent, load her belongings into a carrying-frame and stagger out. The frame caught in the door: as she tore it through, the contents crashed, and a laugh rose in the house; but Earth-tongue sobbed long.

He was larger when he paddled with other children at the edge of the slough; but still very small as he first remembered himself seeing the great, stretching river that drew by with mysterious, swirling noises in its red eddies. He and his little brother were put into a huge pot which his father and another man pushed before them across stream: their hair as it coiled high on their heads was just visible over the edge as they swam. And then followed an interminable trudge somewhere through the dust, relieved only by rides on his father's back, and on his grandmother.

He was older when he shot his first bow; when at dusk he caught a woodpecker in its hole and would not let go though it hacked desperately at his clasped hands, until a half-grown cousin took it from him to imprison under a turned jar for the night. His father wove a cage the next day, and the captive was installed, but remained wild, and one morning was dead. And then came the time when the boys of Mesquite-water challenged those of his settlement on a hot, summer day after the inundation had half dried, and they slung lumps of mud at each other from the ends of long willow poles.

There were other events that must have fallen soon after this period, but which he did not remember: when he rolled his hair into long, slim cylinders, began to measure how nearly it reached his hip, and made his first advances to girls.

Even before this he had dreamed of Mastamho, gigantic on the peak Avikwa'me in the great, dark, round house full of peoples; of the two Ravens singing of dust whirls and war and of the far away clumps of cane waiting to be cut into flutes; and of the river, drawn from its source to wash away the ashes and bones of Matavilya where the pinnacles stand in the gorge at House-post-water. He knew later that he had dreamed these things as a little boy, even while he was still in his mother; he did not yet think about them, except when the old man his grandfather, and his father and uncles, sang of them.

One day a runner came up the valley and shouted pantingly that strangers had appeared from the east at dawn and killed a woman and two children at Sand-back, besides wounding a man and his younger brother. The men leaped for their weapons; the women called in their children, loaded themselves with property, and soon began to track northward in a straggling, excited stream. Earth-tongue pulled down his bow and raked among the roof thatch for such arrows as he could assemble. Then he joined his kinsmen and male neighbors who stood in a group in front of one of the shades, exclaiming and pointing at a smoke that rose down the valley. Bundles of crude, blunt arrows projected behind their hips, shoved under cord belts; and many had clubs dangling from their wrists. Earth-tongue did not own a club: he had never seen battle; and he hung about the outside of the cluster of seasoned men.

Soon, refugees from the nearer settlements began to arrive; and then a body of fighting men from up the valley, bedaubed for war. Earth-tongue's kinsmen merged with them; and as they proceeded south, growing in numbers, they met ever more women and children, and finally those from the point of attack, until, not far away in the cotton-woods, they came upon the men of Sand-back. The enemy were Halchidhoma from far down-stream, they were now informed, not Walapai as at first conjectured. They had avoided the river, traversing the desert to hide in the Walapai mountains and descend at night upon the nearer tip of the Mohave land. They had long since gone off—sixty they were said to number, as they were seen to file over the rocks far above the stream at Pinnacles. They had looted and burnt only the group of houses at Sand-back, killed the woman, and lightly wounded with an arrow one of the men who fought back from a distance: the other reported casualties turned up safe. But the enemy had carried off the woman's head, and would dance about its skin. Earth-tongue gazed at the collapsed houses, their charred posts smoking on the mass of sand; and that night he watched the beheaded woman's cremation. There was much talk of retaliation, but an immediate attack would have found the Halchidhoma prepared or perhaps removed.

So some months elapsed without a move being made; and meanwhile Earth-tongue became married. In the turmoil of the Halchidhoma invasion, as party after party trooped by, he had been attracted by the sight of a girl, barely but definitely passed out of childhood, and only a little younger than himself, who halted, leaning under her laden carrying-frame, behind her mother, as their group paused for an excited colloquy. He saw that the girl noted his eyes on her and glanced away, and he knew, from the people she was with, that her name was Kata. Not long after, he began to find errands or companions that took him to her settlement. Soon a mutual familiarity of each other's presence was established, the purport of which was manifest even though direct speech between the two young people was infrequent and brief. Both were shy; until one afternoon a blind old man, the girl's father's uncle, who knew of Earth-tongue's repeated presence from the references of the family, addressed him and her directly. "Why do you not marry?" he said. "Persons do not live long. Soon you will be old like myself, unable to please yourselves. It is good that you sleep and play together. You, young man, should stay here the night." Neither Earth-tongue nor the girl answered. But he remained through the evening meal and after; and when the house was dark, went silently to where she lay. The next day, he stayed on; the day after, returned briefly to his home; and from then on, spent increasing time at his new abode, where, without a word having been spoken, he slipped into a more and more recognized status. He did not work, unless special occasion called, such as assisting with a seine-net; and Kata only occasionally helped her relatives farm. Instead, they spent much time together, lolling under the shade, toying or teasing each other, or listening to their elders. Sometimes he sang softly as he lay by her, or she bent over him searching his head or untangling his clustered locks, or tried to draw the occasional hairs from his face with her teeth; and ever she laughed more freely. So the days followed one another.

When at last the Mohave were ready, it was announced that they would once for all destroy the Halchidhoma. The entire nation was to move and appropriate the enemy land. Soon they started, most of the men in advance, weaponed and unburdened save for gourds of maize meal at their hips; water they did not have to carry since they followed the river. Behind tramped the women, children, and old men, under loads. Foods, blankets of bark and rabbit fur, fish nets, metates, household property, and the most necessary pottery vessels were taken. The remainder of their belongings and stored provisions were buried or hidden away: every house in the valley stood empty.

For five days they walked. Then the men suddenly surrounded a group of settlements. These were the houses of the Kohuana, a far down-stream tribe, wasted by wars with their neighbors, until the pressed remnant had sought refuge half a day's journey above the Halchidhoma to whom they were united, less by positive friendship than by common foes and parallel fortunes. For the Halchidhoma, too, remembered having once lived populously among the welter of tribes in the broad bottom lands below the mouth of the Gila. With the Kohuana the Mohave had no direct quarrel; and though they arrived armed and overpowering, they proclaimed themselves kinsmen, and anounced that they had come as guests. By night the Kohuana houses overflowed with the mob of Mohave families. Kohuana messengers were dispatched to summon the Halchidhoma to battle at White-spread-rock-place, if they were not afraid. Such challenge the outnumbered people could not find it in their manhood to evade. So the next day saw them in line at the appointed field, barely a hundred strong, against perhaps four hundred that the Mohave mustered after setting a guard over their families.

Earth-tongue went into battle with much inward excitement, but little fear, and listened obediently to the admonitions of his seasoned kinsmen. Even before arrows could reach, the shooting began. Before long, arrows flew feebly by, and then it became necessary to twist sharply sidewise to avoid them. At this distance the two lines shot at each other, taunting and leaping, while, in the rear, half-grown boys and a few old men helped to gather up and replenish bundles of arrows. What the Halchidhoma lacked in frequency of shots, they partly made up in greater openness of target; and before long, struck men began to withdraw temporarily on each side. The Mohave could have made short work by charging in a body with their clubs; but they had asked for an open stand-up fight, and besides found pleasure in the game, which fell increasingly to their advantage. For hours they sweated in the sun, gradually and irregularly forcing the Halchidhoma line back, and shouting whenever one of the foe was carried off.

At last the leaders called that it was time to cease, and defied the foe to resume in the same spot on the fourth day. Then they trooped victoriously home, without a fatality, though a few, weakened from bleeding or with parts of shafts broken off in them, were carried on the backs of companions. Earth-tongue had been struck twice. One arrow had grazed the skin of his flank when he became over-confident and failed to bend his body with sudden enough vigor. Then, one of three shafts that came toward him almost at once had imbedded itself a finger-joint's depth in the front of his thigh, and hung there until he hastily plucked it out. Neither wound bled profusely, especially after a bit of charcoal was reached him to rub in for stanching; and he returned stiff, tired, and proud. The Halchidhoma losses were severer. None of them appeared to have fallen dead on the field; but at least half had been struck, and a number so vitally or often that they would die.

For four days the Mohave treated their wounds, talked of the next battle, and ate their hosts' provisions. Then they set out. But the Halchidhoma had sent their families down-stream and taken up a new stand farther back. Here they joined once more, and the fight went on as before but with ever more preponderance to the Mohave, until these, wearied by the noon sun, contemptuously drew off to the river to drink. The Halchidhoma seized the occasion to run to their children and women, set these across the river, and strike east over the desert. When the victors reappeared, the fugitives were far. The Mohave thereupon decided to occupy their fields and houses until the dispossessed might come to drive them out; which the latter, by this time safely received among the Maricopa far across the desert on the Gila, had no intention of doing. However, the Mohave lived nearly a year in the land of the Halchidhoma, adjusting themselves as they could; and returned only as the next flood and planting time approached, taking the Kohuana along to settle among themselves, where these enforced visitors remained for some years.

Before the stay in the Halchidhoma country was over, Earth-tongue and Kata had drifted apart. The derangement of accustomed residence, enforced with others, Earth-tongue's pride as an incipient warrior, the fact that no child was born, all contributed to separate them increasingly. Each formed new interests while vaguely jealous of the other's; and in the end Earth-tongue brought not Kata but another girl to his parents' house.

Soon after his first child was born,—a daughter, called Owich like the sisters of himself, his father, and his father's father,—Earth-tongue grew restless for adventure, and, the time being one of peace, joined himself to those that would travel. Ten or twenty in number, they would go out: too few to excite apprehension of treacherous intent, too many to be made away with safely. Each carried maize, water, his weapons, and whatever he might wish to trade. On shorter journeys they prided themselves on being able to travel at a trot four days without food, and with only such drink as the desert might afford, chewing perhaps a bit of willow as a relief for the dryness of their mouths. But these hardships they underwent mostly in emulation, or toward the last of a return with Mohave land before them. Again and again Earth-tongue went down the river, through Yuma, Kamia, Halyikwamai, and Cocopa settlements, to the flat shores of the salt sea; east into the Walapai mountains and down into the chasm of the Havasupai, where he saw strange-speaking and strangely dressed Hopi and Navaho, heard of their stone towns, and brought home their belts and, once, a blanket of white cotton.

To the northwest he visited the Chemehuevi and other Paiutes about their scattered springs, and ate their foods of seeds and wild fruits, some familiar, some strange; and mescal and sometimes deer.

Theirs was a strange language too, but he had heard a little from the few Chemehuevi who lived at the northern extreme of Mohave valley and beyond it on Cotton-wood island; and many of his companions could speak more. They went from Paiute band to band, to where the river no longer flows from the north but from the east, beyond the Muddy, and found each group like the last in customs, but of new foods. They listened to the stories of the Paiute, who dreamed of the mountain Nüvant as the Mohave do of Aikwa'me, and to whom they sang their songs, which the Paiute wished to hear.

To the west were many tribes, all different tongued, but mostly easy to understand a little when one knew Chemehuevi. There were the Vanyume on their river that dried into nothing and left them always half-starved; the Hanyuvecha in the range of great pines beyond; northward, about Three-Mountains, the Kuvahye, adjoined by other mountaineers, little tribes, unwarlike, friendly to the visitors, some of whom they hailed as old friends. They offered no smoke, but gave tobacco crushed in a mortar with shells; which Earth-tongue and his companions ate in courtesy, and were nearly all made to sweat and vomit violently thereby. From a crest near here they looked over a vast plain beyond, in which shimmered what one of his companions said were large lakes. He had been there and seen the people, who lived in long houses of rushes,—a hundred fires in line within one house,—and ate rush roots, and slept on rushes, and at night worms came up and troubled the sleepers. And in the tumbled range on which they stood, but beyond them, were the Like-Mohave, a very little like them in speech, but naked, unkempt, and poor. Them Earth-tongue saw, but not in their own houses.

And going out again, he traversed the land of the tribes to the southwest, unfriendly, half-sullen, and dangerous to small parties. The Hakwicha dug wells and ate mesquite; beyond them were people in the mountains, about hot springs, who sang to turtle shells instead of gourds; and still farther, stretching down to the ocean that one could see from their peaks, lived the Foreign-Kamia, speaking almost like the real Kamia, but knowing nothing of farmed foods, eating rattle-snakes, and a hostile lot to venture among. They had some grudges to pay off to the Mohave for plundered settlements, but were not a people to travel far from their homes even for revenge.

The Yavapai, too, Earth-tongue came to know, though theirs was not an attractive country to visit. They dreamed and sang like the Mohave, but of other animals; and some of their stories were the same. Their neighbors and friends were the Roaming-Yavapai, a small-statured, sharp-eyed people, wearing their hair flowing, fierce lance fighters, taciturn, violent, untrustworthy; but inclined favorably to the Mohave in spite of the utter unintelligibility of their speech because they knew them through the Yavapai as traditionally hostile, like themselves, against the Maricopa and that people of innumerable houses, the Pima. These last Earth-tongue never came to know save on the field of battle.

One early summer, as the river was flooding, its rise suddenly stopped. The inundation being wont to grow in interrupted stages the people waited quietly for its resumption. But the water fell back and back. Then some began to declare that it might not rise again, and advised planting at once before the moist ground should dry: but others pointed out that high water was yet due, and had often come late, and that present planting in that case would cause the seed to wash out and be lost. So nearly all waited with concern and much discussing; until finally the river was wholly back within its banks and dropping decisively. Then they knew that nothing more was to be hoped for that season, and men and women hastened to save what they might of the crop. But many of the fields had remained untouched by water, and most of the others were already half dry. In some, the maize and beans never sprouted; in some they came up indeed, but soon wilted; and though the women carried water in jars, only small patches could be effectively served in this hand fashion.

Soon, every one knew that famine impended, and that so few houses would grow even enough harvest for another seeding, that the year after would also be hard to survive. They gathered every wisp of wild seed plants in the uncultivated bottoms; but these wild seeds, too, had come up thin, and the crop of mesquite pods was pitiful. The women labored faithfully, and the children watched over the scattered maize; yet though the grain ripened, the scattered stalks were too few to keep any house through the winter. Some families did not pick even an ear. A moon after harvest time, the crop was consumed; by winter, the last of the other stores. The men fished daily, but the sloughs and ponds had never filled and were soon seined out, and the river's yield was uncertain and far insufficient. Every one was gaunt; the children lay listlessly about; sickness grew.

Earth-tongue's wife, and his older brother's, had planted with his mother in his father's ancestral field, which lay low and was long-proved rich. So they fared better than many. Nevertheless, before spring the emaciated bodies of two children and an old woman had been burnt and Earth-tongue had three times sung himself hoarse as they lay dying.

The young men went out with their bows, and now and then returned with a bird or gopher or badger, but oftener empty-handed. People who had new belongings went to the Walapai to trade for mescal and deer meat. Whole families trudged to visit the Cheme-huevi, until they brought back word that these hosts too were eaten out. At last not a day passed without columns of smoke from pyres visible somewhere in the valley. It was a terrible year and long remembered before the end of another summer brought partial abatement.

So numerous had been the deaths from bowel flux and cough, that shaman after shaman fell a victim to the anger of the kin of those he had attempted to save. Yellow-thigh, a powerful man and not very old, had lost two patients during the famine, and three more at intervals since. Mutterings were frequent; but no one had found opportunity, or dared, to work vengeance on him. One morning, Earth-tongue and a friend, sauntering up valley on some errand, turned to a house before which Yellow-thigh lay, for those there were kinsmen of his. No men were about; and as the two visitors stood in the door, his friend on sudden impulse whispered to Earth-tongue, "Let us kill him." So they sat down for a little and passed the news of the day, then arose, Earth-tongue reaching for his bow and four cross-pointed arrows, with the remark that they were going to shoot doves. The shaman grunted assent and the pair passed out.

For a time they traversed the brush, planning the deed. At the mesa edge they broke two stones to sharp edges, and then returned. Yellow-thigh lay under the shade-roof with closed eyes, breathing regularly. The friend went by him to look into the house, and finding it empty, nodded. Earth-tongue, who had approached, bent suddenly down and struck with all his might at the sleeper's head.

The shaman pushed himself to a sitting position as the blood began to pour from the mangled side of his face. The friend started back, then plunged forward to finish the man, and swung; but his excited arm brought the weapon down only on the victim's knee. Then he staggered off, scarcely able in fright and emotion to drag his own legs. Earth-tongue, seeing the shaman still sitting, strode forward again and with both hands drove the point of the stone through the top of his skull. Two women who had been going through each other's hair in the shadow of the brush fence outside, half turned at the noise and shrieked, while Earth-tongue dashed after his companion, seized his hand, and dragged him forward. They ran through the willows and at last lay down to pant in hiding; and here, after they had quieted, Earth-tongue laughed at his friend's faltering stroke and steps. Then they went on, still keeping to cover, until around the second bend they swam the river.

On the other side, old men were gaming with poles and hoop, and others watched. The two sat down and looked on. Three times, four times, until it was early afternoon, the players bet and threw their poles and one or the other finally took up the stakes. Then Earth-tongue said, "I have killed a shaman, the large man at Sloping-gravel."

"Yes, kill him," answered one of the old men, thinking he was boasting of an empty intent; and a spectator added, "Indeed, it would be well. Too many persons are dying."

"I have killed him," Earth-tongue said again, and they began to believe him. So they went to the houses. Soon word came that the shaman was dead; and then his kinsmen arrived, angry and threatening, and accusations flew back and forth, while Earth-tongue stood unmoved and silent but wary. The kinsmen finally challenged to a stick fight the next day, and withdrew to burn the dead man.

The people of the settlement commended Earth-tongue and promised to engage for him; and in the morning they and all his kin and the kin of those whom the shaman had brought to their death, gathered in the center of a large playing field. Each man carried a willow as thick as his forearm and reaching to his neck; and in his left hand, a shorter parrying stick. The challengers appeared, somewhat fewer in number and with tear-marked faces, but enraging their opponents by crying the names of their dead parents and grandparents. Then the two bodies, spreading into irregular lines, rushed at each other. Each man swung at an antagonist's head, now with his staff held in one hand, now in both. Blows beat down on heads through the guard, rained on shoulders, bruised knuckles, and the willows clashed amid the shouts. Now and then a staff broke and a contestant ran back to seize a new one. The fighters sweated, panted, rubbed blood out of their eyes and staggered forward and back as the lines swayed in the clamor. Once or twice a maddened fighter, running in under his opponent's strokes, seized his hair to belabor him with his parry-club; whereupon shouts of "Bad, bad! no! no! release!" arose and a multitude of rescuers' blows drove him back. The shaman's side were getting the worst of it, but rallied again and again without being driven wholly to their end of the field. Strokes became fewer and feebler. Weary arms could no longer rise. Fighter after fighter leaned on his stick, or sat on the ground in the rear. Each side taunted the other to come on again; and at last they drew apart, every man panting, bruised, and weary, but satisfied at the damage he had inflicted. No heads had been broken and no one died, though some were sick for a few days from maggots that had bred in the scalp under their clotted hair; and then talk died down and the enmity gradually subsided. Earth-tongue won the praise of all the Mohave who were not directly involved.

Once, runners came from the Yuma to invite to an attack on the Cocopa at the mouth of the river. A hundred and twenty Mohave went down. The kohota or play-chief of the northern Mohave asked for captives, although he already had several; and Earth-tongue was one of the men whom he requested to carry food and water for the prisoner's return journey. and to guard against their escape.

The Yuma contingent was even larger than the Mohave one; and the attack was made at daybreak. It was not much of a fight. The first house entered gave the alarm and the settlement scattered amid yells. Only two Cocopa were killed by the Yuma and two young women, sisters, called Night-hawk, captured by the Mohave. The latter stayed with the Yuma four days to watch the scalp dance; but no one of them having touched the corpses, they were not in need of purification, and returned home.

The whole tribe came out to escort them to the kohota's house. There the captives were made to sit down, while the kohota stood up and sang Pleiades. Then men and women, facing each other, danced. When the sun was at its height, they stopped, ate what the kohota's women brought out, then lay in the shade or gambled. In the afternoon the kohota called out a Chutaha singer. Soon the sounding jar began to boom, the people left off their play, and danced: three rows of young men with feathers tied in their hair, one row of old men, and two women standing separate. Then at last, as the sun was coming low, the chief came with rattles in his hand and at the end of a song shouted: "Let him sing who wishes to! Let any woman sing! I appoint no one!" Women grasped the rattles and carried them, one to a Tumanpa singer, others to those who knew Vinimulya and Vinimulya-hapacha; and one was brought to Earth-tongue to sing Raven. Soon all four of the dance series were in progress at different places, while those women who liked Nyohaiva, having persuaded an old man to sing that, began to revolve about him standing shoulder to shoulder. As fast as one song ended, the singers took up another, for the sun had nearly set, and the sweating women clamored for more, while the crowd of people stood about.

With darkness they stopped to bathe and eat and rest, then danced again, singing as before and new kinds too, while off on the side, by the light of a fire, groups of men played hiding game to the Tudhulva songs through the night. In the morning the kohota had the assemblage bathe, fed them once more, and sent them home to return two days later.

This time they danced again all evening, all afternoon, and all night. As the sun rose, the kohota, still singing, took the two captives one by each hand, and walked toward the river. Behind him came the Tumanpa and Vinimulya singers, each with his crowd, and then the mass of people in procession. The kohota, still holding the two girls, ran over the bank, and every one followed. This made Mohaves of the captives, and people were no longer afraid of them. The kohota led them back to his house, where they were to live, and said, "Perhaps these girls will marry and bear children, who, belonging to both tribes, will make peace when they grow up, and there will be no more war." So it came in part. After two years, one of the sisters married, and soon had a child. The other continued without husband. In time, formal peace was made between the Yuma and

Cocopa; whereupon the kohota announced, "Since the tribes are friends now, let us not keep Night-hawk longer." So a party led her to the Yuma, where her kinsmen met and escorted her home. Her sister remained with her Mohave husband.

Earth-tongue was beginning to grow old. His oldest son and one daughter both had children, and his hair showed first streaks of gray. He thought more of his youth, and commenced to remember what he had dreamed then. He knew he had seen Matavilya sick and gradually dying and burned, and his ashes washed away by the river that Mastamho made to flow out of the ground. He remembered too Mastamho's house on Avikwa'me, with the multitudes inside it in rows like little children, and Mastamho instructing them; and how he repeated after him, correctly, until Mastamho said to him, "That is right! You know it! You have it! I gave it to you!" Then he had dreamed how Sky-rattle-snake was at last inveigled from his house far in the south ocean, and his head cut off on Avikwa'me. Earth-tongue saw his joints and blood and sweat and juices turn into eggs. From these eggs hatched Rattle-snake, Spider, Scorpion, and Yellow-ant, who went off to Three-Mountains and remote places, deep in the earth or high in the sky, and from there built four roads to all tribes. When they wish a man for a friend, they bite him and take his shadow home with them. "But another road leads from their house to my heart," Earth-tongue would say, "and I know what they do. And I intercept the shadow before Rattle-snake has led it wholly to Three-Mountains, and sing it back; I break the roads of spittle that Spider has begun to wind four times around the man's heart; and so he lives again."

Then Earth-tongue commenced to be sent for when people were bitten—first his relatives, then others. He would stand up at once and sing to bring a cooling wind; and, reaching the sick person, sing over him from the north, west, south, and east, but not a fifth time, lest he die. Then, sending every one away but a wife or mother, and forbidding all drink, he would sit by the patient all night, singing his four songs from time to time. In the morning the sick person used to get up well.

Fighting interrupted these pursuits. It was a summons again from the Yuma, this time against the Maricopa; and two hundred of the Mohave responded. The seventh night they were on Maricopa soil and met eighty Yuma by appointment; and in the morning advanced to attack. But the Maricopa had got wind of their presence, and when the fight opened were reënforced by a vast number of the Pima. The Mohave and Yuma exhorted one another, and though man after man fell, gave ground slowly, fighting back outnumbered.

At last the enemy ran all in a body against them. Part of the Mohave broke before the shock and fled to the north, ultimately escaping. But sixty of them formed with the Yuma on a little knoll near the Gila, where they stood in a dense mass. As the Pima and Maricopa dashed against them, they dragged man after man struggling into their midst, where he was dispatched with fierce club blows on his head or thrusts into his face. Twice, Earth-tongue leaped out to grasp an opponent and fling him over his back, thus protecting his own skull, while his companions beat the struggling foe to death. The fighting grew wilder. The Pima no longer drew back to shoot but swirled incessantly around and into the dwindling cluster at bay. At last the shouts ceased; the dust began to settle; and all but two of the Yuma, and every man of the sixty Mohave, lay with crushed head or mangled body on foreign earth.

A. L. KROEBER

THE CHIEF SINGER
OF THE TEPECANO

The Chief Singer of the Tepecano

THERE was unusual activity around the house of Don Pancho, a little thatch-roof hut of oval shape, possibly fifteen feet by eight. Two large posts supported a framework of poles on which was laid a gabled thatching of grass. Only toward the center of the house could one stand upright, and a strong push would have sent tumbling outside, the stones heaped in a wall without the use of mortar or mud, which filled the space between the eaves and the bare ground.

The unwonted stir in the house of Don Pancho did not betoken any epoch-making occurrence even in the uneventful history of the little village of Azqueltán which sheltered the remnants of the Tepecano tribe. It was merely that Don Pancho was awaiting the birth of his child. And so the women of the immediate neighborhood gathered inside the hut while the men conversed in low tones without. Francisco alone passed freely in and out. At last, after a longer pause within, he slipped quietly out of the door.

"Gracias a Dios! It is a son," he said quietly and produced from somewhere a bottle of sotol [1] bought on his last journey to the nearest "civilized" village against this very event. The men crowded around him and drank heartily to the health of the newcomer. With true politeness they congratulated the father and then slipped away into the darkness toward their own little hovels. Only the squalling of the infant broke upon the stillness of the mountain air.

Again an air of unusual activity pervaded the village. Word had come that the cura from the neighboring town would arrive that day to say mass. The church and the adjoining curato had been opened and aired, the dirt swept from the floor and the dust from the crude figures of the crucifixion. For the little church was the pride of Azqueltán. A generation ago it had been built of adobe brick and stone quarried by civilized artisans, and its white front faced the torrid rays of the sun as valiantly as it did the sulphurous flames of hell. The little courtyard, too, shone with a freshly-swept air, not a blade of grass nor a speck of green marring its smooth surface.

[1] Agave brandy.

At last sharp eyes detected a cavalcade slowly descending the tortuous path. Hastily Francisco climbed the shaking ladder to the roof of the church and seized the clapper. Well did he realize the importance of his office as mayor-domo of the church! And never while *he* lived would the Sr. Cura arrive without proper greeting! One of the several bells was still uncracked, and to it Francisco devoted particular attention. The bells held a place hardly second to the church itself in Don Pancho's affections, for had they not been imported at enormous expense from that far away capital, the City of Mexico? A final clang and Francisco hastened down the quaking ladder to be the first to kneel before the jocund padre and kiss his hand. Roused by the pealing of the bells the inhabitants of the little valley began to wander in. Reverently they entered the church, kneeling on the brick floor, the men and women on opposite sides, while mass was said.

The service finished, the Aguilars, Francisco and Julia, his wife, stood up, bearing the child. Beside them stood Juan Márquez and his wife, as godfather and godmother. A few drops of water resented, a few ritual words, and Mother Church had gathered another soul to her bosom. José María was the name the cura entered in his record.

But had these intervening weeks been entirely uneventful in the life of little José or Pepe, as he was familiarly called? By no means! Francisco was too conscientious a man to take any chances with his son's welfare. For centuries before the padres had told them of God and Christ, the forefathers had worshiped Father Sun, Mother Moon and Elder Brother Morning Star. In fact it was quite obvious that God *was* the Sun, the Virgin María the Moon and Jesus the Morning Star. For did not the beautiful picture of the Virgin of Guadalupe hanging in the church show her standing on the moon? The two religions could not be antagonistic, but merely supplementary, thought Francisco, as far as he thought on the subject at all. Nevertheless, there was no use arguing with the cura about it, for he would not understand. And so, immediately after the birth of little Pepe, Francisco made four prayer sticks with little squares of colored yarn attached, and went and deposited them at secret altars on the hills to east, north, west and south, breathing a prayer at each place for the health and fortune of his child.

Little José grew up to boyhood, his status in the world a rather anomalous one—a little lower than the half-blood Mexican peon on the rolling country to the south, a little above the pagan Huichol in the mountains, yet despised by both. Yet that worried him little. For was he not surrounded by loving parents and friends and a not ungenerous nature? To north and south stretched the canyon or barranca of the Bolaños, a great rent in the earth's crust, carved out through countless ages by the little silvery rivulet hiding in its bottom. Hardly more than a brook in the dry season, it swelled to an impassable, turbulent torrent during the rains. On either side rose the steep sides of the barranca, those to the east leading to the rolling, flat country populated by the "neighbors," the Mexicans, while to the west the mountains rose higher and higher to form the great Sierra Madre range in which lived the pagan Huichol and Cora Indians. Occasionally small groups of Huichol passed by or through the village on their way to or from their mountain homes, and José peeked at them from behind the shelter of his mother's skirts, and wondered at their strange dress with many little woven bags around the waist, their queer hats, their bows and arrows.

"When I was your age," said old Nestor, his grandfather, "we all dressed as they do now. Then our wives wove us blankets and we made clothes of deer hide. But Ave María! Now we must dress in white cotton blouses and trousers and look like Mexicans!"

José never tired of hearing Nestor tell of the glories of the days gone by, when the Tepecanos were a powerful people and held a great stretch of territory. But wars and pestilence had done their worst and the tribe had gradually withdrawn to the great barranca where José was born. And even there the Mexicans were gradually encroaching. Some married into the tribe, while the more unscrupulous boldly appropriated the ancestral lands and recorded the first titles.

José's earliest impressions, of course, were those of home, to him a wonderful place, and his parents most remarkable people, omniscient beyond a doubt! Surely there was nothing in the world they did not know or could not do! His mother in particular was the busiest person. As the first rays of the sun dimmed the morning star, she arose and put wood on the fire which had been smoldering all night under the pot of beans and under the comal or griddle, and by the time the rest of the family were well awake the little, round, flat tortillas were toasting. These little toasted cakes of thin, unleavened corn dough were the staple food, not only of the Tepecano, but of millions of Mexicans of the peon class. Torn in half and used as a scoop to carry a mess of brown beans and chili sauce to the mouth—ah! Who could ask for anything more savory? Surely not little José. But what a drudgery it meant to his mother! Not that she considered it drudgery—she knew of nothing else, and it was the lot of every woman.

And so Señora Aguilar bent all day—or most of it—over the stone metate grinding the softened, boiled corn into dough. The corn itself, the typical Indian corn with yellow ears, black ears, red ears and ears of all these colors, lay husked in a corner of the house. Every day a few ears would be taken, shelled and put to simmer in a pot with a pinch of lime to soften it. Then it had to be ground on the metate with a stone grinder, patted into shape and toasted on the griddle. At almost any hour of the day could be heard in the hut the sound of the muller grating against the metate, or the sharp "pat, pat" on the cake. When night came at last, a mass of dough was always ready to be prepared for breakfast.

So José watched his busy mother and wondered why she took no time to play with him. Several times a day she took the great water jar on her shoulder and walked slowly with him down the long, winding trail to the little brook which supplied the household—yes, several households—with water. Occasionally, too, they bathed in the clear waters—in the summer. But even then the water was cool and soap expensive, so baths were infrequent. And then the water was full of wonderful animals known as chanes. No one could see them, of course, except in rainy weather, when they appeared as great arcs or bows in the sky, striped with colors, head in one spring and tail in another, as they visited. But ordinarily they were invisible, though their forms were well known. They had the bodies of serpents with horns like cattle. They were to be treated reverently, as they had the power of sickening all who disregarded them.

"Never drink directly from the spring, Pepe," his mother warned him, "or the chan will enter and sting you. Dash the water into your mouth as your father does."

Although corn cakes and beans supplied the major part of their dietary, there were other foods, in season and on a smaller scale, other crops, tobacco, chili-peppers and squash. Squashes did not keep like corn or beans, unless they were cut into long strips and dried. More often the squashes were eaten fresh, at harvest time. A hole was dug in the ground and lined with stones and in this a fire was lighted until the stones were hot. Then the fire was removed and replaced with squashes, and the whole covered and allowed to remain all night. In the morning the squashes were perfectly baked and delicious. But the best part of the squash was the seeds which were toasted, cracked open and the kernels eaten. These were indeed excellent! Occasionally the juicy centre of a large cactus was cooked in the same way.

But with the advent of spring, that was the joyous time! It was the coming of the rains after the long dry season. The spring rains are the most vital factor in the life and economy of the natives of northern Mexico, and on them all interests settle. Then the parched land springs into verdure and the streams burst forth anew. Then the nopal, the "prickly pear" cactus, puts forth new green leaves which can be cleaned of their spines and boiled to an edible tenderness, and the blue and purple tunas appear on their leaves. Then the mesquite and vamuchile trees prepare to produce their fruit. But best of all, it is the time of the pitahaya, that luscious fruit of the organ cactus.

"The pitahayas are ripe! The pitahayas are ripe!" shouted and sang José with the other children, while their elders prepared to desert their villages and repair to the heights where the cacti grew most abundantly, there to gorge themselves until the season passed. All year long the great reed poles leaned against the thatched roofs of the houses, awaiting the joyous spring when they would be used to pick the pitahayas from their high branches.

Seldom it was that little Pepe tasted flesh of any kind. To be sure they kept a few chickens, but the Aguilars were too poor to eat many of them; they were sold to the itinerant trader to take to the larger civilized towns. Too, the dried corn which the chickens ate meant just that much less for the family. Nevertheless José knew and relished the taste of chicken and eggs. A few goats, sheep, pigs and turkeys were kept in the neighborhood, and occasionally the word was passed around that one was to be killed. The wealthier families purchased a few pounds, cut it into strips and hung it up to dry. For a few days, meat was added to the dietary of the Aguilar family. A very few cattle and horses were kept by the very opulent, but these were seldom killed. They represented rather the wealth of the owner and were sold to Mexican ranchmen. But when for one reason or another—generally by accident—one was killed, the word was noised abroad for many miles and, like buzzards, the population gathered to purchase or beg the meat.

"Ah, but it was different in the old days!" exclaimed old Nestor. "Then the country was full of game. Ave María! So many deer! And rabbits and raccoons, ducks and pigeons! But now the Gods are angry at us because we have neglected them and will send us no more deer."

"Is it really the Gods who send the deer, little grandfather?" asked José.

"Surely," replied the old man. "Are they not the pets of our Elder Brother, the Morning Star? When one wishes to hunt deer he must first fast seven days and then go to one of the sacred altars with a prayer stick and beads for payment and recite the old prayer begging Elder Brother to lend him some of his deer. Then he will be sure to shoot them. But he must not eat any of the first deer he kills, but must give it to the other people, and he must be sure to make candles of the fat and burn them. Of course we always used bow and arrows to shoot them, as they would be offended and leave the country if they were killed by other means."

"How interesting!" murmured little Pepe. "And do the Gods keep other animals too, little grandfather?"

"Por Dios, no! The deer are their only pets. But the scorpions are the cattle of the Devil and one must also say a prayer and make a jícara [1] full of pinole [2] with beads in order to drive them away from one's home. And then there are the great serpents which live in the mountains. One must also recite a prayer to get one of them."

"Ave María!" ejaculated José. "Did you eat snakes too?"

"Only small ones," laughed Nestor, "and iguanas. The large serpents we kept in the houses as protectors. They were brought

[1] Gourd cup.
[2] Corn meal.

home and instructed to hold any one who came to the house to rob, and to give the alarm by striking the ground with their tails. But they had to be fed bread every Thursday." Here old Nestor smiled. "At least that's what my grandfather told *me*. I never saw them myself!"

It was many years before little José journeyed from home. There he played with the stones and the household objects, his dog and cat and his pet quail, learning the manifold secrets of the world about him. There were other boys nearby with whom he played; they had their bows and arrows—weapons discarded by their elders long ago—and their toys and dear possessions like boys the world over. There were few household objects for them to break in play, only a few pots and gourds, and, like all Indians, the Tepecanos seldom or never punished their children, preferring that they should grow up loving and with their spirits unbroken. An occasional trip to the nearest Mexican village to purchase cloth or sugar, or to the house of a relation a few miles away was the extent of José's travels. For sweets he had the honey which might be taken from the hollow logs raised on forked posts outside of the house.

Gradually José learned to help his parents and, by the time he was fourteen, he was able to do most of the tasks expected of young men. He accompanied his father Francisco on trips to the hills in search of natural products. The leaves of the agave were one of the most sought-after materials. These they carried home, stripped off the soft green exterior and put the strong interior fibers to dry. This was called ixti, and from it all kinds of cord and rope were made. Many hours José sat, twisting the wheel with which his father made rope. At other times he helped to make adobe bricks, mixing the mud to a proper consistency, pressing it into moulds and leaving it in the sun to dry. His father likewise taught him to weave strong sacks of ixti cord on a simple loom.

Some of his spare time, too, he devoted to that eternal Mexican pastime of hunting buried treasure. Of course he never found any, but the joy of the search was in itself and had he not heard countless tales of fabulous wealth found in caves where it had been hidden during a revolution? One could never tell!

By this time José was old enough to wear the typical costume of the men of the tribe. For a few years he had run naked, but not for long, and during the greater part of his boyhood had worn clothes of a nondescript character.   But about the time of puberty, his mother made him a suit of white cotton cloth consisting of blouse and trousers.   These were so much more comfortable than the tight trousers affected by the civilized Mexicans.   Nevertheless, the laws of the nearby towns prohibited any one's appearing in the streets in the flowing calzones, so in each Indian village was at least one pair of pantalones which were borrowed whenever any one wished to visit town.   The trousers were upheld by a girdle of faja or wool, woven by his mother on a narrow loom with geometric designs in black and white.   A little bag, woven of the same material, known as a costal, accompanied him wherever he went, for in this he carried all his little personal possessions and necessities, such as matches, tobacco and, at times, lunch, as well as the dozens of little knick-knacks dear to the heart of the boy.   In the same way his forefathers carried their sticks to make fire, and his grandfathers their flint and steel.   But in these enlightened days sulphur or wax matches were within the reach of even impecunious Mexican Indians, and José very early learned to smoke cigarettes made of locally grown tobacco rolled in corn husks.   As likely as not he carried the "makin's" on the broad brim of his sombrero, an immense peaked hat of the braided leaf of the agave.   Sandals of rawhide completed his costume.   The hat was extremely heavy, but it was the custom, so José wore it with pride.   But his greatest pride was his machete, that great steel knife carried by every man, which served every imaginable purpose.   No boy was ever half so proud of his first watch as was little José of his first machete.

José helped his father in the labor of the field.   In the winter they made a clearing by cutting and burning down the trees and brush.   This was not a great task, for the rocky and infertile hillsides produced few trees or bushes and the cacti and grass were easily destroyed.   Then, after the first heavy rain of the summer, they went to their field, carrying the seed corn, beads and a jícara full of water in which corn meal had been mixed.   They had already undergone a fast of five days and an ablutionary bath.   It was indeed a very sacred and solemn occasion, for the success of the yield, if not the entire harvest, depended upon them.   For was not Corn the daughter of Father Sun?   So they reverently placed the beads in the center and four corners of the field, and sprinkled the pinole water to the cardinal points of the compass while Francisco, reverently facing the east, recited the ancient prayer, promising Father Sun that they would guard well his daughter and cherish her. Then they made little holes in the ground with sticks, dropped in the kernels and covered them over. But little attention was required until harvest time. Then the corn was gathered with great joy, but the twin stalks, the corn plants with forked stem and two ears known as the milpa cuata, were left standing until the end. Then father and son solemnly walked around the field as many times as there were stalks within it, and recited another prayer, begging permission of Father Sun to carry home his daughter and promising again to guard her well. These stalks, with the ears attached, were then gathered in a sheaf and fastened to the ridgepole of the house, or to a tree. And that evening Nestor told again the old story of how Father Sun sent his daughter Corn to earth to be of service to man and how she was wronged by her husband, Toloache, [1] who used her bounty to support his mistresses, Crow and Badger, so that at last she returned to her father.

"Therefore it is," said old Nestor, "that we must pray hard for only a little corn in place of the plenty which would have been ours. But Toloache was punished by being fastened head downwards to the rock and being required to grant us whatever we may ask of him."

At this story José smiled for he was of the sophisticated younger generation, and he looked upon it as a pretty fable, but old Nestor evidently believed it implicitly.

Practically all the efforts of the people were individual or family affairs. It was only on religious or ceremonial occasions that any communal interests were attempted . But one day at the height of the dry season his father said to José:

"Pepecito, to-morrow we are all going to fish in the river and you are old enough to go along."

The following day found them trudging toward the little river, their costales filled with gordas—tortillas made thicker than usual so that they retained their softness during the day. As they neared the river they were joined by other parties bound in the same direc-

[1] Jamestown weed.

tion. All paths led to a deep hole in the river above a series of rapids where, it was suspected, the fish had all congregated. Here all hands set to work making a tapexte, a weir or mesh of reeds laid together closely in a plane and tied with cord. One of the long edges was weighted with stones so that it sank to the bottom, and thus the entire mat could be dragged up or down the stream, carrying the fish with it. An entire day was consumed in making the tapexte and at nightfall all returned to their homes, worn out with exertion. The next day—ah! That was a wonderful day! Sounds of shouting and splashing filled the air. Dark skins glistened and sparkled in the sun as the fishermen plunged into the deep holes and endeavored to seize in little hand-nets the fish which had been cornered by the great tapexte. And that night fish boiled merrily in the pots of many happy households.

José was of good physical type, of medium height and slim build. His hands and feet were small and well shaped, his features large but not coarse. His eye was dark and sparkling, his hair thick, straight, long and very black, his mustache, beard and body hair sparse. His forefathers used to pluck out their beards, considering that it made them look like the animal world, but he, like the younger generation, cut and shaved his as fashion dictated. His color was a dark brown. He was active, keen and bright when necessary, but inclined to slothfulness. After all, why *should* he do to-day anything he could put off till to-morrow? An unpleasant task, if procrastinated, might settle itself; if a pleasant prospect, why not prolong the enjoyable anticipation? When life contains so little variety, why do everything to-day and have nothing to do to-morrow?

José liked to smoke, of course, but any luxury was too expensive for him to overdo it. And naturally he drank whenever he could get the various distillates of agave which sold in the neighboring villages as mescal, tequila and sotol. He drank to excess, for strong liquor gave him a surcease from monotony—it made him a different person in a different environment and he was glad to seek the change. Of course drunken brawls were frequent and machete wounds occasional, but they were forgiven shortly afterwards and forgotten.

Like all of his people, José was naturally cheerful and from a certain point of view, honest. He would probably have considered it highly commendable to steal anything from a Mexican or a Gringo stranger if he could escape undetected, but he couldn't steal from friends. He was given to boasting—when the boast could not be checked up. Always cheerful, singing and happy, few things worried him. Although very emotional, like all Indians he considered it weak to betray emotion before others. His one outstanding quality was his politeness, and this was of the heart, not a mere outward display; he was always ready to be of assistance to the helpless, sympathetic to the unfortunate. He could hardly be called literate though he could, after intense and laborious cerebration, manage to spell out a message or write a note. What with this illiteracy, his tendency to procrastination, ignorance of all trades and indisposition to continued labor, he would have been a miserable failure in an industrial civilization, although in his native environment he was a valuable member of society.

One year during the dry season, after the harvest of corn was in, José accompanied several other young men of the tribe to a nearby mining town where labor was in demand, and here he experienced his first contact with "high" civilization. Here with pick and shovel he could earn half a peso a day—twenty-five cents. Even at that rate José could save enough to return to the little village in comparative affluence after a few months, for money of any kind was seldom seen there, practically all business being done by barter and one was indeed deeply in debt who owed his neighbor a peso! José's native boss was easy-going and the men were not overworked, but the American foreman was a puzzle to José. Always on the go, he never sat down to rest. And such queer Spanish as he spoke—principally profanity! Then there were such wonderful and incomprehensible machines, there, which did the work of many men, run by steam and electricity: telephones, telegraphs, automobiles and countless other appliances.

But the most joyous days of José's youth were those of the fiestas. Then the natives for miles around, both Indians and "neighbors," gathered in the little pueblo. Ave María! What an assemblage! All the pretty girls with their best petticoats of bright red flannel, their rebozos [1] covering their sleek, black hair, their bright black eyes sparkling with excitement and their white teeth shining. All the men with their white trousers and blouses freshly washed, their hats

[1] Shawls.

freshened up and their machetes polished. All roads led to the little village, most coming on foot, the more opulent on donkeys, mules or horses, for none owned wagons, nor could any wagon traverse the rocky trails. Open hospitality reigned everywhere. Relations who had not seen each other for months, compadres by the scores, old friends, new acquaintances, fell on each other's necks and slapped each other on the back while the bottle of fiery sotol or tequila circulated freely.

Frequently the fiesta began with some communal work on the church, for the church was the center of all activity. Possibly a wall had to be erected and each one helped as he or she was able, the boys and women carrying single small stones, the men carrying frames on which many large stones were piled. An hour or so of combined labor and the wall was built. In the afternoon, sports were the order of the day. Of these the most popular was that of colando al toro, in which the wealthy young men endeavored, each on his pet horse, to ride past a bull, seize him by the tail and overthrow him. How José longed to be able to own a horse and gain the plaudits of the girls by his prowess!

"I might even," thought he, "go to the great City of Mexico and learn to be a famous torero and be the idol of the entire Republic."

At night there were cuetes exploded in honor of the day, which delighted José hugely, and dances to the music of the violin. All day and much of the night the celebration kept up. Little booths and tables were erected wherever vendors sold dainties, and the air was filled with the cries of the merchants.

"Sweet oranges! Four for a half-real!" [1]

"Melon seeds! Perfectly toasted!"

"Peanuts! Peanuts!"

"Sugar cane! The very sweetest!"

"Candies! Who wants them?"

Lucky was the boy who had a real to spend at the fiesta, for a goodly portion of anything would be sold at the standard price of a centavo.

Meanwhile, over in one corner, the men gathered around a Mexican from a nearby town who was running a gambling game with the cards, while his partner dispensed bottles of the agave

[1] Twelve cents.

brandy.   Soon the inevitable vicious altercation would arise.   To be sure it was limited to a violent flood of profanity and only reputation and dignity were injured, but the women shrank away while drunken cries filled the air.   A few cool heads interfered before any irreparable damage was done, but it was not always thus, as a rude cross or two in the neighborhood of the pueblo, marking a place where a soul had come to a violent end, mutely attest.

It was the Christmas season that was particularly celebrated at Azqueltán, for then the old pageant of "Los Pastores" was performed. For weeks before, the performers, all prominent men of the village, were engaged in making their costumes of long, white dresses and their staffs decorated with colored tinsel and tissue paper.   The words and music had been handed down from the days of the first Spanish missionaries, and depicted the adventures of a group of shepherds journeying to the nativity.   José's father, Francisco, played the part of the hermit with a crude mask of wood and an immense rosary of wooden beads.   It was José's ambition to take the part of Satan, who attempted to prevent the pilgrimage.

"José," said Francisco one day, "it is high time you were married. You are eighteen now and most of the boys of your age are married already.   I cannot afford to support you any longer and you must set up for yourself.   I've been hearing a great deal about your affairs with several girls—yes, and with some of our married women too! And it will have to cease."

Here Don Pancho chuckled to himself, for he had a great deal of pride in his handsome son and enjoyed the gossip of his amours. José had learned to be a fair performer on the fiddle and the guitar, and would sit by night with a few other free lances of his own age under the eaves of some straw hut watching the stars come out in the beautiful crisp, evening air and singing melancholy love songs. Most of the girls succumbed to his advances at once, but there was one who rejected them with affected scorn and she, of course, was the one he most desired.   Consequently he began to hedge at his father's suggestion.

"But, little father," said he, "I don't want to get married yet,— possibly I never will!"

"What nonsense!" exploded Francisco.   "It's all right for Gringos to be bachelors; they can hire women to do their work; they can eat in tiendas. But you! Who'll make your tortillas? Who'll make your clothes? Don't be a fool!"

José knew it was up to him to get a wife, but he wished a little more time to press his suit with Josefa, the much-to-be-desired daughter of Cándido Gonzales. "Give me another month, little father," he asked, and Francisco agreed.

So José sought out his grandfather, old Nestor. Bashfully he hesitated and "stalled" until at last the sly old man suspected the truth.

"Come, come!" he ejaculated. "Speak out! What is it, a girl?" José presented his case. The old man swelled up with pride.

"Ah! Of a truth you have come to the right man! You knew your old grandfather was the one to aid you! There is now only one other man in the tribe who knows how to gain the love of a girl! A week from to-night at midnight will be the time. We must both fast for five days before, in order to appease the Gods and María Santísima. Get me a piece of the girl's clothing and I'll find the other things."

José didn't relish the idea of a fast, for he was of the younger generation and took little stock in the superstitions, as he considered them, of the elders. Nevertheless he was now in trouble and, with the natural faith of the helpless man, willing to try anything. So he endured the fast without a whimper and surreptitiously visited the girl's house while she was fetching water from the spring and stole a small article of clothing.

When at last the night came, the old man was in a queer mood of neurotic enthusiasm and excitement, combined with sober dignity in contemplation of his important office.

"Have you the clothing?" he asked eagerly. José handed it to him.

"And now a piece of your own clothing!" A short search brought to light a discarded bit which would serve the purpose.

Carefully the old man made a doll of the clothes of each, one to represent the boy, the other the girl. Then he produced flowers of five narcotic plants which he had spent the day in seeking— güizache, palo mulato, garambullo, rosa maría and toloache—and with these he decorated the boy doll. When the stars indicated the hour of midnight, a candle was lighted and the figures were placed in a large bowl of water, floating. José watched with bated breath. Not that he put much faith in the outcome, but the spell of the magic, the stillness of the night and the temper of the old man, who by this time had practically reached a state of self-hypnosis, had a profound effect. Reverently, and in a low, tense voice the old man recited the ancient prayer begging of the Intoxicated Woman and the Flower Man, that the desired one should be brought to her lover. After this he produced his musical bow and, placing a bowl upside down on the ground, held the bow on it with his foot. Striking the string with two small sticks so that it gave a sonorous twang, he began to sing the old song appropriate for the occasion. Five times he sang it, and then jumped up and walked around the bowl with the floating figures, five times. The charm was then complete. Eagerly he looked into the bowl and found that the two figures had floated together. With a delighted air he turned to José, restraining his high-pitched emotion.

"It is well," he said simply. "The Gods and María Santísima have answered your prayer." José felt relieved, for, although at heart he doubted the efficacy of the charm, the old man's emotion had a considerable effect upon him. So it was with greater self-confidence that in the morning he renewed both his meals and his assaults on the heart of the delectable Josefa, until he felt that he might confidently put the matter to the test.

"Father," said he the following day, "will you speak to Cándido Gonzales about Josefa for me?" His father chuckled.

"So that's the way the wind blows! I guess we can settle the matter. It would be silly of Don Cándido to refuse such a promising son-in-law!"

There were many things to be arranged and the matter of the marriage of one's children was too important an affair to be lightly settled, so old Francisco and Cándido had many long conferences. They debated the matter from every possible point of view and then all over again from the beginning. But even matters of greater pith and moment must eventually be squeezed dry, and at last the time arrived when neither the fertile Don Pancho nor the equally fertile Don Cándido could conceive of another topic of discussion, so they considered the matter formally arranged. The young people would await the next visit of the cura and then be married.

But right there old Nestor interposed a furious objection. Here he was, the Cantador Mayor, the Chief Singer or high priest of the old religion, the keeper of the old customs, doing his best to preserve the tribe from dissolution and destruction because of the anger of the old Gods. The young generation were deserting the Gods and the practices of their forefathers. They no longer attended the old ceremonies, prayed and sacrificed to the Gods, fasted or made prayer sticks. Even the old language had nearly perished and the Gods were so angry that they were permitting the ·tribe to grow smaller and smaller, yearly. It was only the fervor of a few devoted conservatives like himself which still induced the Gods to send their rains in the spring. And would he allow his only grand-son to be married without the practice of the old rites? Por Dios, no! And besides, he was one of the very few men who still remembered the old prayer and it was the custom to pay a peso per night to the one who recited the prayer. He had not the slightest objection to Pepe's being married by the cura—the more Gods the better —but he insisted on his privileges and the observance of the old customs.

So, to please the old man and to keep peace, it was agreed to follow the old customs, and the next Wednesday night the three men, Nestor, Francisco and José, journeyed to the girl's house. Along the narrow, steep and rocky trail they stumbled, finally arriving at the house where they were cordially admitted by old Cándido. Seating themselves by the door, Nestor immediately launched into the prayer which was a long one and recited with great gravity. He spoke in beautiful allegory of the creation of the girl in the heavens, and of her long wanderings before her birth. At last the long prayer came to an end and the party trooped home again.

For five nights on successive Wednesdays and Saturdays, this was repeated and on the last night Cándido, who had been ably coached by Nestor, arose at the end of the old man's speech and spoke in reply, gravely, the traditional response which had served Tepecano brides and grooms for centuries. He admitted that his daughter was lazy and worthless, but appreciated the honor of having her hand asked, and closed with an appeal to the Gods for forgiveness from sins and for health. Then he brought out a white cloth and on it were piled all the girl's possessions and her wedding gifts.

Then all four, the bride and groom and their fathers, seized each a corner, raised the cloth, and the ceremony was complete. José remained with his wife's people for several months while he built himself a new house and put his household in order before taking his bride to her new home. When the good cura came to say mass the next time, the couple appeared before him and were united according to the rites of Holy Church.

One day a melancholy figure appeared before the little hut of Nestor and the old man hobbled out to greet his visitor.

"Enter, enter, little grandson!" he greeted. "Why so sad? What has happened?"

"It is my wife, little grandfather," replied José. "She is quite ill. We have done everything we can for her. All the neighbors have come, and each one has brought her some delicacy and forced her to eat it, but to no avail. Can you not help her?"

The old man puffed up with a mixture of self-conceit, anger and contempt.

"Ah, what could you expect from these old women? They expect to cure sickness by foods and drugs when it is necessary to appease or overcome something! Verily you have come to the right man! Let us see what we can do." He disappeared within his house, made a judicious selection of objects, put them within his sack, and over the trail they went toward the house.

Sure enough, there lay poor Josefa on a mat on the floor of the house. The civilized physician would have diagnosed her malady as malaria and suggested doses of quinine and crude oil—the latter to be administered to the mosquitoes in the pools of stagnant water. A few sympathetic neighbors were gathered around, begging her to try one or another of the dainties they had so carefully prepared.

"Truly, I have done my best, grandfather," lamented José. "I have sucked at the seat of pain as you have told me, but extracted nothing, and I have blown tobacco smoke on her and prayed, but without avail."

"Yes, my son, but one must have practice in such matters and the confidence of the Gods. Possibly it is the work of one of your enemies. It is well that you called me, for none else in the tribe has my power and influence."

Sending the neighbors home, he questioned José with regard to his sins of omission and commission, trying to determine the cause of his wife's infirmity. Had he or she any enemies who might wish to send sickness upon them? José knew of none, except possibly one of her other old suitors. Had he been careful to placate the chanes when he built his new home? José was compelled to admit that he had ignored this matter entirely.

"Ah, my son!" lamented the old man, "you young people laugh at us; you think we are silly, and yet when your own obstinacy leads you into trouble you come to us for aid! Well, that is ever the way of youth. Now let's see what we can do."

He laid Josefa on her back, standing at her feet. Lighting a cigarette made of corn husk and tobacco he assumed a serious attitude which rapidly became almost hypnotic. Taking long draughts of smoke, he faced the four cardinal points in turn, blowing a puff of smoke in each direction, and then in a low tense voice recited a prayer, begging that the illness might pass from her and she be restored to health. Then he blew five puffs of smoke on her hands, feet and forehead and, falling on his knees, began to stroke her body rapidly from the extremities to the seat of pain, at which place he then began to suck vigorously. Finally arising, he spat into his hand a mouthful of blood. His state of tense emotion rapidly disappeared as he said gravely:

"This is a serious matter, Pepito. It is not the chan; if it were, I should have sucked out only spittle. The blood proves it to be witchcraft!

"It is a matter of the greatest delicacy," continued Nestor, "and you are lucky to have one so powerful as I at your service. Even for me it will require a whole week of fasting and praying to diagnose the matter correctly. And even for my favorite grandson I couldn't afford to do it for less than the standard price of five pesos!"

After a half-hour's argument the matter was amicably arranged and for a week the old man bathed, fasted and prayed, and by the end of that time had worked himself into an exalted state which combined with the weakness induced by the fast, made him see visions. On the evening of the seventh day he again appeared before the young man, the gravity of the business evidently weighing upon him very heavily.

"I have seen it all," he said simply. "It was a young man. I couldn't see him plainly enough to recognize him. But he made a figure from a piece of her clothing and stuck a pin into it while another old man prayed that she might sicken and die!"

A wave of hatred passed over José and he cursed the culprit violently. There was no longer the slightest doubt in his mind that old Nestor spoke with authority. He had heard all these old tales about ways of harming an enemy by magical means, but he had never really put any faith in them. And now he was the victim! He ran over in his mind the names of those who might be suspected. There was Pablo Hernandez with whom he had had an argument at the last fiesta, and Pedro Martinez who claimed he had cheated him over a sale of corn last month. Ah, but wait. There was Margarito de la Rosa who had been his pet rival for the hand of Josefa. The more he thought of it, the more certain he was that it must have been he. All right! He would fix him!

Nestor set about his cure with gravity and self-possession, knowing like any doctor that the best half of any cure lay in the confidence of the patient. First he produced his bundle of arrows made of a straight shaft of wood with a large feather from an eagle or a red-tailed hawk, hanging from the blunt end. These were the arrows that attacked evil and sickness. Three of these he stuck in the ground at the patient's head and a fourth at her feet. Then he performed a number of motions with the arrows, which involved changing their positions, pointing them to the four cardinal points and waving them above the patient's head to purify her. Finally he fell on his knees and once again began to suck at the sorest spot in her body. After several attempts on various parts he finally arose with great emotion, his face a livid red from the intensity of his efforts, spat into his hand and showed José—a pin! The latter gasped with astonishment.

Now without doubt the old man had concealed the pin in his mouth before beginning to suck, nevertheless he had worked himself into such an intense emotional state that the fraud was probably quite unconscious. As for José—had he not seen with his own eyes? The very pin which had been stuck into the figure representing his wife had been removed from her body! So that was the game, was it? Very well, it was a game more than one could play at. From that time on he nursed his revenge.

After he had brooded over his wrongs for a long time he again consulted Nestor and told him of his suspicions. The old man nodded gravely.

"Most probably it was he," he assented. "Now that I think of it, the person I saw in the vision was much like him. Of course! I see him very plainly now. And the old man who helped him was that shameless old Heleno Montez who thinks he has more power than I. I'm certain of that. Very well, we'll show them!" And so the two conspirators secretly planned the untimely demise of Margarito and Heleno.

Thus it happened that a few days later they met late one night in a secluded spot on the outskirts of the village.

"There are several methods of bewitching," began Nestor, after crossing himself. "You might as well learn them. One way is to make a figure of cotton and bury it in the cemetery, light a candle and place it at the head of a grave at midnight on Monday, after having fasted all day. Repeat this for five successive Mondays and on the last day get a black stone from the river and hit the earth above the figure five times. Then run home before the candle goes out. The corpse will cause your enemy to sicken and die within five months. But one must fast for the entire twenty-nine days."

José shuddered and looked furtively around into the darkness with the fear of one who dreads ghosts. Neither the method nor the long fast appealed to him. But Nestor, with the air of a devotee, warmed up to his subject.

"But a better way is to make a figure of cotton with hands and feet, head and mouth, wrap it up with the shroud of a dead man and then pierce the head and the heart with five thorns. Pretty soon the victim will fall sick of the stomach and his heart will rot and—may God have mercy on his soul!" Nestor chuckled. "A very pretty way it is, too! That was probably the method they tried on Josefa. Lucky you had me to counteract it!"

Again José's anger rose at the thought of the villainy and he hardened his heart against the malefactors.

"Another good way," continued Nestor, "is to make a clay figure and bury it in an ant hill at high noon. You must fast a day and say the creed seven times while counting your rosary and light a candle. And when the candle goes out, the ants will come up and in five days the enemy will die of boils and hives and fever!"

"That's a terrible death, little grandfather," said José. "We can't do anything like that!"

"Well, there's still another way, the best of all. Few men know this, but I will tell you the secret." His voice sank to a whisper.

"First you must get a bone from the right hand of a dead man. Take this and hide it in the thatch of the roof of your enemy's house when no one is looking. Then in the night he will see a black phantom and the following night a terrifying vision lamenting behind the house. Unless he finds and removes the charm, he will continue being terrified until at last all the people of that house will die from fear of horrible nightmares of poisonous animals—rattle-snakes, centipedes, tarantulas, lizards, spiders and scorpions!"

But José had heard enough, and was on his way home as if all these noxious creatures were after him. Others might dabble in witchcraft if they pleased, but it was not for him! His difference with Margarito he would settle with fist or machete!

This experience brought José more closely into contact with old Nestor. Besides he was getting on toward middle life and beginning to recover from the agnosticism of youth and to take an interest in the old religion and customs of the forefathers. These, he was well aware, were kept alive by a few devoted old conservatives like Nestor who believed that it was only their fidelity which kept the tribe from complete annihilation by the Gods, angry because of the neglect of the younger people. The younger people regarded the conservatives as harmless old fools and their religious practices as amusing superstitions. In this they were encouraged by the padre who was anxious to see all the old beliefs rooted out. Nevertheless he knew enough of human nature to realize that little could be accomplished by coercion and force, and enough of church history to remember that the Church had always found it better to reinterpret the old pagan beliefs and incorporate them into the faith rather than to battle against them. Consequently the conservative group considered themselves perfectly good Catholics and saw no antagonism between the new and the old religions. Nestor found José in a receptive mood when he approached him on the topic.

"José," said he, "it has always been a matter of great regret to me that my only grandson has not been one of the few who have kept faith with the ancient Gods of the pueblo. But that is the nature of youth. I too, up to your age, took little part in the ceremonies, although at that time all of the elder generation were loyal. But now you have arrived at the age of discretion; your advice is sought and your example has considerable influence. I know you no longer laugh at our beliefs; you have frequently questioned me about them. But you have never affiliated yourself with us. Delay no longer, dear little grandson. Father Sun is stretching out his hand toward you to gather you unto him. This is the fifth of January. To-night we celebrate the feast of the Pinole. Come and join us!"

There was an air of ecstasy about the old man and of hysterical emotion, due, as José realized, to the long fast in preparation for the feast, as well as to the narcotic peyote. José saw that a refusal would anger the old man and, besides, he felt a curiosity as well as a real religious interest in the proceedings.

"I will go," he said shortly.

As the sun sank behind the western mountains José and Nestor followed the winding trail toward the place where the ceremony was to be held. Just at dusk they arrived at the patio situated on the top of a small hill. Of course in his boyhood days José had frequently visited the patios where the ceremonies of the conservatives for untold generations had been held. He knew their general form well—a flat circular ground with a place for a fire in the center, a ring of stones which served as seats for the communicants, a circular path without this for the dancers, and a rude altar built of stones to the east. But now everything assumed a new significance.

On arriving, Nestor and José gravely made the requisite five ceremonial circuits of the ground, after which they bowed before the altar, while old Nestor recited a prayer in a low voice. José knew enough of the old Tepecano language to get the sense of the prayer which begged permission of the Gods to prepare and decorate their temple. After this, they set to work and cleared the ground of all growth until it presented an even surface, swept it smooth and started a fire in the center.

Nestor then busied himself at the altar for a long time, and José observed that he had opened his box and taken out many objects of ceremonial importance which he placed in their proper positions on the altar. For a long time he busied himself there, carefully unwrapping every object and giving great care to its placing. José, sweeping the court and nursing the fire, watched him out of the corner of his eye. At last the old man turned and called to him.

"Joselito," said the old man, surveying his work with the pride of a good craftsman, "it is well that you should understand the meaning of all our religious objects. Doubtless you have heard malicious gossip and lies concerning them from the unbelievers of the village. They have told you that we worship idols here, and are in league with the Devil in opposition to our Holy Catholic Faith. Lies! All lies! We worship God here just as we do in the church with songs and prayers. Our dear cura is the leader of that branch of the church, and I of this. He needs his chalices and his sacraments just as I need the ceremonial objects you see here. Just as the blessed images in the church protect the town from evil, so do these bring us health, relief from sickness, and rain for our crops. Look here! This white cloth is the tapexte—it represents the heavens filled with great white rain clouds. These little square objects of colored yarn on a frame, you know well. They are chimales, shields, and represent the face of God, the Sun. Consequently they shield us from every influence and we even fear to make them until after the rainy season for fear they might keep away the rains! These arrows you know too. They are our active defense from sickness and evil and are hung with the feathers of the royal eagle and the red-tailed hawk."

"Why only those?" interrupted José.

"Because they are the most powerful, swift and strong; therefore the arrow will fly fast, hard and straight. It is with these arrows that people are cleansed from sickness and evil. Then these sticks with tufts of cotton wound on them are bastoncitos. The cotton, of course, represents the great rain clouds, and these also serve to cleanse and purify and to bring the rains for the crops. All of these things you have seen and know fairly well. But these little objects of great importance you probably do not know."

Nestor pointed to the front of the altar where lay six or eight jícaras. Some of these were decorated with designs made of small glass beads of different colors set in beeswax on the outer and inner surfaces, but all of them contained various small objects resting on beds of cotton. Many of them were natural stones of strange and unusual shapes and colors, others were little bone carvings and similar objects made by the ancient populations of this region, and occasionally found by the present people. A few others were, although neither of the observers realized it, manufactured objects from other lands.

"These," said old Nestor solemnly, "are the cidukam which are sometimes called our 'idols.' Of course they are not. But they are very powerful and rare and are carefully guarded. One finds them here and there, where they are left by the Gods that those with faith and observation may find them. They protect him from evil and sickness and bring to him health, wealth and happiness. I, as Chief Singer, have the largest number of most powerful ones which protect not only me, but the entire pueblo. And yet they care so little for it that the people laugh at my valuables and refuse to attend our ceremonies. But let them beware! The Gods will not bear with this neglect forever! Already things are not as they were in my youth. Then the rains were longer and heavier, the corn grew more bountifully and the deer were more plentiful. While I last, I will keep the faith, but who will follow me? Not one of the younger generation knows the prayers, the songs or the details of the ceremonies! Well, at any rate, I shall have done my best to save them from the consequences of their neglect."

"Here," he exclaimed, pointing to a spherical object resting on a bed of cotton in a beautifully decorated jícara, "here is the most powerful object in the collection. There is not another one in the tribe—yes, there cannot be another like this in the whole world."

He raised the globe reverently and lovingly from its bed. Now an American schoolboy would have recognized it as a large glass marble with the white corkscrew veins in the center. But to Nestor and José it was a wonderful object, and they feasted their eyes on the beautiful and regular shape and color.

"This is surely the spirit of the rain," said the old man softly. "See! It is transparent like the water and in the centre the whirling rain descends. Ah! If that should be lost or taken from the country, the rain would surely follow it and we would all die of drought and starvation!" He put it back into its place reverently.

"Here is a representation of the moon, white and round; this one is evidently the spirit of the deer. See how closely it resembles one with its horns! Here is doubtless an ear of corn, and this one here is certainly intended for a chimal. And these—but here come more people!"

Into the light of the fire brightly blazing in the center of the patio came three elderly men. José knew them well, of course, as prominent in the conservative party. They walked five times around the circle and stopped before the altar and breathed their prayers before stepping out to greet the two. From this time on, the communicants arrived slowly, until by eight o'clock about a dozen had congregated, almost entirely elderly men. A few women also had come, but these made a fire for themselves outside the circle and took no part in the ritual.

Presently Nestor brought out a bow of the type used by the hunters of old, and tightened the string until it gave forth a resonant twang when plucked. Then, scooping out a hole in the ground in front of his seat, he inverted a gourd bowl over this and held the bow, string uppermost, on the bowl with his foot so that it served as a resonance chamber. Two small sticks were selected and the ceremony was about to begin. First, however, he called José to him and formally recited to him another of the old speeches, handed down by tradition through centuries, delivering to him the care of the fire for the night. Then he seated himself on his central seat, and on either side sat another old man. In each hand they held one of the ceremonial arrows which they had taken from the altar. These were waved slowly, and pointed in turn to east, north, west and south while the old man recited the traditional prayer opening the fiesta. This done, he settled himself on his seat and, taking the two sticks in his hand, struck the bow with a sonorous twang. Then he began to sing in a low voice to the accompaniment of the monotonous twang of the bow. José followed the example of the other men by getting up and dancing around the circle with a solemn, slow tripping step, stopping to face outwards for a moment at each of the cardinal points, and particularly to the altar at the east.

And so the long night passed. Around Polaris swung the bright stars, shining as they can only in the crisp air of high altitudes. All night long with but brief intermissions the old man sang. Only four

songs there were in all, but these were very long and full of monotonous repetition.   They told of the origin of the Gods and of the
world, and of the coming of the rain to refresh the world with its
life-giving water.   José tended the fire conscientiously and danced
with the other men for at least a portion of every song.

At last above the rim of the eastern hills appeared the glowing
Morning Star like a heavenly torch, and all greeted it reverently.
Soon the great sun himself began to spread the light and warmth of
his glow abroad, and finally showed his face radiant above the eastern
hills.   Seldom had he seemed more majestic to José and seldom had
his warmth been more welcome, after the chilliness of the night.

About this time Nestor finished his last song to the Sun and the
ceremony was almost over.   Once again the other two old men took
their places beside him on the stone seats and once again were the
arrows pointed to the cardinal points while the Chief Singer recited
the prayer to close the ceremony.   Then, one by one, all the men
approached the altar where they were given little tamales [1] to eat,
while Nestor purified them of all sickness and evil by waving over
them an arrow, the feather of which had been dipped in peyote
water.   A few drops of the water were placed in the hand of each,
and then water in which corn meal had been mixed was sprinkled
over every one present, over the altar and the seats.   The sacred
objects on the altar were collected and replaced in their box, all the
attendants, led by Nestor, made their five ceremonial circuits of the
patio and the ceremony was completed.   José went home and slept
the rest of the day.

Although José still affected to ridicule the beliefs and practices
of the conservatives, yet the ceremony he had witnessed had really
quite an effect upon him.   And he began to show a live concern
for the old religion, studying it almost as would a scientific investigator.   Many were the conferences and long talks that he and Nestor held together, the old man an intensely enthusiastic informant,
the young man an interested listener and keen inquisitor.   Of course,
like all the Tepecanos, he already understood the basis of the old
religion, how the trinity of Father Sun, Mother Moon and Elder
Brother Morning Star watched over and protected their people;
how Father Sun had sent his daughter, the Corn, into the world that

---

[1] Cooked corn meal wrapped in corn husk.

they might have sustenance, and how the Gods sent the welcome and necessary rains in the spring and summer, that the corn might flourish, requiring only that the people worship them with song and dance, with arrows and chimales. But all of the minor esoteric details opened a new field of interest to him. He learned the many set prayers which were enjoined for various occasions, the ritual songs sung at the four principal ceremonies, that of the Rain in April, the Ripe-corn in September, the Corn-meal in January and the Twin-corn in March. He heard of the tabus of fasting and continence enjoined upon the Chief Singer and, above all, of the influence and power of the magic peyote which played such a large part in all observances. He learned to make the various kinds of arrows and chimales and to know their special powers. He learned the locations of the altars, and particularly the four principal ones to the cardinal points, in each of which was a habitant spirit, and how to each pertained a special color—green to the east, gray to the north, black to the west and white to the south. He came to realize that the religion was practically based on the securing of rain, for which the Gods were petitioned with prayer and song, and placated by sacrifices and fasting, for rain was the one essential to human life.

José became particularly interested in the little cactus root known as peyote, that dried, shriveled-up little thing which produced such a wonderful effect when eaten. Such a feeling of ecstasy and exhilaration, of joy and insensibility to fatigue, did they produce that they were certainly powerful instruments of the Gods, if not near gods themselves.

"It is a kind of corn," volunteered Nestor of the peyote, "just as the deer are corn." By that he meant that it was a food sent by the Gods, for he knew well that it was the root of a cactus growing in a country far to the east.

"When I was young," he continued, "we journeyed far to the east to gather the peyote root just as the Huicholes do to-day. But now that I am old and there is no one to take my place, I must buy it from them."

Then and there José swore that he would accompany the next Huichol party to the eastern country in search of the strange plant, for he was still young enough to feel youth's passion for visiting strange lands. He had frequently seen parties of peyote-seekers passing through the village and had struck up an acquaintance with some of them, envying them their gaudy costumes and long trip. Now he would go with them and himself bring back the peyote!

"May the Gods be with you, Joselito!" fervently prayed old Nestor. "Would that I were young enough to accompany you! But I shall fast and pray for you. When you return with the peyote you will have fulfilled one of the requirements for the office of Chief Singer, and I will go to my forefathers in peace, knowing that you will take my place. It is now October and some of the Huichol men will be about starting out. You have frequently heard me mention my old friend Benito Torres who left Azqueltán as a youth to live with the Huicholes, and who has risen to be one of the most respected men of the tribe. Go to him and he will befriend you. Go with God!"

It was a bright, warm day in October when José set out for the Huichol country. Josefa had filled his sack with gordas and his bule [1] with water. Tobacco, matches, his machete and blanket were the rest of his equipment. He waved farewell to his wife and started up the hills to the west. Higher and higher he climbed, now scrambling up a slope of rock talus, now following a trickling stream up a ravine, now skirting a fertile hill with the hay still slightly greenish from the recent rains. The little river in the bottom of the great barranca grew smaller and smaller, until at last it was lost to sight entirely, behind the hills of the upper edge. The heat grew perceptibly less as he climbed and the pine trees appeared singly and then in groups. The first night he spent by the side of a blazing pine fire on the edge of the mountain forests, while he listened to the howl of the wolves or the snarl of a jaguar or mountain lion.

Early in the morning he was off again, still going westward through the pine groves until at last he began to see the fields and houses of the Huichol. The houses were much like those of his tribe except that none was of adobe. They were also arranged in villages, but in every village was one larger house which served as the temple, in place of the open-air altars to which he was accustomed. The people looked very much the same, but their dress was different. They wore scarfs, belts and little pouches woven in designs of bright colors, wide hats with feathers, and their legs were bare to the knees. They looked askance at the traveler in the conventional cotton trou-

[1] Gourd bottle.

sers of the Mexican peon. One or two accosted him in the Huichol language. It was a queer tongue to him, with many sounds he had never heard before and was confident no civilized man could ever reproduce. He replied in Spanish, but was not understood until one of the middle-aged men who had worked in the nearby mining town, and there acquired a small Spanish vocabulary, happened along. From him José learned that Benito Torres lived on a little ranch a few miles beyond the village. Arriving there about sunset he kicked aside the snarling dogs which, as everywhere in Mexico, prowled about the house, and called aloud. A middle-aged man came out of the house.

"Cafhövan, armano!" José greeted him. The man, after a moment of silent surprise, smiled and countered:

"Cafhövan api! It is a long time since I have heard that greeting in Tepecano," he continued in Spanish, "and the language has about failed me. Enter! Enter! Here is your home! Julia! Bring food and drink for my brother Waköri!" Waköri is the name given the Tepecanos by the Huicholes.

"I am called José Aguilar," said the traveler, "the son of Francisco and grandson of Nestor."

"Ah, yes! Francisco and I were boys together, and many pranks we played on Nestor. He himself was a young man then. How long ago that was! But when I was younger than you, I saw the way things were going. The Mexicans were encroaching on our lands, the cura came and built the church and we were made to give up our communal land and each man take a piece for himself. As if the Gods ever intended their land to be owned like a machete or a hat! As well divide up the air and the water in the river and make the new-born babe pay to breathe and drink! Ave Maria! And then they began to bring in strong drinks; they wanted us to put our legs in those long trousers you wear now, to give up our old language and speak Spanish and to foreswear the old religion. I saw the way it was going and said, 'Not for me! Not for Benito Torres!' And I took my blanket as you have done and came up here with the Huicholes where I have spent a long, happy life following the mandates of the Gods. You are wise to have done likewise. I welcome you!" And he threw his arms around the younger man in a welcoming embrace.

José was pleased and yet troubled.

"Yes, little uncle," he replied at last, "it is quite true. There is little of the old left now in Azqueltán. Only old Nestor and a few of the other old men keep to the old faith. But I am of the new order. These are the clothes I have always worn; Spanish is my language, Catholicism my religion. I cannot change to the old order any more than you to the new. And yet the new is inevitable; I see it even here."

Benito nodded a sad acquiescence. "Yes, it is a losing fight. Even here the old is passing. I have not postponed it for these people, but only for myself by coming here. In a century or so there will be no Huicholes, no Tepecanos, no Coras, only Mexican peones of Indian blood. But why then have you come here?"

José explained his mission, at which the sad face lighted up again.

"It is well," he said. "I too went with parties several times after I first came here. But it is a task for young men. You know it involves harsh restrictions of fasting and great endurance?" José insisted he was prepared for them.

"Very well, then. In a very few days a party begins the preliminary fast. I will speak to their leader and you shall join them."

And so it happened that through the good offices of Benito, José was accepted among the peyoteros and prepared to take his part in the work. He adopted the dress and paraphernalia of the party, taking bow and arrows and several small tobacco gourds. The evening before the departure he bathed and prayed, as he might not bathe again until the return from the long journey. There were nine other men in the party, including a leader who was the only one allowed to make fire while on the long trip. Several burrows were taken along, to carry tortillas on the journey and bring back the peyote on the return. Nevertheless they were expected to fast much of the time, and several men of the party ate little but peyote during the entire forty-three days they were away on the journey.

Bidding an affectionate good-by to their wives and families, the little party started out. Instead of passing by Azqueltán, they struck eastward down the slopes of the wooded mountains and out onto the rolling plateau, dry, hot and sandy. Day followed day in monotonous repetition, night followed night. Generally in single file they walked, dirty and hungry, but with their minds fixed on the goal before them—the attainment of the little cacti which would protect their villages and bring them rain. Across the well known trail they went, camping each night in a certain place, so that the faithful watchers at home knew each night exactly where they were. This trail had been followed for centuries and went along the most inaccessible route, away from roads and villages, so that the pilgrims were seen by very few of the Mexicans of even the more inhabited parts of the country they traversed.

But at one spot when the journey was about half ended, not far from the great City of Zacatecas, they came to a road which could not be avoided. It was made up of short logs of wood laid parallel, and on these were fastened long, snaky iron rails. José, though more civilized than the others, had never seen anything of the kind before, but one of the other men who had made the journey before, explained by signs that an immense monster, dragging behind him houses full of people, ran at tremendous speed along the road, as a horse drew a cart along a dirt road. From the description José recognized it as a railroad, as he had heard about railroads when an open-eyed boy, from an itinerant peddler.

Eastward, ever eastward they pressed, until two full weeks had passed, when the leader of the party informed them that their destination was but five days' journey away and that from that time all restrictions must be rigidly observed. They were to walk in single file continuously, and eat nothing but peyote for the rest of the journey. In a few days José began to see the first little peyote plants, but the leader affected not to notice them, although as the party pressed on the plants grew more abundant. At length, on the nineteenth day, when they had covered about three hundred miles, the leader called a halt. Trembling with emotion, superinduced by hunger and fatigue, he cried:

"There is the peyote, appearing as a deer!"

At that, all drew their arrows and shot at a peyote plant, taking care not to hit it. Then from the loads on the burrows various ceremonial objects were produced—arrows, chimales, bastones and other objects not used by the Tepecanos—which were deposited as sacrifices to the Gods and to the peyote. For the next three days all collected the little cactus roots until the burros were loaded down and the men wore strings around their necks. On the fifth day after arrival they started their long journey homeward.

By this time the supply of tortillas had become entirely exhausted and José, in particular, being more accustomed to regularity of food, and less accustomed to the diet of peyote, suffered greatly. The others appeared not to be greatly affected, for they consumed many peyote roots and walked with the sprightly, springy step that certain kinds of intoxication produce, though their thin limbs and drawn faces betrayed the strain upon them. Now and again inhabitants of the country gave them food, but these were rare occasions and for the greater part they covered the first fourteen days of the return trip in a daze, sustained only by the stimulus of peyote and their nerve.

But at last the fourteen days were over and they approached the spot where, the leader informed them, a party from the village would meet them, five days' journey from home, with loads of tortillas. And so indeed it happened! How good the corn cakes, bone dry after five days in the scorching sun! With renewed strength they continued their way to the edge of their pine forests, where they hunted deer for several days to obtain the meat demanded for the return feast.

A few days later, a body of thin and famished men, their figures only just beginning to recover from the privations of the long journey, but their heads high with elation and consciousness of probity and of duty well performed, their burros laden with sacks of peyote and deer meat and their necks bedecked with strings of peyote, marched down the street of the principal village. The tabu upon washing would not be removed until the great feast, and they presented a bedraggled and filthy appearance, yet they were heroes to the stay-at-homes in the village as they entered the temple and deposited their cherished strings of roots. Then they again began to hunt deer in order to have plenty for the great Peyote Fiesta in January.

But José was anxious to get home. He felt that he had done his share and should be excused from the month or more delay in preparation for the fiesta in which he had but little interest. Benito took his part also and urged that he be allowed to depart. Many of the shamans took exception, fearing that such a rupture of all the regulations of peyote-gathering might anger the Gods and work harm. But finally Benito's argument that harm, if any, would fall upon the culprit and his people in Azqueltán and not on the Huicholes, carried the day, and José was wished god-speed, loaded with gordas made by Benito's wife, Julia, and sent on his way.

How beautiful the great barranca seemed as he first emerged from the edge of the pine forests and saw the gaping chasm below! What joy to make out the little cluster of adobe and thatch shacks with the little white church in the center! As he neared his house, his loving wife ran out and embraced him. How good it was to be home again, and how much better were her tortillas than those of any of the Huichol women!

But only a few minutes did he tarry at home in spite of his long absence, for Josefa said at once: "Old Nestor is sick unto death and has been asking for you hourly. He has kept track of the time you have been away, and says you should be home about this time and that he will not go until he sees you again."

Hastily José ran along the winding trail which led to the house of the old man, and as he neared it he heard the doleful wail of an old shaman singing one of his curing songs. On his blanket on the floor lay the old man, surrounded by his ceremonial arrows and other sacred paraphernalia. As José entered, he smiled and motioned to the shaman to stop singing.

"It is useless," he said simply. "I know my time has come. Sooner or later it comes to all of us. But I knew you were coming to-day, my boy. I dreamt it last night, and I would not go until I saw you. I see you have brought the peyote for me. Well, it will never benefit me. Stay! Give me a drink of it now. It will make my head clearer. But the rest of it you must keep for yourself. You are the only one of the tribe who has fulfilled the requirement for Chief Singer by going to the peyote country. And besides, you know all the songs and prayers and all the intricate details of our ceremonies. And I will leave you all my cherished valuables, my arrows, my chimales and my cidukam. They will help you in every need, and while you cherish them the Gods will allow no harm to befall the pueblo. Francisco! Baldomero! Must he not be Chief Singer after me?"

"It is true," spoke Francisco. "José, my son, you are young in years, but old in experience and knowledge. Will you not do as grandfather wishes?"

Reluctantly José agreed.

A few days later a straggling procession wound its way to the little cemetery behind the church while strong hands bore a plain black box containing the body of old Nestor. The burial customs of old had been entirely forgotten, and even if they had not, Francisco would have taken no chances with fate by having the old man buried outside of consecrated ground. But nevertheless José managed to slip a few of the old man's most cherished sacred things into the box with him. Later José went to the principal altars in the hills to deposit other things, besides journeying to the seat of the cura to pay to have masses said for the rest of his soul.

For a year or so José fulfilled his office as Chief Singer dutifully, but then the restrictions and fasts began to pall upon him, and he shirked the duties and finally abandoned them altogether. Some of the conservatives remonstrated with him, but he replied that he could not see but that they had just as much rain and corn, without performing the ceremonies, and no more sickness and famine than when the ceremonies were performed, in which he was certainly borne out by the facts. And not long afterwards, when a "Gringo" scientist came to the village to study the language and customs, he was glad to sell all of Nestor's sacrosanct valuables at a high price and call it a good riddance.

J. ALDEN MASON

THE UNDERSTUDY OF TEZCATLIPOCA

The Understudy of Tezcatlipoca

THIS story [1] is a mirage of thin words and bodiless phrases.   It paints on a film of mist things that are long ago and far away, and lifts up a pale reflection of cities and grandeurs lying below the horizon of our times, never to be resurrected in fact.   It presents in a vaguely understandable fashion, strange beliefs and philosophies that a wonderful society of human beings created out of their common thought and supposed necessities.

Have you ever tried really to understand the Past, not so much the material Past of quaint costumes and accoutrements, as the immaterial Past of ideals, ambitions, and enthusiasms?   Have you ever wilfully imprisoned your present spiritual being in the emotional matrix of an age that is dead?   In the hall where the glum old faces of your ancestors stare out from dull frames upon your unimagined new life, have you ever paused to gaze back into those dim presentments, and to think how impossible to-day would be the quest of the Pilgrims, or of the Crusaders?   And when, not so long ago, a Gothic fantasy in gently treated stone crumbled before the war-saddened eyes of the world, did this fearful thought impress itself upon you: No man in all Christendom can ever re-carve those shattered prophets or re-groin those airy arches in the dread sincerity of the first builders?

Now, it is not the stone that changes, nor the chisel, nor the loves and hates of individual men and women: it is the over-soul of society that passes.   For, out of our herded life of tribe or nation, comes an over-soul that directs our hands and implants in our minds the seeds of duty, the impulses of sincerity, and the recognition of all the needs which we think are absolute, but which, in a larger view, are merely relative.   The cloud forms of communal emotion that constitute these over-souls, flame and fade like the western sky and never twice assume the same shapes and colors.

In Mexico, before the steel-clad soldiers of Cortes landed at Vera Cruz, there was a civilization that ran back into a twilight of the

---

[1] At the request of the author, there has been no editing.—E. C. P.

237

gods. Centuries of accumulating art and ceremony had enriched the first crude thoughts of savages coming out of desert camps to abide in houses of mud and stone, amid maize stalks and squash vines. Cities and indeed, empires, had risen, flourished and fallen. There had come into being those slaves to the ideal of ritual whom we call priests, and those slaves to the ideal of political grandeur whom we call kings. And back of all these were gods to whom sacrifices were duly given for benefits received. And the people, commanded by their over-soul, raised gleaming temples on stately pyramids for their gods, and built palaces with bright gardens for their priest and kings. And, moreover, they gave honors and rewards for success in trade and war and they set the marks of class upon certain men and their children. This is a story of their sincerity. . . .

That wise old man, bent from much climbing of temple stairs, but with the steady, believing gaze which comes from watching the stars, foretold the distant event with deceptive clarity. He was reader of the fates and keeper of the calendar in Quauhnahuac, and after grave study of his painted books he resolved the tangled interests of greater and lesser gods in the new-born child. So he said to the father and the friends who crowded round: "Let him be called Macuilquaultli, Five-eagle, after the day on which he was born, and let him be well taught in all that a chief should know. He shall acquire grace, skill, and a knowledge of all arts, for he shall come to rule in a high place. Thus it is written: he shall govern the City."

The father of Five-eagle was a Captain among the armed men of Quauhnahuac, a bearer of standards, and a councilor in matters of state. He proudly bore the insignia of high success in war against the strange-tongued people of Tolucca. Yet, Quauhnahuac was not a city of warriors. The populous capital of the Tlahuica (as you may know from that Cuernavaca of sunlight and indolence which survives) lay deep below the mist houses of Ajusco, in a valley where waters dance and flowers flame. To be sure this people had come out from the Seven Caves with the Azteca and other tribes, but they had passed down from the cold highlands and had prospered under the benign protection of Xochivuetzalli, goddess of flowers, and patroness of all the arts that give beauty to the world and take vigor from it.

Five-eagle, at the age of eight, left the shaded portico of his father's courtyard, where the fountain bubbled in a gleaming pool and where imprisoned birds sang, to study and sleep in one of the Great Houses with other youths. He was a slender boy with a pleasing and thoughtful face. Under the instruction of the old warriors he acquired only a careless skill in the hurling of lances, and took little pride when he won his set in the battering contests with wooden swords and shields of cane. Rather he preferred to beat out the thundering war songs of his people on the two-lipped drums. In this he became proficient beyond all others, and in his hands the rubber-tipped drumsticks set up wild, nerve-racking rhythms that soon had young men and old whirling in a mad dance and chanting a song of the old nomadic days. Or, hidden among the trees he would play lonesome melodies on flutes of clay.

He knew the narrow hunting trails that led across the hills to the haunts of deer and wild turkey. He knew the great lava flow that stretched, in twisted and forbidding ridges, along the sides of the high mountain which separated Quauhnahuac from the Valley of the Five Lakes. He had climbed the pinnacles of black desolation on this lava desert and descended into its caverns of whirring bats.

Often in the shade of a market shrine Five-eagle would encounter the aged priest of the calendar who had laid the gorgeous prophecy upon him. This wise old man knew there was no end of knowledge, for he squatted with his books unfolded on the ground before him, and diligently made other books. But always he laid aside his brushes and his sheets of lime-sized paper when the youth drew near. First he would explain what calculation was being written down, and then expanding to the breadth of his subject, he would tell his young disciple how time ran in wheels of days and years and ages, and how the cycles of the Morning Star fell now for good and now for evil fortune, and how the gods ruled the hours in turn. He taught the boy to calculate in high numbers, to make hieroglyphs and read history, and to draw with a sure skill the faces and distinguishing marks of all the gods.

And sometimes, at the dead of night, he took the youth with him to the top of the high pyramid and before the very door of the temple itself. Below them lay the sleeping city amid soft rustlings of the wind and sweet smells of hidden flowers. The ravines were in deep shadow except where a thread of water gleamed faintly. The palm-thatched huts of the common people were huddled in the folds of the valley, with here and there a chieftain's house built round a little court. The barracks and public buildings were placed on the four sides of larger squares, and in the dark of night their plaster walls showed ghostly white. In the market places still glowed the coals of dying fires, about which were massed the muffled figures of men who had brought their packs to market from afar. It was a solemn hour when mysteries crowd in upon the soul, and a still more solemn station. With heads together, speaking now and then in hushed and reverential voices, they studied the multitudinous stars as these swung grandly around the pole in a march of majesty across the eternal depths of heaven. And they kept their vigil until the great white Star of Morning hung like a splendid jewel above the calm snows of Ixtaccihuatl, the White Woman. Then the blue of the East turned to pearl and rose; new smoke streamed upwards through roofs of heavy thatch; the city stirred and the markets filled with sellers and buyers; the yellow Sun had given another day.

Once Five-eagle and the old priests journeyed together to the ruined site of Xochicalco, where one fair temple was still used in religious services. But the walls of a hundred more lay in shapeless heaps of fallen stone. In front and on either side, the terraced hill dropped off to great depths, but behind it rose another hill to a commanding height with a stronghold on its crest. The priest related fragments of history of this all-but-forgotten capital, shards of myths with names of kings and empty dates to signify resounding triumphs. Then he spoke sadly: "The glories of the great pass like the smoke of Popocatepetl, leaving the skies serene."

"But Tenochtitlan," broke in the youth, "tell me about that famous city, for surely you have been there and seen its wonders. Once from the top of Ajusco I looked down, far down, across the lava, and I saw the five lakes like five mists in the valley, and there was Tenochtitlan shining like a jewel. And I saw the roads that lead out from the land like a spider's web."

"Tenochtitlan: yes, I have seen it, and its gardens and temples are rich and beautiful. Its priests and warrior chiefs have much jade and green feathers of the quetzal. Yet Tenochtitlan is youngest of all the cities of Anahuac. Many ages older are Chalco, Colhuacan, Atzcapotzalco,—and Tezcoco, too, where ruled the loved singer. They say that Tenochtitlan was nought but a rock amid the reeds of the great lake when the Azteca came in bondage and distress. But these sought favor of Tacuba to fish and build floating gardens. Then came Acamapichtli and his sons, so that the fishermen went forth to fight, and their god Huitzilopochtli gave them victory. And now the ancient cities have fallen, save only Tezcoco, in all the valley. Those Azteca of Tenochtitlan go now to Colima and Tuxpan for tribute and captives, and even past Cholula to the lands of the Zapoteca. Their traders first go forth with shining goods to spy out the way; then their warriors fall like the lightning flash. Only the wild Tarasca have turned them back, and those of Tlaxcala, fighting behind stone walls."

So the priest of the calendar told the long history of Mexico, and he described the great feasts that fell, one each twenty days, till the year was done. He discussed the signs and powers of the various gods who thirsted for the blood of human sacrifices and hungered for hearts that were freely given.

"But they say," said Five-eagle, "that in ancient times we gave only flowers to our Xochiquetzalli. Now we must offer children to her or she will be displeased."

"They," replied the priest softly, "are the most precious flowers! And to her who gives should be returned gifts as precious. Yet, I think pride of place enters sometimes into sacrifices, and that there is human boasting where the altars are piled too high. If only the Cause of All, to whom even the gods are quarreling children, would speak the last truth, so that man might understand! But if Tlaloc calls for a sprinkling of blood before he will give us showers of rain, then it is indeed just that he should have his blood. Without rain the world would die. Yet Huitzilopochtli, under whose standard fight those of Tenochtitlan, is a god of war alone. He can promise only plunder. He is a little god suddenly grown to commanding stature, so that all the cities pay tribute to his children. But Tezcatlipoca is the great one of all the land; he is the Magician to whom nothing is hidden—may he remember us only in gentle mood!"

There stands to this day in Cuernavaca a graven bowlder bearing a shield, a sheaf of arrows and a record in hieroglyphs of the fatal hour when the painted warriors of Tenochtitlan swept down upon Quauhnahuac. Then the City of Flowers withered before a rain of flint and a wind of flame. And among the men and women carried away as slaves or more honorable sacrifice was Five-eagle. This young man had disclosed, in the stress of that sudden attack, the qualities of true leadership. Out of the confusion he had emerged at the head of his people, leading them vainly against the foe. Yet he was captured at last and taken to Tenochtitlan without degradation, wearing still his earplugs of jade, sandals, and the embroidered mantle of his rank.

And then the prophecy of his birth was justified. For, because of his beauty, his daring and his arts of music and song, Five-eagle was raised to wealth, honor and the power of kings. He was made that other Tezcatlipoca to live among men and enjoy life and be granted every wish while the year turned slowly round to the feast of Toxcatl. His laughter meant good fortune to all the land, and his momentary sorrow spelled calamity. But at the end, replete with every honor, accomplished in every grace, surfeited with every joy, he must go freely under the black knife of glass. And the offer of his youth must be made so that the youth of Tezcatlipoca should be eternal, so that his powers should not wither with the creeping infirmities of time, so that his mysteries should still give forth life and happiness to the sad tribes of men.

What wonderful beings are the gods that men have imagined out of hopes and fears in the twilight of faith! They are creatures of beauty and terror, shaped from stars and storm winds and green waters and from the subtle and powerful beasts. Or they rise still higher to the very form and mind of their creator, man. They loom forever majestic, immortalized by the sincerities of human sacrifice, by prayers and incense and devoted lives, by ceremony and all its pictured train of magnificence and centered power, by temples and songs and statues that artists, in the grip of common thought, yield up and create. They are the over-souls of nations made visible from afar. But to their makers they are the blinding light of a great presence.

And what more gallant god ever bestrode the heavens than Tezcatlipoca of the Mexicans? He was a Lord of Magic, inscrutable, pitiless, magnificent. He combined the wisdom of white hair and wrinkled cheeks with the reckless joy of never-passing youth. He was swift and cunning and unconquerable, making and breaking fates, snaring his brother gods in wizard traps. He was not alone the Smoking Mirror in which the world lay reflected, he was the Sun that looked down into the hearts of men, he was the prowling Jaguar, he was the night wind stealing across land and sea. Yet in his proper guise he was Youth with all its wiles and enchantments: Youth that was graceful, debonair, beguiling as music, subtle as the perfume of flowers,—but cruel, swift and terrible as the lightning bolt.

The greatest feast of the Mexican year was the feast of Toxcatl, made in honor of Tezcatlipoca. It fell in the springtime when thirsty fields called for rain. Scarcely had one young warrior, chosen from the clean-limbed and accomplished prisoners of a sacred war, been sacrificed on the last day of his fictitious glory than another stepped into the empty rôle. And, as had been said, it was the fate of Five-eagle, after his arrival at the Aztecan capital, to be chosen as a fit candidate for this dramatic death. With a true knowledge of the symbolism and significance of the ceremony in the emotional fabric that then was Mexico, he assumed the part proudly, and made ready his mind to play out the drama to the end, with minute regard for all the details and effects.

A retinue of pages, the sons of chiefs and great merchants of Tenochtitlan, accompanied him in his daily wanderings about the city. These were six in number. They were dressed in fine liveries and it was their duty to see that their master, whom they addressed as Tezcatlipoca, did not fall into sad thoughts. A sacred college of girls embroidered new garments for Five-eagle and each day braided fresh garlands of fragrant blossoms to hang about his neck. Later, from this house of virgins, it was fated that four maidens should be chosen to act as his brides, during the last month of his earthly life, the month of Toxcatl, crowded with gayeties and tears.

So Five-eagle, as the Youth of Toxcatl, walked through the public squares of Tenochtitlan and over the many bridges that spanned its canals, and on the great wall that held back the storm winds of the lake. Clothed in the bright habiliments of divinity, with a laughing retinue, he played upon his flutes and chanted songs and danced. And no one in all the city remembered to have seen an understudy of the great God of Magic in other years so skilled in all the graces or so well taught to tread the brief stage of vanity and pride. Five-eagle, a captive from the enslaved city of Quauhnahuac, where Xochiquetzalli had been worshiped in happier times, ruled great and small in Tenochtitlan.

He chanted many songs that the people loved, but none that was so great a favorite as a splendid lament of fallen soldiers, a requiem of the young men who died in the sacred service of arms. All Mexico knew this song composed by a famous ruler of the Toltec cities whose name was a smile and a benediction after the passing of many years.

> Words like the saddest, drooping flowers I seek
> I, the Singer, weaving my tears in song,
> For Youths, alas!—broken as spears are broken!
> And the women weep in darkened corners
> But the men lift up their heads in pride.

A valiant song it was, full of high courage and the will that conquers death. Upon such songs as this, planted deep in human hearts, rest the brave deeds of nations.

So Five-eagle passed through Tenochtitlan with his pages by his side, in the white mantle of Tezcatlipoca, with a garland of fragrant blossoms about his neck. His chanted verses charmed the market and the court to silence and tears, but when the song was done there was sudden laughter, and he was pelted with flowers by a gay throng. And he was invited to enter the houses and to eat of the choicest fruits, and to rest under canopies of those rare trees with crowns of cardinal, that now we call poinsettia.

Among the girls who did service in the temple of Tezcatlipoca, according to the law of consecration that none might escape, there was one who had come to look upon Five-eagle as more than a man, perhaps,—but less than a god. Once, as she had thrown across his shoulder a wreath of her own weaving, he had looked at her with unclouded eyes and a faint, steady smile. And she had turned away, thrilled and chilled with awakened interest in life and sudden visions of death. In the days that followed she wove other wreaths and awaited his coming at a certain place. And though she greeted the Youth of Toxcatl with a smile, she turned away in tears.

A kindly priest saw and understood. He knew that women were used to weep and moan for all the fine burst of glory that death might bring to the stilled flesh. Women, in the thoughts of Aztecan poets and philosophers, were flowers blooming near the ground. They were crushed beneath the feet of Huitzilopochtli leading his men to war. They could not be trusted for supreme sacrifices, and must be caught by surprise and trapped in the midst of revelry.

By the water gate against Tlaltelolco, when night was falling and mists were stretching filmy hands across the lake, the priest spoke to the girl of Tenochtitlan, "My child, are you envious of the gift that must be given cheerfully to a god who knows all thoughts? Do you dare love the consecrated sacrifice of Toxcatl?"

"Then why do those of the upper skies put seeds of love in our hearts to grow and bloom when it is spring?"

"That sometimes we may climb, my child, to heights where only the mind rules. The Youth of Toxcatl is a captive of Quauhnahuac. He fought bravely; he will die bravely that the city and all Mexico may prosper. Should he falter, he will live as a vile slave unworthy of a bright death; he will live as a vile slave condemned to life—beneath the whip. Daughters of Tenochtitlan may not mate with slaves."

She stood rigidly by the wall as the priest spoke, a mutinous and tragic figure, with yellow flowers in her hair. On the towers of the water gate the torches were being lighted so that belated fishing boats might find their way into the city. The stars were beginning to twinkle faintly.

"But twenty days remain for that gallant boy," said the priest softly, "for to-morrow is the feast of Huey Tozoztli, the great Humility, and then begins the month of Toxcatl, of such gladness and sorrow. Twenty days mean much when there is new love to be gathered and enjoyed. There are four who shall be his brides, impersonating in name and dress those four gracious beings of the ninth heaven to whom the love of Tezcatlicopa is given. If you might be the first of these, would your mind be content and filled with happy thoughts? Would you teach your will to strengthen his and not let your soft tears plunge him in worse than death, you to despair and the land to disaster?"

A new light shone in the eyes of the girl. "See how I shall laugh to the last," she said, "and be happy in the noon of love and in him who is noble." So among the gifts that came vicariously to Five-eagle, as the impersonator of Tezcatlipoca, there was a humble gift of love for him alone. But this is a tale of the stupendous lights and shadows that pass, not of those little ones of love and hate, forever found in human hearts.

When the sun rose after the feast of Huey Tozoztli, Five-eagle was installed in a royal house with many rooms and a wide court. Then the dancing that began with the sun ended with the paling stars. They dressed the hair of Five-eagle as if he were a leader in the army and they put new jewels upon him. When he went out into the streets of the city, the people knelt as he passed and bowed their heads and prayed. But in the temple many things were prepared behind the veil.

On the tenth day before the feasts of Toxcatl a priest in the common livery of the God of Magic stepped out into the market-place and, while the multitude of buyers and sellers stood in silent awe, he played a summons on his clay flute. The shrill notes were directed first to the east and then to the north and west and south, so that the universe might be aware. When the signal notes had died away, every one bent forward and, having taken a bit of earth upon a finger tip placed it in the mouth as a sign of humility and abnegation. Then they wept strongly and threw themselves upon the ground, invoking the darkness of nights, the invisible winds, and other unknowable manifestations through which the great god spoke, imploring that men upon the earth be not forgotten, nor overwhelmed with labors, nor left in misery and despair. And because the God of Magic could look into secret deeds and thoughts, the thieves and murderers and those whose deeds had been secret and sinful were struck with great fear and sadness, and their faces altered with fright so that men knew their guilt. With tears they pleaded for clemency to an intangible, invisible presence, while incense carried their prayers upward. And the strong men of war bowed themselves in great agonies and begged for strength against all enemies, that they might return from their forays with many captives. So the shrill notes of the flute opened the floodgates of fear throughout the great city and there were tremblings and tears. In the still air, threads of smoke rose upward; now they were white from fragrant copal, now black from evil-smelling rubber.

On the fifth day before the feast of Toxcatl, the high priest of Mexico that in those days was Tizoc, locked himself in an inner room of his palace while his courtiers bowed low and acknowledged Five-eagle as lord. A day of submission was granted to each quarter of the city, and with pomp and pageants the temporary powers of an empire were conferred upon the impersonator of Tezcatlipoca. And the grandeurs crowded into these days kept sorrow from the eyes of a love which could see too clearly.

Before dawn of the last day, the priests went into the temple and removed the old garments from the stone image of Tezcatlicopa and refurbished it with new clothes, and adorned it, moreover, with feather ornaments and bangles and spread over it a bright canopy. Then they drew back the curtains of the temple so that the world might see the hard and splendid image. As this was done, a high priest came out with flowers in his hand, and played again a summons addressed to the east and the north and the west and the south.

When the multitude had gathered in the principal court of the city, before the temple enclosure with its serpent walls, a procession formed behind Five-eagle and the stone image of the god and two priests who carried ladles of incense. Five-eagle was seated on a gorgeous litter carried high on the shoulders of men. Behind him rode the high priests of the cults of magic with their bodies painted black and their hair tied at the nape with white ribbons. Then a throng of youths and maidens, comprising those specially dedicated to a year's service in the temple of Tezcatlipoca, rushed forth with a rope of surprising whiteness in their hands, encircling with it the line of gorgeous litters. This rope was made up of threaded popcorn and was symbolical, so they say, of the thirstiness of the fields. The boys were dressed in mantles of open network, and the girls in new smocks with gay embroideries at neck and hem, but all of them wore necklaces of popcorn and turbans as well. Then the priests, leaning forward, took long strings of the white corn to wrap around their heads and to loop over the sides of the litters. Then the procession moved slowly forward over a road of green leaves strewn with flowers. On the ground, too, were strewn needle-like tips of the maguey with which many penitents perforated tongue and ears till they were bathed in blood that glistened horribly in the sunlight. And there were others in the long procession who lashed themselves with knotted cords. But such are the ways of frenzy whenever the souls of men are stirred in common.

It would prove over-tiresome should all the happenings of the marvelous day be related in full detail. There was a solemn sitting in state on the summit of the pyramid of Tezcatlipoca and before the door of the temple, where stood likewise the grim idol of stone, while complicated dances were being enacted in the court below. And Five-eagle, with a precise and certain artistry, wasted no moments of the triumph forecast at his birth and compromised in no feature his dignities and obligations.

The water pageant came at the end of the long, brilliant day when the sun was dropping towards the mountain crests. There was a long line of the largest canoes, laden with flowers and colored streamers and surmounted with awnings and sunshades. In the first of these Five-eagle sat erect on a royal seat with his brides beside him. The waters of the lake were calm, with pale reflections of gossamer clouds, and the boats struck a wide wake that found the distant reeds and willows.

Still there was laughter and gayety, but that one who in fantasy was a goddess of mountain crests had floating mists in her eyes while her lips formed a tremulous smile. On her black hair rested softly the hand of a lover, mortal at heart, but divine in a subtle play of mind over substance.

"O little Lady of the House of Mists, see how your white fogs cling to Ajusco, dropping dew on the cosmos flowers that Xochiquet-zalli loves."

"They are mists of a joyful sorrow, my Lord, they are mists of sorrow that obscure the world to-day that it may be fairer to-morrow."

"Then tell me that no shadows shall lie across your heart to-morrow when the fishing boats enter the canal at sunset. Tell me there shall be no shadows but only content in what has been, O my precious Lady of Mists."

"Youth of Toxcatl, there shall be no weeping."

At a rocky point called Tlapitzahuayan the procession of canoes came to land. Here the courtiers and the four brides of the Youth of Toxcatl took merry leave of him, and he set out with his six boys for Tlacuchcalco, a nearby ancient temple, neglected and unused except on this one occasion of the year. A winding trail led to a rocky field of cactus and acacia to a temple mound overrun with desert growths. A broken stair climbed upward to a crumbling sacrificial chamber whose doorway was nearly closed by yellow orchids and thorny vines. Behind this humble screen, the thirsty knife of the great Magician awaited its draft of blood. The boys of the retinue followed in the footsteps of Five-eagle, and from the shore rang out a last sally of uplifting laughter.

At the foot of the temple stairs they took from his shoulders the white mantle of the god who must be kept youthful at the cost of youth, and they unwrapped from his waist the gayly brocaded breechcloth, and they took from his feet the sandals, and from his ears the disks of apple-green jade, the last symbols of his year of earthly power. Only around his neck remained the necklace of flutes. He was a naked mortal, come, in the last humility of all men, to make the sincere gift of his life itself to a jealous and implacable god. With a gallant smile Five-eagle dismissed his pages and mounted the broken stairs; pausing on each step to break a flute between his two hands. Only a moment later and a human body, naked, horribly gaping at the breast, came crashing down the temple stairs, staining the brambles and the stones with blood.

.   .   .   .

We can know the Past only as a masquerade of the Present. We can imagine only those smells and colors which have come into our nostrils and have passed before our eyes. To-day there are no gods, you say, and it is true that terrible Siva and the sweet face of Christ fade back into the haze that covers unbelief.

Yet, to-day, how many a young Icarus plunges gladly to his death from dizzy heights. Does Necessity make us invade the airy kingdom of the birds or the green depths of the sea? Or are we driven to these conquests by the lusts and sincerities of a new commanding over-soul, built out of song and fellowship and ordered lives of work and play? For the harnessed Powers enslave their busy masters, and the new-found gods of Speed and Thrill count victims as freely offered as that Youth of Toxcatl, who bravely climbed to the bloody altar of his sacrifice in Tenochtitlan that is no more. The soul of the Machine comes forth to rule the prostrate nations that another age may see a strange mirage thrown upward on the pale mists of romance.

HERBERT SPINDEN

HOW HOLON CHAN
BECAME THE TRUE MAN
OF HIS PEOPLE

How Holon Chan Became The True Man of His People

A YOUTH of seventeen sat on the summit of the loftiest pyramid in the city, and gazed moodily out over the surrounding temples and palaces, and the thatched huts of the more lowly folk beyond, to the grasslands, which swept as far as the eye could reach in every direction.

He was naked save only for a sash-like cotton breechclout, so arranged that one end fell between his legs in front, the other in the same position behind, the ends being elaborately broidered with green feathers. A pendant of beautifully carved jade hung about his neck. Ear-plugs of the same material and sandals of deer hide with feather tassels completed his costume. In height he was under five feet and a half, slender, supple, small as to hands and feet, and a pleasing, warm golden brown in color. His eyes were black and narrow and in their placement somewhat slanting. His nose was aquiline and long, and merged into his flattened forehead in one straight line. During his babyhood his head had been bound between two boards to secure this very effect, an effect of beauty and distinction among his people. His hair was black, glossy and long. It was braided and then wrapped around his head except for a small queue which hung behind.

The time was the month of August 531 A. D.; the place, Tikal, the greatest metropolis of the Old Maya Empire; and the youth himself, no less a person than the ruler-to-be of the splendid city stretching at his feet, as well as of many smaller dependencies beyond the waste of grassy savannas which bounded his vision.

His discontent was of long standing and arose from a condition which he could not alter. His father, Ahmekat Chan, the preceding "True Man" of Tikal, had died two years before, leaving this boy, Holon Chan, as his sole surviving child and heir. The government of the state during the period of his minority had been carried on under the regency of his paternal uncle, Ahcuitok Chan, High Priest of Itzamna, aided by the powerful priesthood of this god, head of the Maya Pantheon; but now the people were clamoring for the

251

investiture of Holon Chan in the supreme office, so that certain of the highest ceremonies, which only the True Man might perform, could be celebrated once again, and indeed Ahcuitok Chan was only awaiting the conclusion of the current five-year period to invest his nephew as True Man of Tikal. Itzamna, Lord of Heaven, had indicated through the mouthpiece of his priests that this event should be solemnized on the closing day of this period, and preparations for it had now been going forward for some time.

Now the boy had little heart for his coming dignity. His had always been a roving nature; he was a child of the open air, a lover of the forest fastnesses and solitudes, better suited to the humble lot of wood gatherer or corn planter than to that of ruler of a people.

The great discoveries of the preceding century, of large and wonderfully fertile lands far to the north of his own domains, had fired his imagination, and he burned to lead his people to this new land of promise, where the gods were said always to smile, and the corn-fields to yield bountifully. Nor had these hopes always been without foundation. Once he had an older brother, named Chac Chan, who was to have succeeded their father as True Man, but while on a communal deer hunt, this brother had been bitten by a poisonous serpent, the deadly wolpuch, from whose bitter sting none ever recovered, and had died, leaving Holon Chan next in line of succession. And now the time was come when the exacting demands of his position, the elaborate ritual, which would fill his every hour, and the cares of the council chamber, would deprive him of every vestige of personal liberty.

The Maya people at this time, in Maya reckoning the close of Katin 18, were at once at the zenith of their power, and at the threshold of their decline. For generations now, the heavily forested lands which originally had surrounded their cities, towns and villages, had been gradually transformed under their primitive methods of cultivation into grassy savannas. This method of cultivation consisted in felling patches of the forests at the end of the rainy season in January or February, in burning the dried trees and bushes at the end of the dry season in March or April, and in planting after the first rains in May. The following year a new patch of forest was sought and the process repeated, nor was the first patch planted again for several years until a new growth of bush had come up, since experience showed that the use of the same cornfield two successive years would yield only a half crop the second year. This method of cultivation however, had two serious defects: not only was the greater part of the land thus always held idle, but also there eventually came a time when woody growth no longer came back to replace the original forests. Instead only perennial grasses would grow, and gradually the whole countryside was transformed into savannas. These savannas the Maya could not cultivate since they had no means of turning the sod, and they were thus obliged to go ever farther and farther from their homes in order to find suitable land for planting their corn. But the limit to which even this expedient was practicable had been reached at last. The cornfields now lay two, and even three days' journey from the cities, and people were beginning to lose faith in deities who permitted living conditions to remain so intolerable, and who either could not, or would not make possible the cultivation of the savannas.

Holon Chan was not the only one whose eyes turned ever more anxiously toward the north, to Yucatan, where life was said to be so easy, and Yum Kax, Lord of the Harvests, always so propitious; and many a humble corn planter had stolen away with his family through the great northern forests to this new land, in spite of the stringent laws against such a procedure. Both priesthood and nobility were strongly opposed to this disintegrating movement, and oracle as well as law was being invoked to prevent the abandonment of the country. But, despite threats of divine wrath and the swifter punishment of men, for the death penalty had been exacted more than once for this very offense, a steady stream of people was pouring out of the Old Empire region, northward into Yucatan; it was whispered for example, that the priests of Itzamna at the Holy City of Palenque could scarcely muster enough temple servants to till the fields of the god himself. This news could not be repeated openly, but more and more people were coming to believe that the old land was accursed and that the only salvation of their race lay in a general exodus to the north. Indeed every one saw that if some way was not speedily found to cultivate the grasslands, the people would be starved into moving elsewhere.

Meanwhile the priests were holding forth every inducement for greater piety and religious zeal. It was said that the people were lax in their offerings, and the gods were offended. The sacrifices must be redoubled. And latterly, with the approaching accession of Holon Chan as True Man, the auguries and oracles had foretold that this event would usher in a new era of abundance and prosperity, the like of which had never been before. The boy, the priests widely circulated, was born on a lucky day, of which Yum Kax, Lord of the Harvests, was the patron, and the death of his older brother, far from being a calamity, had been a direct intervention of the gods in order that the chosen of Yum Kax should sit in the council chamber and rule over them. Thus was the Lord of the Harvests to be appeased, and thus would prosperity return once more to the people. High hopes therefore were entertained for his rule, and while in other happier days, Holon Chan might possibly have been permitted to renounce in favor of his uncle, the times were too troublous, and the future too uncertain thus deliberately to offend the Harvest God.

Of all these things the boy had been thinking as he sat on the temple summit, watching the shadows lengthen over the glistening white walls of the city. Finally with a sigh he jumped to his feet. The sun was setting behind the distant savannas, a great, glowing, red disk, as Holon Chan turned to enter the sanctuary of Itzamna to sacrifice to the god. A single aged white-robed priest squatted in the outer corridor guarding the sanctuary, but since the boy always had the right of entry because of his rank, the old man scarcely looked up from his meditations as Holon Chan drew aside the elaborately embroidered cotton curtain and passed within.

The sanctuary was dark save only for such fitful light as came from a brazier of burning incense and two small windows not more than eight inches square, one at either end of the long narrow room. As the curtain fell behind him, the boy stooped to a shallow platter by the door, selected from it a small, round ball of incense, the gum of the copal tree, painted a brilliant peacock blue for ceremonial use, and advanced to the brazier. In the half light, a wooden image some eight feet high could be distinguished standing on a stone platform against the back wall. It was in the form of an old man, with prominent Roman nose, toothless lower jaw, and piercing green eyes, made of two discs of highly polished jade which caught and shot back the flickering light. The head was surmounted by an elaborate headdress carved in the likeness of the Plumed Serpent, and the whole figure was brilliantly painted in red, blue, yellow, green, white and black.   A necklace, breast-pendant, ear-plugs, anklets and wristlets of heavy, rich jade completed the costume of the image. Holon Chan placed his offerings on the brazier and prostrated himself before the image.   However disinclined he might be to follow the path Itzamna had chosen for him by removing his older brother from the line of succession, it never entered the boy's head to evade the responsibility thus thrust upon him.   He came of an old and distinguished family which had ruled the state of Tikal for more than four centuries.   From that distant ancestor of his, who had first led the people to their present home, down to his father, all had been brave men used to facing crises and shouldering responsibility, and this latest son of the Chan race had no other thought than to do likewise in the present emergency.   And so he prayed long and earnestly for wisdom to meet the many problems of the future, and above all for some means of alleviating the terrible agricultural problems which were threatening the very existence of his people.

The prayer over, Holon Chan left the sanctuary and, nodding to its aged guardian in the outer corridor, he prepared to descend the pyramid.   The swift twilight of the tropics had already dissolved into night.   Above, the stars blazed forth in the cloudless sky; below, the darkness was picked out here and there with little glowing points of red, the cooking fires of his people, who were busily preparing for the great ceremony of his investiture, now but three days distant.

Carefully picking his way down the steep stairway, Holon Chan crossed the broad, paved plaza at its base, and ascending a low terrace, entered a long building of cut stone, which had been the home of his family for generations.   It was a single story in height, more than two hundred feet long and three ranges of rooms in depth. These all had the typical Maya arched ceiling, were narrow and long, and lighted only by the exterior doorways and small, square windows about six feet above the floor.   The largest room in the palace, a chamber sixty feet long, ten feet wide, and eighteen feet high, was entered directly through the central doorway.   At one end was a raised stone platform with a wooden seat.   This was without a back and the arms were carved to represent jaguar heads.   Above there was a canopy of green featherwork. This was the council chamber of the state.

Through this chamber Holon Chan passed to the living quarters at the rear, and, clapping his hands, he summoned a slave to serve the evening meal to him as he sat cross-legged on the floor. Presently the slave returned bearing dishes of tortillas and black beans, a bush fowl, and a bowl containing an aromatic drink made of cacao. Holon Chan inquired for his uncle, and he was told that he was at the monastery of Itzamna. After eating, and rinsing out his mouth with water, a not-to-be-forgotten custom of gentlefolk, Holon Chan withdrew to his own room, and lying down on a bench covered with soft skins soon fell asleep.

Early the following morning, Holon Chan arose, and after a bath in a wooden tub, hollowed from a mahogany log, he dressed, but partook of no food, since custom decreed that he must fast throughout the period of his investiture. Thus he waited for his uncle to fetch him to the assembled priesthood of Itzamna. This first day of the induction ceremonies was to be given over exclusively to mental tests, quizzings by his uncle and the other priests of Itzamna, in the monastery of the god just behind his temple. It was proper for Holon Chan to appear before the priests without any emblem of rank, and presently when his uncle came to lead him thither, he was dressed as any other boy of his age, a simple breechclout encircling his loins, and leather sandals on his feet.

Of the many subjects Holon Chan was questioned about during that long day, we may only touch upon a few. First his uncle asked him to recite the complete ritual of the New Year's feast, one of the most important ceremonies of the Maya year. Other old wiseheads questioned him as to the stars, when would the next eclipses of the sun and moon take place, when would Venus next appear as evening star? Clean sheets of fiber paper were set before him, pigments and brushes were brought in, and he was told to write the current date, giving the phases of the moon therefor, and the presiding deity. All these tests he went through creditably, and the old men nodded approval. Next a fowl was brought and the boy was told to kill it and read the omens from its entrails. Again he acquitted himself with credit, and the old priests were satisfied with his knowledge of this important part of the Maya ritual.

In conclusion his uncle again took the lead, and put searching questions to him as to the condition of the people—how many heads of families were there in the tribe, and how many man-loads of corn were required to support the average family for a year? With which cities he should strive to ally himself, and which to avoid? How migration to Yucatan could best be discouraged? When the boy replied it could neither be discouraged nor prevented unless the Harvest Lord permitted corn to be grown on the savannas, a few of the older men shook their heads, but the great majority of the priests signified their approval of this sage answer. After these tests he was led from the monastery back to the palace, and later his uncle informed him that the priests had adjudged him to be worthy and well qualified to be made the True Man of the state.

The second day was even more strenuous than the first. The day was devoted to numerous rites of purification, in which by sweatings and blood-lettings he was supposed to be purged of all sin and wickedness, and thus fitted for the high office he was about to assume.

Following this the priests led him to the Temple of Purification. Here, in an inner chamber, he removed his clothes and crawled, naked, into a low stone closet. A bowl of water stood at the back of this low cell, and presently the priests passed in through the small doorway five or six large, rounded, heated stones wrapped in leaves. The doorway was now closed by a slab of stone, and Holon Chan dropped these heated bowlders, one at a time, into the bowl of water. Each succeeding bowlder raised the temperature of the water, and soon clouds of vapor filled the cell. From time to time more hot stones were passed in and the boy thus kept the water boiling. Beads of sweat broke out over his body; he almost suffocated, but still he served the steaming bowl with heated stones, and still the temperature rose. Every pore streamed and he gasped for breath. When it seemed as though he could stand it no longer, the slab was suddenly removed, the vapor rushed out and he was left panting and faint from the heat and his hunger, and the first step toward ceremonial purification was over.

Next they gave him a violent emetic, which left him completely prostrated from weakness. With the characteristic stoicism of his race, however, he uttered no complaint, but presently gained sufficient strength to pass on to the next trial, a cruel and painful

letting of blood.   His uncle bade him put out his tongue and through
the end of it, he thrust a sharp stone awl.   Waiting priests caught
the blood on little balls of cotton and these were borne off to the
sanctuary of Itzamna as an earnest of his faith and purification.   At
sunset a small fiber cord with thorns caught in it every few inches
was passed through the still open wound, cruelly lacerating the
flesh, and fresh blood drawn to offer to the god in renewed proof
of his constancy of purpose.   That night Holon Chan was so exhausted that he slept without stirring, until awakened before dawn
to prepare himself for the long day of meditation and prayer in the
sanctuary of Itzamna which preceded the actual investiture at
sunset.

Preparations for this ceremony had been going forward now for
a long time.   It has been told how Itzamna had indicated that the
investiture of the new True Man must coincide with the unveiling
of the great stone shaft which had been erected to commemorate
the end of the current five-year period of the Maya Chronological
Era.   As much as a year before, this shaft had been quarried, transported to the Great Plaza of Tikal, set up there and a high fence
of thatch built around it to conceal it from the people until the moment of its unveiling.

Ahcuitok Chan in consultation with the most learned astrologer
priests of the state had carefully calculated what would be the
nearest solar and lunar eclipses to the day of dedication (then still
nearly a year ahead).   Other astronomical phenomena important
during the current five-year period, had been compiled, together
with a record of the principal events of the period.   These matters
had been written down in the Maya hieroglyphic writing, on pieces
of fiber paper coated with a sizing of fine white lime, which served
as working drawings for the artisans who were to carve the shaft;
and finally the likeness of Holon Chan himself, gorgeously appar-
eled as he would be at the ceremony of investiture, had been laboriously carved on the front.   This monument, which was to mark the
ending of the current five-year period, 9.18.0.0.0. 11 Ahau 18 Mac
of the Maya Era, was at last ready, and would be unveiled at the
proper moment, namely the instant of sunset on the closing day of
the period.   This had to be so, since to the Maya, time was conceived and measured in terms of elapsed units (like our own astro-

nomical time), and not until the final day of the period came to its end, that is at sunset on the last day, could the monument commemorating that period be formally dedicated thereto.

But now all was in readiness for the great festival, upon which, as has been noted, so many and such high hopes had been builded. For the past several days, people had been pouring into Tikal. From the farthest outlying villages men, women and children were moving toward the religious and governmental center of the state. The surrounding savannas were filled with temporary shelters of thatch, and booths had sprung up everywhere for the barter of tortillas, beans, squash, sapotes, cacao, bush meats, gourds, pottery, mats, featherwork, hides, cotton stuffs, and even beads and pendants of jade, the most highly prized of all materials by the Maya.

The Great Plaza of Tikal had been filling with people since midnight, eager to catch the first glimpse of their future ruler as he was being conducted at daybreak to the sanctuary of Itzamna for prayer and meditation. His learning tried and tested by the wise men of the state on the first day; his body purged of sin and wickedness by rites of purification, and his fortitude and earnestness of purpose established by his giving of blood to Itzamna on the second day, there remained only that he should cleanse his soul of any lurking grossness, by prayer and meditation, and he would then be ready for the most solemn moment of his life, his formal consecration as the True Man of his people.

After rising, Holon Chan bathed, and donned again the simple girdle worn by common folk, in token that he had not yet received the supreme rank, and passed into the council chamber. Here all the great dignitaries of the state, the high priests of the different Maya deities, the chieftains of the dependent towns and villages, the collectors of taxes, deputies, and other officials had assembled in gala costume—magnificent cloaks of featherwork, gorgeous panaches of plumes, mantles of deer hide, heavy necklaces, pendants, earplugs, wristlets and anklets of jade—each in his bravest display. Naked male slaves stood about the council chamber with lighted torches of fat pine in their hands, for the hour of dawn had not yet come, and these cast a fitful light over the company. Outside on the terrace, in front of the palace, the musicians were assembled with long, wooden drums, rattles and flageolets.

High on the topmost point of the roof of the sanctuary of Itzamna stood a priest scanning the eastern horizon for the first sign of the orb of day. As dawn approached, the multitude stirred faintly and with common consent all eyes turned to the portals of the palace. Slaves with short staves were seen to open a passage through the crowd and stand on either side to keep the way cleared. Suddenly a piercing cry falls from above. "Lo, the Lord of Day cometh." The musicians strike up, and move in ordered rank down the terrace stairway and across the plaza. First come temple boys with brooms, sweeping the way, followed by others swinging braziers of incense from which clouds of heavy, black, aromatic smoke wreath upward. Next appear the temple chanters clad in white, singing an ode of welcome to the Lord of Day; next, a troop of the palace guard in quilted cotton armor, armed with stone-pointed javelins and shields of skin. Following these are the lords of the dependent towns and villages, and the higher civil officers of the state; these last, with their gorgeous cloaks of featherwork, furnishing the brightest spot of color in the procession. Next are the lower orders of the priesthood of Itzamna, a long file of white-robed figures moving slowly forward.

Now Ahcuitok Chan leaves the palace surrounded by the higher priestly dignitaries. He is magnificently dressed, a cloak of rich featherwork hanging from his shoulders and falling over the jaguar skin draped around his body. His jade necklace is a work of art, beautifully carved human heads hanging in front and back, and over each shoulder. Delicate, tendril-like feathers of the quetzal, the royal emblem, hang from a brilliantly painted wooden helmet carved to represent a serpent head, the patronymic of his family, Chan. Indeed he wears all the insignia of the True Man save only the Double-headed Ceremonial Bar which ancient practice decrees may only be borne by the True Man himself. Follows last the simply clad boy of seventeen in whose honor all have assembled.

The procession moves slowly across the plaza and ascends the steep stairway to the sanctuary of Itzamna above. The musicians, sweepers, incensers and chanters take positions on either side of the temple doorway on the summit of the pyramid, now bathed in the first rays of the rising sun. The soldiers form a double cordon on each side of the stairway from bottom to top, between which the rest of the procession passes, dividing at the top and arranging itself on either side of the doorway. Even Ahcuitok waits at the entrance for his nephew, and when the boy has at last reached the summit, he takes his hand and leads him within, followed only by the highest officers and priests.

The crowd now dispersed since nothing visible to the eye of the common folk would be going forward until the close of the afternoon, although within the sanctuary itself the ceremony would be continued all day. When the higher officers of the state had all assembled in the outer corridor of the temple, Ahcuitok Chan, still leading his nephew by the hand, approached the curtain guarding the sanctuary, and drew it aside, at the same time motioning the boy to enter. After Holon Chan had passed within, Ahcuitok Chan let the curtain fall behind him and seated himself on his haunches outside the doorway, all the others arranging themselves about the chamber in the same position.

Now followed a long and wearisome vigil both for those without the curtain and for the hungry tired boy within. Etiquette proscribed conversation lest it should interrupt the devotions of the suppliant in the sanctuary, and time hung heavy, as the hours dragged by.

All day long Holon Chan prayed to his father Itzamna in the semi-obscurity of the holy place, leaving his orisons only long enough to replenish the brazier with little balls of incense or quench his thirst from a bowl of water by the door. He had now fasted so long that he was light-headed, and it seemed to him that at times the wooden image of the god smiled down upon him, even answered his prayers for guidance and gave him counsel; at least so he told his uncle when the latter came to fetch him for the investiture an hour before sunset. But this one was a wise old man, well acquainted with the frailty of the flesh and the hallucinations born of an empty stomach, and he only nodded wisely, and did not press for further particulars.

In the outer corridor all was astir for the final act of the great drama. As Holon Chan stepped out of the sanctuary all prostrated themselves in obeisance. A priest now stepped forward, and painted his legs, arms and torso with a bright red pigment, encircling his eyes with a heavy band of the same color, and adding a large red daub to each cheek. His plain breechclout was now removed, and a heavily embroidered one wound around his loins instead. Next anklets and wristlets of jade were fastened around his ankles and wrists, and a heavy collar of the same material hung about his neck. This was richly embellished with four large medallions of jade, one in front, one behind, and one over each shoulder, beautifully carved to represent the human face; a fringe of smaller jade heads hung from the collar. Square jade ear-plugs were fitted into the lobes of his ears, and a jade ring slipped on his finger. These were, in truth, the state jewels; precious material gathered by succeeding generations of True Men to adorn their own persons.

A magnificent jaguar skin, tawny orange-red dappled with rosettes of black, was hung from his shoulders, the long tail dragging on the ground. Finally the serpent crown was placed upon his head. This was an ornate affair of cedar carved to represent the head of a snake with widely distended mouth. It was painted a brilliant green, the mouth being red; the eyes were formed by two pieces of highly polished, jet-black obsidian, the teeth being inset pieces of white shell. From the head of the snake rose a shower of quetzal plumes, the tail feathers of an hundred of these rare tropical birds, obtained with infinite hardships from the cold mountain ranges far to the South. These delicate tendrils of plumage floated down behind the boy, and as the evening breeze caught them, swirled around him, enveloping his body in a mist of translucent green.

The hour of sunset was at last drawing near. The priest on the roof of the temple above shouted down a warning that the Lord of the Day was nearing the horizon. The Great Plaza and its surrounding terraces had, in the meantime, filled with people; every pyramid-stairway and summit thronged with spectators. A body of priests had taken positions by the thatched fence around the monument, ready to fell it at the instant of sunset. All the officers of state and the priests, including Ahcuitok Chan, indeed all save only Holon Chan himself passed out of the temple, and arranged themselves on either side of the doorway. Before Ahcuitok Chan, stood two priests supporting a brilliantly painted wooden staff; one end carved to represent the Sun God, the other end, the Rain God, the whole shaft being hung with green feathers. This was the Double-headed Ceremonial Bar, the emblem of supreme authority of the state, only to be carried by the True Man.   Throughout his regency even Ahcuitok Chan had never used this insignia of the highest office.

The sun was now all but touching the horizon; the watcher above uttered a piercing cry, and the multitude below stiffened to attention. Sixty silent seconds passed and then the watching priest chanted: "Lo, the Lord of Day passeth."   Suddenly from the temple doorway into the full radiance of the setting sun, now gilding the brilliant company gathered on the pyramid's summit, stepped the new ruler, resplendent in the flashing green of jade against his crimson body, his cloak of glossy jaguar skin gleaming in the sun, his form swathed in a shimmering mist of green, the swirling tendrils of quetzal hanging from his headdress.

A mighty roar of acclaim loosed itself from the spectators below. The drums on the summit pealed a roll of welcome.   At the same instant the fence of thatch around the monument was beaten to the ground; the sun, striking at last fair upon its front, made glow every detail of carving.   From the True Man above, to his exact counterpart sculptured on the front of the newly unveiled monument below, every eye turned and turned again.   The mighty cheer continued. The chosen of Itzamna and Yum Kax, he who would bring back fertility to their sterile fields, was at last proclaimed ruler.   Ahcuitok Chan took the Ceremonial Bar from the waiting priests and, advancing to his nephew, placed it horizontally in his outstretched arms: "Hail, Ah Holon Chan, son of Ahmeket Chan!   I invest thee with the rank of True Man of Tikal, and may the Great Itzamna grant thee long life, and to thy people prosperity everlasting!"

Ah Holon Chan, no longer a boy, and now entitled to a man's designation (the male prefix Ah) advanced to the edge of the pyramid and, raising the Ceremonial Bar, signaled for silence.   A profound hush fell upon the multitude.

"Oh People of my blood, my single purpose, my single thought from this moment henceforth till the Father of Heaven, Great Itzamna, calls me hence, shall be your welfare.   May the Lord of Life guide me through the perils which beset our race, and endow me with wisdom to rule you justly and well, and above all to find that way which once again will bring prosperity and abundance to our failing fields.   Oh People of my blood, accept this my solemn vow of consecration to your service."

The sun had set, a rosy afterglow enveloped the boy in a haze of mysterious light. It seemed, to the breathless thousands in the plaza below, as though the Lord of Life were actually infusing the new ruler with that wisdom for which he had so earnestly prayed. Profound silence reigned. Swiftly the twilight fell. A few stars began to twinkle through the sky. At last in the gathering gloom the boy was seen to turn and pass within the temple. And then the multitude began to melt away until the court was empty. . . .

SYLVANUS G. MORLEY

THE TOLTEC ARCHITECTURE OF CHICHEN ITZA

The Toltec Architect of Chichen Itza

THE battle is over, the once glorious Chichen Itza has fallen and all because of the love of a woman. Hunac-eel, the king of Mayapan, the conqueror, is being borne into the ruined city. There are no shouts of welcome, no crowds gathered on the tops of such buildings as have escaped destruction. Many of the former citizens have been killed, others are held prisoners, later to be enslaved, and still others have fled far to the southwards to find a resting place in Peten Itza.

Chac-xib-chac, the king of Chichen Itza, had fallen on the field of battle, fighting for his bride. She was also of noble lineage and it was she whom Hunac-eel had dared to desire, although she was the bride of his friend and ally in the famous League of Mayapan which now was to be disrupted after an existence of two hundred years.

The wedding of Chac-xib-chac and Tibil had been marked by the pomp and luxury customary in royal marriages of the Mayas. There had been games and dancing, feasting and song. The kings of Mayapan, Uxmal, Izamal and the other kingdoms of Yucatan, had been present. Chichen was in gala dress. The festivities were at their height when, without warning, Hunac-eel and his followers from Mayapan rushed up the broad but steep stairway of the royal residence and burst into the very chamber of Chac-xib-chac and his bride. His retainers, worn out by too much feasting, had made but a feeble resistance. Hunac-eel fled with the reluctant bride to his home at Mayapan.

There followed a long and devastating war. Chac-xib-chac had been able to induce all the surrounding kingdoms except that of the Xius to join his forces. The Xius alone remained neutral. Hunac-eel, on seeing the hosts against him, had called to his aid a body of Mexican warriors who happened to be in Tabasco. The war raged for many years. Izamal was conquered, and one after another of the famous cities fell into the power of Hunac-eel and his foreign allies. Finally he attacked Chichen itself, killed Chac-xib-chac, and, aided by the novel machines of war of the Mexicans, sacked the city.

And now, the conqueror was making his triumphal entry. His son, also the son of Tibil, accompanied him, a youth just arriving at manhood. There was also in the train of Hunac-eel a young Mexican named Pantemitl. Pantemitl had been trained as a warrior, but his activities had taken a more peaceful turn. He had had a minor part in the erection of the great Temple of the Sun, at Teotihuacan in his homeland. Hunac-eel had recognized the young man's abilities as an artist and architect; he was just such a man as Hunac-eel needed in order to carry out his plan of building a greater and more glorious Chichen.

Hunac-eel soon returned to Mayapan, leaving behind him Taxcal, his son, and installing a Governor to rule the city.

Taxcal and Pantemitl, the young architect, soon became the greatest of friends. Pantemitl was engaged in building a wonderful temple, erected on a high pyramid, with stairways on the four sides. He had brought with him the ideas of his country which were new to Yucatan. He had carvings of the feathered serpent made for the entrance to the temple and for one of the great stone stairways. The people of Chichen marveled at the art of the foreign country which was blossoming in their city.

Among the inhabitants, of whom many were serving as slaves to the usurpers, was a worker in jade. The beauty of his carvings had brought him renown. His craftsmanship was unequalled in all the country. It was he who was called upon to furnish all the head and breast ornaments and beads, for the regalia of those who impersonated the gods of the Mayas in the festivals which came every twenty days. With his daughter the old jade worker lived in a thatched hut on the outskirts of the city. The girl was beautiful. Her frame was small, and she had bright brown eyes with features sharp and finely chiselled. There was a subtle refinement about her which is common even to-day to all Maya women, especially when they are young. Nicte, the Flower, was a dutiful daughter and when she was not grinding maize she liked to spend her time sharpening the stone tools, and collecting the reeds needed by her father in his jade work. Like the other women, she took little part in the great religious spectacles performed so frequently in the temples. And now more than ever her father kept her at home, for he feared lest by chance she be selected as an offering to the new gods, introduced by the Toltecs who had come to the city in the armies of Hunac-eel. However her beauty attracted the attention of Pantemitl when he came to visit her father, who was making the jade and obsidian eyes for the many figures of the feathered serpent set up by the young artist.

Pantemitl was about to complete a wonderful Ball Court at Chichen, for the game of tlachtli which formed a part of the religious life of the Mexicans. The people of Chichen looked with favor at the introduction of this game into their city, as they were fond of spectacles. The court consisted of two massive and parallel walls of masonry. Near the top and at the center of each wall there projected a stone ring which was carved with the feathered serpent design. But the court itself was a very small part of the whole undertaking. There were two beautiful temples at either end, and the most wonderful of all buildings on the top and at the end of one of the walls. The outside was decorated with friezes of tigers alternating with shields. The portico of the building was borne by two serpent columns with a stone altar between, consisting of fifteen carved and painted human figures, supporting in their upturned hands a flat stone as a table. The stone jambs of the doorway were carved with warriors and the carved wooden lintel had the Sun God upon it. Inside the temple itself Pantemitl painted the scenes of the battles of Hunac-eel and his enemies. He introduced into this fresco also many scenes of domestic life; he had even dared to paint in women and the very house of Nicte. This was sacrilegious according to the ideas of Taxcal who believed that women should not be represented in a temple of the gods, as they had no part to play in the religion of his fathers.

Now Taxcal, too, had seen Nicte and had begun to covet her. His friendship for Pantemitl had given place to rivalry and bitter enmity. The quarrel had reached the ears of the Governor of Chichen who was forced to take cognizance of it as it was interfering with the completion of the architectural work. The Governor's position was difficult. He feared the wrath of the king and yet he hesitated to take the side of Taxcal as the people had made Pantemitl, the Toltec, a hero on account of the part he was playing in rebuilding their city. Besides, the Governor had learned that Hunac-eel was being surrounded in his city by the Cocomes, descendants of the Itzas themselves. As these people were conquering everything before them, perhaps Hunac-eel was no longer to be feared.

The decision of the Governor was to let the gods solve the outcome of the quarrel. He ordered the two rivals to play the first game of tlachtli in the inauguration of the new court. The gods of the Ball Court would determine the victory; their solution would be a just one. It was decided, therefore, that the winner of the game could claim the jade worker's daughter as his prize. The other should be given to the gods, his heart cut out and offered to their images. This practice, so common in Mexico, was comparatively unknown in Yucatan. Here was a chance, thought the Governor, of providing a worthy sacrifice to the new gods.

Each youth eagerly accepted the wager of gaming for their gods and Nicte. As for Nicte, she was virtually a slave, her choice in the matter played no part. And yet she was inclined strongly toward the prince, a man of her own race, as against Pantemitl, the foreigner.

The day dawned for the inauguration of the Ball Court. News had gone out of the unusual circumstances connected with the first game. People were coming from all the surrounding towns, even from Itzamal, many leagues distant. The usual stakes were mantles, gold, and jade ornaments, but sometimes men played themselves into slavery. To-day the loser is to give his very life. The crowd line the top of the massive walls, the Governor and his suite sit in the portico of the Temple of the Tigers, other dignitaries fill the two small temples at either end. Sacrifices are made to the gods of the Ball Court in these three temples. There are songs and dances in the court itself, by gayly dressed youths. Priests in the superb regalia of their offices are entering the enclosure in solemn procession. Prayers are offered and the ball is thrown about the court four times in the direction of the four points of the compass.

The two young men, each with five friends as fellow players, enter the court. A hush falls on the multitude, followed by a murmur of admiration when they see the stalwart youths, their bodies glistening with paint, and their breechclouts covered with gold and jade ornaments. Pantemitl is the favorite in the betting, as he it is who has caused Chichen to rise again as a city second to none in the whole peninsula. Taxcal and his players have the rubber ball, bouncing it steadily down the court towards the ring of their adversaries.

The ball hovers a moment at the hole but falls back again. It lands squarely on the hip of Pantemitl, who leaps high into the air to receive it. He and his fellow players have had long practice with the game in Mexico and this fact now begins to show itself. Pante-mitl bounces the ball to a companion, and from one to the other it quickly passes until he finally receives it again, directly in front of the ring of his opponents. With great dexterity he throws it squarely through the hole and the game is ended.

According to the rules, the mantles of the spectators belonged to the victor but on this occasion none rushed from the court. All were preoccupied with the tragic ending of the game. For Taxcal had fallen exhausted at the feet of Pantemitl who raised him and carried him to the Tiger Temple. Here the Governor received them. Taxcal's father was no longer to be feared, as word had come that he had been driven out of his city by the Cocomes. By sacrificing the son of Hunac-eel the Governor realizes that he will curry favor with the new conquerors of Mayapan.

The Governor decides, therefore, to have the sacrifice at once. Priests are dispatched to prepare for the ceremony in the portico of the famous Pyramid Temple, hardly a stone's throw from the Ball Court. The sacrificial stone is ready to receive its offering, and Taxcal is a youth without a blemish, as demanded by the gods. Resistless, he allows himself to be arrayed in the magnificent robes of sacrifice. He is regaled with incense from vases of burning copal, and is almost buried in flowers. Pages follow him in the procession of priests as they wind their way up the hundred steps of the pyramid. According to Mexican custom, believed to be the impersonation of a god, he is treated with all possible honor and respect.

At the top of the staircase, relinquishing his flowers and his mantles, he is received by six priests with locks matted with the blood of previous victims, their ears hanging in long strips where they have been cut as acts of penance. Led to the sacrificial stone, he is thrown on his back upon it. Five priests hold his arms and legs while the sixth, clad in a scarlet mantle, dexterously opens his breast with the famous sacrificial knife, its wooden handle carved with the intertwined bodies of two serpents. Inserting his hand into the wound, he tears out the palpitating heart. Holding it first toward the setting sun, he casts it at the feet of the image of the god to whom the temple is dedicated.

When Pantemitl next made his way to the jade maker's hut he heard from a distance singing and wailing, and was surprised to see crowds of people gathered. Presently he learned with horror that his beloved Nicte had offered herself for sacrifice. She had announced that she too would die, a sacrifice to the gods, in the sacred well of the Itzas.

Priests were already preparing the ceremonies. The sixty days of fasting had begun. Gifts and incense were brought and Nicte, lying on her couch, was being dressed in white robes and garlanded with flowers. In despair and contrition, Pantemitl spent the time in his Tiger Temple, painting over the door of the frescoed chamber the scene of the sacrifice of his rival. In the chamber behind the temple he carved scenes of warriors and civilians paying homage to the God of the Feathered Serpent. These he hoped would find favor with the gods and free him from his unhappy feelings.

The Cenote of Sacrifice, a huge natural well, was situated only a short distance from the temple which had been the scene of the death of Taxcal. Into the cenote the most precious possessions of the people were thrown as offerings to the gods. Virgins were considered especially welcome to the gods and the dark waters, three score feet from the surface, held many victims.

At the break of the sixtieth day, the procession starts from the house of the jade cutter. Numberless bowls of copal incense, incrusted with amulets, are burned, carved wooden staffs, with heads made of stone mosaics or covered with gold masks, are being carried by the priests, all to be thrown into the dark waters. The maiden herself is dressed in finely woven textiles, heavily ornamented with golden bells and jade beads. She wears on her breast a gold plaque on which the sacrifice of her lover is depicted. Nicte is to die for the love of Taxcal, but to all the others it is an act of supreme devotion to the gods.

The procession winds its way to the Great Pyramid and from there a broad avenue, lined with images, leads to the Cenote of Sacrifice. As the band of worshipers are encircling the holy well, the priests with the maiden take their places in the small temple directly at the brink. More incense is burned and the precious offerings are thrown into the water, with prayers and songs in praise of the gods of the cenote. In the silence which follows, the main actors reach the roof of the temple whence, in a few moments, the maiden is cast into the depths beneath. As the ripples widen out to the edges of the great pool, prayers are chanted supplicating the gods to receive graciously the offering. . . .

Worn out with work and with sorrow, Pantemitl could stand the strain no longer, and he sickened and died. Just before his death he completed a small replica of the Pyramid Temple planned to receive the ashes of the poor queen, the mother of Taxcal, Tibil, who had requested that she be buried in the city of her fathers.

The death of Pantemitl cast the city into mourning. His great achievements had made of him a hero. His masterpiece, the Pyramid Tomb, was completed, and the people demanded that this beautiful temple with its crypt be made the tomb of its architect. Offerings from all covered the pyre on which his body was burned. His last wish was that the ashes of Taxcal should be mingled with his. . . . The final rite is about to begin. A beautiful alabaster jar, one of the most precious possessions of the city, a gift from a visiting monarch from a distant country, is carried in the procession of priests to the top of the Pyramid Tomb. It holds the ashes of Pantemitl and of Taxcal. Reverently the vase, surrounded by offerings of jade, is lowered from the floor of the temple through the stone-lined shaft until it rests in the natural chamber below the mound.

ALFRED M. TOZZER

WIXI *of the* SHELL-MOUND PEOPLE

Wixi of the Shellmound People

ON THE BEACH

"HERE'S another! Here's another! Here's another!"

It is the excited voice of a naked, gesticulating youngster, little more than three years old, who is pointing to a tiny hole in the smooth surface of the tide beach at his feet.

"Yes, yes, child, I am coming," is the reply, in soft, affectionate tones, by a woman a few steps away.

"But I am hungry, I am hungry," comes the insistent, half-petulant voice.

"Well, you can't have any clams now, you know. Mark the one you have and run along to find some more. Soon we shall go home."

At this the child stoops unsteadily and with a rough, pointed splinter of bone draws a circle around the hole, then patters away along the wet beach.

Presently his mother comes forward, with a rough basket in one hand and a short, stout, pointed stick in the other. She is barefooted and bareheaded. Her only garment is a sort of skirt made of loose bark strands, reaching from the waist to the knees. Her heavy, glistening, black hair is fastened in two locks hanging down in front, partially covering her breasts. Her complexion, a shade darker than that of the child, is the color of a smoked, reddish brick or of a certain shade of Oriental bronze. Scarcely more than twenty years old, she has a fine, comely figure.

Having reached the spot indicated by the child, the young woman sets the basket down. Then, grasping the stick with both hands, she drives it into the firm beach mud and with a single, deft, prying motion brings to the surface a good-sized clam. She picks it up, throws it into the partly filled basket, and proceeds a few steps to where the child is calling her anew.

Similar scenes are being enacted on every hand. Women and children, numbering close to one hundred in all, are scattered along the beach for nearly half a mile; a hundred yards or so beyond there is another, somewhat smaller group. In both groups the women and older children are busy with the digging-stick, while the younger children run about over the beach locating the clams. Presently there is a curious splash near the edge of the receding waters. The splash is repeated once or twice and with it a chorus of voices rings out.

"Wixi! Wixi!" (Stingaree! Stingaree!)

A dozen or so half-grown children come running from different directions, all shouting vehemently, "He's mine! He's mine! I saw him first! I saw him first!"

There is nothing actually to be seen, except perhaps a small area immediately off shore where the water is unusually muddy. Into the water the children rush, keeping clear of the roiled spot, and when ranged partly around it on the sea side, they begin to poke into it with their sticks. Very soon there is another violent splash and a large, monstrous looking creature is seen to lift itself almost bodily out of the shallow water.

"Wixi! Wixi! We've got you!" shouts the chorus. "We've got you!"

The steadily receding water soon reveals the cause of the excitement—an extra large eagle ray, a kind of flat-fish, in outline something like an immense butterfly, plus a long whip-like tail, near the root of which appears a sharply-pronged, bony excrescence which can inflict a severe wound. Wixi is an ugly fellow, and as he lies there in two or three inches of water, flopping spasmodically, lashing his tail viciously from side to side, the children plant their sticks firmly in the ground, making a sort of fence around him, while they stand back out of reach. But, the moment the monster subsides, all pound and punch with their sticks, screaming and carrying on like a pack of fighting dogs. Finally, the oldest of the children, a girl of ten or eleven, manages to insert her digging-stick in the creature's eye. A few violent lashings, and the ray lies still.

The girl remains leaning on the stick, holding the great fish firmly transfixed. The other children fall over each other in a scramble to get near it. All seek to pierce the dead body with their sticks and to pull it away. But their implements are too weak and dull. Some grasp with their fingers at the slimy thing, but to no avail. The girl stands unmoved.

In their rage some of the children suddenly turn upon her. In an effort to defend herself, she lets go her stick, and at the same moment the big ray is pulled away, but not by any of the original claimants. During the tumult a boy of thirteen or fourteen had approached unnoticed from the larger group of clam gatherers, and had wound the tail of the ray two or three times around his hand. Now when the girl's hold on the stick is released, he jerks the ray away and starts to run as fast as his legs can carry him toward his own people, the body of the big fish dragging behind him over the slippery mud.

There is a tremendous uproar. Some of the children attempt to follow, but they are soon outdistanced. The girl who killed the ray, finally realizing what has happened, bursts out: "You took my wixi! You took my wixi! You—wixi! You—!" Her voice chokes with sobs. But her epithet is taken up by a chorus of voices in both groups of clam diggers, those of Kawina and those of Akalan: "You wixi! You wixi!"

But the boy pays no heed. When he reaches the shore proper, he winds the ray's tail a few more times around his hand, swings the immense body over his shoulders, and disappears among the marsh weeds in the direction of his home.

Wixi! Wixi! Thus the boy is nicknamed for life.

AT BREAKFAST

It is still early morning on San Francisco Bay. The tide is going out, and the sun, just topping the eastern hills, is reflected in the placid waters as in a great oval mirror. On the horizon beyond the expanse of the waters of the bay, the sunlight glitters on the snowy summit of Mt. Hamilton; to the left, looms the hazy outline of Mt. Diablo; and to the right, glorious in the clear sunlight, stands green-clad Mt. Tamalpais, guarding the entrance to the broad channel heading north into San Pablo Bay. The surface of the channel is slightly choppy, because here passes out to sea the collected volume of the great rivers that drain the interior mountains and valleys. The shore of the bay is low and marshy, lying in sweeping curves. Along these curves faint blue smokes rise at intervals against the shadowy background of the hills. These smokes mark settlements, of which there are along the entire bay shore about two hundred, strung like pearls on a necklace.

In one of the curving arms of the bay, smoke ascends from a grayish spot in the marshland, some three hundred yards back of the shore line. It is the village of Kawina. Four miles farther east, directly on the water front, lies the village of Akalan. Beyond that the shore line turns, and other settlements hug the shore at every point where a fresh water streamlet empties into the bay.

The clam diggers are straggling along the beach toward home. A number of young men from Akalan have gone to the head of the cove a few rods away. They are engaged in dragging a dozen or more curiously shaped bundles of dried tule-rushes down the muddy slope to the tide channel, which drains the extensive marshes ranging along the entire east base of the potrero. When the clam gatherers left home the channel was dry, but the tide already is fast returning and the breakfast bringers have to be assisted across.

It is a lively, not to say noisy, occasion. The older children glide down the slippery mud into the water, and flounder across amidst laughter and shouting. Only the women with their baskets, and the smaller children cross by ferry; for these tule bundles are boats or, rather, floats. Some of them carry only from four to six persons, others as many as fifteen. The ferrying proceeds rather slowly, to the lively chatter of the women. The children have run on ahead, up the grassy incline to the village.

The grass suddenly ceases at the foot of a blackish eminence on which the village stands. The eminence is about twenty feet high and of an irregular contour, the slope in places being gradual, in others steep, while the top is roughly flattened. On approaching nearer, the whole mound-like structure appears to be composed of the shells of clams, mussels, and oysters. There is an occasional brightly colored abalone shell. Here and there are scattered pairs of deer antlers, and the wing bones of ducks, geese, and other birds with feathers still attached. Crushed or broken bones of various animals lie everywhere. And there are fish bones. Flies are swarming about; the odor is far from enticing. Closer inspection would reveal the presence of ashes and charcoal, as well as a goodly number of bowlders and pebbles of crackly surface. The impression is that of a huge ash pile or refuse heap. And yet on top of it all stands the village!

The village is an irregularly grouped cluster of about thirty hive-shaped huts, with openings facing either south or east. The huts themselves are constructed on a framework of slender poles set in circles from twelve to sixteen feet in diameter, the top ends being bent together and intertwined some eight or nine feet above the ground. Over this is placed a layer of twigs and grass, and this again is covered with earth and sod. Only the top is left open for the exit of smoke. This morning, however, the fires are out in front of the doors, each family having its own.

A number of fair-sized bowlders form a ring around the edge of the dying embers. Ranged about each of these circles, within reaching distance, are seated the members of the family. Even the older men, who do not condescend often to eat with the women and children, are present. They are mostly grizzled, ill-kempt, sluggish looking fellows, who have barely had time to rub the sleep out of their eyes. Through the rainy winter months they have been comparatively inactive, the women have been doing the work; but now it is April and the warmth of spring is bringing them out of their hibernation. Soon they will be off for the entire summer, and fall to leading an active life among the hills where food is not so easily obtained as it is on the bay shore, though it can be had in greater variety if all hands, including the men, make the effort.

The clams brought in from the beach are being distributed, and the older folk place them, just as they are, on the hot rocks around the fire. The smaller children watch intently and yet uneasily, having repeatedly been scolded for poking their fingers against the sizzling shellfish lying nearest on the rocks. Suddenly some of the clams open up, ready to eat. They have been cooked in the most admirable fashion in their own juice. In the group around the fire, next to one of the rear huts, are seated a very old man, a middle-aged woman, two children, and a half-grown boy. It is the boy Wixi, who has just proposed to his mother to boil some of the fish.

"Boiled fish! Boiled fish! Who ever heard of boiled fish?" blurts out the old man in a cracked voice. He is blind, or nearly so, judging from his dull, deeply sunken eyes. His hair, as well as his straggly beard, is white, and his face and neck are seamed and wrinkly, suggestive of tanned alligator skin. His body is thin and frail, his hands shaking.

"Well, fish *could* be boiled," Wixi retorts. "You boil acorn meal and you boil buckeye meal and you boil lots of things. Why couldn't you boil fish?"

"Why couldn't you boil fish? Why couldn't you boil fish?" the old man screams, his whole frame trembling. "You couldn't boil fish because—because nobody ever did such a thing! Chakalli didn't tell us to boil fish."

This sort of dispute has been an almost daily occurrence for many moons, since the time of the boy's initiation ceremony, when he began to assume the responsibilities of manhood. His father, as Wixi would say, is away. A shaman, he had failed to cure the poisoned wound of a certain chief, and he had been quietly waylaid on the trail. Since then, his family had had to suffer partial disgrace.

That was some years ago, and the boy, thrown thus early upon his own resources, had learned through stress of circumstances to practice a number of new devices. He discovered that by suspending a grass mat in a vertical position by means of an upright stick to serve as a support, he was able alone to sail his tule float speedily before the wind. Other young men would have copied his device, only they had elders in direct authority and were prevented. But Wixi, being already something of an outcast in the village, was suffered to do much as he pleased, his feeble old grandfather being in no position to check him.

On this occasion, Wixi, instead of arguing with the old man, dips his hands quickly into a basket standing in a slight hollow, well away from the fire, and brings out four or five small rocks dripping with water. He throws them to one side, and by means of a couple of sticks, pulls several rocks out of the fire and drops them, one by one, into the basket, half full of water. There is a momentary splutter and rise of steam, and then the water in the basket begins to boil. Wixi places several chunks of the stingaree in the boiling water, and in a short time is eating boiled fish.

DRAKE PASSES

The fires have flashed more than once from mountain to mountain and have been answered not only by Akalan, but by every one of the two hundred settlements on the bay shore. The principal event, one for which no predetermined signal existed, was the passage along the California coast of the *Golden Hind,* early in the summer of 1579. The great captain, Sir Francis Drake, did not see the Golden Gate because of the heavy fog, but the watchers on Mt. Tamalpais saw his ship and did their duty as best they knew. Before evening of that day, every dweller on the bay shore (those on the coast could see for themselves) understood that Wasaka, the Eagle who brought the original fire to the Mutsun people while they yet lived in the far North, had passed by.

Three or four weeks later, when the vessel returned from the North, and was drawn ashore for repairs within the shelter of Point Reyes, the signals were revised as a result of messages brought to Tamalpais by runners from the Tamalaños, otherwise known as the "peaked-house" people, who lived directly at Drake's landing place. This time the Mutsunes were informed that it was not Wasaka, but the great Chakalli himself. Chakalli, the "Man Above," or the "Great One Above," was much in their thoughts, but to have him visit was an event foreboding ill. Nearly every one wished to flee from his presence. As it turned out, the visitor conducted himself peaceably and in due course went away, leaving few of the Mutsunes any the wiser.

Drake's Bay, as it happened, lay in the country of the Miwok people, who spoke a different tongue from the Mutsunes and who, besides, were ordinarily jealous of their territorial rights. But a few of the Mutsunes had gone around by sea, Wixi among them. Wixi was the only one from Akalan who had gone, and the adventure proved a turning point in his life. He came back somewhat of a hero, at least in the eyes of those of his own age, the older men holding aloof. Wixi had learned many wonderful things during his few days' sojourn with the bearded white men, among them that other people used sails to drive their boats. If any doubted the story that he told, he had but to exhibit the proofs: a small mirror, a couple of strings of colored glass beads, a square of red cloth, and, above all, a truly marvelous thing, a knife of metal. These things were given Wixi by the great captain himself, in the general exchange of presents that followed one of the Indian dancing ceremonies that we read of in Drake's own log book.

IN THE COUNCIL LODGE

In early manhood Wixi had become fairly conscious of his own strength and skill, as well as of his power to direct and improve the life of his people. He had decided, however, to wait his time. The old men would slowly give way or would "disappear." Why quarrel? Besides, it was not his nature to hurry. His patience was shown in still another way, namely, by the fact that he was not yet married. According to custom his parents should have chosen and purchased a wife for him; but, having no parents, or at least only a mother who accepted his assistance and submitted to his authority, the matter was left largely to himself. He had indeed performed the acts that entitled him to a wife. That is, he had carried presents of food, and skins for clothing to the door of the girl he had chosen, and she had silently accepted them. Still he did not bring her home, because she was not acceptable in his own village, because she belonged to the neighboring village of Kawina. She was none other than the girl to whom he owed his name, the girl from whom he had wrested the stingaree.

Now the people of Kawina were not friends of the people of Akalan. Nevertheless, Wixi had met Mahúdah again and again, both on the beach and in the hill country, and, somehow, they had settled their quarrel and were friends.

Wixi had waited and yet, contrary to his expectations, the sentiment of his village people continued to harden against him. True, more and more power and authority fell to him, but the stern opposition of the old men was doing its work. Admired though he was by the younger generation, none dared to stand by him openly. He was constantly meeting the old men in council and they listened respectfully enough to his words, but stood solidly against him whenever he suggested departure from the ways of old.

One night in the council lodge at Akalan, the small blaze in the centre reveals Wixi and about a dozen of the old men looking unusually stern and solemn. The pipe is passing around the circle and the War Chief—the youngest man present, barring Wixi—is stating the purpose of the meeting.

"For many winters," he is saying, his eyes averted to the roof, "for many winters we have all been troubled about the future of our tribe. We have not known what to do. The white man has come to the land. We thought first he was Wasaka, and later that he was Chakalli. But he is instead a powerful enemy. He has done us no harm. That is good. He is killing our enemies, the Longhairs beyond the Mutsun waters to the South. That is good, too. He has taken away some of our neighbors, the Miwok. And that also is good. But some day, when the clouds float high in the sky, he will discover the way into the Mutsun waters and then why should he not kill and enslave us also?"

There is a nodding of grave heads all around and some exchange of furtive glances, in part directed toward Wixi, who is seated alone opposite the main group of elders.

"In these circumstances," the speaker continues, this time looking sharply in the direction of a very old man central in the group, "in these circumstances some of us have thought it well to have Kakari, our Peace Chief, tell us the ancient story of our people, so that together we may judge from past experience what is best for the future."

Every one present, including Wixi, nods his head, and the word is taken up slowly and deliberately by the feeble old man, Kakari, the Peace Chief.

"The story of the Mutsunes," the old man begins, "is long. It would take many nights to tell it all. I shall tell only two or three things that happened and which will show us what the 'Great Ones Above' expect us to do."

"Yes, yes, what they expect us to do," echo the hearers.

"Long ago," the old man continues, "when the Mutsun people first came to this water, they were poor. They came on foot from the far North. They had no boats and they had no bow and arrow. Wasaka had brought them fire and they had the digging-stick. That was all. Our people first went to live at Old-Old Akalan. At that time the place was not an island, it was a part of our own long Mutsun hill that shelters us here on the west. And while they lived there Chakalli came. He came from the 'Great Ones Above' and he brought with him the boat and the bow and arrow and the pipe and many other things. These he gave to the Mutsunes and he showed them also how they were to be used. But later, Coyote came along and told them how to make different ones and to use them differently. That made Chakalli angry and he struck at Old-Old Akalan with his digging-stick, the lightning, and, missing the village, knocked a big piece out of the hill beside it. This shook the ground and when the piece, struck off the hill, fell into the Mutsun water, over where it runs out to the big sea, the Mutsun water came up high and ran through the hole made in our hill, and Old-Old Akalan became an island. The piece knocked out of the hill also became an island, Mutsun Island, where our young men rest and wait for the tide when they go out to the big sea after abalones. Then Chakalli went away, but he did not go back to the 'Great Ones Above,' for every now and then the earth shakes and we know that somebody else has disobeyed instructions."

Here old Kakari paused. It was becoming plain to Wixi why the meeting had been called. But there was more for him to hear.

"After Chakalli went away," went on Kakari, "the Mutsun people had to move. The beach around the small island was not large enough to give them the clams they needed. Moreover, the driftwood for the fire would not lodge near the village as before. It all went through the new channel made by Chakalli, and across to where now live our neighbors the Earth People at Kawina. Some of it came up here. Therefore the Peace Chief of that day—Walen was his name—advised the people to move across to Kawina, but he himself remained with the 'Old People' at Old-Old Akalan (i. e., he died), and with him were left all the things that Chakalli had brought. To-morrow we shall sail over to Old-Old Akalan to see them.

"The Mutsunes had made other boats, as well as bows, arrows, and everything, all copied after those brought by Chakalli. And they had no difficulty in sailing across the water to Kawina.

"All went well for a long time at Kawina. Then trouble came once more. Coyote had brought a basket from the North, which he gave to the young women of the Miwok people over across the water at Tamalpais. He told them to boil food in it. They did so and liked it. Later on, the Miwok people told some of the young men from Kawina, who were over there looking for wood for new bows. Chakalli must have heard about it all, for he struck the earth a fierce blow over near where the bearded men came with the great white-winged ship. Chakalli's blow made a long, deep rent in the earth, and the big sea came in and filled it. You can see it there to-day. At that time the water also came up, and drowned many of the Mutsun people at Kawina, although they lived on a high mound they had made, like the one we now live on. Only the top of the mound was left above the water.

"Soon after that the Mutsun people left Kawina, or Old Akalan, as they called the place. Many of them went east and south, making new homes all around the Mutsun water. Our people alone came over here, where they have been ever since. Those are the stories of Old-Old Akalan and of Old Akalan."

Old Kakari's strength is being spent, and he leans back against the wall. But presently he goes on: "After we came over here, all went well again for a long time. Every one did as he was told by the elders, and Chakalli was pleased. One day the earth shook again and the water went away from around Kawina or Old Akalan. Our people thought it was Chakalli making ready for their going back to live once more near the 'Old People.' But before they could move over, Coyote came down from the North with some of the Earth People, who settled at Kawina. Coyote brought with him also the cooking basket and the fishing net."

At this point the anger and resentment of the listeners are expressed by low growls and explosive breaths through set teeth. Wixi alone, leaning forward with his elbows on his knees and his chin resting in his hands, remains silent.

Old Kakari makes a last effort: "The Earth People, the Poma, belong in the North. They do not belong here. Some of them speak our tongue, but they are not our people. At first we made war upon them, but Coyote was too clever for Chakalli. Yet though we are now at peace, we never marry their women, nor they ours. We are neighbors, not friends. To-morrow we shall go to see the proof of what I have told you. Katka (Be full of crickets)." And with this formula of conclusion the Peace Chief ceased.

After a few moments of silence he leaned once more back against the wall as if in deep sleep. No one spoke, but, one after another, the listeners arose and left the council house. Outside, the night was black and no sound was to be heard except the sigh of the breezes over the marsh grass.

PROOF

At daybreak a large tule float stands out from the high, pointed cliff forming the southern extremity of Potrero San Pablo, and heads straight for Brooks Island. In a moment the swiftly paddled float is gone from sight. It carries all the men who were in the council lodge except one. Wixi is not there. The float left Akalan while the night was yet black, and the paddlers were obliged to feel their way along the shore as far as the pointed cliff, and to wait there until the island became faintly visible. Fortunately, this happened before they themselves could be observed from the home village, for their mission to Old-Old Akalan is secret.

The skiff slips behind a large outlying rock and the next moment grates on a low, narrow, curving sand bar connecting the rock with the island proper. As the men step ashore, they see emerging out of the dim north a small float bearing one paddler. The solitary boatman lands on the opposite side of the sand bar, a few yards nearer to the island. It is Wixi. He draws his float across the ridge to the south slope of the bar, to lie with the other float. It is a precaution, lest sharp eyes at Akalan or Kawina discover that visitors are on the island.

With the War Chief in the lead, the men proceed a few rods to the northwest corner of the island, which slopes conveniently to the beach. Bearing onward to the north shore, they walk eastward across a noticeable rise of ground toward a number of buckeye trees. Tall grasses and weeds cover the place. It is the mound left by the people of Old-Old Akalan. Here rest the bones of the oldest ancestors of the Mutsunes.

Having passed over the summit, the War Chief sights a line in the direction of the two oldest buckeye trees, and stations Wixi on the line. The older men he directs to sit down. He himself walks briskly to the nearest of the two trees, and returns again with steady, measured steps straight toward Wixi. As he walks, he counts the steps on his fingers. At a point half-way down the east slope of the mound, he suddenly comes to a halt and with a significant nod of his head motions every one toward him. From one of the men he takes a digging-stick, draws a rough circle around his standing place and says, "This is the place. Dig!"

The men drop to their knees, partly to keep hidden in the tall grasses, and none dares to stand up again for it is now almost sunrise. Some take to loosening up the earth with digging-sticks, and others scoop up the loosened portions with large abalone shells. In this way they make a hole several feet in diameter. Presently, at a depth of about two feet, they uncover the bones of a full-grown person with arms and legs doubled up tightly against the body. All exclaim under their breath. From the presence, next the skeleton, of a mortar and pestle, as well as certain bone awls and needles, the old men know that these are the remains of a woman. The spirit of the implements which the woman used in daily life, had gone, they would say, with the spirit of the departed to her new dwelling place in the far West.

Deeper down, perhaps five or six feet, the workers come to another skeleton. On the breast of the body, they uncover a large, beautifully shaped obsidian blade. Close to the shoulder are found a number of arrow points, just as they were left when the wooden shafts decayed away. Near one hand lie, side by side, two highly polished, steatite tobacco pipes. On either side of the skull is a disk-shaped ear pendant of iridescent abalone shell, and all about the neck and shoulders are many beads of clamshell. The workers are agreed that these are the remains of a great man and the War Chief emphatically declares them to be those of the ancient Peace Chief Walen, himself. All the old men demur to this, however, contending that Walen, according to the traditions, was buried, not in the black refuse material left by the inhabitants of Old-Old Akalan, but lower down in virgin soil.

All through the day the digging continues, and skeleton after skeleton is taken up—men, women, and children. Each was originally buried beneath the floor of the hut in which he or she died, and in the course of time, as shells and ashes accumulated above their bones, a new hut was built, again to be destroyed with the succeeding death.

As the men dig deeper and deeper, the paraphernalia of the dead become fewer and fewer, and even where anything at all is present, the object is crude and unfinished. There are no more pipes, no beautiful obsidian blades, and no fine, ivory-like awls or needles. What can it mean? Did the ancestors of early days not possess these things? Some such thoughts are surely passing through the mind of some of the workers, certainly of the War Chief, for he suddenly declares his belief that they are not digging in the right place. But the old men only smile and work on.

At last, shortly before dark, there are signs of bottom to the mound material. Real earth is beginning to appear, and before long human bones are turned up. Very soon the complete skeleton is laid bare. No implements have been found, but every one's attention is centred on a bright red spot near the extended right hand of the skeleton. It is a quantity of paint powder, such as has been noticed to accompany several of the men skeletons. The War Chief, now visibly excited, grasps a sharp-edged abalone shell and eagerly cuts into the red substance. The next moment the shell drops from his hand. He, with the rest, is staring blankly at seven large, beautifully clear quartz crystals—the whole of Walen's treasure! . . .

It is morning. The remains of the dead have been replaced and all obvious traces of disturbance removed. Let the "Old People" of Old-Old Akalan rest until the sea removes them! Wixi has labored hard and is weary in body, but in spirit he is a new man. Has he not had proof from the graves? Knows he not for a certainty that the life of the Mutsunes has not stood still in the past, and is he not determined that it shall unfold and develop in the future? . . .

The old men are sleeping after their arduous work, continued far into the night. Wixi alone has watched restlessly for the dawn, and when the cliff across the Mutsun channel is distinctly visible, he puts off with his featherweight skiff. He is scudding along with swift, sure strokes and is already near enough to the opposite shore to see a woman waving to him from the top of the bluff. It is Mahúdah, who has watched for his return since the evening before. The sun's first rays are just beginning to play around her as she stands there on high, and Wixi is raising his paddle in the air to wave recognition. At that moment Mahúdah utters a loud, piercing scream and turns to run from the edge of the precipice. Portions of rock and earth fall to the beach, and a rising cloud of dust obscures the figure of the fleeing woman. A moment later Wixi is raised on the crest of a tremendous wave, which carries him with the speed of a swooping eagle directly against the face of the cliff.

The old men of Akalan, awakened by the first tremors of the earth, witness the whole scene. Most of them simply shake their heads. But the War Chief, affecting solemnity, announces: "Chakalli has struck! The old order remains."

N. C. NELSON

ALL IS TROUBLE
ALONG THE KLAMATH

All Is Trouble Along the Klamath

A YUROK IDYLL

(MRS. OREGON JIM, from the house Erkigér-i or "Hair-ties" in the town of Pékwan, speaking) : You want to know why old Louisa and I never notice each other? Well, I'll tell you why. I wouldn't speak to that old woman to save her life. There is a quarrel between her and me, and between her people and my people.

The thing started, so far as I know, with the bastard son of a woman from that big old house in Wáhsek that stands crossways—the one they call Wáhsek-héthlqau. They call it that, of course, because it is *behind* the others. It kind of sets back from the river. This woman lived with several different men; first with a young fellow from the house next door, and then, when she left *him*, with a strolling fellow from Smith River. When she left him for a Húpa, they all began to call her *kímolin*, "dirty." Not one of these men had paid a cent for her, although she came of good people. She lived around in different places. Two of her children died, but a third one grew up at the Presbyterian Mission.

He had even less sense than the Presbyterians have. He came down to Kepél one time, when the people there were making the Fish Dam. It was the last day of the work on the dam. The dam was being finished, that day. That's the time nobody can get mad. Nobody can take offense at anything. This boy heard people calling each other bad names. They were having a dance. The time of that dance is different from all other times. People say the worst things! It sounds funny to hear the people say, for example, to old Kímorets, "Well, old One-Eye! you are the best dancer." They think of the worst things to say! A fellow even said to Mrs. Poker Bob, "How is your grandmother?"; when Mrs. Poker Bob's grandmother was already dead. It makes your blood run cold to hear such things, even though you know it's in fun.

This young fellow I am telling you about, whom they called Fred Williams, and whose Indian name was Sär, came down from the

Mission school to see the Fish-Dam Dance at Kepél. He was dressed up. He went around showing off. He wore a straw hat with a ribbon around it. He stood around watching the dance. Between the songs, he heard what people were saying to each other. He heard them saying all sorts of improper things. He thought that was smart talk. He thought he would try it when he got a chance. The next day, he went down by the river and saw Tuley-Creek Jim getting ready his nets. "Get your other hand cut off," he said. "Then you can fish with your feet!" Two or three people who were standing by, heard him. Tuley-Creek Jim is pretty mean. They call him "Coyote." He looked funny. He stood there. He didn't know what to say.

Young Andrew, who was there, whose mother was from the house called "Down-river House" in Qóvtep, was afraid for his life. He was just pushing off his boat. He let go of the rope. The boat drifted off. He was afraid to pull it back. He went up to the house. "Something happened," he told the people there. "I wish I was somewhere else. There is going to be trouble along this Klamath River."

The talk soon went around that Coyote-Jim was claiming some money. It was told us that he was going to make the boy's mother's father pay fifteen dollars. "That's my price," he said. "I won't do anything to the boy, for he isn't worth it. Nobody paid for his mother. Also, I won't charge him much. But his mother's people are well-to-do, and they will have to pay this amount that I name. Otherwise, I will be mad." As a matter of fact, he was afraid to do anything, for he, himself, was afraid of the soldiers at Húpa. He just made big talk. Besides, what he wanted was a headband ornamented with whole woodpecker heads, that the boy's grandfather owned. He thought he could make the old man give it up, on account of what his grandson had said.

The boy went around, hollering to everybody. "I don't have to pay," he said. "I heard everybody saying things like that! How did I know that they only did it during that one day? Besides, look at me! Look at my shirt. Look at my pants." He showed them his straw hat. "Look at my hat! I am just like a white man. I can say anything I please. I don't have to care what I say."

Every day somebody came along the river, telling us the news.

There was a big quarrel going on. I was camped at that time, with my daughter, above Metá, picking acorns. All the acorns were bad that year—little, and twisted, and wormy. Even the worms were little and kind of shriveled that year. That place above Metá was the only place where the acorns were good. Lots of people were camped there. Some paid for gathering acorns there. My aunt had married into a house at Metá, the house they call Wóogi, "In-the-middle-House," so I didn't have to pay anything. People used to come up from the river to where we acorn pickers were camped, to talk about the news. They told us the boy's mother's people were trying to make some people at Smith River pay. "He's the son of one of their men," the old grandfather said. "They've got to pay for the words he spoke. I don't have to pay." The thing dragged on. Three weeks later they told us the old man wouldn't pay yet.

Somebody died at the old man's house that fall. The people were getting ready to have a funeral. The graveyard for that house called Héthlqau, in Wáhsek, is just outside the house door. They went into that kämethl, in that corpse-place, what you whites call a cemetery. They dug a hole and had it ready. They were singing "crying-songs" in that house where the person had died.

Tuley-Creek Jim's brother-in-law was traveling down the river in a canoe. When he got to Wáhsek he heard "crying songs." "Somebody has died up there," they told him. "We better stop! No use trying to go by. We better go ashore till the burial is over." Tuley-Creek Jim's brother-in-law did not want to stop. "They owe some money to my wife's brother," he said. "One of their people said something to Jim. They don't pay up. Why should I go ashore?" So they all paddled down to the landing-place. They started to go past, going down-river. A young fellow at the landing-place grabbed their canoe. "You got to land here," he said. "My aunt's people are having a funeral. It ain't right for anybody to go by in a canoe." The people in the canoe began to get mad. They pushed on the bottom with their paddles. The canoe swung around. Coyote-Jim's brother-in-law stood up. He was pretty mad. They had got his shirt wet. He waved his paddle around. He hollered. He got excited.

One of the men on the bank was Billy Brooks, from the mouth of the river. "Hey! You fellow-living-with-a-woman-you-haven't-paid-for!" he said to Billy Brooks, "make these fellows let go of my canoe."

Billy was surprised. He hadn't been holding the canoe. And anyway, he did not expect to be addressed that way. "Läs-son" is what he had heard addressed to him. That means "half-married, or improperly married, to a woman in the house by the trail." Brooks had had no money to pay for a wife, so he went to live with his woman instead of taking her home to him. That is what we call being half-married. Everybody called Billy that way, behind his back. "Half-married-into-the-house-by-the-trail" was his name.

When Billy got over being surprised at this form of address, he got mad. He pointed at the fellow in the canoe. He swore the worst way a person can swear. What he said was awful. He pointed at him. He was mad clear through. He didn't care what he said. "Your deceased relatives," is what he said to Coyote-Jim's brother-in-law, in the canoe. He said it right out loud. He pointed at the canoe. That's the time he said "Your deceased relatives." "All your deceased relatives," he said to those in the canoe.

Coyote-Jim's brother-in-law sat down in the canoe. Nobody tried to stop the canoe after that. The canoe went down-river. Billy Brooks went up to the house. He waited. After a while the people there buried that person who was dead, and the funeral was over. "I've got to pay money," Billy Brooks said to them then. "I got mad and swore something terrible at Coyote-Jim's brother-in-law. That was on account of you people. If you had paid what you owed to Coyote-Jim, Coyote-Jim's brother-in-law wouldn't have gone past your house while you were crying, and you wouldn't have held his canoe, and he wouldn't have addressed me as he did, and I wouldn't have said what I did. Moreover, Wóhkel Dave was in the canoe, and when I said that which I said, it applied to him, too. I feel terrible mean about what I said. I've got to have trouble with both those men. There were others in the canoe, too, but they are poor people, and don't amount to anything. But Dave is a rich man. Now all this trouble is on your account, and you've got to pay me two dollars and a half."

The old man at Wáhsek was in trouble. "First my mouse says to Coyote-Jim what should not in any case have been said," the old man complained. (We call illegitimate children "mice," because they eat, and stay around, and nobody has paid for them.) "Now on account of what my mouse said, all this other trouble has happened."

Everybody was talking about the quarrel now. That is the time they left off talking about the old man's troubles, and began talking about what Billy Brooks said to the Coyote's brother-in-law in the canoe, and to Wóhkel Dave. It finally came out that the fellow who was steering the canoe, and who called Billy Brooks "Läs-son," was out of the quarrel. His deceased relatives had been referred to, but, on the other hand, his father had only paid twenty-five dollars for his mother, so nobody cared much about him. He talked around but nobody paid any attention, so he decided that he had better keep still about it, and maybe people would forget that he had been insulted.

Wóhkel Dave, however, was a man of importance. His people were married into all the best houses up and down the river. Everybody was wondering what he and Brooks would do. Billy Brooks was kind of a mean man himself. He had a bad reputation. One time he even made a white man pay up for something he did. The white man took a woman from Brooks' people to live with him. Brooks looked him up, and made him pay for her. Everybody was afraid of Brooks. Some people said, "Brooks won't pay. He's too mean. He's not afraid. He'd rather fight it out." Other people said, "That's all right, as far as ordinary people are concerned. Wóhkel Dave, though, is not ordinary. His father paid a big price for his mother. She had one of the most stylish weddings along the river. Dave won't let anybody get the best of him." People used to argue that way. Some said one thing, and some said another. They used to almost quarrel about it.

Suddenly news came down the river that Billy Brooks was going to pay up for what he said. Some one came along and told us that Billy was going to pay. "He offered twenty-five dollars," this fellow said. The next day we heard that Dave wouldn't take it. He wanted forty dollars. They argued back and forth. It was February before they got it settled. Billy had to pay twenty dollars in money, a shot-gun made out of an army musket, bored out, and a string of shell money, not a very good one. The shells were pretty small, but the string was long—reaching from the chest bone to the end of the fingers.

The next thing that happened is what involved me and old Louisa. It came about because Billy didn't have twenty dollars in cash. He had to get hold of the twenty dollars. About that time, certain Indians stole some horses. They were not people from our tribe. They were Chilula from Bald Hills, or people from over in that direction somewhere. Those people were awful poor. They couldn't pay for a woman. They couldn't pay for anything. They had to marry each other. In the springtime they got pretty wild. They were likely to do things. This time they took some horses from a white man. This white man complained to the agent at Húpa. So some soldiers from Húpa went out to chase these Indians. Billy Brooks was a great hunter. He has been all over everywhere, hunting and trapping. The soldiers needed a guide. They offered Billy twenty-five dollars to serve as a "scout" for the Government, to chase these Indians. So Billy, because he had to have twenty dollars, went as a scout, that time.

The soldiers went to Redwood Creek. Billy Brooks went along. There was a sergeant and six men, they say. Two of the men went to that Indian town six miles above the mouth of Redwood Creek, the name of which is Otlép. That town belongs to the Chilula. These two soldiers went there, looking for the men who stole the horses. There was trouble after a while at that place. The soldiers got into a quarrel with the Indians.

The trouble was about a woman. One of the soldiers wanted her, but the woman would not go with him. She did not feel like it. I don't know exactly what happened, but the soldier insisted, and the woman insisted, and finally her relatives told the soldier that if the woman didn't want to, she didn't have to. There was a fight that time. There was a tussel about the soldier's revolver. Somebody got hit over the head with it. The front sight was sharp. That soldier had filed down the sight on his revolver, to make it fine. That sight dug into a man's face, and cut it open, from his jaw bone up to his eye.

There was big trouble there that time, they say. Everybody got to hollering. That woman had a bad temper. She hit a soldier with a rock. She broke his head open. The man whose face was cut open went for his gun. He couldn't see very well. He didn't get the percussion cap on properly. He tried to shoot the soldier, but the gun wouldn't go off. The cap had dropped off the nipple. The soldier saw the Indian aiming the gun at him, so he fired at the Indian. There was blood in the soldier's eyes, for the woman had cut his head open with a rock So he missed the Indian who was aiming at him, but he hit old Louisa's nephew, Jim Williams. The bullet went through his thigh. Two years passed before Jim Williams could walk straight after that.

Now that is the trouble between old Louisa and me. Her nephew was hurt, and she blames Billy Brooks, because Billy Brooks was with the soldiers, helping them, the time this happened. Billy would never "pay up" for this. One time it was reported that he was going to pay, but he never did.

Now Billy is a relative of mine by marriage. His sister married my father's brother's oldest boy. That old woman, whose nephew was shot, doesn't like me, because I am a relative of Billy who guided the soldiers.

One time she played me a dirty trick. My nephew was fishing with a gill-net on the river here. The game warden made a complaint and had him arrested, for he had one end of his net fast to the bank. That old woman, that old Louisa, went to Eureka and told the judge there, that one end of the net was fast to the bank. They say she got money for doing that. Somebody said she got two dollars a day. My nephew was put in jail for sixty days. I am not saying anything to that old woman, but I am keeping a watch on her. If anybody talks to her, then I have nothing to do with them.

One time a white man from down below came along this river, asking about baskets. He wanted to know the name of everything. He was kind of crazy, that fellow. They used to call him "Häpó'o," or "Basket-designs." He was always asking, "What does that mean?" or "What is the name of that?" He wanted to know all about baskets. He talked to old Louisa for a day and a half about her baskets. Then he came through the fence to my house. I wouldn't say a word to him, and he went away. My friends won't talk to Louisa, or her friends. It will be that way forever.

It all goes back to that boy Sär. If he had not talked about

Tuley-Creek Jim having only one hand, Jim's brother-in-law would not have paddled past a house where there was a person lying dead, and his canoe would not have been seized, and there would have been no quarrel about the canoe, and Billy Brooks would not have sworn at anybody, so he would not have had to pay money, and he would not have hired out as a scout to the Government, and the fellow in Redwood Creek would not have been shot, and old Louisa would not have testified about my nephew. To make people pay is all right. That is what always happens when there is a quarrel. But to put my nephew in jail is not right.

I'll never speak to that old lady again, and neither will any of my people.

T. T. WATERMAN

SAYACH'APIS
&
NOOTKA TRADER

Sayach'apis, a Nootka Trader

TOM is a blind old man, whose staff may be heard any day stumping or splashing along the village street of his tribal reservation, or up or down the hillside that slopes to the smoke-drying huts massed by the Somass river. He is an honored member of the Ts'isha'ath, a Nootka tribe that is now permanently located a few miles up from the head of Alberni Canal, the deepest inlet on the west coast of Vancouver Island. The Ts'isha'ath fishes and harpoons along the river, the length of the "Canal," and down among the hundreds of islands that dot Barkley Sound, the first of the large bays north of Cape Beale that are carved out on the stormy coast line of the island.

Tom's early life was passed at the now abandoned village of Hikwis, whose row of houses looked out upon the main water of the Sound, but for decades he has led an uneventful existence in his river reservation and its vicinity, old summer fishing-grounds that were conquered in the first instance by his people from an alien tribe. Within convenient reach are the slowly booming white men's towns of Alberni and Port Alberni, where one may lay in a supply of biscuits and oranges for a tribal feast, or make periodic complaint to the Indian Agent. Tom is now old and poverty-stricken, but the memory of his former wealth is with his people. The many feasts he has given and the many ceremonial dances and displays he has had performed have all had their desired effect—they have shed luster on his sons and daughters and grandchildren, they have "put his family high" among the Ts'isha'ath tribe, and they have even carried his name to other, distant Nootka tribes, and to tribes on the east coast of the island that are of alien speech. Nowadays he spends much of his time by the fireside, tapping his staff in accompaniment to old ritual tunes that he is never tired of humming.

Tom's present name is Sayach'apis, Stands-up-high-over-all. It is an old man's name of eight generations' standing, that hails from the Hisawist'ath, a now extinct Nootka tribe with which Tom is connected through his father's mother's mother, who was herself a Hisawist'ath on her mother's side. The tribe is extinct, but its personal names, like its songs and legends and distinctive ritualistic ceremonies, linger on among the neighboring tribes through the fine spun network of inheritance. The name "Stands-up-high-over-all," like practically all Nootka, and indeed all West Coast names, has its legendary background, its own historical warrant. The first Nootka chief to bear the name, obtained it in a dream. He was undergoing ritualistic training in the woods in the pursuit of "power" for the attainment of wealth, and had not slept for a long time. At last he fell into a heavy slumber, and this is what he dreamed: The Sky Chief appeared to him and said, "Why are you sleeping, Stands-up-high-over-all? You are not really desirous of getting wealthy, are you? I was about to make you wealthy and to give you the name Stands-up-high-over-all." The ironical touch is a characteristic nuance in these origin legends. And so the name, a supernatural gift, was handed down the generations, now by direct male inheritance, now as a dower to a son-in-law, resident at some village remote from its place of origin. This is the normal manner, actually or in theory, of the transmission of all privileges, and though the owner of a privilege may be a villager a hundred miles or more distant from its historical or legendary home, he has not completely established his right to its use unless he has shown himself, directly or by reference to a speaker acquainted with tribal lore, possessed of the origin legend, the local provenance, and the genealogical tree or "historical" nexus that binds him to the individual, that is believed to have been the first to enjoy the privilege.

Tom did not always have the name of Sayach'apis, nor need he keep it to the end of his days. He assumed it over thirty years ago on the occasion of his great potlatch, a puberty feast in honor of his now deceased oldest daughter. At that time he had the young man's name of Nawe'ik, now borne by his oldest son, Douglas. It is a name belonging to the Nash'as'ath sept or tribal subdivision of the Ts'isha'ath, and was first dreamt by Tom's maternal grandfather. It is thus a name of comparatively recent origin, nor does it possess that aura of noble association that attaches to Tom's present name. Its exact meaning is unknown, but it is said to have been a command—"Come here!"—of a spirit whale, dreamt of by its first possessor. Tom assumed it at a potlatch he gave to his own tribe when he was not yet married. It was just about the time that the discovery of placer gold in the Frazer river was bringing a considerable influx of whites to British Columbia.

Before this, Tom was known as Kunnuh, a Nitinat young man's name, "Wake up!", which is again based on the dream of a spirit whale. The Nitinat Indians are a group of Nootka tribes that occupy the southwest coast of the island, and Tom's claim to the name and to other Nitinat privileges comes to him through his paternal grandfather, himself a Nitinat Indian. The name originated with his grandfather's father's father's father, who received it in a dream as he was training for "power" in whaling. It was assumed by Tom when he was about ten years of age, at a naming feast given the Ts'isha'ath Indians by his Nitinat grandfather. It displaced the boy's name Ha'wihlkumuktli, "Having-chiefs-behind," this time of true Ts'isha'ath origin and descending to Tom through his paternal grandmother's father's father, who again received the name in a dream from a spirit whale. This ancestor was having much success in whaling and, becoming exceedingly wealthy, was "leaving other chiefs behind him." Tom was given the name at an ordinary feast by his paternal grandfather.

The earliest name that Tom remembers having is Tl'i'nitsawa, "Getting-whale-skin." When the great chief Hohenikwop had his whale booty towed to shore, the little boys used to come to the beach for slices of whale skin, so he made up the name of "Getting-whale-skin" for his son. The right to use it was inherited by his oldest son, but was also passed on to the chief's younger sister, who brought it as a dowry to the father of Tom's paternal grandfather. Tom himself received the name on the occasion of a mourning potlatch given by his paternal grandfather in honor of his son, Tom's father, who had died not long before. Before this, Tom had a child's nickname, in other words, a name bestowed not out of the inherited stock of names claimed by his parents, but created on the spot for any chance reason whatever. Such nicknames have no ceremonial value, are not privileges, and are therefore not handed down as an inheritance or transferred as a dowry. Tom has forgotten what his nickname was.

At the very outset, in the mere consideration of what Tom has called himself at various times, we are introduced to the two great social forces that give atmosphere to Nootka life. The first of these is privilege, the right to something of value, practical or ceremonial. Such a privilege is called "topati" by the Indians, and one cannot penetrate very far into their life or beliefs without stumbling upon one topati after another. The second is the network of descent and kinship relation that determines the status of the North West Coast Indian, not merely as a tribesman once for all, but in reference to his claim to share in any activity of moment. The threads of the genealogical past are wound tightly about the North West Coastman; he is himself a traditional composite of social features that belong to diverse localities, and involve him in diverse kinship relations.

As far back, then, as he can remember, Tom has been steeped in an atmosphere of privilege, of rank, of conflicting claims to this or that coveted right. As far back as he can remember, he has heard remarks like this: "Old man Tootooch has no right to have such and such a particular Thunder-bird dance performed at his potlatches. His claim to it is not clear. In my grandfather's days men were killed for less than that, and the head chief of the Ahous'ath tribe, who has the primary claim to the dance, would have called him sharply to order." But he has also heard Tootooch vigorously support his claim with arguments, genealogical and other, that no one quite knows the right or wrong of. And as far back as he can remember, Tom has been accustomed to think of himself not merely as a Ts'isha'ath, though he is primarily that by residence and immediate descent, but as a participant in the traditions, in the social atmosphere, of several other Nootka tribes. He has always known where to look for his remoter kinsmen, dwelling in villages that are dotted here and there on a long coast line.

The first few years of Tom's life were spent in a "cradle" of basketry, in which he was tightly swathed by sundry wrappings and braids of the soft, beaten inner bark of the cedar. Even now he has a vague recollection of looking out over the sea from the erect vantage of a cradling basket, looped behind his mother's shoulders. He also thinks he remembers crying bitterly one time when left all by himself in the basket, stood up on end against the butt of a willow tree, while his mother and four or five other women had strayed off to dig for edible clover roots with their hard, pointed digging-sticks.

During the cradling period, Tom was having his head, or rather his forehead, gradually flattened by means of cedar-bark pads, and the upper and lower parts of his legs were bandaged so as to allow the calves to bulge. The Indians believe that they do not like big foreheads and slim legs, nor do they approve of wide eyebrows, which are narrowed, if necessary, by plucking out some of the hairs. Later on in life Tom was less particular about his natural appearance, having been well "fixed" by his mother in infancy. Like the other men of his tribe, he has never bothered to pluck out the scanty growth of hair on his face. Some of the Indians of Tom's acquaintance have tattooed themselves, generally on the breast, with designs referring to their hunting experiences, or to crest privileges— a quarter-moon or a sea lion or a pair of Thunder-birds,—but Tom has never bothered to do this. Aside from the head-flattening of infancy, Tom has never had any portion of his body mutilated, unless the perforation of his ears and the septum of his nose, for the attachment of ear and nose pendants of the bright rainbow-like abalone, strung by sinew threads, be considered a mutilation. These pendants, which he and other Indians have long discarded, were worn purely for ornament; they had no importance as ceremonial insignia.

In spite of the fact that neither razor nor tweezers have ever smoothed out the hairy surface of his face, Tom has not altogether neglected the care of his body. To prevent chapping, he has often rubbed himself with tallow and red paint, and in his younger days he was in the habit of keeping himself in good condition by a cold plunge, at daybreak, in river or sea. The vigorous rubbing down with hemlock branches which followed, until the skin all tingled red, helped to give tone to his body. He could not afford to miss the plunge and rub-down for more than two or three days at a time, if only because to have done so would have brought upon him the contempt and derision of his comrades. No aspiring young hunter of the seal and the sea lion could allow himself to be called a woman. In the course of his long life Tom has painted his face in a great variety of ways, whether for festive occasions, or in the private quest of supernatural power in some secluded spot in the woods. Some of these face paints—and there are hundreds of them in use among the Nootka—are geometrical patterns, others are emblematic of supernatural beings and animals. Many of them, like the songs and dances with which they are associated, are looked upon as valuable privileges.

It is long since Tom has worn or seen worn native costume—what little there was of it—but he distinctly remembers the blankets and cedar-bark garments that his people wore when he was a boy and, indeed, well on into his days of manhood. The heavy rains of the Coast, and the constant necessity of splashing in and out of the canoes along the beach, made tight-fitting garments and cumbrous foot- and leg-wear undesirable. The Nootka Indians wore no clinging shirts or leggings or moccasins. They are a barefoot and a bare-legged people. Those of the men who could afford more than a breechclout wore a blanket robe loosely thrown about the body, either a hide—of bear or the far more valuable sea otter—or a woven blanket, whether of the inner-bark strands of the "yellow cedar" or the long, fleecy hair of the native dogs. The women wore cedar-bark "petticoats," which are nothing but loosely fitting girdles, fringed with long tassels of cedar bark. In rainy weather, they also wore woven hats of cedar-bark strands or split root fibers, round topped and cone-like. When the weather was thick and heavy with rain—and this happens often enough in the winter—both men and women wore raincapes of cedar bark or rush matting. The children ran about completely naked.

The food that Tom was accustomed to in his early days did not differ materially from his present fare. It was then, and is now, chiefly fish—boiled, steam-baked, spit-roasted, or smoked. In all his early haunts, in the houses and along the beach, everywhere he was immersed in grateful, fishy odors. From the earliest time that he can remember anything at all, he has been daily confronted by some aspect of the life of a fishing people, whether it be the catching of salmon trout by the boys with their two-barbed fish spears; or the spearing or trolling or netting of salmon by the older men; or the getting in the sea of herrings with herring rakes, of halibut with the peculiar, gracefully bent halibut hooks that every Indian even now has kicking around in his box of odds and ends, of cod with twirling decoys and spears that have two prongs of unequal length—"older" and "younger"; or the hanging up of salmon in rows to dry in the smoke houses, so that this all-important fish may still contribute his share of the food supply, long after the last salmon of the late fall has ceased to run; or the splitting up of the salmon by the women as a first preliminary to cooking; or any one of the hundreds of other scenes that make of a fisher folk a fish-handling and a fish-eating people.

Second in importance to fish are the various varieties of edible shellfish and other soft bodied inhabitants of the sea—mussels and clams and sea urchins, sea cucumbers, and octopuses. The flesh of the octopus or "devil-fish," though not an important article of food, was considered quite a dainty, and feasts were often given in which it figured as a special feature, like crab apples or like the apples or oranges of present-day feasts. Far more important than these mushy foods, though probably subsidiary, on the whole, to salmon and other fish, was the flesh of sea mammals—the humpbacked whale, the California whale, the sea otter, the sea lion, and, most important of all, the hair seal.

Tom has harpooned his fill of seals in the course of his life and, like most other Nootka men of the last generation, has done a considerable amount of commercial sealing for white firms in Behring Sea. He has caught a few sea otters, which are now all but extinct, but no sea lions or whales, though he claims to have the hereditary privilege to hunt these animals, and to possess the indispensable magical knowledge without which their quest is believed by the Nootka to be doomed to failure.

Boiled whale and seal meat were highly prized and there was no more joyous event to break the monotony of tribal life than the towing to shore of a harpooned whale, or the drifting to shore of a whale carcass. In either case the flensing knives were quickly got ready, the carcass cut up, and feasts held in the village. Tom remembers how excitedly—he was then but a boy of ten or so—he once reported the appearance of a drifting whale carcass a quarter-mile from shore, how the whole village rushed into its canoes, and how they laboriously floated it on to the sandy beach, with their stout lanyards of cedar rope wound with nettle-fiber. The whale was cut up carefully, under the direction of a "measurer" into its traditionally determined portions, which were then distributed, according to hereditary right, to those entitled to receive them. Tom himself got the meat about the navel as a reward for his find. There was an unusual amount of whale oil tried out that time, and the fires at the feasts leaped higher than ever as the oil was thrown upon them, lighting up in lurid flashes the house posts carved into the likenesses of legendary ancestors.

Tom ate very little meat of land animals in his early days. Indeed, like most of the Coast people, he had a prejudice against deer meat and it was not until, as a middle-aged man, he had come into contact with some of the deer-hunting tribes of the interior of the island, that he learned to prize it, though even to this day venison has not for him the toothsome appeal of a chunk of whale meat. Fish and meat were the staples, yet not the only foods. The women dug up a variety of edible roots such as clover and fern root, which made a welcome change, while blackberries, salmon berries, soapberries, and other varieties, frequently dried and pressed for winter consumption, added a sweetening to the somewhat monotonous fare. One relish Tom has never learned to enjoy—salt. All the older Nootka Indians detest salt in their food.

As Tom grew up, he became initiated into the chief handicrafts of his tribe. He got to be rather skillful at working in wood, both the soft red cedar and the hard yew and spiræa, familiarizing himself with the various wood-working processes—felling trees with wedges and stone hammers, splitting out planks, smoothing with adzes, drilling, handling the curved knife, steaming, and bending by the "kerfing" or notching process. Even in his youngest years, iron-bladed and iron-pointed tools had almost completely replaced the aboriginal implements of stone and shell, but the forms themselves, of the manufactured objects, underwent little or no modification down to the present day. In the course of his long life Tom has made hundreds of wooden articles of use—boxes with telescoping lids, paddles, bailers, fish clubbers, adze handles, ladles, bows, arrow shafts, fire drills, latrines, root diggers, fish spears, and shafts for sealing and whaling harpoons. He has also assisted in making dugout canoes, and has often prepared and put in position the heavy posts and beams of the large quadrangular houses that were still being built in his youth. On the other hand, Tom has never developed much aptitude in the artistic decoration of objects. Such things as paintings on house boards and paddles, or realistic carvings in masks, rattles, ornamental fish clubbers and house posts, are rather beyond his power and have had to be made for him, when required, by others more clever than himself. The one thing that Tom grew to be most proficient in was the preparation of house planks of desired lengths and widths. When he was a young man, he would travel about in canoes from village to village with the stock of planks he had on hand, and trade them for blankets, strings of dentalium shells, dried fish, whale oil, and other exchangeable commodities. It was through trading, rather than through personal success in fishing or hunting, that Tom amassed in time a considerable share of wealth, and it was through his wealth and the opportunity it gave him to make lavish distributions at potlatches or feasts, rather than through nobility of blood, that he came to occupy his present honorable position among his tribesmen.

While Tom and the other men, when they were not busy "potlatching" or visiting some relative, or taking a run down to Victoria, were engaged in fishing and sea mammal hunting and wood-working, the women prepared the food, dug for edible roots, gathered clams, and spent what time they could spare from these and similar tasks in the weaving and plaiting of blankets, matting, and baskets. What receptacles were not of wood were of basketry, while mats of various sorts did duty for tables, hangings, and carpeting. The materials of these baskets and mats, the omnipresent cedar bark and the rush, frayed easily, so that the women were kept constantly busy replenishing the household stock. Even now one can hardly enter a Nootka house without seeing one or more of the women twilling mats and baskets with strips of softened cedar bark or twining the cedar-bark strands into cordage and bags, or threading a rush mat with the long needles of polished spiræa. In the old days, there was always in the house a great clatter of breaking up the raw, yellow cedar bark with the corrugated bark beaters of bone of whale, annd of loosening up the hard strips of red cedar bark into fibrous masses with the half-moon shredders. The women could work up the bark into almost any degree of fineness; indeed, the cedar-bark "wool" that was used to pad the cradles is almost as soft and fluffy in feel as down or cotton batting. When Tom was a boy, the women made only plain, unornamented baskets, whether twined or twilled, and ornamented the mats with sober, but effective lines of alder-dyed red and mud-dyed black. Since then, however, they have taken to making also trinket baskets and plaques of the peculiar wrapped weave, beautifully ornamented with realistic and geometrical designs in the black and white weft of grass. This art came to Tom's people from the Nitinats or Southern Nootka, who in turn owe it to the Makah of Cape Flattery. Trade with the whites is the chief incentive in the making of these finer specimens of basketry.

Nowadays the Nootka live in small frame houses, a family, in our narrower sense of the word, to a house. It was not so when Tom was young. The village of Hikwis, in which he was raised, consisted of a row of long plank houses, each constructed on a heavy quadrangular frame of posts, which were the trimmed trunks of cedars, and of crossbeams of circular section resting on the posts. The roofing and walls were of cedar planks, running lengthwise of the house. The floor was the bare earth, stamped smooth, and a slightly raised platform ran along the rear and the long sides of the house. On the inner floor one or more fires were built, the smoke escaping through openings in the roof, provided by merely shoving a roofing plank or two to a side. Tom early learned not to stand erect in the house any more than he could help. The smoke circulating in the upper reaches of the house, particularly in rainy weather when the smoke-hole rafters were closed, was trying to the eyes, and people found it convenient to sit or crouch on the floor as much as possible. Some of the houses, like the one in which Tom was brought up, had paintings or carvings referring to the crests or legendary escutcheons of the chief of the tribe, tribal subdivision, or house group. In Tom's house the main escutcheons were two Thunder-birds, face to face, painted on the outside of the wall planks; a series of round holes cut in the roof, and one in front that served as a door, all representing moons; and paintings of wolves on the boards that ran below the platforms. The chief of the house group, together with his immediate family, occupied the rear of the house; other families of lesser rank, kin to the chief by junior lines of descent, occupied various positions along the sides. Slaves were also housed in the long communal dwelling. They were not, like the middle class, undistinguished relations of the chief's families, but strangers, captured in war or bartered off like any chattels. The mat beds of the individual families were made on the platforms and were screened off from one another as required.

In such a house Tom early learned his exact relationship to all his kinsmen. He soon learned also the degree of his relationship to the neighboring house groups. He applied the terms "brother" and "sister" not only to his immediate brothers and sisters but to his cousins, near and remote, of the same generation. He distinguished, among all these remoter brothers and sisters, "older" and "younger," not according to their actual ages in relation to his own, but according to whether they belonged to lines of descent that were senior or junior to his own. Primogeniture, he gradually learned, both of self and progenitor, meant superiority in rank and privilege. Hence the terms "older" and "younger," almost from the beginning, took on a powerful secondary tinge of "superior" and "inferior." The absurdity of calling some little girl cousin, perhaps ten years his junior, his "older sister" was for him immensely less evident because of his ever present consciousness of her higher rank. As Tom grew older, he became cognizant of an astonishing number of uncles and aunts, grandfathers and grandmothers, of endless brothers-in-law—far and near. He was very much at home in the world. Wherever he turned, he could say, "Younger brother, come here!" or "Grandfather, let me have this." The personal names of most of his acquaintances were hardly more than tags for calling out at a distance, or at ceremonial gatherings.

Along with his feeling of personal relationship to individuals there grew up in Tom a consciousness of the existence of tribal subdivisions in the village. The Ts'isha'ath tribe, with which he was identified by residence, kinship, and upbringing, proved really to be a cluster of various smaller tribal units, of which the Ts'isha'ath, that gave their name to the whole, were the leading group. The other subdivisions were originally independent tribes that had lost their isolated distinctness through conquest, weakening in numbers, or friendly removal and union. Each of the tribal subdivisions or "septs" had its own stock of legends, its distinctive privileges, its own houses in the village, its old village sites and distinctive fishing and hunting waters that were still remembered in detail by its members. While the septs now lived together as a single tribe, the basis of the sept division was really a traditional local one. The sept grouping was perhaps most markedly brought to light at ceremonial gatherings. Tom learned in time that of all the honored seats recognized at a feast, a certain number of contiguous seats in the rear of the house belonged to representatives of the Ts'isha'ath sept, a certain number of others at the right corner in the rear to those of another sept, and so on. Thus, the proper ranking of the septs was ever kept before the eye by the definite assignment of seats of higher and lower rank.

But it must not be supposed that Tom's childhood and youth were spent entirely in work and in the acquirement of social and ceremonial knowledge. On the contrary, what interested him at least as much as sociology was play. He spun his tops—rather clumsy looking, two-pegged tops they were—threw his gaming spears in the spear and grass game and in the hoop-rolling game, hit feathered billets with a flat bat, threw beaver teeth dice (though this was chiefly a woman's game), and, when he grew older, took part in the favorite game of "lehal," the almost universal Western American guessing game, played with two or four gambling bones to the accompaniment of stirring songs. More properly belonging to the domain of sport was the somewhat dangerous game of canoe-upsetting, in which the contestants upset their canoes and quickly righted them at a hand-clap signal. This was an especially favored game of Tom's. All through his life, up to the time that he lost his sight, he was as instinctively familiar with the run of water, the dip and lurch of a canoe, and the turn of a paddle, as with the movements of walking on the land. Indeed, for days on end, at certain seasons, his life flowed on insistently to the very rhythm of rising and falling wave.

In at least one class of activities and beliefs Tom constantly received definite instruction from his father and maternal uncle. This was the world of unseen things, the mysterious domain of magic, of supernaturally compelling act and of preventive tabu. There were hundreds of things he must be careful to do or to avoid if he would have success in hunting and fishing, if he would be certain that unseen but ever present powers favor him in his pursuits or, at the least, desist from visiting harm upon him. He must be particularly careful not to anger the supernatural powers, among whom are to be counted the fish and mammals of the sea, by contamination with unclean things—and most obnoxious of all unclean things is the presence or influence of a menstruating or pregnant woman. For instance, a sealer or hunter of sea lions must not drag his canoe down to the water's edge, but have it carried over, as otherwise it might run over offal or some spot through which a menstruating woman had passed, and thus carry with it a scent that would frighten away the game. And one must be careful about his speech when hunting on the sea. A curious example of this is the fiction by which fur seal hunting is spoken of as gathering driftwood, the fur seal himself being referred to as "the one that sits yonder under a tree." It would not do to let him know too precisely what is going on while he is being hunted! The various tabus that Tom has learnt and practised in the course of his life are almost without number, and his practical success and longevity he ascribes in no small measure to his religious observance of them all.

The tabus are largely preventive measures. But Tom learned that there are more positive ways of working one's will in the world of magic. One of these is the use of certain amulets on the person, hidden in the house or woods, or in connection with hunting and fishing implements. As a general good-luck amulet, Tom was fond of wearing in his hat the spine of the "rat-fish." When his father was about to die, he called Tom to him and whispered in his ear an important secret. This was that the chief life-guarding amulet of the family had been a fire drill that was secreted at the bottom of an old box filled with all sorts of odds and ends. Its efficacy depended largely on the fact that hardly anybody knew of it. In general, secrecy helps tremendously in the power of all magic objects and formulæ. An Indian likes to withhold as much as possible, even from his nearest kin, until economic urgency or the approach of death compels him to transmit the magical knowledge to some one that is near and dear to him. Some of his most powerful amulets Tom would secrete in the canoe or hide under the cherry bark wrappings around the hafts of his hunting spears. These amulets were of all sorts, but chiefly fragments of supernatural animals—blind snakes, crabs, spiders, or the like—obtained in the woods.

Some men are fortunate in getting power for hunting, fishing, wealth, love, doctoring, witchcraft, or whatever it may be, from supernaturaι beings or visitations. Amulets are often obtained in connection with these experiences, which regularly take place in mysterious or out-of-the-way places—the open sea, a remote island, the summit of a mountain, the heart of the woods,—and of all mysteries, it is the mystery of the dark woods that most fascinates and inspires with dread the coast villager, so much at home on the sandy beach and on open sea spaces. The supernatural givers of power are a variegated and grotesque lot—mysterious hands pointing up out of the earth; the scaly, knife-tongued, lightning serpent; fairy-like beings; treacherous tree nymphs; hobgoblins; ogres; and strange hybrid animals that seem to have stepped out of nightmares. All these denizens of the supernatural world have power to bestow that may not with impunity be refused. This power, once obtained, must be carefully husbanded by the observance of requisite tabus.

Tom has not had as many supernatural experiences as some men, but he has nevertheless been favored by two or three striking visitations. A gnome-like being of the beneficent, wealth-giving class known as Chimimis, once appeared to him as he was sitting out at dusk in company with two other men. Though these companions had their eyes directed at the Chimimis, they could not perceive him. Tom alone, speechless with astonishment, saw him place two spears on the roof of the house, walk off to the neighboring house, and disappear, so it seemed, in a log. When Tom came to himself, he scraped off those parts of the spear shafts that the hand of the Chimimis had gripped. He preserved the scrapings as an amulet and, in time, became one of the wealthiest men of his tribe.

At another time Tom obtained power from a supernatural being known as "Full-eyed," a diminutive, brownie-like creature. He was lying very ill in the house, gazing steadfastly at the fire, when the popping up of a little cinder caused him to raise his eyes. He saw what seemed to be a child circling the fire in a counter-clockwise direction, which is the exact opposite of the Nootka direction in dancing. He knew immediately that it was Full-eyed. The brownie carried a small storage basket on his breast, and picked up from the floor anything he could lay his hands on. Though Tom had been unable to sit up straight, this supernatural experience infused him with such sudden strength that he was now easily able to sit up. He believed also that, from this time on, wealth rolled into his house more rapidly than ever. The third of Tom's supernatural experiences was less striking than the other two, but apparently equally potent in its practical results. Tom was reclining on the sleeping platform of the house, in the dead of winter, when he observed a strange thing in one of the storage baskets on the box that marked the head of his bed. He noticed that a big black bumblebee gave birth to an infant bee. This seemed remarkable and evidently significant in view of the fact that the young bees ordinarily come into being in the summer, only. Because Tom was sole witness to so strange an occurrence, he was more than ever favored in the accumulation of wealth.

Such extraordinary occurrences as these are clearly in the nature of accidents; they cannot be relied upon for the necessary aid in the successful prosecution of life's work. The standard, and on the whole, the most useful means of securing this necessary aid is by the performance of secret rituals. Nothing came to one who did not undergo considerable hardship in training. This Tom learned early in life. If he wished to be a successful fisherman, or a hunter of sea mammals, or a land hunter, he had to retire at certain seasons to secret places in the woods, known only to the respective families that frequented them. Here, for days on end, he would bathe, rub himself down with hemlock branches until the skin tingled with pain, pray to the Sky Chief for long life and success, and, most important of all, carry out secret, magical performances based on the principle of imitation. If he wished to obtain power in sealing, he would build effigies of twigs representing the seal, the harpooning outfit, and the hunting canoe. The aspirants for success would dramatize the future hunt in its magical setting. He himself performed imitative actions and offered continuous prayers for success. These periods of preparation tested physical endurance to the utmost; fasting, continuous wakefulness, sexual continence, and the observance of all sorts of tabus formed part of the training. There was little that one could not learn to do, if only he were hardy enough to undergo the necessary magical preparation. Such young men as were fired with extraordinary ambitions, say unusual success in whaling or the acquirement of potent shamanistic power, would train the will and chasten the cries of the flesh for incredibly long periods, their spiritual eye fixed singly on the austerities of magical procedure.

Tom never devoted himself to unusual rigors in the acquirement of magical power. He contented himself with the normal routine enjoined upon those planning to seal, to spear salmon, to troll, to catch halibut with hooks, to spear cod with the aid of decoys, to accumulate wealth, to prepare for ritualistic performances, and to obtain enough shamanistic power to withstand the attempts of evil-minded people to bewitch him. He never ventured upon the more difficult and exhausting procedures required to make a successful whaler or hunter of sea lions. Of the more unusual types of secret ritual, Tom attempted but one. When past middle-age, he was fired with the ambition to learn how to interpret the speech of ravens. The ravens are believed to be the supernatural messengers of the wolves, the most austere and eerie of all beings, in the belief of the Nootka. Could Tom have learned to unravel the mysteries concealed in the croakings of these supernatural birds, there is little doubt that he would have been able to advance in ritual power far beyond his fellow tribesmen. Unfortunately he found the quest of this difficult knowledge too exhausting, too baffling. Tom acknowledges his failure with a sigh.

The secret rituals could only be performed at auspicious periods, when the moon was waxing and when the days were becoming progressively long. It was for this reason that Tom was always very careful to keep track of the passage of time, of the recurrence of the moons. If some neighbor, less wise and observant, committed the error of taking one moon for another and of performing magical rituals out of season, Tom would say nothing. He would smile and keep counsel with himself, knowing well that his neighbor's efforts when the hunting season came around, were doomed to failure. While Tom was one of those that never went out of his way to bewitch his neighbors or to spoil their luck, he was naturally not altogether displeased when they put themselves at a disadvantage. It was none of his business to correct them, to strengthen the hands of possible rivals.

Medicine men gained their power in a manner perfectly analogous to all other quests for magical assistance. The difference was simply that they sought aid of such beings as were known to grant power to cure diseases and to counteract witchcraft. The material guardians and amulets obtained by medicine men, generally certain birds and rarer fish, were locked away in their breasts.   When required for the detection of sickness, for the cure of the diseased, or for the overcoming of an evil opponent, they could be called upon to fly invisibly to the desired goal and to return at will.   Tom himself obtained a modicum of power from the mallard ducks, but not enough to warrant his considering himself a regular practitioner.   He had, also, a certain inherited, shamanistic power, or rather privilege, that came to him from a Nitinat ancestor.   This is why at public shamanistic performances which form part of the Ts'ayek cult, Tom's oldest son has the right to initiate shamanistic novices at a certain point in the ceremonial procedure, though he himself is not a practising medicine man.

Many Nootka are accused of gaining power to bewitch their enemies or rivals, whether by the handling of their food, nail parings, and body effluvia, or by the pronouncing of direful spells in connection with the name and effigy of the hated person.   Tom never indulged in such mean spirited pursuits, but he is very sure that many of his acquaintances have done so.   It is the constant fear of witchcraft that even to this day causes the Indians to keep many dogs around the house, and to lock their doors securely at night.   The barking of the dogs is useful in calling attention to malevolent "pains" or minute disease objects that wander about, particularly at night, while the locking of doors is essential in denying these objects an entrance.

The great supernatural beings of Nootka belief, such as the Sky-Chief, the Thunder-bird, and the Wolves, loomed very large in Tom's life, whether in prayer or in ritual.   Certain Nootka are more deeply religious than others.   They are more fervent in their prayers and they work themselves up to a greater ecstasy in the performance of rituals that are sacred to divine powers.   In contrast to men of this type, Tom has always been rather sober, not a skeptic by any means, but not an emotional enthusiast.   His knowledge of religious ceremonials is vast, but the spirit that animates this knowledge is rather one of order, of legal particularity, not of spiritual ecstasy.   The practical economical world, the pursuit of gain, has always been more congenial to Tom's temperament.   This does not mean that Tom is a rationalist in matters relating to the unseen world.   Only the educated or half-educated half-breeds are rationalists, and more than one of them has angered Tom by his ill-advised attempts to disturb him with skeptical arguments. However, there has been no change in Tom. He knows, as firmly as he knows his own name, that when the rumble of thunder is heard from the mountain, it is because the Thunder-bird is leaving his house on the peak, flapping his wings heavily, as he makes off for the sea to prey upon the whales. He knows also that when those that are not blind like himself tell him that there has been a flash of lightning, it is because the Thunder-bird has dropped the belt wound about his middle. This belt is the lightning serpent, zig-zagging down to the earth or coiling in a flash around a cedar tree.

Aside from the elementary problem of making his living, a Nootka's main concern is to earn the esteem of his fellow tribesmen by a lavish display of wealth. It is not enough for him to accumulate it and to live in private ease. He must, from time to time, invite the other families of his tribe, and the neighboring tribes, to public ceremonies known as potlatches, in which one or more of the important privileges to which he is entitled are shown and glorified by the distribution of property to the guests. The exhibiting of privileges may take several forms. The most important of them refer to ancestral crests, which may be shown in a dramatic performance, as a picture on a board, or latterly, on canvas, or symbolized in a dance. Ceremonial games are another frequent type of exhibitions of privileges at certain potlatches. Nearly all privileges have their proper songs, which are themselves jealously guarded privileges, and which are sung on these occasions.

There are two considerations that make the public performance of the more important privileges a matter of the greatest moment. In the first place, a man must clearly indicate his right to its performance by recounting the origin myth that it dramatizes, and by tracing his personal connection with the originator of the privilege. In the second place, he must be careful to distribute at least as much property as has already been distributed in his family, in connection with the public presentation of the privilege. If it is at all possible, he will try to exceed the record, so as to add to the public prestige not only of himself and his immediate family, but of the privilege itself. Should he fail in either of these essential respects, he is shamed. Hence, an important potlatch is not to be lightly undertaken. It requires much careful thought and preparation, and it necessitates the gathering of enough wealth to pay for all the services rendered by singers and other assistants, to present substantial gifts to the guests, and to feed the crowd of men, women and children that are present at the ceremony.

A potlatch is not often given as a mere display of wealth. Nearly always it is combined with some definite social or religious function, such as the giving of a name, the coming to marriageable age of a daughter, marriage, a mourning ceremony, the Wolf ritual, or a doctoring ceremony. Potlatching in its fundamental sense, in other words the giving away of property to the guests, is an essential of practically all ceremonies, big or little, religious or profane. Every potlatch involves at least three parties, the giver, the guest or guests, and the person in whose honor the potlatch is given. The last of these is generally some young member of the family whose prestige is thus furthered early in life, but it may be a stranger who has done the giver a service. There are different kinds of gifts. Certain of them are ceremonial grants to which the highest in rank of the tribe are entitled, but which they are expected to return with one hundred per cent interest at a subsequent potlatch. Another class of gifts, which feature the most important and picturesque part of the potlatch, is made to the highest in rank among the guests. There is no rigid rule as to the return of these gifts, but in practice they are nearly always liquidated at a return potlatch, with gifts of an equal, and in many cases greater, value. Finally, towards the end of the potlatch, there is a general distribution of smaller amounts to the crowd. Less careful account is taken of the return of such gifts than of the first two types. In part, the giving of a potlatch amounts to an investment of value, though it is doubtful whether, among the Nootka, the greater part of the expenditure incurred at a potlatch ever returned to its owner.

A potlatch serves not only a definite social and economic purpose for its giver, but affords, as well, an opportunity for minor distributions of property, such as public payments for services, on the part of other individuals present. Indeed any announcements of importance, such as the handing over of a privilege or a change in name, would be most appropriately made at a potlatch. The assembled tribesmen and guests were, to all intents and purposes, witnesses to such announcements.

Tom began to give potlatches on his own account when still quite a young man. The first one of any importance that he was responsible for, was a potlatch in honor of his niece's husband. This was a man of low birth, whom Tom had vowed to have nothing to do with. When his niece, however, gave birth to a child, Tom relented and, in order to wash away the stain on his family's honor, he called together thirty of his relatives, and distributed four guns and a blanket to each. He also sang two of his privileged songs, which he then and there transferred to the child as its due privilege. This potlatch not only marked a reconcilement with his low-born nephew, but gave the little youngster a fair start in life in the race for status. The next of Tom's potlatches was a Wolf ritual, in which he himself performed two of the ceremonial dances, those of the Thunder-bird and the Wolf circling about on all fours.

Some time after this, Tom resolved to marry a Ts'isha'ath girl named Witsah. In spite of the fact that she was a member of his own tribe, Tom wooed the girl not as a Ts'isha'ath, but as a member of a Nitinat tribe, among whom he had kinsmen on his father's side. As his own father was dead, he had ten of his Nitinat uncles woo the girl on his behalf. The wooing is always an important part of the marriage preliminaries, and consists chiefly in the placing of objects, symbolizing one or more of the privileges of the suitor, outside the house of the girl's family. The suitor himself is not present. Sometimes the objects are refused, when the suit may be continued until an acceptance is gained, though this does not necessarily follow. The suitor privileges deposited by Tom's representatives consisted of ten fires and a carving, representing the lightning serpent. These were accepted and returned to Tom's uncle as an indication of willingness on the part of the bride's parents to proceed with the marriage ceremony. Not long after the return of the privileges, the marriage ceremony was celebrated among the Ts'isha'ath people. The money distributed at that time by Tom and his Nitinat relatives constituted a bridal purchase, but when Tom's first child was born, the property then distributed was returned to Tom and the Nitinats with interest.

The greater part of the marriage ceremony consists of the performance of ceremonial games, each of which is accompanied by special songs, and followed by distributions of property. These games symbolize the difficulty of obtaining the hand of the bride, referring as they do to legendary tests that suitors were compelled to undergo in the past, before they could be admitted by the bride's father. One of the tests, for instance, might be the lifting of an especially heavy stone, or standing for some time without flinching between two fires. According to legendary theory such tests should be endured by the bridegroom himself, but in actual ceremonial practice any one of the bridegroom's party may be the winner in the contest, and receive the prize from the bride's father or whoever of her people is the proud possessor of that particular marriage-game privilege.

Some time after his marriage Tom gave two potlatches in a single month. The first of these was a puberty potlatch in behalf of a younger sister of his. The second was a birth feast or, as the Nootka term it a "navel feast" for his first child, a boy. About a year later Tom invited the Ucluelet people, one of the Nootka tribes, to a feast at which many dance privileges were performed and much property distributed. By this time Tom was getting to be pretty well known among the tribes of the west coast of Vancouver Island, for his rapidly growing wealth and for his potlatches. It was, therefore, no surprise to him, though it proved very gratifying, to have the chief of the Ahousat, one of the most powerful of the northern Nootka tribes, especially invite him to a potlatch at which he was given four of the chief's ceremonial songs. In return, Tom gave a potlatch to the Ahousat and the Comox, a tribe of alien speech from the east coast of the Island. He distributed four hundred blankets to the former, three hundred to the latter.

A year or two after this potlatch, occurred the decisive event in Tom's social career. This was the birth of his first daughter. The most magnificent Nootka potlatches are generally given in connection with a daughter's puberty ceremony. Ever since his marriage, Tom had been hoping to be able, in the fullness of time, to make a record in potlatching among his people, and to show his most valued privileges at the puberty potlatch of a daughter. Now that he was actually blessed by the arrival of a little girl, Tom's plans took immediate shape. He set about the accumulation of property with more zest than ever, driving many a sharp bargain with the Indians and whites, and he revolved frequently in his mind what tribes he was to invite, and what dramatic displays, dances and songs he was to use at the great ceremony. His first concern was to build a large house of native construction that the guests were to enter when invited to the Ts'isha'ath people. Appropriate timbers for posts and beams are not easy to find, especially since the white man's sawmill has made its appearance in the country. Hence, Tom was indefatigable in making inquiries of various persons and keeping his eye out for sufficiently large and conveniently located cedars. As he found such trees, he had them felled, hauled up to the Ts'isha'ath village along the Somass river, and put in place as opportunity presented itself. The actual construction of the house was thus spread over a period of some ten or fifteen years.

At one time an unfortunate casualty occurred. One of the heavy crossbeams fell to the ground, fortunately without injuring any one, but the event was considered an ill omen. Nevertheless, Tom did the best he could to ward off the evil influence by having a dance performed in honor of the spirit of the beam. Special songs that he possessed for this purpose were sung at the time.

Tom hoped that he could have the house completed before his daughter arrived at maturity. He was doomed to disappointment. His house still lacked one of the crossbeams and all the lighter woodwork, when his wife announced to him one morning that their daughter had come of age, was menstruating, in other words, for the first time. There was nothing for it but to have the puberty ceremony performed at once, reserving the main puberty potlatch for a few months later. Tom painted his face red and invited the neighboring Hopach'as'ath tribe to the puberty ceremony, the "torches standing on the ground," as it is termed.

This ceremony marks the beginning of the period of seclusion of the girl. She is painted and ornamented for the occasion, generally with legendary insignia belonging to the family, is made to stand in front of two long boards painted with representations of Thunderbirds and whales, and has water thrown four times at her feet. Four or ten poles, the so-called "torches," are lighted and later distributed with gifts to those entitled to receive them. Songs of various types are sung, particularly satirical songs twitting the opposite sex. Ceremonial games, some of them anticipating later marriage games, are also performed and prizes are distributed. After a general distribution of goods, the guests depart, leaving the girl to fast for four days and to enter upon a secluded period of various tabus behind the painted boards in the rear of the house.

After the puberty ceremony, Tom proceeded to Victoria to lay in his store of supplies for the impending potlatch. He bought an enormous number of boxes of biscuits, and to this day nothing pleases him more than to tell of how he compelled the white merchant to give him a special rate on the unusual order. As soon as the provisions were safely deposited at his village, Tom invited twelve tribes to his potlatch. To the nearer tribes he sent messengers; the more remote tribes of the east coast he invited in person. When the appointed day arrived, the Ts'isha'ath found that they had on their hands by far the largest number of guests that had ever visited the tribe at a single time. It was the proudest moment of Tom's life. Everything went well. There was enough food for all, the distributions of property were generous, and all the privileges were interestingly presented. There were a considerable number of these privileges performed, one or two of them being fairly elaborate dramatic representations that were new even to the most northern Nootka tribes, great potlatchers though they are. Tom's hereditary claim to the performances, the dances and the songs, was carefully explained by the ceremonial speaker. The ancestral legends were in every case recounted at length. Tom's title to the special crests of the whale and the Thunder-bird was duly set forth. The explanation of the carved house posts took the speaker back to the creation of the first Ts'isha'ath man from the thigh of a woman. Due account, as usual in these origin legends, was taken of the flood. The potlatch securely established Tom's position among the Indians of the Island. To this day it is often referred to by the Ts'isha'ath and their neighbors. Tom's family was "put high" as never before. More than once, Tom's grandson has found himself, when visiting comparative strangers, say among the East Coast tribes, received with open arms and honored with gifts of great value, all on the strength of his grandfather's potlatch.

Tom's potlatching career did not end here. Some time later he invited the Kyuquot, a Nootka tribe adjoining the Kwakiutl. At this potlatch he gave a dramatic representation of a number of privileges, including two Thunder-birds, a spouting whale, the supernatural quartz-beings known as He'na, and a supernatural bird known as Mihtach, a sort of mallard duck that haunts the top of the mountain called "Two-bladders-on-its-summit." The Heshkwiat tribe of Nootka was the next to be invited to a potlatch. A year or two after this, the second greatest ceremonial event in Tom's career took place, in the form of his second Wolf ritual or Tlokwana. The ritual was given for the special benefit of his oldest son Douglas and his newly married wife. These were the chief initiates in the ritual. Curiously enough, Tom's little grandson, as yet unborn, was also initiated. This is an extreme instance of the tendency of the Nootka Indians to heap honors upon their offspring at the earliest possible opportunity.

The Wolf ritual is the most awesome, the most fascinating and fear-inspiring ceremony that the Nootka possess. Whatever religious exaltation or frenzy they are capable of, finds expression in this elaborate ritual. The performance, which generally lasts eight days, preferably in the winter, is dominated throughout by the spirit of the wolves who are believed to be hovering near at the outskirts of the village. The more important parts of the ceremonial are open to only such members of the tribe as have been initiated. Many tabus must be observed by those participating, and an attitude of high-minded seriousness must be maintained throughout. In the old days, frivolity during the more strictly religious parts of the ritual, aside of course from the ceremonial buffoonery, was very severely punished by the marshaling attendants. Spearing to death on the spot was the penalty for infraction of the most sacred tabus.

The ritual begins with the songs and other ceremonial activities of an ordinary potlatch. Rumors are set going of the appearance of wolves in the neighborhood of the village. These rumors, accentuated by tales of narrow escapes and bloody casualties, act powerfully upon the imagination of the children, who are soon reduced to a state of panic. All of a sudden the lights are extinguished, and the four "wolves" break through the side of the house. In the confusion that ensues they make off with the youngsters that are to be initiated. From this moment, begins the ritual proper. A certain number of the tribe have the hereditary privilege to "play wolf," that is, to act as wolves during certain parts of the ritual beyond the confines of the village, to make off with the novices, and keep these as supposed prisoners in the woods.   For a number of days, there are supposed to be unsuccessful attempts to take back the captured novices, but the wolves remain obdurate until certain songs are sung, when the novices are brought out in view of the people and the series of attacks finally succeeds in routing the wolves.   The novices are supposed to be frenzied by the spirits of various supernatural beings that possess them.   They must be brought back by force.   Those privileged to do so lasso them, and, to the accompaniment of sacred songs, the struggling novices are conducted to the potlatch house, whistling furiously all the while.   The hubbub of mingled whistling, drumming and simultaneous singing of many distinct ritual songs, continues for the greater part of the night.   The din is indescribable. During the following day is performed the most sacred episode in the ritual.   The whistling spirits that possess the novices must be exorcised by means of sacred dances and songs.   A purification ceremony of bathing in the river or sea follows.   The remainder of the ritual consists of the performance of a number of special dances, each of which is appropriate to the particular supernatural being that is supposed to have possessed one of the initiates.   There are many of these dances, varying greatly in their prestige as privileges, and in their character of religious frenzy.   Probably the most austere of the dances is that of the supernatural wolf, who crawls about in reckless pursuit of destruction and has to be restrained with great difficulty by a number of attendants.   Other dances represent various types of woodsy creatures or ogres.   Many of them are pantomimic representations of animals, while human activities of various kinds are represented in still others.

With this Wolf ritual Tom's ceremonial activities gradually lessened.   He continued to take an active interest in whatever potlatches were given by his family, and he often helped with his advice and active coöperation in the singing of songs and the delivering of ceremonial addresses, particularly of the formal speeches of thanks. Now that he had done his share in establishing the glory of his family, Tom sat back and allowed his eldest son to take the initiative, at least in theory, in all ceremonies affecting their standing in the tribe.

It is long since Tom has been able to do useful work.   He is entirely dependent on his oldest son's family, with whom he lives, but they do not feel his presence to be a burden.   For one thing, he is uniformly good-natured, very talkative about his own past and in judging his neighbors, and always ready to help with his advice in matters of importance, whether it be the preparations for a potlatch or some contested sealing claim. But back of the garrulous, shabby Tom of the present, looms up the Tom of the great potlatches of former days. It is to this Tom that his children and grandchildren almost entirely owe the high standing that they maintain among their people.

When Tom dies he will be put in a coffin and buried in the ground. This was not the old Nootka custom. The more important families had caves in which their deceased members were put away; others were laid in burial boxes or rush mats which were then put up in trees back of the village. Near the place of the burial there would be put up a grave post, constructed of roof rafters of the house, on which would be painted one of the crests of the deceased.

Though the old burial customs are no longer followed, some of the beliefs and practices attending death have not yet died out. Thus, the immediate personal effects of the deceased, as well as considerable additional property, are always destroyed. In the old days the whole house might be burned down, and tales are told of how the mourning survivors would move off to another spot to build them a new house. In all likelihood there will be performed immediately after Tom's death a ceremony intended to comfort the family of the deceased and to induce Tom's spirit to leave the house and its vicinity. Tom's soul will have left his body in the shape of a tiny shadow-like double of himself, through the crown of his head, to assume eventually the form of a full-fledged ghost. It is safe to assume that the tabu of the dead person's name will be carefully observed. Not only will Tom's name not be mentioned by his tribesmen for a stated period, but all words that involve the main element of his name will be carefully avoided. This element denotes the idea of "distant." People will have to get along as best they can without it, whether by beating about the bush, by stretching the meaning of some other element so as to enable it to take its place, or, if need be, by borrowing the corresponding element, provided it be of different sound, from some other dialect. Wailing sounds will be heard in the village for some time after Tom's death, and it is very likely that at a mourning potlatch a number of privileges belonging to the family, say four songs, will be thrown away.   Such privileges are tabued during the mourning period.   At the end of the mourning period, which may be anything from a year to ten, another potlatch is given by one of the family and the tabus are lifted.   When that time arrives Tom's name will have passed into native history.   The name Sayach'apis, "Stands-up-high-over-all," will then be freely referred to with pride or with envy.

EDWARD SAPIR

WINDIGO
A CHIPEWYAN STORY

Windigo, a Chipewyan Story

I

BEHIND the Hudson's Bay Company's post at Fort Hearne, they were wrestling for wives. Forgotten were the words of Catholic priests on the sanctity of marriage, forgotten the precepts of Episcopal missionaries. In the twinkling of an eye those high-flown, newfangled notions had been swept aside by the deep rooted usage of ancient days. The Indians had been peaceably playing at "Button, button, who has the button?" with half the spectators staking shirts and blankets on the issue of the game. The real fun started when drunken Ramsay MacCrae reeled into the crowd and hugged Blanche Lecouvreur. Her husband sent him staggering to the ground, but the toper rose and, thrusting his fingers into Lecouvreur's face, challenged him to an old-time combat for his spouse.

There was no more guessing game after that, there was genuine sport. Ramsay was laid low, but he had set the example and another young swashbuckler fell foul of Casimir; and so it went on. There was nothing riotous about the affair, it was as nicely regulated as a prize fight. There was never more than one contest at a time for no one would miss part of the spectacle by engaging in a side show of his own. The wrestlers pulled each other about by the hair and ears, after the approved Athabaskan fashion before attempting other holds. What amusement when Angus had thrown the gauntlet to little Gordon and was on the point of carrying off buxom Peggy by default! But there was still more laughter when the crafty wag of the camp, supposed to be cowering in a hiding-place, popped out of his tent, his skull cropped, ears and body glistening with grease, and, seizing his handicapped adversary by his long locks, dragged him to the ground. Cries of encouragement and admiration filled the air. One wagered his gun on a friend's victory, another staked his net or tent. The women fought for, looked on stolidly while the battle was waging, but when Ramsay had fallen, Blanche heaved a sigh of relief, and Peggy could not suppress a sneer at her would-be captor.

Others were hauled away whimpering, but with Marie every one knew that she was wailing only to satisfy the proprieties, for she was well rid of her brute of a husband who had nearly beaten her to death after his last journey.

But the climax came when big Douglas thrust his paw in Pierre Villeneuve's face. To be sure, Louise was as comely as any young matron in or near the settlement, yet until now the bullies had refrained from challenging her husband. Every one respected her for her virtue and her kindness; and every one, too, was fond of Pierre. He was such a harmless, easy-going, good-natured chap, so handy with packstrap and toboggan, a prime companion after a two days' trip without food, keeping up his blithe old ditty about *"ma belle patrie"* or warbling some native melody, when every one else was ready to sink down from exhaustion. But what was all that to crazy Douglas when he was in drink and lusting for a woman? He had the advantage of four inches in height, and of at least two stone in weight,—good enough reason for trying for a prize. Still, Pierre was no mean antagonist with his sinewy, agile frame and his widely famed strength of grip. Nor was it long before Douglas discovered that he had caught a tartar. Twice he was on the point of scoring, only to have Pierre wriggle unhurt from his grasp. At last a cry of anguish from Louise as the inevitable was about to happen. Douglas had lifted her husband and was about to hurl him to the ground. But then things happened quickly, no one knew how, and Douglas lay stretched out on the ground panting. He limped off with a sprained ankle, amidst the mocking and jubilations of Pierre's friends, while even his backers had sportsmanship enough to congratulate the conqueror.

Then through the laughing, shouting, gesticulating crowd a Titanic figure elbowed his way. In the midst of the din and excitement the strange half-breed's approach had passed unnoticed. He had arrived only yesterday, with a letter of credit from the Company of Gentlemen and Adventurers' Trading into Hudson's Bay. His name was George MacDonald; beyond that nothing was known about him. What a frame was his! Beside it, huge Douglas looked puny. Pierre seemed a mere babe. MacDonald was not a man of many words. He strode towards Louise, lightly touched her arm and said, "I want you." She shrank back shrieking, and Pierre rushed at the giant in a blind fury, only to be firmly grasped and gently deposited on the ground.   Once more he leaped at his conqueror but was caught in a vise-like grip and laid low again, raging and impotent. In his madness he unsheathed his knife, but now Casimir and Gordon pinioned his arms and the crowd shouted, "Peace, peace!   The stranger has won fairly!"

MacDonald stood there calm and supercilious.   "I have won," he said to Louise, "come."   Without looking back he walked towards his tent, and the woman followed sobbing.   That was the last wrestling bout that day.

II

MacDonald stayed at Fort Hearne and built himself a cabin at the other end of the post.   He went off for a few days and returned with a retinue of Slaveys.   Then he began trading against the Company itself.   He had a way of dealing with the Indians that no other man had.   He paid less, rather than more, for their furs, and disdained to coddle them with gifts and favors.   Yet, when the peltry hunters caught a silver fox or some other valuable fur, the prize went to the gruff giant's shack rather than to the Company's warehouse.   There was no competing with him.   One factor was sent to relieve another, but without avail.   At last the Commissioner himself braved the journey to the Fort, bought out MacDonald, and set him up as head of the post.

Now, things began to hum at Fort Hearne.   Never had such a factor been seen as MacDonald.   He spoke Dogrib and Chipewyan and Cree and French as well as his father's Orkney Island brogue: there was no hunter for hundreds of miles with whom he could not converse in his own tongue.   He was on his feet from morning until night and kept every one else on the go.   As a freetrader he had beaten the Company at its own game.   With the Company's prestige behind him he allowed no freetrader to raise his head.   By fair means none could compete, and who dared try force or trickery against MacDonald?   In the long winter evenings, when boresome hours of sloth were whiled away with story telling, strange tales began to circulate about the big factor.   Since little or nothing was known of his early life, imagination ran riot.   Angus knew that the factor could transform himself into a wolf, and hunt deer thus disguised. Casimir pictured him in his youth, pulling cargo-laden scows, single-handed, that were wont to be towed by a half-dozen strapping Indians. Jean had it from an aunt that MacDonald had once swum a river in pursuit of a bear, had stabbed it with a knife and carried the carcass twenty miles to camp. Some said he was bulletproof, and others with a tincture of Christian lore spoke of his pact with the devil. He grew into the central figure of a new mythology.

The hero himself moved across his stage with the saturnine grandeur of a Norse god. He never boasted, never faltered, never failed. He ran unscathed through rapids never attempted since two parties of canoemen had been capsized and drowned. He walked toward the cocked gun of a drink-crazed competitor, and calmly knocked it out of his hand. MacDonald did not know what it was to be afraid.

Between the trader and Pierre a curious relationship developed. The factor of course used men as pawns, and knew a good lieutenant when he saw one. But for Pierre he showed more consideration than was due to even the best of assistants. Perhaps it was because Louise prompted kindness to her former husband; perhaps there was some spontaneous sentimentalism for a man he had wronged. However that might be, Pierre became a sort of attendant-in-ordinary on MacDonald, his companion on trips of inspection and the rarer jaunts of pleasure.

For Pierre, his sullen, imperious master became the one and only subject of interest. He studied his habits and gestures and speech. He had set out eager to detect weakness, but his prying skepticism had changed to grudging admiration, and later to despondent amazement. He had begun by hating his wife's abductor, and he came to hate with an ever intenser hatred the man who was without peer. It was not merely the giant's strength or dauntless courage, it was the way he had with men. How he ordered about Casimir or Angus or Ramsay! A word was enough to quell rebellion. Again and again, in the beginning, Pierre had resolved to bid him defiance, yet when the moment came his resolution had failed. Yes, people liked Pierre and after a fashion they respected him, but that was a different thing. It was not in him to issue commands to others. If he ever mustered courage to do so, they would think he was putting on airs and laugh in his face, so that he would slink off in shame and humiliation. Why were men born so different? Why was *he* not born superior to the rest, like MacDonald? Why born at all only to be lorded over by another? Thus he brooded and brooded for hours at night, losing all hope and joy in life.

Then one day, unexpectedly, his despair was lifted. He had been on a fruitless hunting trip with the factor, and the two were approaching the post at the close of a rainy day. They were walking through a dense wood. Both were drenched to the skin, and Pierre was nearly exhausted. Suddenly, odd fancies crossed his mind. Weird tales of childhood, retold round many a winter camp fire, surged in memory and would not down. At dark, the forest was peopled with mysterious beings. The Windigo were about then—cadaverous shapes with glaring eyes, and feeders on human flesh. They lurked in the shadows of trees, and rose upon wayfarers from the depths of the swamps. What chance of escape when they had once sighted a victim? Rattling their skeletons, they flitted after him faster than a hawk can fly, tore him apart like a rabbit or swallowed him whole. The very wood Pierre was now traversing had been once entered by a trapper who was never seen again. Pierre began to feel oppressed by a sense of uncanniness. He peered cautiously into the gathering darkness, then glanced eagerly behind him. He was glad MacDonald was near. The great man could protect him if any one could. Pierre felt reassured, yet it was best to take no chances, so he hurried on.

Of a sudden there was a snapping of boughs, and he heard his name called as if in mockery as a long form swished through the wood, and a grim face was gaping at him not ten feet away. He turned in horror and fled towards MacDonald, crying, "Windigo! Windigo!" as he pointed at a spot ahead. But MacDonald did not smite the ogre with one of his huge fists, or seek to grapple with it as he was said to have once wrestled with a bear. His face turned an ashen hue, his mighty body was quivering like an aspen. That was the half-breed of it. Then with a bound he ran through the wood as fast as his legs would carry him, down to the river bank and along the rocky water front, till at length he caught sight of the big warehouse. There he paused panting, with the cold perspiration on his forehead. Pierre had followed as swiftly as he could, and at last overtook his master. Both were trembling from head to foot and MacDonald kept muttering, "Windigo! Windigo!" Thus they walked toward the Fort. And Pierre felt happier than he had ever been since that wrestling bout when he had lost Louise: for all his way, MacDonald was afraid of the Windigo!

III

Casimir was dangerously ill. His appetite was gone and his limbs seemed paralyzed. There came rumors that a famous Cree doctor was visiting the Chipewyan of a nearby settlement, and Pierre was dispatched to lure him to Fort Hearne with promise of fabulous fees. The Cree consented. He was a garrulous old man and on their joint trip Pierre tried to sound him about his powers, but on that subject he was mum. "You will see," he answered, and Pierre was obliged to wait.

When they arrived at the Fort, the medicine man erected a little booth and had himself thrust in, with his hands and feet firmly tied. He sang his incantations and the lodge began to shake. It seemed filled with strange beings, for unearthly sounds were heard, followed by a death-like silence. Opening the lodge they saw the conjuror unbound, and as if awakening from a trance. He proclaimed that the spirits had visited him and declared that Casimir would recover. Next, the patient himself was stretched out in the booth and the doctor entered it, stripped stark naked. He knelt and sang and blew at Casimir's heart, sucked at his breasts, and talked as if with his guardian spirits. Then he swallowed a stick three feet long, and retched it up again, announcing that all was well. In sooth, Casimir was carried from the tent clamoring for food, and in a week he was able to walk about. Then his kin showered gifts on the great magician, and all the other Indians sought to curry favor with him by every manner of attention.

Pierre was less ostentatious than others in his entertainment of the old sage, but sometimes when the rest were fast asleep he would steal to the conjuror's tent with liquor and tobacco, to ply him with questions about the magic art. And after a while his host's reticence waned. He even confessed to having bewitched a rival by drawing his image on the ground with an arrow pointed at his heart. Yet when Pierre hinted that he, too, had a strong enemy on whom he would fain cast a spell, the old fox hedged and said that sorcery was a dangerous business. Some men had power of their own, and could hurl the evil charm back with redoubled force against the sorcerer. Besides, he himself was old and wanted to live his few years in peace.

When Pierre found it hopeless to make the Cree bewitch his master, he changed his tactics. What was the truth about the Windigo? He had heard his mother tell about them, but did they really exist? That proved a less delicate subject for the medicine man. He himself had never seen a Windigo, but he knew all about them from another conjuror. Yes, the Windigo were dangerous spirits and fearfully strong. How strong? Surely no stronger than the factor? Why, they would rend him asunder like a dry twig. They swooped down upon men to tear out their vitals, and played ball with their skulls. There was a way to gain their favor, but it was very hard. If one fasted for three or four days in a wood they haunted, and freely offered them of one's flesh, they were pleased and might adopt him as their child. True, they were likely to swallow the sufferer whole, but when they spewed him out he was like one of themselves ever after, fierce and cannibalistic. The other Indians had better keep a wide berth of such as these, or placate them by gifts lest they break loose and destroy every one in sight. And now Pierre himself recalled a gaunt man who had terrorized the camp of his childhood, and whose bare glance had thrown timid folk into convulsions.

Pierre slipped home and sat musing for a long time. Should he tempt the spirits of the woods? Would they answer his prayer? What if they ate him before he could make his offering? Yet, why should he live? He had lost Louise; and her captor was master of Fort Hearne. Life mattered not, unless the Windigo chose to bless him.

The next day he entered the wood he had traversed with MacDonald that memorable evening. He ate not a morsel of food all day, and continued his fast next day, praying to the Windigo. At last he mustered up courage, gashed his chest with a big knife, and offered his body to the spirits. Then he fell down in a dead swoon. When he woke up, there was joy in his heart for all his pain. A Windigo had really come and blessed him! It had seized him as a boy seizes a moth, but when it saw the blood streaming from his breast it took pity on him, swallowed and disgorged him. Next spring he was to wreak vengeance as a Windigo. He must merely bide his time.

As he walked homeward, he exulted in his new powers. Why not try them for a joke? He, too, would show people his strength now. The first man he encountered he would terrify into fits. Yonder was Angus, mending a net in front of his tent. He would do as well as the next. Pierre quickly stepped up to him, and assuming a ferocious grimace, he cried, "I am Windigo! I have come to eat you!"

But Angus burst into a guffaw, "You a Windigo! You, who never hurt a fly! You are crazy. You've been drinking. Go home and sleep it off!" Pierre slunk home like a whipped cur, and threw himself on his bed crestfallen and humiliated. The Windigo had blessed him, yet he could not be Windigo. It was not in him. Even the Windigo could help only men like MacDonald. Thus he lay in impotent grief till exhaustion brought sleep. Then the Windigo loomed in sight and whispered, "In the spring, fool! I said, in the spring!"

IV

Spring came, and word reached Fort Hearne that the factor was to meet a fleet of scows at Fort Batise. That was a post he had never visited, so he summoned Pierre to make ready for the trip as his guide. They laid in an ample stock of provisions, for it was a long journey and there might be a protracted wait for the boats at their destination: Hudson's Bay Company transports do not run on schedule time. One fine morning the two men set out in a canoe, struggling up-stream against the powerful current. Now and then they landed to shoot some partridges, and one day MacDonald killed a moose. Otherwise there was little to relieve the monotony of the journey. From morning till night, not a soul crossed their path. With MacDonald lapsing into his wonted silence, hours would pass without a sound but the splashing of the paddles and the quaint, plaintive notes of Pierre's Red River melodies. Once in a while an abandoned site, with tent poles standing, suggested former human occupation. Every night the two men camped near the water edge, played a game or two of cribbage, and then stretched out to rest till four or five o'clock the next morning. And in the night Pierre would hear strange sounds, and as they grew nearer they turned into words: "In the spring! In the spring!"

When they reached Fort Batise, the post was all but deserted. The Company's trader had gone on a hunting trip and the dozen Indians in his charge were scattered though the woods. A single half-witted breed was holding down the Fort, and pointed out the uninhabited island, already known to Pierre, where the scows from time immemorial had been unloading the cargoes destined for Northern posts. The factor and Pierre paddled across and threw their bedding into a long, tumble-down shack reserved for the Company's servants. It was still somewhat too early for retiring, so MacDonald suggested a walk, and they set out for a stroll through the dense wood.

Pierre had been unusually silent that evening, as though by contagion with the factor's taciturnity. Now, of a sudden, his tongue was loosened. Did MacDonald know why the post had never been transferred to the island for all its fine landing place? The Indians would not live there, they never came there alone, for the spot was haunted, they said. It was called Simon's island. There was a long story about it, a foolish tale, but one the Indians told about their camp fires as though it were true. Of course Simon had really lived; Pierre remembered him well from the days of his boyhood—a ne'er-do-well, not a bad sort, but one always in bad luck. First, none of the girls would have him, then he got married and his wife died in childbirth. He would get a job towing a boat, stumble over a windfall on his first trip, and break his leg. It was always that way with poor Simon. When he gave up tracking, he became a pelt hunter. For years he roamed over the country and eked out a miserable livelihood. At last he had a stroke of luck and caught a silver fox. Now he thought he should live in plenty. But while on his way to the nearest trader's, he fell in with another trapper. They slept side by side, and in the morning the stranger and the silver fox were both gone. High and low, Simon looked for them, but in vain. Then he turned crazy in his grief and became a Windigo. Whomever he chanced upon, men or women, he killed and ate. The Indians made up parties to hunt him like a wild beast. He laughed at them; he was Windigo. They could never catch him. Then some time after, those who had hunted him were found murdered in their tents, and people ceased pursuing him. Now they tried to buy him off. As soon as he had been sighted near a camp, heaps of meat were piled up outside the settlement, and the handsomest clothing was laid beside the food. Then he would leave the camp alone—till some fine day the fancy seized him once more, and he stole into a camp to gratify his craving. That was long ago, and Simon had died on this very island, where he lay buried. Yet the natives believed that his ghost still walked as a Windigo from time to time, though the Company said it was all nonsense and put up its shack there, in defiance of Indian tales. Of course the Company knew best.

MacDonald had been listening with growing attention, and throughout the tale Pierre's gaze had been riveted on his features. Had not a faint tremor passed down his spine when he first heard the word "Windigo"? Had he not caught his breath when he learned of the ghost's reported wanderings? And why this sudden turning on his heels at the close of the story? Pierre was whistling a tune on the return walk, and the factor roared at him to keep still. He was plainly nervous; the tale had done its work.

Arrived at the cabin, MacDonald picked up his bedding and muttered, "Perhaps we had better go across to the post, we won't be able to sleep here for mosquitoes." He did not expect Pierre to have faith in his pretext; neither did he expect to be openly flouted by his meek companion. But Pierre, looking him up and down, asked drily, "Afraid of Simon's ghost?" "Afraid of nothing!" thundered MacDonald, hurling his blankets on the floor and glowering at his mate. He began to pace the room with giant strides. There was no doubt of it, he was troubled. He would not play cribbage. He was too tired, he said. MacDonald, who had never been tired before! So, soon both men sprawled out on the floor covered with their four-point blankets. But neither fell asleep.

After a while MacDonald rose softly, and tiptoed toward the door. Perhaps he could make his way to the bank unnoticed, and put the river between Simon's ghost and himself. But Pierre was wide awake and staring at him in the gloaming of a Northern night. "I was just stretching a bit," the big man offered in explanation, and Pierre did not even deign to tell him he lied. He sat up against the door now, and was eyeing the factor steadily, scornfully. The big man was nonplussed. What was Pierre's game? How could he be so calm in a haunted spot? A mad hatred against him suddenly rose in MacDonald's breast. He would brain this puny dolt with a blow of his fist, and say he had been drowned in the rapids. Then he would escape to the post and no soul would know of his weakness. Still Pierre sat looking at him with his gun across his knees. MacDonald cared little for the gun. There was at least a chance for him to take Pierre by surprise, and wrest the weapon from his grasp, and when had MacDonald been afraid to take chances? But there was something in Pierre's gaze that cowed and subdued him. So he merely sat up facing Pierre and the door, with neither uttering a word.

As the minutes passed, strange noises became audible. The floor was creaking and the door began to rattle, and over on the other bank the dogs were barking as dogs never barked before. There was a something—was it a bat?—that kept flitting against the roof, and on the door came an unaccountable rhythmic tapping. The factor fidgeted and peered in this direction and that, while Pierre sat now six feet away, immobile and pitiless. Then there was a different sound. A slow, heavy tread was coming up from the water edge. It was approaching the shack from the rear, passed round and got to the door. MacDonald sprang to his feet, but the steps went on, and he sank on the floor relieved though faint. But what was that? The steps were coming closer again: the wanderer was circling the shack a second time. Yet it seemed he had no intention of coming in, for, without halting at the door, the mysterious being started on its third round. But if it cared not to enter, neither was its purpose to leave the inmates in peace, for a fourth circuit began.

Now Pierre burst forth: "It is Simon! He is walking round four times, then he will stop and pay you a visit." MacDonald leaped up—a beast at bay, afraid to stay, afraid to go out now, straining to hear the weird footfalls first passing away then returning, ever more and more distinct. And now there was a dead halt at the door. Would it fly open and usher in the hideous shape of Simon's ghost? The door remained closed. But now Pierre rose with a grim laugh, dropping his gun. He walked toward his master and thrust his thumb at his face. "Simon has come to see us wrestle. I will wrestle you for Louise. Simon has made me Windigo. I will throw you and kill you and eat you, and he wants to look on." Fearlessly and madly he sprang at the giant's throat. The factor had not watched him, he had not heard his speech, he was still looking and looking at the door. Where now were those puissant arms that had held Pierre like an infant at Fort Hearne? Limp and powerless, they were hanging from a twitching heap that fell resistless at the first impact. Pierre beat him and kicked him and choked him. Without knife or gun, with his bare hands he murdered the great factor. And then—he was Windigo!

He rose jubilant. The Windigo had spoken truly: his enemy lay conquered. What next? Return to the post and tell of his deed? Would they believe him? They would say he was drunk or crazed, *he* who could not kill a fly. They would say some enemy of Mac-Donald's, a party of freetraders perchance, had shot him from ambush. And *he* would be once more good, meek Pierre Villeneuve. It had all been in vain. To kill MacDonald was nothing, nothing even to regain Louise. He wanted to be master like the dead giant, and that he could never be.

He staggered to the door ·and flung it open. What was that? A pallid face recoiling in terror, a horror-stricken cry of "Windigo!" and a man fleeing to the river and paddling across. He had forgotten the breed he had bribed, on plea of a practical joke, to cross from the post and prowl round the shack. The man had peeped in and seen everything. Now Pierre was saved, now he had won. His witness would spread the news and warn the people against the new Windigo. Pierre was greater now than MacDonald had ever been. His fame would travel from Hudson's Bay to the Rocky Mountains and from the Red River to Fort Macpherson. How they would pamper him—Crees and half-breeds, Chipewyans and Slaveys—as he roamed over their country that now was his. He would steal their furs and eat their game and kidnap their wives, snapping his fingers in their faces. He was master now, for now he was Windigo.

ROBERT H. LOWIE

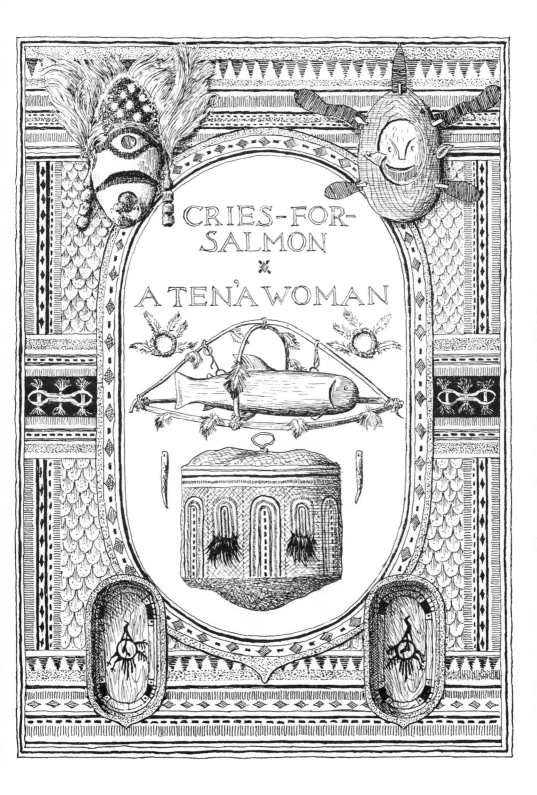

CRIES-FOR-
SALMON

A TEN'A WOMAN

Cries-for-salmon, a Ten'a Woman

YOU ask me to tell you the story of somebody's life at Anvik, my home in Alaska. I will tell the story of the woman who gave me the moccasins I showed you—there is more to tell about a girl than a boy. But I shall have to tell about a boy, too, for you can't tell about the girls without telling about the boys.

When Cries-for-salmon was to be born, they called in Havetse-kĕdtsa, Their-little-grandmother, an old woman of experience, to help. For three days after the birth Their-little-grandmother stayed by the side of the bed of skins, nor might the mother leave her bed without the permission of Their-little-grandmother. I don't know much about these days because boys and men do not stay in the house at this time; they go to the kadjim (the men's house). All I know is that the after-birth is wrapped in a cloth, and placed in the fork of a tree—the after-birth is a part of the body and you would not want to destroy it, just as when you cut yourself, you wipe off the blood with shavings and place the shavings in the fork of a tree. Even what is left of an old garment you would not destroy, you would not throw it into the fire as the white people do, but put it into a bag which in course of time you will place in a spruce tree. Whatever is put away in the woods is thought of as being still a part of the village, so that when a ceremonial circuit has to be made of the village, a half mile or so of woods is covered so that these things in the trees may be included.

The baby's cord is tied around the wrist or the neck of the baby with sinew, and left on for two or three years. An ax head is placed on the body of a boy baby for a certain number of days—I don't know how many, nor what they put on top of a girl. Should a white person come into the house at this time, the object is removed. If the child dies under three or four years of age the object, the ax or other thing, is put with the corpse. I don't know why, and when I have asked the old men they would answer, "Who of us knows?" as they often answer when they *do* know but have not enough confidence in you to tell. Besides, young fellows are not

337

expected to ask questions; you must learn by overhearing, and coming that way to understand.

For twenty days after Cries-for-salmon was born, her father had to stay at home, indoors, "under his smoke hole," as people used to say when they lived in igloos or underground houses. Nowadays, all or almost all live in frame houses. During these twenty days a man is not to touch any object made by white people, more particularly things of steel or iron, knife or ax or ice pick. Copper, got in trade from the coast, which has been melted down and hand beaten, a man may use; and he would eat out of dishes of wood or bone. Work tools of any kind he would not handle, unless in a household emergency he had to go to the forest for wood or game, when he would first go to the dyiin, the shaman, to get a song to sing in the circumstances. For this song, as for other songs, the shaman would be paid loftak—skins, meat, or oil.

Even if a man goes out during the twenty days, he should be careful not to pass over the water of a stream or lake—it would be othlang, and the fish would cause a skin eruption in the child. Our skin is usually very smooth and clear, and whenever any one has an eruption or rash we know it is from othlang.

Had Cries-for-salmon been born in the spring, then the following fall her father would not go eeling—that too would be othlang and it would cause a dearth of eels. Nor would a man go eeling for a year after a death in his family. If you knew how much we depended on eels for food, you would understand why we have to be so careful. The first sign of the eel coming is the finding of an eel in the stomach of a lush, the fish which is our main food in winter. Some one may find an eel in a lush, miles away from the village, and then at once he sends word, and the men go out to the places on the river where the channel is narrow and there are good feeding grounds for the eel. Here they come so thick that they cause the water to rise, and you have but to throw them out on the bank with a stick. As people eel together in this way, every one would know if a man went eeling after a death or birth in his family.

As with work after a birth in his family, so with amusements—a man should not take part. He should sit quiet, with his head down, for at this time he is supposed to be in connection with his spirits. His spirits are not any stronger than the strongest songs he has, and at this time a man must be watchful lest his songs lose their virtue or power, or lest from violations of the rules the baby die.

When Cries-for-salmon was restless as a little child, and cried, no doubt her mother called out to her, "Lia! the Evil One! Keep quiet!" to scare her. (To abuse any one, people will say, Li dená! Blood of the Evil One.) And when Cries-for-salmon was able to walk, she was watched all the time by her father or mother, for she had to be taught from the very beginning not to step on anything pertaining to the welfare of the family that might be lying on the floor. Should a stick be lying there, for example, that was being worked for an arrow or fish trap, the little girl would have to walk around it, not over it. The spirit of the boy is stronger than the spirit of the girl, so a boy may step where he pleases.

And the girl, as she grows a little older, has to be taught to be extremely careful about whatever she finds on the floor, of bits of food, of bone or feather or hair or skin. It is a rule that all such waste bits be put separately into baskets by the women, and carried to the haunts, in forest or on river, of the creatures to which the bits belonged. Cries-for-salmon would go along with her mother to see how she dumped into the river from her canoe the feathers of duck or goose or swan, that they might change back into birds such as they had come from—as the feathers drifted down the current, although invisible to her, Cries-for-salmon was told, they became birds again to return to feed in their old haunts of mud and goose grass. Similarly she saw her mother empty out fish bones to become fish, and she saw her take to the forest the bones of game animals. Were such bones left on the floor and stepped on, it would be othlang.

Sometimes, as men sit on the floor with their heels drawn back to the buttocks, or as they sit cross-legged, left leg over right, with a bowl of food propped on their legs, a bone may snap out on the floor instead of back from their fingers into the bowl. It is a spirit of the family, a hungry spirit, who is after the food. The spirit of the food goes to feed the family spirit, and although the particle is picked up and taken to the forest, it has lost its power, it will not become animal again.

When we men kill willow or ruffed grouse (ptarmigan), we take out some of the tail feathers and throw them on the ground, giving them back to the forest to become birds again. I remember that the first time I shot a grouse I took out some feathers above the tail. The fellow with me laughed. "That is not right," said he. "It is the tail feathers you must take." In selling grouse to the Mission, people will first skin them, just as they will first pluck the geese or ducks they sell, and remove the entrails. Similarly, they skin and clean the rabbits they sell. (Before a ceremonial the men engage in a rabbit drive. They pick out an island or a point of land, and spread out, each man in sight of another. Each yells and beats on the trees to scare out the rabbits, and then they form the arc of a circle and close down to the water. They keep the rabbits for the feast, but a few they may sell.) Bear meat and lynx meat they would not sell at all to white people.

We do not eat rabbit meat in summer and no doubt Cries-for-salmon was told, as are other children, that it was wormy. She was told, too, never to eat in the dark, lest she swallow the eye of the Evil One, which in going back to the Evil One, would choke her. Nor in eating meat should she cut off a piece in her teeth. In pouring out tea or liquids, Cries-for-salmon was taught to be very careful to pour only to well below the brim, almost an inch below, not to risk spilling. If the cup ran over it would be othlang to the person served—he would fail to run down his game, to catch fish, or to do well in leadership—and to overcome the othlang he would have to go to the shaman for a song.

In all these particulars a girl has to learn how to behave, how to carry herself. A young man is rated by his ability in making snowshoes and in running down game, fox, deer and, before the portaging of the whites drove them out, caribou. A girl is rated by her ability in handicrafts and in providing food, but she is also esteemed for her household behavior. If she is gifted with strength, with virtue, as she grows old she is likely to have given into her keeping an old wooden bowl which has been passed down from generation to generation of women, within the same rank, to be used in ceremonies to honor hunters of distinction. Moreover, the presents of a careful woman are welcome. People hate to see a young man as he grows up wear things made by any or everybody. Were he to wear mittens or boots or parki (shirt) made by a careless woman, his own ability might be reduced and his spirits weakened.

Cries-for-salmon was taught, like other little girls and boys, never to sing or whistle when eating, and never to imitate at any time in the winter the birds of summer—that would prolong the winter, perhaps making it run into two winters (a frequent expression of the narrator meaning that the already short summer is further shortened), and so causing famine. Nor was Cries-for-salmon ever to make snowballs or snow images. There is but one time a snow man may be made—when people want a freezing spell in the spring. Travelers are afraid of being caught away from home by the spring floods. One early spring I remember that there were many traders at Anvik when it turned warm. The men had to get home to make their fish camps and set their fish nets. Some of them had a portage of twenty miles to make through tundra and woods. The soft snow in the woods and the slush would tire out their dogs. So they went to the shaman and got permission to make a snow man to face the north, and draw from it the cold winds. As image maker they chose an unmarried man who had been born in a month of changing weather.

Snow fights the children may not play, but they play at war in another way. Almost anything will start a sham fight. Perhaps a child will call the family of another child dirty or say, "My father has more skins than yours." Then they gather fireweed, strip the stalks and use them for spears and darts. These weapons take the skin off your forehead, but the more you bleed the better you like it, and you never cry, no matter how hard hit. Two or three boys will pretend to be killed, the girls will set up a wail, they have a big feast, and they make friends again.

The boys play, too, at duck-hunting and deer-stalking. They will make a duck of grass and fasten it to a long, slender stick. Then they put it into a muddy place and throw short wooden spears at it. The game should be played only in the spring, for if it is played later it will cause famine. It is a very exciting game, and often, out of season, we boys would carry cans of water into the woods to make a duck pond out of sight of the old people.

To play deer-stalking, boys take a bunch of grass and make it into the figure of a deer. For the belly they insert strips of salmon. They set the figure up on sticks and then go off into a cover of stumps and grass. One boy says to the other, "I see a deer."

"Where?" "Over there." They creep up on it. They shoot, and the boy who sends his arrow nearest to the heart is deemed the killer. They skin the deer, talking all the while—"How fat it is, how limber."—"It was hard to get." They take out the dried fish, the killer cuts it up and, as would an adult, he sees to it that the food is divided up among the hunters. When a man returns from a long and successful hunt he goes to the kadjim, while his wife prepares the food and invites all the people to come and partake of it. She goes from house to house, saying, "Come and drink tea and eat meat." (By "meat" she would always mean bear meat, as that being the most powerful meat, is called just meat. Other flesh she would call deer meat, porcupine meat, etc.) Similarly when a woman gets a full trap of fish all the people are invited to eat.

Little girls and boys together play at fishing and housekeeping. The boys will gather willows and make them into a great bundle, a foot and a half thick and fifteen feet long. They choose a shallow place in the river where there are little fish, and they lay the willow trap in an oval. After the catch the girls take the fish to cook, and boys and girls pair off together to make fish camps like their elders. Once when I was about ten, I paired off with Cries-for-salmon. She got roots to sew into a basket, and grasses to make a doll. She sang to the doll and pretended to nurse it. I went into the woods and gathered bark and wood. I shot a squirrel and a little bird with my bow and arrows, and Cries-for-Salmon skinned the squirrel and picked the bird and cooked. We even made a kadjim to have a feast in. In winter, we children built snow houses and snared rabbits and stole pieces of dried meat or salmon from home. It is not stealing unless we are caught. But our games in winter were cut down.

I wish I could tell you about the time when the children, girls and boys, are turned over to the shaman, that they may belong to the village, to be a part of the village. I know there is a ceremony at that time, but I don't know much about it. At that time I was at the Mission house. The children are little—about four or five years old. Henceforward, should anything happen to the family, the village would look after the child, and the village is responsible for the child's learning as much as possible about village custom. The old men talk to the boys, and the old women to the girls. They tell them old stories to teach them what they may not have learned at home.   Of course there are other stories that people tell; but these are never told except at night in the kadjim and in the early part of the winter before it is time to prepare for the big ceremonies, to make the masks and rehearse the songs.   Many of these stories are about the bird nobody will ever kill, Raven, who can change himself into anything and who made the Yukon river by drawing a furrow with his feet, and the hills and mountains, by carrying earth. And many stories are about the beginnings of a town, of how it was started by a couple who survived a massacre and of what happened up to the present day. . . . It is improper to tell a story when nobody is listening, so every other sentence or two somebody must say "hen, hen" to show that there is a listener.

There is a ceremony for getting a name, too, which I know little about.   Persons may be named according to what they do or according to their character.   One girl I know is called Swollen-face; another, Pointing-at (she had a mean habit of pointing her finger [index finger of left hand] at people in scorn); another, Does-not-like-any-one (i. e. men; she would refuse suitors) ; another, One-the-Evil-One-does-not-like.   This last girl got her name because she was never sick or subject to epidemics; she had good eyes; she was big at heart; she was a successful basket maker and net maker and rabbit snarer; she had a cheerful face and looked helpful, just the opposite of the kind of woman who hurts people by looking at them in scorn, and of whom people are afraid.   I know a man called He-creeps-towards because his gait is stealthy, as if he were stalking something.   Because of the way the name is given, and because it has so much meaning the name is little used.   You go around it.   A man will call out "Look here!" and his child will recognize his father's voice and know it is he who is being called. When the Mission children call a village child by his name, it makes him very angry.

We go on now to when Cries-for-salmon is a big girl.   When she first menstruated, she was placed in the corner of her father's house to be out of sight of young men, and to stay so for a year, as we count by moons.   The space assigned to Cries-for-salmon was just long enough to lie down in.   In this corner Cries-for-salmon had to keep all the things she used, more particularly her own cup and bucket of water. When no one was about, she went to fill the bucket, but, as with her other things, she had to be scrupulous about not leaving the bucket where young men could by any chance come in contact with it. Girls are supposed not to go outdoors at all; but if a girl has to go, she must walk with head bent so that if she passed by a young man her eyes would not get a direct line on his eyes, or his eyes on hers. That would be othlang. The man would lose his hunting and fishing powers and what I may call his community power. (For example, he would not know how to speak in meeting, where there are rules for speaking in order to cut out loose talkers.) Once I went to Cries-for-salmon's house while she was in the corner. We do not knock on the door like white people, and I would have gone in, making the customary quavering sound of hihihihihihi and saying something perhaps about the weather, expecting to be told to sit down and to be served with food—a guest is never allowed to leave without food—but Cries-for-salmon's father saw me approaching and met me at the door, saying, "Let us go to the kadjim." I knew what that meant; he had a daughter in the corner; he was protecting me.

In the corner, a girl wears continually a beaded forehead band to which bear claws are attached. Her behavior during this time determines whether or not she is to be a worthy woman for life, and how skilled she will be in the domestic arts. For at this time she makes everything she is going to use after she marries—what I have heard the students here (at Hampton Institute) call a hope chest. She learns to sew, to make beadwork and porcupine-quill work, to make baskets, and fish nets. The first few months she is not allowed to cook, but towards the close of the period the cooking, the bulk of the housework, indeed, is put upon her. And it is then that suitors take notice of her work and accomplishments. They notice whether the seams of the boots and mittens she has made look strong and durable; whether her bead embroidery is fine, whether she is industrious and competent, how she carries herself. A man knows how important to his welfare the character of his wife is. A man has to run his chase, but, after he marries, that is all; his wife does all the hard work. She gets wood and water, she snares grouse and rabbits, she sets fish traps, and she prepares all the clothing and all the food, not only for the family but for the ceremonies at which the man is called upon to contribute.

But there is more to tell about the girl in her first stage, as well as about the feeling about women until they have a change of life, until they are old. If a girl goes into the corner in the summer, when we are all at the fish camp, her family, in returning to winter quarters, will probably have to cross the river or go along it. This happened, I recall, in the case of Cries-for-salmon. Her father had to go to the shaman. He went to Salmon-clubber, who lived with his two wives and several families who had followed him because of his services, to settle down twenty miles or so away from Anvik. Cries-for-salmon's father gave Salmon-clubber what he asked for—several bundles of fish, some seal oil, and a deerskin. And then Salmon-clubber went into a trance and, as the feeling he had in it was good, he gave permission to the family to move. Cries-for-salmon had to stay in the bow of the canoe, crouched down that her head might not be above the gunwale, and her face had to be covered over. Had she not observed these rules, it is likely that some time later a rash would have come out on her face.

Salmon-clubber would have had to withhold permission had any men been out hunting ducks or geese, as they do hunt after the fishing season closes. The birds and animals are sensitive, as you would say, to girls "in the corner." To have animals respect them, men must respect their songs. After I returned home in 1917, I went on a bird hunt—this was in the spring. I got only one goose and one crane, and the other five men got much less, too, than usual. On our return one of the old men said to me, "My son, are you thoroughly familiar with all our rules? I have been talking with the shaman and he has seen you bathing where the girls bathe. There are three girls in their first stage." "How did you know?" "We have ways of knowing." And he used one of the phrases the old men use which we do not understand. The old men talk to us, only on the outside of things. They tell us enough for us to understand if we think as they think. He went on, "It was because of that, you got so little on your hunt, and the snow fell and heavy northwest winds blew. . . . We could put you aside; but we think too much of you; and I speak to you as a friend." Had I been stubborn or not seen through what he meant at this time or another, I would have become known for it from one village to the other, and it would be hard for me to get a wife.

This old man knew, of course, that boys of the Mission were apt to be careless of the old rules. He may have seen the boys for example, go into the basement of the girls' dormitory, a violation of a strict rule, for, until a woman is old, she is, as we say, in an unfavorable state, and she should never be above the head of a man. In the spring, families move out to the fishing grounds where they open the season by making canoes or boats they will use. In cutting the wood they use a whipsaw. Now it is a rule that if a man and a woman are sawing together the man must always stand at the higher end of the saw, the woman below. Similarly, in putting away the fish in the cache, the post-built storeroom, the man must do the overhead work; a woman would never work on a rack above a man. In the kadjim, women sit on the floor, and men overhead on the benches which they also use to sleep on. Not only the Mission house, but other houses built on the American two-storied plan are making it difficult to follow this rule of overhead.[1]

Again, while a woman is still young she should not be present at a birth. Nor may she eat a certain species of duck or their eggs, and "meat" i. e. bear, she may not eat.[2]

During the menstrual periods, for about a week, were a young man to come into the house or a man to stay home, it would cause the woman pain at childbirth, so at these times a woman's husband leaves their bed and goes to stay in the kadjim, sleeping there with the boys and young men. A boy leaves his mother, to live at the kadjim as soon as he has courage enough, perhaps at fourteen or fifteen. If plucky, he may go earlier; but if a weakling, he may not go until he is eighteen.

During her periods, a girl or woman will protect men against herself if she can. For example, if a boy starts to wrestle with a girl—to fuss her, as you say, only it is not done your way, a boy wrestles and throws a girl down, and tumbles about, it is much gayer

[1] What an interesting illustration of how custom and belief may be affected by a change in material culture, caused by foreign contact!

[2] The Rev. J. Jetté notes that a peculiar fear of bears is universal among Ten'a women, concluding that the fear is due to the bear tales in which the bear is represented as peculiarly hostile to women. The view that the tale is the outcome of the fear is also tenable.

and more lively—the girl, if she is in her period, will claw his face to make him leave her alone. The old people see him scratched up and they know why, and they laugh at him. . . . Once when Cries-for-salmon's mother was in the kadjim at a ceremonial, she was called upon to dance on the skin she was giving to the shaman for a deceased relative. We saw her hesitate. "Go ahead. What's the matter with you?" some one said. She was in her period. "That's all right," they said to her. "Stand on one corner of the skin. We'll fix it up." She took her place with Cries-for-salmon next to her, and they went through their own dance, their eyes on the ground, and making the motions with their arms that belonged to the dance. . . . In this way, you see, Cries-for-salmon learned the dance that belonged to her mother.

Like all dancers, the girl and her mother faced the doors of the kadjim—there are two doors, the outer of bearskin, meaning strength, the inner, about four feet away, of wolferene, meaning speed and skill. The space of about four feet, between the doors, allows for the first door to close on the person entering on all fours, and shut out Li, the Evil One, before the second door is opened. When masks are set out under their covers they, too, face the doors. The smoke hole of the kadjim has a cover of bear gut. Below it, in the center of the floor, is the fire. The kadjim is always warm. After the fire flares up, it is killed with split logs.

There is a ceremonial in the kadjim for a girl after she comes out from the corner. I know that she wears a new parki given to her by her parents or by her suitor; but I have never seen the ceremonial and I can't tell about it.

As I said before, a girl may have a suitor while she is in the corner or before—that is a young man, who has noticed her and knows he wants her, has set to work for her family. He cuts wood for them and fetches water and gives them the bulk of his game. If he does enough to create an interest in him on the part of the old people, they will accept him. The girl herself has no say. Even if she likes him, if the old man does not like him, thinking he has not done enough, the young man can not get the girl. On the other hand, the girl may not like the young man whom the old man likes. As soon as she came out of the corner Cries-for-salmon was married to a man her father liked because he had done so much. This man,

Thleg'athts'ox, Fish-skin-hat, after giving loftak, had also to get the consent of the shaman, or perhaps it was the chief of the village. Cries-for-salmon did not like Fish-skin-hat; and yet although his father is a miser, Fish-skin-hat himself is a good man of ability and power—songs had been bought for him and his name was one no ordinary fellow would have.   (For such a name a man must have powers and must live up to them.)

Cries-for-salmon's parents knew that since Cries-for-salmon would be a woman of ability, a good snarer and fisher, a woman who would be highly esteemed for the amount of fish she could cut up in a day, and for the skill and rapidity of her sewing, she should get a husband equally competent, one who would run his chase well, who would save his furs and trade.   The old people knew, too, that unless Cries-for-salmon got a good husband, it would be a slave's life for her.   She would have to work for her husband's relatives as well as for him.   For the first two or three years, a girl will live on with her man in her parents' home; but then he builds his own house and takes her to this house.   It may be near her parents' house, but it belongs to her husband.   She will leave it, if she quarrels with him, and is scolded or beaten up by him, and she will return to her parents' house, or to her grandmother's or nearest relative's, to stay there until he comes for her.

Fish-skin-hat belonged to Anvik, but Cries-for-salmon had seen little of him before he began to come in at night to visit her.   Older boys and girls do not go about together in the day time; you never see them paddling together in a canoe.   A girl would not speak to you on the road.   If she wants to talk, it must be in the dark or under the cover of a roof—under cover because, as people say, "There is some one watching you."

After the ice breaks up and people live in tents, when a man wants to take a girl, he will slip in at night under the tent wall to the side where he knows she sleeps, and he will slip out again when the birds begin to make noise.   People of position see to it that nobody visits their daughter this way, except the man she is to live with openly after a while, i. e. marry.   Parents would say to a girl, "You watch yourself."   If the wrong young man came in, the girl would know because he would not make the signs agreed upon, holding her perhaps in a certain way, and parents would expect the girl to cry out and wake up the family. But—some people are careless, and there are young men who do browse about. Sometimes the family will so embarrass the young man that he has to marry the girl; they will say that the girl has conceived by him—"from him she has man inside." A man who persisted in not marrying in these circumstances, would be shunned by the other girls.

At the ceremonies, young men see the girls in a formal way. The chief will appoint a girl to be a man's partner, sohaldid. When I returned home in 1917, the chief appointed three girls to be my partners, and two of the three girls, Cries-for-salmon and one other, accepted. During the intervals of the ceremonial, your partner invites you to her house, and sets out, for you to eat and drink, tea and whatever the season has produced, bear, caribou, etc. What you can not eat you are expected to carry away, and you judge the girl according to the generosity of her service. Always there is great lavishness in setting out food. At bear feasts, for example, the woman serving would set out ten times more than I could eat. (Never forgetting at the conclusion to give me a bowl of water to wash with and a cloth, that I might not take out carelessly any waste particle.) The dance leaders call out for the presents. When you give them, you go through a short dance. Once when it was my turn, two women, thinking I did not know the dance, got up, without being asked, and danced in my place. One woman was gifted with bear songs, the other, with hunting songs. I had given some tea in bulk. A cupful was given to every one present except to me, the giver, and then of what was left over they gave first to the shaman, and then to the elders and so down. On another occasion I received a skein of twine, an ax, a saw, a steel trap, two large white fish, and some ice cream of seal oil, berries, boneless fish and snow. Somebody made a joke. "We have given him things as if he were married. He ought to go and take some of these old women around here who are looking for old men." I did not like the ice cream, so I gave it to Cries-for-salmon who saw to it, as a partner is always supposed to do, that my presents were taken out and put away. Women give feasts to men, where the women dance and give out presents, inviting the men between dances to eat. The day following, the men give the feast to the women, seeing to it likewise that the women get all they can eat. I may say here that it is the interest a man expresses in the feasts, in the ceremonials, that helps to make him a chief. Who helps most at these times and at other times (whenever one man can help another, help is expected of him) qualifies as a chief.

The sohaldid or partner relationship lasts. Whenever you return to the village where your partner lives, she will provide for you. Married women as well as unmarried are assigned as partners, and this sometimes makes trouble with the husband. But I remember one case where all the trouble was made by the missionary. Two men had each the other's wife as partner, and after a while they agreed each to take his partner as his wife, that is they exchanged wives. Five years later the missionary heard about it and, although by that time one of the women was dead, he decided to make the other woman go back to her first husband.

With the marshal and me he went at night to Myuli's house. They knocked. "Who's that?" called Myuli. . . . "Why don't you come in the light as we do when we want to speak to any one?" . . . The woman went to the door. A woman always goes to the door, as the newcomer might be an enemy, and she goes to protect her husband. The missionary wanted the marshal to arrest Myuli on the spot. "Do you think I am a white man to run away?" asked Myuli. . . . Myuli got sixty days, the other man thirty days, and the woman six months. "I can't see through this," Myuli said to me, "the other man was satisfied, I was satisfied, and she was satisfied, and now they come and break up things for us." . . . Myuli sent in food to her after he got out, and after she got out they lived together again.

At the ceremonies the old men saw that I was well provided for, and because I had been away four years I was given a seat with the chief men of the village; and people tried to attach me to Anvik in other ways. Women are the berry gatherers, and so women would ask me to come and eat berries at their houses. At other times men would invite me. Once one of the chiefs met me as he came in from a hunt. He invited me to his house to eat. Instead of saying, however, "Do you want to come now?" or "Let's go," he said, "Wait a while." From that I understood that he did not want me to follow him directly to the house because he had a daughter in the corner, and I knew too that he wanted me to become a suitor. He was afraid if I went along with him I might ask a question about her in the open sky—that would be othlang.

More than once an old man would say to me, "We want to see you settled down with a good-hearted girl who will take good care of you and keep to the customs. We don't want to see you with a Mission girl. They don't amount to much, they have lost their pride." (You see the Mission girls don't have to make their clothing or look ahead. Because of famines we always look ahead. People become greatly alarmed when they are down to a few skins, etc.; they are prudent, they watch themselves—except in ceremonies when they give away everything.)

And the old man might go on to say, "A man is no more than his wife. You must use your head enough to get a village girl. If you will go with the right kind of a girl here, we won't say anything. We don't care if you slip in at night and slip out again." Some one else then might laugh out and make a joke. "If you went in you might upset a bowl and have to get out!" Being a Mission boy they thought I might be awkward.

People do not want young men to marry out of their village, and so, just as soon as a boy kills his first game, as soon as he can run his chase down and trap—perhaps he is only sixteen or so—they want him to take a girl. Nor do people welcome foreign suitors. They suspect them. A man never gives up connections with his own people—at ceremonies, for example, men who have wandered off may return home, and then they sit in the old place with their own people, even if the wife's people are there too. Outsiders are invited to ceremonies. Two messengers are sent out to carry the invitation to other villages. From the masks the messengers wear, people know whether the performance is to be a mask ceremonial, a spirit ceremonial, or an ordinary "feast." In the old days of raids of one village upon another, when all but the chiefs and the girls were killed, a foreigner might betray his wife's people to his own people, telling them of weakness from an epidemic or from lack of warriors for various reasons, or telling about an abundance of stored food. And so even now people are suspicious of foreigners. If you do not marry within your village, they joke about you—they joke so much that it makes it disagreeable.

When I had volunteered to go into the American army, people

said to me, "If you died among us, we would see to it that you were sent off right; but if you die on a battlefield you might be blown to pieces; men would track over you."

"I am not afraid," I answered.

"You are not afraid; but we want to look out for you. . . . Give a minx skin to the shaman; he thinks highly of you, he would not expect much to safeguard you." Three men and two women came to me to urge this. Finally the shaman himself came. He said, "I will not ask you to pay anything. Let me but tattoo on your back the image of cross-guns."

"No," I said, "it would not do when I came to be examined by the white army doctor."

"I will give you a skin-tight shirt with the cross-guns on it. You can take off the shirt before the examination."

"No, in the army you may wear only what the government gives you to wear."

"Well," ended the shaman, "we will perform secretly to protect you." The idea about the cross-guns was that as a spirit will not go against a spirit of its own kind, with the image on my back other guns and bullets would not attack me.

Again last year when I had the influenza here, and they wired home about it, my friend Cries-for-salmon gave fifteen dollars in gold to the shaman to have him visit me through his fox, the one who carries his messages. Weasels and wolferenes, wolferenes are the most powerful of all, may be messengers for the shamans, but the commonest messenger is the fox. The fox is swift and sly.

A boy should marry among his own people, but it is not customary for him to marry near kin, a first cousin. To have relations with a sister is othlang. Of such a boy, people would say, "There are so many girls, yet he did not have the courage to go with them, he went with his sister." If he did go with his sister, he would be thinking at the same time of another girl. And for this reason, a sister, realizing she was a substitute, would feel outraged. A really weak-minded boy would even go with his mother. It is possible, for it is all in the dark, and no one speaks; merely some one will come, some one will go.

Cries-for-salmon has a brother who is dead or, as we say, "has gone." In telling of his death you will hear about the death rites and the way the people mourn. I will tell you, too, of a woman relative of Cries-for-salmon, who died.

But first I would tell you of another relative of Cries-for-salmon who has been such an invalid since the birth of her first child that she can not sit up, and who will never have another child. She had been a woman who menstruated with the waning moon—the character of such women, it is thought, is poor. So, as women do, she went to the shaman to have him regulate her periods to fall with the growing moon—the best hearted, best natured women menstruate at that time. Again there was a time when this woman was much frightened because the menstrual flow did not stop. This time she asked an old woman shaman—sick women are apt to go to women shamans and to the wives or widows of shamans, and sick men, to men shamans—if she should consult a white doctor. "Yes," said the old woman, "we don't know what is going to happen nowadays." Since the whites have come people have lost self-confidence. Formerly they were far more certain that the cause of sickness, of an epidemic, let us say, was not keeping the rules.

Well, when Cries-for-salmon's relative was sick after her first child was born, she went again to the man shaman. On this occasion the shaman expressed a desire for her, but she refused. Ordinarily women will not refuse the shaman. Nor would their husbands expect them to. The old women tell you never to go against the will of the shaman. "That is one of the things you will have to watch," an old woman once said to me. Nevertheless Cries-for-salmon's relative refused, and she has been sick ever since, and ever since the other women have sneered at her.

Her husband, too, has been down and out. They were poor to start with, he lived in one of the few underground houses left at Anvik, and now he has only three poor dogs, bale-back dogs we call them, nor can he borrow a dog team. Not long since, he was charged with stealing green fish (fish fresh from the trap) from another man's cache. "Why did you steal?" the old men asked him. "Don't you know if you are hungry we will feed you?" And so they would. Food would be given to any one who was hungry, although sometimes in return he might be asked to help at the fish traps or in making snowshoes. With us it is only when a man is put into a mean position, when he has lost pride in himself, that he will steal. In this case, the man denied the theft, so the old men kept at him. "Why do you deny?" they asked. "We know what you have done. Don't you know that there is somebody watching you?" You see, since it is customary for the young men to be most of the time in the kadjim, except when they are away hunting or in other settlements—on their return they go directly to the kadjim to tell the news and to give the jokes they have heard about the persons they know—the old men know pretty well what the young men are about, where they are. Besides there is the shaman. A man believes that the shaman knows what he is doing all the time. It is just because of this knowledge that the shaman is head of the village.

It is not only for cures, and to buy songs for hunting and trapping, that people go to the shaman: the shaman has to blow upon the masks which we put on to represent other beings (when we put them on we are not ourselves), and the shaman has to give power to the dancers by blowing on them at the ceremonies or, as we say, the annual performances, of which each has its own name. Until the shaman blows on it, a spirit mask is just like any other mask. Besides downy feathers, from the leg and breast of duck and goose, are fastened to a spirit mask and from the forehead there is the quill of a goose feather with a downy tuft tied to the tip. The masks of the fun makers are not blown on. The fun makers come out at intervals to give the dancers time to rest. The fun makers are usually young men, but sometimes a witty old man will act. I remember one old man—he was a shaman—and one of his jokes. He acted like a woman and he said, "Half of me belongs up river and half down river. How are you going to 'fuss' me?"

Men may wear female masks. There are certain parts women may not take, so men act for them. But there are female masks that women wear. Women never wear male masks. Women sing in the kadjim, too, to big drums, four feet in diameter, made of a sea animal's stomach on a spruce frame—five drums that can be heard a mile or more away. There may be as many as a hundred and fifty persons singing at one time in the kadjim. But in the powerful dances—the hagerdelthlel—ordinary women do not sing, only the wives of chiefs and shamans.

After a mask is made, it belongs in the kadjim for a year, and some man will appropriate it to wear for the year—or longer if he likes, and if he performs well what the mask represents. The shaman does not make the masks—he is too busy. He is charged with the welfare of the whole village, and he may be called upon in any emergency—at an eclipse, for example. Once long ago, it is said, there was a great famine, the winter ran into two winters, and Moon said to the shaman, "Whenever I go out of the sky, the people may not look, they should go inside and cover the smoke hole until I have performed my duty." Since then, at an eclipse, the shaman will send out fast runners to cry out, "Moon has gone under the sky! Stay indoors!" The shaman himself will go on top of the kadjim and chant and go through the motions the moon taught. When the moon reappears, the shaman will reënter the kadjim where every one has been sitting silent,—if a dance had been on at the time, it had stopped. The following morning all form a long line, the shaman in the lead. They encircle the village, forming an arc starting from the river and ending at the river, and, as I said before, taking in a half mile of woods above the village and half a mile below. They drum and sing and go through certain motions, each having a bundle of fish on his back.

There are many other times, too, when the shaman takes charge or tells people what to do. I remember a great to-do over a frog that appeared in a house in the middle of the floor. The house had been built in the fall, after the ground was frozen, and one warm day in the dead of winter the frog thawed out of its hole and came out on the floor. This was an othlang, and it had to be righted at once. The shaman had to be paid to find out about it. Such an incident would never be forgotten.

Muskrats come out from their holes in the bank of pond or lake, when the ice breaks loose in the spring. If a muskrat came out before, say in February or March, this, too, would be othlang and would have to be righted.

Sometimes a whale will stray up the Yukon River, and when this happens, unless the whale is killed, there will be a great famine. Once, a whale went up river as far as Tenana, about nine hundred miles. There was great alarm, and one of the shamans, a shaman of medium powers (there are shamans of high, medium, and low powers; nowadays, however, there are no very great shamans who, as in the ancient days, can do everything; nowadays some shamans do one kind of thing, others, other things), this Tenana shaman went out single-handed and speared the stray whale. It was forty to fifty degrees below zero, he was nude from the waist up, and from the great exposure and the great strain, within a few days he died. The people were so grateful to the shaman for saving the village that they made a carving in split spruce of the shaman spearing the spouting whale, to place near his grave-box.

When the caribou and deer began to decrease at Anvik, the people became greatly alarmed, they were afraid it was because of something they had done, and they consulted the shaman. When he came out of his trance, he told them to paint seven deer on the board over the ridge pole of the grave-building of a certain shaman who had been a great hunter of caribou. Each deer was to represent a year's kill. Once, long ago, to preclude othlang, the shaman ordered a man to be thrown off the side of a certain mountain.

At every death the shaman has to give the death stroke, that is, when it is time to send the spirit of the deceased away—on the fourth day for an ordinary person, some days later for a person of distinction—the shaman has to strike the corpse on the chest. He sends him on his journey under the river to the village of the spirits—kethagyiye—a way where there are, at intervals, pillars of fire at which the dead may warm himself, and may cook. At the time of giving the death stroke, the shaman also drives away all the evil spirits that are around the village.

I mentioned a cousin of Cries-for-salmon who died in childbirth. Her child was born alive, but as it was a girl and as the family were ordinary people—the deceased woman was a sister of the invalid woman I told about—the baby was put in the grave-box of the mother, in her bosom. Strong families with many songs, with spirit powers and hunting powers, might save babies in these circumstances, particularly a boy baby; some woman in the family would adopt him. But the girl baby of an ordinary family would certainly not be let live. I remember the case of a girl baby the Mission people wanted to save. They took her, and she had the best of care from them, but in four months she died.

Should a child die while it is still creeping, it is wrapped in something the animals will not devour, like bark, and placed in the woods under a spruce sapling. As long as the tree lives, the spirit of the child lives, too, under its protection. The spirit dies with the tree. . . . I may say here that in getting wood or bush from the forest we do not take all there is in any place. We depend on the wood and bark. If we destroyed it, we would become vagabonds.

The death of Cries-for-salmon's brother was by drowning. He had been drinking with the white trader, they were out in a boat together, the boat upset, and the Indian was drowned. When Cries-for-salmon's mother heard the news, she rushed out of the house, wailing with heart-rending cries, pulling her hair, and stripping herself to her waist. "My son, why have you left me?" she cried, looking to the North where the dead live. We could hear her cries a mile away, and we knew from her wailing songs the family of the deceased. Distinguished families have their own songs, and they make a greater outcry at death. Cries-for-salmon's mother is a woman with power. She has many strong songs. Her father had been a great hunter, with wolferene and bear songs. She is always consulted in the village, she knows her power, and there is no one to check her or to talk about her. So she stripped to the breeches—an ordinary woman would be afraid to strip lest people would talk— and she threw herself into the ice-cold water. She wanted to go on with her son, he was the only son left her. But they pulled her out. And they pulled out her husband who had also thrown himself in.

After two or three hours, they found the body and took it home, transporting it in the oldest or most worn-out canoe at hand. As the spirit of the drowned man was supposed to be still in the water, nobody was allowed to go into the water. It would cause othlang. People were told not to use that channel for a year, and women were not to set out their fish nets in a place where there was a good place for pickerel. The evil spirit of the place might pull them over-board. I recall another place in the river where there are sand bluffs where, unless people pay homage, they do not feel safe.

As usual, the mourners made new garments, new mittens, new moccasins, and a new cap for the dead man. The second night they danced and sang old songs, and the third night they danced to new songs. Cries-for-salmon's brother was a good bear hunter, so they danced bear dances which showed how a bear behaves and which would promote the increase of bears. Had he been a good seal hunter or hunter of other animals, similarly they would have danced seal dances or other animal dances. Besides, had he died during a good game year, they might have carved the game animal on his grave-box. I recall a hunter with a good heart, who died in a good deer year, having a string of deer carved on his grave-box—to continue the abundance of the deer.

During the mourning time of work, of dancing and feasting, the corpse is placed so that the dead man can see what is going on and absorb it all. He is in a sitting position or, even if he is laid out, as happens nowadays, the body is propped up. The dead man has to report in the village of the dead how his favorite food was placed near him and how he was honored, up to the last. On the sixth day, after waiting for relatives from another village to arrive, after the death stroke,—in this case the white man was not allowed in to pray, for everything was done in the old way,—the dead man was put in the grave-box in a sitting position, his eyes open, frozen open, and his hands placed in a position to show his interest. He is thought to return to his grave-box from time to time, more particularly in summer, and he wants to see what is going on. For this reason, too, the sinew corded grave-box is set on a hillside overlooking the river, the face of the corpse turned towards the river, that the dead may see who are passing and what is going on in the village; likewise that the dead may be near his food supply, i. e. the fish in the river. In the late autumn, after the leaves have fallen, the older women take bits of their most valued food, salmon and, since the coming of the whites, biscuit, to place by the side of the grave-box for the dead to eat, and to bless the givers. At the same time the men, if not the old women, will put the grave place (tudatonte, where the body lies stiff, as we say) in order, removing vegetation and restoring implements to their place. Thus engaged, every one will be continually breathing out to the North. Towards spring these attentions to the dead are repeated, on a smaller scale.

At death, food is put near the head of the corpse in the grave-box and, in the case of Cries-for-salmon's brother, the bows and arrows of the deceased were tied to a cross piece supported by upright sticks by the grave-box; but, as he was not a shaman or chief, no roof was built over the grave-box nor was the box ornamented. The dead man's things were given away to relatives; his rifle in particular was given to a member of the family distinguished for his ability and for his songs. After the distribution was complete, they set fire to the man's house, to drive away the evil spirit.

Cries-for-salmon's brother, like most men to-day in Anvik, had only one wife—formerly a man might have as many wives as he could support, generally he had two wives, sometimes three. And she had not yet reached middle-age, the time when women tattoo lines on their chin—they tattoo according to the songs they have or their husband has, a shaman's wife will have more lines than a chief's wife—nevertheless, she decided not to marry again and she bobbed her hair. In this way she showed, even to men from other villages who did not know about her, that she grieved and that she was unwilling to associate with one without her husband's power. She wanted to prolong his powers, and to keep the atmosphere she was left in by him, from going over to another man. Having his atmosphere and songs, she was strong and she felt spurred to care for herself, to accomplish almost anything.

Sometimes a dying person will send for one to whom he wishes to pass on his powers. Then the dying one looks to the North, breathes on the other and spits on him (spittle is a part of you). Once, Cries-for-salmon said to me, "I think a great deal of you. I would do almost anything for you, and I would like to give you some of my power, but if I did, I would die within the year. I must live for my children—providing the Good One sees fit for me to live." Cries-for-salmon spoke this way to me because a while before she had said something to me which I did not understand, and it hurt her. An old man present said, "You can't expect much of him" (as a Mission boy). So Cries-for-salmon said to me, "With all the white man's knowledge, you have no intelligence whatsoever. Had I completed my duties to my children, I could tell you more."

Many widows do not bob their hair, but even so, unless a woman were of no account, she would not remarry within the year, she would wait two or three years. A woman is esteemed not only for waiting, she is valued according to the way she cared for her husband before he died, when he was helpless. A man's feelings are badly hurt if he is neglected in these circumstances.

If a man and his wife died at the same time, let us say, from eating poisonous berries, "devil berries" people call them, the two would be buried in the same grave-box. I had to move such a box once—the Mission wanted to make some use of the place. A string of beads fell out, not the kind we use to-day, these were very old, I think, got from Siberia in trade. They asked me for the beads in the village, but I kept them—until they disappeared. The people wanted them very much.

The deceased is referred to as "the one who has gone from us." The term for dead is used only of animals. Once I referred to some one as dead. They said, "What! He is not a dog. You are referring to a human being." Nor is the name of the dead ever mentioned; but people think of them, and whenever they think of them they turn to the North and breathe out. (A prolonged, gentle expiration, as Reed showed me.) So on return from a hunt, passing the cemetery, a man will take a berry, eat half, and throw half in the direction of the cemetery, to some chief dying in a good season, and then look to the North and breathe out.

I recall a visit up river I paid to Shagrūk where lives my mother's sister. "My grandmother," I said to her. "Whose blood is this addressing me?" she asked. When she knew me, she began to wail, looking to the North—she was recalling my mother: "My sister, my sister, and here is my blood come again to me!" People think that if ever they said anything disrespectful about the dead, they would be laughing, as we say, at their own corpse. (In thinking of the dead, people appreciate the experience awaiting them.)

About Christmas time there are ceremonials for the dead for three or four days. Persons who have lost their relatives in the past year are called upon by the shaman to contribute the bulk of the feast. "Who will contribute so many bundles of salmon?" asks the shaman, "so many sacks of seal oil, so many sealskins or caribou skins, so many cords of sinew (for sewing), the œsophagus of a white whale (used in trimming)?" People eat to their heart's content. Sometimes they eat for the dead, sometimes they set aside the food—the best that can be got from the woods and waters. The missionaries are told that these are merely social feasts. Not that many of the old ceremonies have not indeed been cut out at Anvik. If a ceremonial can not be performed fully, in the proper way, people do not want it performed at all. Yet it is much against the wish of the people to go without their ceremonials. The "feasts," as I have often told the missionary, are the only amusements of the people, and they would like to keep on with them just as they do at the conservative village of Shagrūk.

T. B. REED AND ELSIE CLEWS PARSONS

AN
ESKIMO WINTER

An Eskimo Winter

THE skin boat, propelled by the oars of the women, approached the shores.   On the bundles of caribou skins which were piled up in the stern, steering cautiously through the floes of drift ice that dotted the surface of the sea, sat Pakkak, the boat-owner.   The boat was heavily laden and a strong tide was running so that the women had to exert themselves, two on each oar, to make headway.   Pakkak's son accompanied the boat in his kayak.   He had been out seal hunting in order to keep the traveling party supplied with provisions. The seals lay on the narrow deck of his boat which zig-zagged swiftly through the water, propelled by the strokes of the single paddle which he held in the middle, and which struck the water, now at the right and now at the left.

The young man was the first to reach the shore.   He brought his boat sideways close to the beach and climbed out of the small central hatch in which he had been sitting.   He took off his harpoon and lance, his bird spear and float from under the holding thongs.   Then he unlashed the seals, and hauled them ashore.   After everything had been taken off, he lifted the light boat out of the water, turned it over, put his head into the opening and carried it up the shore.

Meanwhile, the whole party in the large boat had reached the land.   It was nearly high water.   The travelers jumped ashore. The children and old people scrambled out of the boat, and the tent covers, poles and household goods were taken ashore.   The caribou skins, which were the spoils of the summer's hunt inland, were deposited on a dry spot.   While the women climbed the barren hills to gather brush for building a fire, the men hauled up the boat, and put up the tent.   The framework was quickly set up, the skin cover was thrown over it, and the lower part of the skin was ballasted with stones.   When the women came back, the shrubs were put down in the rear of the tent.   They were covered with heavy caribou skins, and thus the bed of the family was prepared.   The seals were put down at the right and left of the doorway, inside.

363

After a short time, the boats of Pakkak's brothers came in. They had started together in the morning, but had made unequal progress through the lanes of water that opened between the shifting ice floes. After unloading the boats, the brothers also put up their tents.

Some of the women had piled up the fuel nearby. Pakkak fanned into flames the smoldering slow match which he was carrying along. As soon as he had obtained fire, the shrubs were lighted. Meanwhile, the hunter had opened one of the seals and removed the skin with the attached blubber. He cut off pieces of the blubber and threw them into the flames. The rectangular kettle, hollowed out of a block of soft soapstone, was filled with water and placed over the fire. The seal meat was put into it, and soon the water began to boil. When the meat was done, the men and women had finished their work, and Pakkak stood next to the kettle and shouted, "Boiled meat, boiled meat!"

The men sat down in a circle near the fire. The women formed another circle. Pakkak took one piece of the meat out of the kettle, and handed it to one of the men; he gave another piece to one of the women. The first person bit into the meat and cut off a mouthful close to his lips. Then he passed the meat to his neighbor, who in the same way cut off a mouthful and passed the meat on. Thus, the whole company was provided for.

The travelers were tired from their exertions, and retired to their beds in the rear of the tent where the whole family lay down, their heads toward the door. They covered themselves with the large blanket of caribou skins which extended over the whole width of the bed from one side of the tent to the other.

Pakkak and his brothers, and Usuk, the half-witted old bachelor who lived with them, were the first to arrive at the place of the winter village, but within a few days other families came, who had been hunting in various districts. Men and women would sit together until late at night, telling of their summer experiences and of their success in hunting. Pakkak and his brothers had been hunting on the shores of the inland lake to which they used to resort, where they had fallen in with large herds of caribou. Some of the men drove the animals into the water, while others pursued them in their frail boats. The animals were easily overtaken and killed with the lance.

Pakkak was the oldest one of five brothers who were all skillful hunters, and provided well for their families. They were renowned for their daring and enterprise. Therefore, their friendship was valued and their enmity feared. Pakkak was held in particular awe, for he was not only strong in body and skilled in the use of the knife, lance and bow, but he was endowed with supernatural powers. As a child he had sat on the knees of the old medicine man, Shark, who had been known to visit the moon and the great deity that controls the supply of sea animals. Through contact with him, the supernatural power had passed into Pakkak's body, and now his services were needed whenever sickness and famine visited the village. Thus it happened, that Pakkak and his brothers were both sought as protectors and shunned as possessed of unusual power.

Pakkak did not misuse his power, but one of his brothers, Ikeraping, was rash in anger and overbearing in manner, and he was feared and hated. If it had not been for the combined strength of the brothers, the people of the winter village would have agreed to do away with Ikeraping in order to rid themselves of his aggressions.

Among the later arrivals was No-tongue, whose party had been unsuccessful in the summer hunt. He had hunted in the narrow valleys between the ice covered highlands, and by mischance he had come at a time when the caribou had left for another feeding ground. He had only a few skins for his whole family, hardly sufficient to provide himself, his old mother Petrel, his wife, Attina, and his children, with the necessary winter clothing. However, he was not greatly perturbed. He relied upon good luck and the help of his friends who might be expected to assist him, in case they should have skins to spare.

Gradually, one party after another arrived, and on the island which a short time ago had been solitary and quiet, little groups of huts sprang up and there was great activity. The women were busy with their household duties, getting fuel and mending clothes, while the men went out hunting in their kayaks and brought home game for their evening meal. The skins of the seals were scraped by the women, and stretched on the ground to be dried and later on worked into tent covers.

The wind had shifted seaward, and the floating ice had been driven away from the shore. It was getting cold, and the ponds began to be covered with a thin sheet of ice. Before the sea began to freeze over, it was necessary to bring the dogs back from the islands on which they had been placed over summer, and where they lived on what they could find on the beach or what they could hunt on the hills. Only a few of them had been taken along on the summer hunt, and with them were brought back a few litters of pups that were carefully nursed by the women.

When the new ice began to form on the sea, the hunters could not go out any more in their boats, because the sharp edges of the ice would have cut the skin covers. For a few days, all were confined to the land. The hunters brought in ptarmigans and hares, but everybody looked anxiously forward to the time when the ice would be strong enough for the hunters to go out. A few days without new supplies are likely to empty the larder all too quickly. Besides, it was getting cold, and work on winter clothing could not be started until the sea was covered with ice. The Sea-Goddess would take bitter revenge if such a sin were committed.

This year the weather was favorable, and the anxious days between summer and winter were not needlessly prolonged. After three cold days, the men could go out on the sea ice and wait at the edge of the open water for the seals to come up to breathe. Since the wind had brought back the drifting ice, the stretch of open water was not very wide, and the seals came near enough to be harpooned without difficulty, and to be drawn up to the ice. It was even possible to venture out in the open water in the kayak, for the ice was not forming very rapidly. Thus an ample supply of meat was obtained.

Meanwhile, the women were busy scraping and cleaning the caribou skins, and making the winter clothing for the family—the warm shirts and drawers of young caribou skins, and the heavy jackets and trousers of heavy skins; the stockings of light skins of young caribou, and the boots made from the skin of caribou legs, with soles of ground sealskins. Poor No-tongue had just enough for his family, and a few skins to spare. Unfortunately the catch of the whole community had been rather light, notwithstanding Pakkak's good luck.

From now on, the men went out regularly every morning and came back in the evening, generally with an ample catch. One day they had gone out again and were scattered along the edge of the ice, watching for seals. During the day the sky clouded up, and a strong, seaward wind began to blow. It increased in strength, and an ominous cracking of the ice gave warning of danger. Hurriedly the men loaded their sledges, and sped landward. Under their feet the ice began to crack and to yield to the pressure of the wind, but they succeeded in reaching land before the floe gave way and drifted out to sea.

Only No-tongue's sledge was missing. He had been hunting on a projecting point of ice, and before he was even aware of his danger, the whole point had broken off and was rapidly drifting out to sea. There was nothing for him to do but yield to his fate, and see whether the gale would exhaust itself soon, and whether by chance the floe that carried him might be blown back to land. Fortunately he had just killed a seal. He flensed it and made a little shelter of the fresh hide. His lance had to serve as a tent pole. He protected his tent cover against the wind by piling snow all over it. He made a receptacle for the blubber out of a piece of skin, and thus improvised a little lamp. Fortunately, too, he carried his fire drill and a little of the moss which is used for wicks; so that he was able to start a little fire in his shelter. The gale was still blowing, and the angry waves threatened to break up the floe on which he was drifting. When day dawned the land was far away. Soon, however, the wind subsided, and a swift tide carried the ice floe back, nearer and nearer the land.

It had grown very cold. An icy slush was forming on the surface of the sea and the waves were rapidly calming down. The breaking up of the floe which seemed imminent through the night was no longer to be feared and immediate danger of drowning had passed. Still it was doubtful how the drift would end. With the changing tide, the current changed again, and the floe drifted away from the shore. The play of tides continued for days. Now the shore seemed near, so that the hopes of No-tongue were raised to a high pitch, and now the shore receded. In these days of anxiety No-tongue never lost courage, but, mocking his own misfortune, he composed this song:

> Aya, I am joyful; this is good!
> Aya, there is nothing but ice around me, that is good!
> Aya, I am joyful; this is good!
> My country is nothing but slush, that is good!
> Aya, I am joyful; this is good!
> Aya, when indeed, will this end? this is good!
> I am tired of watching and waking, this is good!

His endurance and patience were finally rewarded. After a week of privations, he reached the shore not very far from the winter village. A few days of hard travel over the ice covered sea, and rocky hills brought him home to his family and friends. They had almost given him up for lost.

.   .   .   .

As it grew colder the light tent no longer offered adequate protection. The women sewed a new cover of sealskins and gathered loads of brush. They placed them on the outside of the summer tent, and spread the new covers over the whole structure. The door flap was also transformed into a solid wall, and only a low opening was left, through which the people had to pass, stooping down low. This darkened the inside of the tent, which before had been fairly light because the front part of the tent cover was made of the transparent inner membrane of sealskin. Therefore the lamps were put into place. The long, rectangular entrance of the tent with its roof-shaped cover still served for keeping provisions, but just in front of the beds, the soapstone lamps—long crescent-shaped vessels —were placed. The wife of the tent owner took her seat on the bed in front of the lamp, where she sat in kneeling position letting her body rest between her heels. The lamp was filled with blubber that had been chewed to release the oil, and the straight front edge of the lamp was provided with a wick of moss which, when carefully treated with the bone pointer, gave an even, yellow flame that lighted and heated the hut pleasantly.

Soon the snow began to fall, and the autumnal gales packed it solid in every hollow in the ground, and piled it up against the sides of the huts. The heather-like shrubs were deeply buried under the snow, and all domestic work had to be done inside. The soapstone cooking vessels were placed over the lamps, and all the meals were prepared in the house. The entrance to the hut was protected against the cold by a low passage, built of snow. As it grew colder, the snow accumulated, and most of the people exchanged their tents for snow houses. The men cut out of an even snow bank blocks about thirty inches by eighteen inches high, and six inches wide. These they placed on edge, in the form of a circle. At one point, the upper edge of the row was cut down to the ground, and then sliced down to the right, so that it slanted up gradually. At the place where it had been cut down, a new block of snow was put on, leaning against the end of the first row and slightly inclined inward. One man was cutting the snow blocks outside, while his helper was placing the blocks from the inside,—each block being inclined slightly more inward so that a spiral wall was gradually formed. Finally the key block was inserted, and the builder cut a little door through which he came out. In the rear half of the circular room, a platform was built for the bed which was elevated a couple of feet above the ground, and at the same level, at the right and left of the entrance, a bank was erected. The bed platform was covered with shrubs and skins. The tent cover was used to line the inside of the snow house, being held to the wall by means of pegs and ropes, thus protecting the snow against the heat of the living room. The lamps were put in place on each side of the front of the bed platform, and the pots were hung over them. In front, just above the door, a window was cut which was covered with a translucent sheet, made of seal intestines sewed together, and a series of low vaulted structures was erected in front of the door, forming a passageway which protected the inside against the wind.

When everything was done the family moved into the snow house. Two families occupied one house and each housewife had her seat in front of her lamp. The stores of meat were placed on the platforms at the right and left. Now the regular winter life began. It was bitter cold. The dogs huddled together in the entrance passages of the snow houses.

Early in the morning, the men went out to the sledges. The shoeing of the runners, which were made of split and polished bone of whale, was covered with a thin sheet of ice. The hunter took some water in his mouth, and allowed it to run slowly over the shoeing. Then he polished it with his mittened hand. After the icing had been made smooth, he turned the sledge right side up.

The harpoon was lashed on, the knife was suspended from the antlers that form the back of the sledge, which are used in steering it through rough ice. The hunters then put the dogs in harness. The light team started down to the beach. During the continued cold weather, the rise and fall of the high tides was forming a broken mass of heavy ice on the beach which, as the winter progressed, was constantly increasing in thickness. A beaten path led down through the broken masses to smooth floe. The sledge sped down, and the hunters went off to the sealing ground. At first the unwilling dogs had to be coaxed to go forward, and even spurred on by cries and by the use of the short handled whip, which the driver handled with skill and accuracy, calling upon the lazy dogs, and hitting them at the same time with the points of the whip. Gradually, the dogs warmed up, and ran along swiftly over the smooth floe. When they reached a part of the ice that was broken up by gales, and in which the uplifted floes were frozen together, the driver had to lift his sledge over the sharp edges and broken masses, and progress was slow and difficult.

Finally the hunting ground was reached. The dogs took the scent of the breathing hole of a seal, and they rushed forward with such speed that the driver could hardly restrain them. At some distance from the hole he succeeded in stopping his team. He tied the dogs to a hummock so that they should not run away and then he inspected the seal hole to see whether it was still being visited by the seal. It was completely covered by snow, and discernible only to the experienced eye. He piled up a few blocks of snow on which he sat down. He laid his harpoon down cautiously, and waited. For hours he remained seated there, waiting for the snorting of the seal. The slightest noise would frighten away the wary animal, and, notwithstanding the intense cold, the hunter could not stir. At last he heard the seal. Cautiously he lifted his harpoon, and sent it down vertically into the snow. It hit the seal which tried in vain to escape. The hunter broke the snow covering of the hole, and hauled the animal upon the ice where, with a swift blow on the head, he killed it. Before he loaded it on his sledge he cut it open, and took out the liver which served him as lunch.

Meanwhile the short day had come to an end! The dogs were harnessed to the sledge, and the hunters returned home. When they arrived, they unloaded the sledge, unharnessed the dogs, and took off the heavy outer clothing. The hunter patted his coat carefully to remove the ice formed by the freezing of his breath. Then he put his coat in the storeroom and entered the house. As soon as he came in he took off his sealskin slippers, bird-skin slippers and stockings, which protected his feet against the cold, and his wife placed them on the rack over the lamp to dry. Then she looked them over and mended them carefully so that they should be ready on the following day.

When all the hunters had come back, those who had brought home no game flocked to the house of one of the successful hunters, who butchered his seal and gave to each man a share to eat in the house, or to take home to his family. They talked over the events of the day until late at night.

This life had been going on quietly for all, without exciting events, when No-tongue's youngest child became ill. The boy refused food and drink, and household remedies did not avail. In her anxiety for the life of her darling, Attina appealed to Pakkak and asked him to find out what ailed the child, and if possible to cure him. Pakkak went to No-tongue's hut. As soon as he came in, the lamps were lowered. He sat down on the bed facing the rear wall of the hut and began his incantation. His body shook violently when he called his protecting spirits to help him. He uttered unintelligible sounds and cries.

Finally his incantation stopped. He addressed himself to Attina and said, "Have you sinned? Have you eaten forbidden food? Have you done forbidden work? What tabus have you transgressed?" She had asked herself what she might have done to bring about her child's sickness, and she remembered that she had scraped the frost from the window of her house, and that she had eaten seal meat and caribou meat on the same day.

She replied, at once, "I confess! I have scraped frost from the window of my house. I have eaten caribou meat and seal meat on the same day. I have sinned."

Pakkak replied, "It is well, my daughter that you have confessed. Now the evil consequences of your sins are forgiven. The black halo that I saw surrounding your body, and that has affected your child, has disappeared and the boy will soon recover."

The lamps were lighted again.   The confession of Attina's transgressions had appeased the supernatural powers and therefore the parents hoped for the recovery of their son.

For a while the little boy seemed to improve, but suddenly he suffered a severe relapse, and before the help of Pakkak could be summoned, he died.   At once No-tongue prepared to bury the boy. He stuffed his own nostrils with caribou hair to prevent contamination by the exhalation from the corpse.   The limbs were tied up with thongs and No-tongue carried his dead child out of the hut and up the hills.   There he cut the thongs, and thus released the soul of the child. No-tongue covered the body with a vault of stones, being careful that no stone should weigh on it.   He deposited the child's toys and returned home.   For three days the whole family stayed in the house. No-tongue did not go out a-hunting.   Attina did not clean her lamps. She did not move the caribou skin of the bed.   She did not mend any clothing.   To transgress these rules would have resulted in new misfortunes.

After four days all the members of the family threw away their clothing which had been contaminated by the breath of the dead child, and it was only with the greatest difficulty that they secured enough skins from their neighbors to make a new set for the whole family.   Through the charity of friends they were finally provided for.

The death of the child, and the cares of the family weighed heavily on the mind of Petrel, No-tongue's mother.   He himself was lighthearted and consoled himself with the thought that they might have other children in the future; but she was an old woman, and felt that she could not carry the burden of her years much longer.   She loved her son and her grandchildren, and the thought haunted her mind that she might die in the hut, and that they might be compelled to throw away another set of winter clothing and be exposed to the hardships of the winter without adequate protection.   If only she could die away from home, and thus spare her dear ones the consequences of another sickness and death.   The thought preyed on her mind and finally she resolved to end her own life.

The long Arctic night had set in, and only at noon came the sun near enough to the horizon to spread the faint light of dawn over the ice and mountains.   One night when it was bitterly cold and the snow was drifting, lashed by a strong wind, old Petrel left the house and walked across the ice to a small island. There in a nook of barren rocks she piled up a wall of stones, and sat down behind it, in order to allow herself to freeze to death. Her thoughts dwelled with her children, and she was satisfied that she was not going to die of sickness in her bed, for then her future life would have been one of agony and torture in the lower world where there is only want and famine, where cold and struggle prevail all the year round. By choosing her own death she looked forward to a happy life in the upper world. There she was going to play ball, and her friends would see her joyful motions in the rays of the Aurora Borealis. She would enjoy comfort and plenty and the cares of this world, as well as the tortures of the lower world would be spared her. Her limbs became numb with the cold and she went to sleep, her mind filled with pleasant visions.

During the night Attina roused herself to trim her lamp. She chanced to look about, and noticed that Petrel was not there. She called her husband who at once guessed what had happened. He gave the alarm and soon all the sledges were out. No tracks were to be seen in the drifting snow, and the whole party scattered in different directions to search for the old woman. To right and left along the coast, north and south they went on their sledges. Usuk, the bachelor, who did menial work for Pakkak, had joined the party. He, the despised and ridiculed one, found the old woman in time to save her from death. Notwithstanding her resistance, he carried her to his sledge, and hurried home. She was taken into the house, covered with a warm blanket and scolded for the unnecessary worry that she had given to her family and to her neighbors. She was ill-satisfied with her rescue, but submitted to the friendly influence of her light-hearted son.

It seemed that with this event the ill luck of No-tongue had spent itself, and the rest of the winter passed quietly. The weather was propitious and no long continued gales kept the hunters at home. The snow was hard and crisp so that the hunting ground could be reached without difficulty. Early in February, the first rays of the sun struck the high mountains and although the cold was still intense, the daylight made hunting and work easier.

Now and then visitors came in from distant villages to see their relatives. Everybody flocked to the hut where they were visiting, to hear the news. There was much to tell about success in hunting, about marriage and birth, sickness and death. For months, the village had been cut off from all intercourse with the outside world, because the strong currents that washed the foot of the promontories prevented the formation of ice, and only after the cold had continued long enough, was the sea covered by a continuous floe, which allowed the villagers to travel unhampered from place to place.

One day a number of travelers were discovered, whose sledge, dogs and gait did not seem familiar. The news spread rapidly through the village and the women and children assembled on a point of vantage, straining their eyes in an attempt to discover who the visitors were. Soon, Pakkak recognized an old friend who lived many days' journey away, and whom he had not seen for many years. He shouted, "There is Eiderduck." When the women knew that the visitors were friends of Pakkak, they burst forth in song and laughter. They waved their arms and jumped about. The frightened children hid, crying, behind their mothers. Most of the men went down to the ground ice to meet the strangers, and to help them to unload their sledges. Pakkak led Eiderduck and his companions to a snow house, and treated them hospitably with frozen seal meat.

While they were eating, the people crowded into the house. They sat on the bed platform, and squatted on the floor until there was no more room. Those who could not get into the house crouched in the entrance to get a glimpse of the visitors, and to hear what they had to say. All the older people had some friends in the villages through which the travelers had passed, and therefore their reports were listened to with keenest interest, interest which communicated itself to the younger generation, who thus learned about the family relationships and the history of all the people who lived many miles up and down the coast line.

One of the saddest stories that Eiderduck had to tell was that of some people who had been caribou hunting in the fjord Muddy-Water. In the fall, when they were preparing to move camp, the frost set in very suddenly, covering the sea with ice. Heavy snows fell in calm weather. The sledges and the dogs sank deeply into the soft snow so that the people were practically unable to move. Soon they were starving. Many died. In one house lived an old woman with her three sons and a daughter. Her oldest son, Powlak, decided to go to the neighboring village to seek aid of the people. He left his only surviving dog with his mother, that she might use it for food after he was gone. Then he started on his dangerous tramp through the soft snow.

A short time after Powlak had left, his mother missed the dog. She went in search of it, and found that its footprints led to one of the neighboring huts and did not come out again. For some time no sound had been heard in that hut. She thought that the people were dead and she had avoided going in. Now, however, when she needed the dog, she overcame her fear. She called in through the entrance and found that the people were alive, although hardly able to stir. She asked, "Is my dog here?" The house owner denied that it was there, saying that she had not seen it. The old woman, however, searched, and finally when she lifted the heather on the bed she found its skinned body. She became very angry and took the meat. The people were so weak and famished that they could not resist. She took the dog home and she and her children lived on it. Her neighbors soon died of exhaustion. The pangs of hunger had so hardened Powlak's mother, at other times a kind-hearted woman, that she only thought of her own salvation, and felt no pity for the sufferings of others.

When Powlak reached the neighboring village, he found that the people had caught two whales in the fall of the preceding year. He told them that the people in Muddy-Water were starving,—that a few had tried to reach other places, but that they must have perished in the attempt, since nothing had been heard from them. Powlak's friends were very kind to him. They gave him food to eat and for a few days they did not let him return to his starving mother. They said to him, "Stay here. Why do you want to perish? Your mother, your brothers and your sister are certainly dead by this time." Powlak, however, said, "I am sure they are alive." When he insisted on returning as soon as he had recuperated, his friends gave him an old dog and a whale-bone toboggan which they loaded with whale meat, skin and blubber. He started on his way back.

When he reached his home after untold difficulties, he went to the window of his mother's hut and asked, standing outside, "Are you all dead?" His mother replied, "There is life in us yet." Then he went in, gave them the whale meat and whale skin, and learned of what had happened during his absence. The food which he had obtained gave him the strength to go out, and he had the good fortune to find a seal hole and as the season progressed, conditions became better and he was able to supply his family with food and clothing. A great number of the villagers, however, had starved to death. . . .

It was late in the night when the crowd began to dwindle leaving Eiderduck and the other visitors to sleep.

.   .   .   .

As the season progressed and the sun rose, the seals whelped. The skin of the young seal is white and wooly and highly prized for warm clothing. Therefore, the whole village set out to hunt for them. The dogs take the scent of the seal hole, and the poor pup is dragged out with a hook and the hunter kills it by stepping on it.

One day when Pakkak was out hunting young seals, he found himself suddenly confronted by a great polar bear, which was also out in pursuit of seals. He always made it a point to raise good hunting dogs, and the large wolf-like gray creatures were eager to attack the bear which tried to escape. Pakkak never hesitated when there was a chance to get a bear. He cut the traces of two of his strongest dogs, which ran in pursuit. When the bear saw that the dogs were about to overtake him, it climbed an iceberg and took its position on a narrow ledge where its back was protected by the sheer ice wall. It sat up on its haunches. The dogs scrambled up the slippery ice, and when Pakkak saw that they held the bear at bay, he cut the traces of the others, jumped off the sledge, and approached lance in hand. His knife was hanging in its scabbard at his side.

The bear defended itself with its paws and teeth, and already one of the dogs lay bleeding on the ice. The bear, however, could not move on account of the swift attacks of the dogs. Pakkak approached fearlessly. With a swift throw he tried to pierce the bear's heart. His position was dangerous. The bear held the ledge, and by a single movement of its forelegs might throw the hunter down the steep side of the iceberg. With a swing of its powerful forelegs, it broke the lance. If Pakkak had not jumped back, he might have been caught in the embrace of the bear. There was nothing to do now, but attack the bear with the long hunting knife. He approached again, and watched until the bear, turning to the worrying dogs, exposed its side.   Then with a powerful stroke, Pakkak stabbed it in the side.   However, he was not quick enough, and, with its claws, the bear tore a deep gash in his shoulder.   Then it rolled over, and fell down to the ice floe.

Without paying any attention to his wound, Pakkak skinned the bear and butchered it and rolled it on the sledge.   He spliced the traces of the dogs and turned back home where his success was greeted with joy.

Then Pakkak tied the bladder and gall of the bear, together with his drill, to the tip of his spear which he put upright in the ground in front of his house.   By this rite, the bear's soul which remains for three days with the body, must be appeased.

The people asked Pakkak about his wound and his battle with the bear.   He scoffed at the danger in which he had been pretending that to kill a fierce bear was to him no more of a task than to harpoon a harmless seal.   His wife tended his wound, which was so deep that it took weeks to heal.

.   .   .   .

One day, No-tongue had been out sealing with Pakkak's brother, Ikeraping.   As luck would have it he was very successful, while Ikeraping, the strong and skillful hunter, had not killed a single seal.   This annoyed Ikeraping, who was ashamed to go home without game.   Therefore, he demanded of No-tongue that he should give up his seals to him.   No-tongue refused, but Ikeraping became so furious and aggressive that No-tongue, who was by nature timid, gave way and let him have what he wanted.   The injustice, however, rankled in No-tongue's mind.   It was not the first time that Ikeraping had lorded it over No-tongue, and No-tongue was afraid that sometime, in a quarrel with Ikeraping, he might be killed.   No-tongue talked the matter over with the other people, but they were all too much afraid of Ikeraping and Pakkak and their brothers, to venture to do away with the aggressive Ikeraping.

Now No-tongue was prompted to leave the village in which he had spent many years.   For a long time he had been talking of the distant home from which he had come with his mother, when he was a very young man.   At that time he wanted to see the world, and he had drifted from village to village along the whole coast line until finally he had settled down with his wife.   The memory of his old home had never left him, and he longed to go back and see his relatives and the scenes of his childhood. The quarrel with Ikeraping strengthened his decision to leave this year, despite the ties which held him to the village where his children were born and were growing up.

Although the feeding of many dogs was a burden, on account of the large amount of meat they demanded, No-tongue had strengthened his dog team by raising a number of pups. He had now an excellent team of ten dogs. His sledge was in good repair. And so, before the melting of the snow made traveling difficult, No-tongue was determined to depart. His wife would accompany him into the distant country which, to her, was a foreign land. It would take several years to accomplish the journey.

The departure of No-tongue was the beginning of the breaking up of the winter village. The families were already planning for the summer hunt. Soon, the brooks would be running. The walrus would come near the shore. Whales would come blowing in the open water. Salmon would ascend the rivers. Young geese would be plentiful, and the caribou would come back. The time of happiness was approaching of which No-tongue once sang:

> Ayaya, beautiful is the great world when summer is coming at last!
> Ayaya, beautiful is the great world when the caribou begin to come!
> Ayaya, when the little brooks roar in our country.
> Ayaya, I feel sorry for the gulls, for they cannot speak,
> Ayaya, I feel sorry for the ravens, for they cannot speak.
> Ayaya. if I cannot catch birds I quickly get plenty of fish.
> Ayaya!

FRANZ BOAS

DISTRIBUTION OF NORTH AMERICAN TRIBES

Names of Tribes Described in This Book Are Printed in Bold Type

APPENDIX

NOTES ON THE VARIOUS TRIBES

Crow

The Crow Indians number about 1750. They now occupy a reservation in southeastern Montana between Billings, Montana and Sheridan, Wyoming. This is near the center of their historic habitat, for their two main bands, the River Crow and Mountain Crow, roamed respectively from the Yellowstone-Missouri confluence southwards, and from east-central Montana southward into Wyoming.

In point of language, the Crow belong to the Siouan family, forming together with the Hidatsa of North Dakota a distinct subdivision. There is no doubt that some centuries ago they must have formed one tribe with the Hidatsa, since the languages are very closely related. In culture many differences have developed between the two tribes; e. g., the Hidatsa were always semi-sedentary tillers of corn as well as hunters in historic times, while the Crow remained pure nomads before white influence. On the other hand, some important traits persisted in both groups after their separation. The principal enemies of the Crow were the Dakota; to a somewhat lesser extent the Blackfoot and Cheyenne.

The most important publications on the Crow are:

CURTIS, EDWARD S. The North American Indian. vol. IV, New York, 1909.
LOWIE, ROBERT H. Social Life of the Crow Indians (*Anthropological Papers of the American Museum of Natural History,* vol. IX, part 2.). New York, 1912.

    Societies of the Crow, Hidatsa and Mandan Indians (*ibid.,* XI, part 3.). New York, 1913.

    The Sun Dance of the Crow Indians (*ibid.,* XVI, part 1.). New York, 1915.

    Notes on the Social Organization and Customs of the Mandan, Hidatsa and Crow Indians (*ibid.,* XXI, part 1.). New York, 1917.

    Myths and Traditions of the Crow Indians (*ibid.,* XXV, part 1.). New York, 1918.

    The Tobacco Society of the Crow Indians (*ibid.,* XXI, part 2.). New York, 1919.

[1] The notes for this appendix have been contributed, except in a few instances, by the respective authors of the tales.

Blackfoot

At the time of discovery, these Indians resided east of the Rocky Mountains in what is now Montana, and Alberta, Canada, and were grouped into three tribes: Blackfoot, Blood, and Piegan. The Piegan were the largest and dominant tribe, but all were in the habit of speaking of themselves as Blackfoot. How this name originated is not known, though there is a story that it was given them by other Indians because their moccasins were always stained with the black loam of the rich prairies of Alberta.

Closely affiliated with the Blackfoot were the Sarsi, a small Athabascan-speaking tribe, and the Prairie Gros Ventre, closely related to the Arapaho. Thus the Blackfoot group—confederacy of early writers—was composed of at least five distinct tribal units. Their nearest cultural contemporaries are the Plains-Cree, Assiniboin, Crow, and Shoshoni.

The Blackfoot speak a language belonging to the great Algonkian family of eastern North America. The presumption is, therefore, that they migrated from the woodlands of the east to the western plains, but this was very long ago.

The surviving remnants of the tribe now number less than 5,000, fully half of whom live in the State of Montana, and less than half of these are of pure descent.

For further information on the Blackfoot and other Plains tribes, the reader is referred to:

North American Indians of the Plains (Handbook series, No. 1 American Museum of Natural History, 1912), by Clark Wissler, and the following monographs by Dr. Wissler, published in the *Anthropological Papers of the American Museum of Natural History:*
Mythology of the Blackfoot Indians. vol. II, part 1.
The Material Culture of the Blackfoot Indians. vol. V, part 1.
The Social Life and Ceremonial Bundles of the Blackfoot Indians. vol. VII.
Societies and Dance Associations of the Blackfoot Indians. vol. XI, part 4.
Sun Dance of the Blackfoot Indians. vol. XVI, part 3.
Some Protective Designs of the Dakota. vol. I, part 2.
Societies and Ceremonial Associations in the Oglala Division of the Teton-Dakota. vol. XI, part 1.
Riding Gear of the North American Indians. vol. XVII, part 1.
Costumes of the Plains Indians. vol. XVII, part 2.
Structural Basis to the Decoration of Costumes among the Plains Indians. vol. XVII, part 3.
Decorative Art of the Sioux Indians (Bulletin, American Museum, vol. XVIII, part 3.).

Menomini

The Menomini are a small tribe (1745 in number) of the Algonkian stock, who formerly lived on the west shore of Green Bay, Wisconsin, and who now dwell on their reservation, about forty miles inland from their former headquarters, on the upper waters of the Wolf River, one of their old hunting grounds.

In culture the Menomini belong to the Central Algonkian group of Woodland Indians, and have long been closely associated with the Siouan Winnebago and the Algonkian Sauk, Fox, Potawatomi, and Ojibwa.

Dr. Skinner's publications on the Menomini are as follows:

In the *Anthropological Papers of the American Museum of Natural History,* vol. XIII which is composed of:

Social Life and Ceremonial Bundles of the Menomini Indians.

Societies and Ceremonies of the Menomini.

Folk Lore and Mythology of the Menomini Indians,[1] and in *Indian Notes and Monographs,* Museum of the American Indian, Heye Foundation:

Medicine Ceremony of the Menomini Indians. vol. IV, 1920.

Material Culture of the Menomini Indians. (unnumbered), 1921.

[1] In collaboration with John V. Satterlee, a Menomini.

Winnebago

The Winnebago number to-day about 3000 people of whom 1100 to 1500 live in Nebraska directly north of the Omaha reservation, and the rest in Wisconsin, mainly in Jackson county but scattered all over the region directly to the north, east and west of that county, also. When first discovered, toward the middle of the seventeenth century, they occupied the region between Green Bay and the Wisconsin River to the west, and their villages extended to the southern portions of Lake Winnebago to the south. Toward the end of the seventeenth century and beginning of the eighteenth century, we find them as far west as the Mississippi and as far south as Madison, Beloit, and even northern Illinois. While, unquestionably, they had been in part forced into this region by the war-like activities of the Fox Indians, there seems sufficient evidence to show that they had always roamed over the greater part of this country.

After their discovery by the French, much of their time was spent in fighting with the Foxes by whom they seem generally to have been defeated. They were, from the beginning, exceedingly faithful to the French. To what degree they were influenced by the French missionaries and traders, it is difficult to say, but in all probability this influence was greater than has generally been supposed. After the cession of the old Northwest to the United States, they remained rather quiet but were definitely implicated in the Black Hawk War.

About the middle of the nineteenth century, they were forcibly transferred to Nebraska but many of them made their way back to Wisconsin, and these, together with scattered Winnebago, who had managed to escape the enforced transference to Nebraska, form the majority of those now living in Wisconsin. Since their partial removal to Nebraska, a number of minor differences in dialect and customs have developed between the two divisions. The division in Wisconsin is undoubtedly the more conservative.

The immediate neighbors of the Winnebago were the Menomini to the north, and the Fox to the south; with these tribes they were always in intimate contact. With the Menomini they seem always to have been on peaceful terms, but with the Fox they were frequently at war. They seem to have known the Potawatomi quite well, and the Ojibwa fairly well. The eastern Dakota they also knew to a certain extent. In the main, however, they knew their Algonkian neighbors (Menomini, Fox, Potawatomi) best and they were profoundly influenced by these tribes in their material culture. The mythology and certain religious notions of their Central Algonkian neighbors they also adopted, but these seem to have been kept apart and distinct from their old Winnebago mythology and religion. In their social organization, they were totally uninfluenced and, on the contrary, influenced their neighbors profoundly.

They present the interesting spectacle of a people entirely surrounded by alien tribes, absolutely cut off from all communication with groups speaking related languages and having similar civilizations, who nevertheless have preserved many archaic Siouan cultural traits. What they have, however, they have in part completely assimilated, in part kept distinct.

BIBLIOGRAPHY

RADIN, PAUL. The Ritual and Significance of the Winnebago Medicine Dance. (*Journal of American Folklore,* vol. XIV, pp. 149–208. 1911.)

Winnebago Tales. (*Journal of American Folklore,* vol. XXII, pp. 288–313, 1909.)

Social organization of the Winnebago Indians. In Geological Survey of Canada. (Museum Bulletin, 10. Anthrop. ser. 5. 1915.)

The Peyote Cult of the Winnebago. (*Journal of Religious Psychology,* vol. VII [1914], pp. 1–22.)

Autobiography of a Winnebago Indian. (University of California Publications in American Archaeology and Ethnology, XVI [1920], No. 7.)

The Winnebago Indians. (Report of Bureau of American Ethnology.) (In press.)

Meskwaki

The Meskwaki Indians at present live in the vicinity of Tama, Iowa, and are 350 in round numbers. Officially, all are listed as full-bloods, but the fact is that there is a good deal of old white (French and English) mixture—practically none within the last sixty years. And many have Sauk, Potawatomi, and Winnebago blood. On the rolls the Meskwaki are carried as Sauk and Fox of the Mississippi; but this is due to the fact that the Federal government long ago legally consolidated the two tribes, though they are, even to-day, distinct in language, ethnology, and mythology. Fox is but one of the many synonyms for the Meskwaki Indians.

Their native name, me sgw A ki A ki, in the current syllabary, means "Red-Earths."

The Meskwaki linguistically are closely related to the Sauk and Kickapoo, more remotely to Shawnee, and to the Penobscot, Malecite, etc., of Maine and adjacent parts of Canada. They are also comparatively close to the Cree and Menomini. Culturally the Sauk, Fox, and Kickapoo are very near each other, and show woodland traits predominantly, with touches of those of the plains. They are also close to the adjacent Siouan tribes. The physical type of the Meskwaki has not been worked out; from Michelson's unpublished data it would appear that beside a mesocephalic tribe, a brachycephalic one also occurs. This last is probably due to intermarriage with Winnebagos. Moderate occipital deformation occurs owing to the use of hard cradle boards; and so the problem is not simple, for moderate deformation is not always easy to detect.

A practically complete bibliography on the Meskwaki is given by Michelson, *Journal of the Washington Academy of Sciences,* vol. IX, pp. 485, 593–596. Since that time (1919) but little has appeared. A number of volumes on the Meskwaki by Michelson will eventually be published by the Bureau of American Ethnology.[1] The most important publications on the Meskwaki are:

MAJOR MARSTON. Letter to the Rev. Jediah Morse, 1820.

FORSYTH, THOMAS. Account of the Manners and Customs of the Sauk and Fox Nations of Indians' Traditions, 1827. (This, and the preceding are readily accessible in E. Blair's Indian Tribes of the Upper Mississippi and Great Lakes Region, vol. II, pp. 137–245).

JONES, WILLIAM. Fox Texts, 1907.
    The Algonkin Manitou (*Journal of American Folklore,* vol. XVIII, pp. 183–190 [1905]).
    Mortuary observances and the adoption rites of the Algonquin Foxes of Iowa (Congrès International des Americanists, XVI: 263–277 [1907]).

[1] See The Owl Sacred pack of the Fox Indians. Bulletin 72, Washington, 1921.

Algonquian (Fox) (revised by Truman Michelson: Handbook of American Indian Languages, Bulletin 40, of the Bureau of American Ethnology part 1; pp. 735–873 [1911]).

MICHELSON, TRUMAN. Preliminary report on the linguistic classification of Alqonquian Tribes (28th Annual Report of the Bureau of American Ethnology, pp. 221–290b [1912]).

Montagnais

The Indians of the Algonkian linguistic stock known in literature as the Montagnais, inhabit the vast region north of the St. Lawrence river from the coast of Labrador on the Atlantic, westward through to the St. Maurice river near Quebec, and northward to the height of land dividing the Arctic watershed from that of the St. Lawrence. They number not far from 3,000 souls widely scattered in small bands comprising certain dialectic and ethnical groupings. Within certain limits they are nomadic, subsisting entirely by hunting and fishing, never warlike except in their resistance to the Iroquois, docile and orderly. They were visited early in the 17th century by Jesuit missionaries who have left us the only specific literature dealing with their mode of life. Their culture is characterized by extreme simplicity, almost barren in its social, political and ceremonial aspects though rich in the field of activity concerned with hunting, fishing and traveling. Roughly speaking, the Montagnais group lends itself to a threefold division, the ethnological and dialectic peculiarities following somewhat the same limits: those of the coast, the typical so-called Montagnais; those of the interior of the northwestern part of the Labrador peninsula, and those of the northeastern interior. The latter have come to be known as the eastern Naskapi. The whole group is closely related to the Cree of Hudson's Bay, outside of which area its next closest affinities lie with the Wabanaki group of the region south of the St. Lawrence, from New Hampshire to Newfoundland.

Iroquois

The Iroquois Confederacy consisted of five, later six, tribes, speaking the Iroquois language. In addition to these tribes there were others belonging to the same linguistic stock, such as the Hurons, the Cherokee, and others. The Confederacy or League of the Iroquois was formed towards the end of the sixteenth century and embraced, at that time, the following tribes: Mohawk, Oneida, Onondaga, Cayuga and Seneca. In the beginning of the eighteenth century they were joined by the Tuscarora.

The original area occupied by these tribes embraced the following district: nearly the entire valley of the St. Lawrence, the basins of Lake Ontario and Lake Erie, the southeast shores of Lake Huron and Georgian Bay, all of the present New York State except the lower Hudson valley, all of central Pennsylvania, and the shores of Chesapeake Bay in Maryland, as far as Choptank and Patuxent Rivers.

According to some computations, the number of Iroquois villages about 1657 was about twenty-four; towards 1750 their number may have grown to about fifty. Towards the end of the seventeenth century, the total number of confederated Iroquois may have reached 16,000, which is also the approximate number of the present Iroquois, including numerous mixed breeds, who occupy a number of reservations in northwest New York and southeastern Canada.

The tribes of the League are usually classed in the so-called Woodlands culture area. They have, however, developed a civilization which is greatly specialized when compared with other tribes of that area, especially in social and political organization. The Iroquois exerted a powerful influence on some of their neighbors, notably on some of the eastern Algonkian tribes, whose socio-political organization bears unmistakable traces of Iroquois influence. The Iroquois of the League greatly developed a consciousness of what to-day might be designated as a historic mission. Their leaders believed that the Great Peace, for which the League stood, was fated to spread over all of the Indian tribes. In their attempts to induce other tribes to accept the principles of the League, they carried on an almost unceasing warfare against such tribes as the Neutrals, the Algonkians and the Sioux, and their combined forces proved irresistible to their less efficiently organized neighbors. Ultimately, they were checked in the south by their own relatives, the Cherokee.

BIBLIOGRAPHY

HALE, HORATIO. The Iroquois Book of Rites.
MORGAN, LEWIS H. The League of the Iroquois (The 1904, one volume edition.)

PARKER, A. C.   The Iroquois Uses of Maize and Other Food Plants.

    Handsome Lake Doctrine.

    The Constitution of the Iroquois League.

HEWITT, J. N. B.   Orenda and a Definition of Religion.   (*American Anthropologist,*
    vol. IV, 1902.).

    Iroquoian Cosmology (21st Annual Report of the Bureau of American Eth-
    nology.).

    Seneca Fiction, Legends and Myths (32nd Annual Report of the Bureau of
    American Ethnology.).

GOLDENWEISER, ALEXANDER A.   Summary Reports on Iroquoian Work (Geological
    Survey, Ottawa, Canada, 1912–13, 1913–14.).

Lenape or Delaware Indians

The Lenape or Delaware Indians were once a numerous people forming a confederacy of three closely related tribes: the Unami or Delawares proper, the Unalachtigo or Unalatko, and the Minsi or Muncey, first encountered by the whites in what is now New Jersey, Delaware, eastern Pennsylvania, and southeastern New York, but at last accounts reduced to some 1900 persons, scattered about in Oklahoma and in the Province of Ontario, Canada, with a few in Wisconsin and Kansas.

Algonkian in language, their culture was typical of the northern half of the Eastern Woodland area, being most nearly related, as might be expected, to that of the Nanticoke and other Algonkian tribes adjoining them to the south, and that of the Mohican of the Hudson valley and of the Long Island tribes; and resembling in many general features the cultures of the New England tribes, of the Central Algonkian peoples, and of the Shawnee. The culture of the Lenape, that of the Minsi, in particular, also shows some special resemblances in addition to the general ones common to the whole Eastern Woodland, to that of the Iroquois tribes, although the latter speak dialects of an entirely different language.

Among the works dealing wholly or mainly with Lenape ethnology are the following:

BRINTON, DANIEL G. The Lenape and their Legends, Philadelphia, 1885.

HARRINGTON, M. R. Some Customs of the Delaware Indians. (*Museum Journal of the Museum of the University of Pennsylvania,* vol. I. No. 3.).

Vestiges of Material Culture among the Canadian Delawares. (*American Anthropologist,* N. S. vol. X, No. 3, July–Sept., 1908.).

A Preliminary Sketch of Lenape Culture. (*American Anthropologist,* N. S. vol. XV, No. 2, April–June, 1913.).

Religion and Ceremonies of the Lenape (in press).

Political and Social Organization of the Lenape (in Ms.).

Material Culture of the Lenape (in Ms.).

Lenape Folklore (in Ms.).

HECKEWELDER, JOHN. An Account of the History, Manners and Customs of the Indian Nations who once inhabited Pennsylvania and the neighboring States. (Transactions of the American Philosophical Society, vol. I, Philadelphia, 1819.).

LOSKIEL, GEORGE HENRY. History of the Mission of the United Brethren among the Indians in North America, London, 1794.

SKINNER, ALANSON. The Indians of Greater New York, Cedar Rapids, 1915.

The Lenape Indians of Staten Island. (*Anthropological Papers of the American Museum of Natural History,* vol. III, New York, 1909.).

The Indians of Manhattan Island and vicinity.   (Guide leaflet No. 41, American Museum of Natural History.)

ZEISBERGER, DAVID.   David Zeisberger's History of the Northern American Indians. Edited by Archer Butler Hulbert and William Nathaniel Schwarze. (*Ohio Archaeological and Historical Quarterly,* vol. XIX, Nos. 1 and 2, Columbus, 1910.)

Creeks

The Creek confederacy was based upon a number of tribes speaking the Muskogee language, usually called Creek, but many other tribes were taken into the organization in course of time, most of them speaking related tongues but a few of entirely distinct stocks. From estimates made by early writers it would seem as though the Creek population had increased from about 7000 in 1700 to 20,000 at the time of the removal (1832). This shrunk again after that date so that the Indian Office report of 1919 gives 11,952 "Creeks by blood," to which must be added 2141 "Seminole by blood," 585 "Florida Seminole," and 192 Alabama in Texas. The Seminole and Alabama formerly belonged to the Confederacy. Probably this includes a great many individuals with very little Indian blood, because the Census of 1910 returned only about 9000 all told.

When first known to Europeans the tribes of this connection occupied the eastern two-thirds of Alabama and all of what is now Georgia, except the northernmost and easternmost parts. Some of the Indians, then found upon the Georgia coast, seem afterward to have moved into the hinterland to unite with the confederate body.

The confederacy was gradually extending itself by taking in smaller peoples driven from their own country or suffering from more powerful neighbors, among them the Yuchi and a part of the Shawnee. Even the Chickasaw, though sometimes at war with them, had a sort of semi-official membership and it is probable that more of the tribes east and south would have been gathered into the league had it not been for the coming of the whites. They were, however, equalled and probably excelled in numbers by the Cherokee on their northeastern border, and the Choctaw to the southwest, with both of which tribes they waged bitter wars as well as with the Apalachee and Timucua southeast of them. These differences were, however, aggravated considerably by the rival Spanish, English, and French colonists. It should be understood that the Creek Confederacy was a growing American national organism, comparable to the Iroquois Confederacy, the states of Central America and Mexico and some of those of the Old World.

BIBLIOGRAPHY

ADAIR, JAMES. History of the North American Indians.
BARTRAM, WILLIAM. Travels.
    (His paper in vol. III, American Ethnological Society. Trans.)

Bossu, M. Nouveaux Voyages, etc., (Alabama Indians.), 1768.

Gatschet. A Migration Legend of the Creek Indians, (vol. I in Brinton's Library of Aboriginal Literature; vol. II in Trans. Academy of Science of St. Louis.).

Hawkins, Benjamin. A Sketch of the Creek Country, (Georgia Historical Society Collections, vol. III, 1848.).

Swan. Schoolcraft, Indian Tribes, vol. V.

Swanton, John R. Early History of the Creek Indians and Their Neighbors. (Bureau American Ethnology [in press]).

Appendix

Apache

The various Apache tribes of Arizona number about about 5000. They are about equally divided between the two adjoining reservations, San Carlos and White Mountain. Their habitat was the upper drainage systems of the Salt and Gila Rivers. Culturally, they are related to the Pima and the Yuman-speaking Yavapai and Walapai to the west. They are related also linguistically, and in pre-Spanish times culturally, to the Navaho who live north of them. In a general way they participate in the social and religious life characteristic of the whole Southwestern area.

BOURKE, JOHN G. The Medicine Men of the Apache (9th Annual Report of the Bureau of American Ethnology.)

GODDARD, P. E. In the *Anthropological Papers of the American Museum of Natural History*, vol. XXIV:
  Myths and Tales from the San Carlos Apache. part 1.
  Myths and Tales from the White Mountain Apache. part 2.

Navaho

The Navaho are an Athabascan tribe of nomadic or semi-nomadic habit occupying a reservation in northeast Arizona, northwest New Mexico and southeast Utah. In 1906 they were roughly estimated at 28,500. Sheep raising and weaving are their main industries. In many ways their ceremonial life appears like that of their neighbors, the Pueblo Indians, but the relationship of the two peoples in ceremonialism, as in other respects, has not been studied.

BIBLIOGRAPHY

MATTHEWS, WASHINGTON. Navaho Legends (Memoirs American Folklore Society, V. 1897. [See bibliography]).
    The Night Chant, a Navaho Ceremony. (Memoirs American Museum of Natural History, VI, 1902.)
FRANCISCAN FATHERS, THE. An Ethnologic Dictionary of the Navaho Language. 1910.
GODDARD, P. E. Indians of the Southwest. (Handbook Series, No. 2. American Museum of Natural History, 1921.)

Zuñi Indians

Zuñi is one of the towns of the Pueblo or Town Indians of the southwest. It is situated about the middle of New Mexico, near the Arizona border. The population of Zuñi and its outlying settlements is estimated at about 1600.

The Pueblo Indians live in about thirty towns in New Mexico and Arizona, and number about 10,000. They are usually classified according to language into four or five stocks, the Hopi of Arizona, the Ashiwi or people of Zuñi, the Keres of Acoma and Laguna to the west and, to the east, of five towns on the Rio Grande, and, also in the east, the Tanoans including the Tewa and the people of Jemez.

When the Spanish conquistadores came up from Mexico into this country, they found the people distributed more or less as they are to-day, although since that time many old sites have been deserted and new sites built upon. With increasing protection for life and property, there has been a tendency to move down from the mesa tops to the better watered and more fertile valleys.

At the arrival of the Spaniards, and no doubt long before, the people were not only builders, but skillful potters and farmers, practising alike dry farming and irrigation. From their economy and complex ceremonial life, they may be considered the northernmost fringe of the maize culture area of Middle and South America, that great reach which included the Inca Kingdom of Peru and the Mayas and Aztecs of Mexico.

Wheat, peach trees and watermelons were brought to the Pueblo Indians by the Spaniards, as well as sheep, cattle, horses and donkeys. And the Spaniards established Franciscan missions and a secular governorship, thereby affecting religion and form of government, to what extent is still an open question. Less obscure, but no less interesting is the effect that modern industry is having upon the culture; as might be expected, American trade has been disintegrating, but entirely destructive it has not been, as yet.

The ceremonial Mr. Culin describes, belongs either to the Thlewekwe Society or to the Big Fire-brand Society. See "The Zuñi Indians," pp. 483–8, 502–1. After the dance, the saplings with butts tapered and painted red are thrown down a rocky pitch in one of the buttes of the mesa to the north. Specimens may be seen in the American Museum of Natural History and in the Museum of the University of California.

That the skull acquired by Mr. Cushing was of questionable authenticity is a fact at present known at Zuñi; for it is said there that it was because of this Tenatsali came to his premature death.

BIBLIOGRAPHY

CULIN, STEWART. American Indian Games. (24th [1906] Annual Report of Bureau of American Ethnology.)

CUSHING, F. H. Zuñi Fetiches. (2nd [1880–1] Annual Report of Bureau of American Ethnology.)

My Adventures in Zuñi. (*The Century Magazine,* N. S. III, 1882.)

Outlines of Zuñi Creation. Myths. (13th [1891–2] Annual Report of Bureau of American Ethnology.)

Zuñi Folk Tales. New York & London, 1901.

Zuñi Breadstuffs. (Republished in *Indian Notes and Monographs,* vol. VIII. Museum of the American Indian, Heye Foundation, 1920.)

DUMAREST, N. Notes on Cochiti, New Mexico. (Memoirs American Anthropological Association, vol. VI, No. 3. 1919)

FEWKES, J W. (For Hopi monographs see his Biography and Bibliography.)

KROEBER, A. L. Zuñi Kin and Clan. (*Anthropological Papers of the American Museum of Natural History,* vol. XVIII, part 2. 1917.)

PARSONS, E. C. Notes on Zuñi. (Memoirs, American Anthropological Association, vol. IV, Nos, 3, 4. 1917.)

Notes on Ceremonialism at Laguna. (*Anthropological Papers of the American Museum of Natural History,* vol. XIX, part 4. 1920.

American Anthropologist, vols. XVIII, XIX, XX, XXI, XXII, XXIII.

Journal American Folklore, vol. XXIX No. 113; vol. XXXI, No. 120; vol. XXXIII, No. 127.

Man, vol. XVI, No. 11; vol. XVII, No. 12; vol. XIX, No. 3; No, 11; vol. XXI, No. 7.)

STEPHEN, A. M. (For articles on Hopi ceremonials see *American Anthropologist,* vol. V; *Journal American Folklore,* vols. V. VI.)

STEVENSON, M. C. The Zuñi Indians (23rd [1901–2] Annual Report of Bureau of American Ethnology.)

The Sia. (11th [1889–90] Annual Report of Bureau of American Ethnology.)

VOTH, H. R. (Several valuable monographs on Hopi ceremonials in the Anthropological Series of the Field Museum.)

Havasupai

The Havasupai are a small Yuman-speaking tribe whose permanent village is in Cataract Canyon, a southern tributary of the Grand Canyon of Colorado, in northern Arizona. Their hunting territory is that portion of the Arizona Plateau seen by tourists to the Grand Canyon. The tribe numbers 177 (214 in 1881) and is therefore dependent on friendly relations with the neighboring Walapai, who share their tongue, to the west, and the Navaho and pueblo-dwelling Hopi to the east. Their enemies were the Yavapai and Apache south of their range and the Paiute, north across the Grand Canyon. Of the little that has been written about these people, the following are dependable:

COUES, ELLIOT. On the Trail of a Spanish Pioneer. The Diary and Itinerary of Francisco Garcés. (A curious record by their discoverer, written in 1776), vol. II, pp. 335–347, 403–409. New York, Francis P. Harper, 1900.

CUSHING, F. H. The Nation of the Willows. (A vivid account of the country and the first description of its people.) *Atlantic Monthly,* vol. I, Sept., Oct., 1882, pp. 362–374, 541–559.

SHUFELDT, R. W. Some Observations on the Havesu-pai Indians. (Proceedings, U. S. National Museum, Washington, D. C., 1891, vol. XIV, pp. 387, *et seq.*)

SPIER, LESLIE. The Havasupai of Cataract Cañon. (*American Museum Journal,* New York, December, 1918, pp. 636–645.)

(A full account of tribal customs is to be published by the same author in the *Anthropological Papers of the American Museum of Natural History.*)

Mohave

The Mohave are of Yuman stock. They have lived for more than three centuries in the bottomlands of the Colorado river where the present states of California, Nevada, and Arizona adjoin. Down-stream to the mouth of the Colorado were half a dozen kindred but often hostile tribes, of whom the Yuma proper are the best known survivors. The mountains to the east, in Arizona, were held by still other Yuman groups—Yavapai, Walapai, Havasupai—of rather different habits from the river tribes. To the north and east, the deserts of Nevada and California were occupied by sparse groups of Shoshonean lineage.

The Mohave may have numbered 3000 in aboriginal times. In 1910 the government counted 1058. Part of these had been transferred to a reservation down-stream at Parker.

BIBLIOGRAPHY

BOLTON, H. E. Spanish Exploration in the Southwest. (pp. 268–280 contain a translation of Zárate-Salmerón's Relacion or account of Oñate's expedition of 1604–05.) New York, 1916.

COUES, ELLIOT. On the Trail of a Spanish Pioneer. The Diary and Itinerary of Francisco Garcés, 1775–1776. New York, 1900.

WHIPPLE, A. W., EWBANK, T., and TURNER, W. W. Report of Explorations for a Railway Route near to the 35th Parallel of North Latitude from the Missouri River to the Pacific Ocean. part 1, Itinerary; part 3. Report upon the Indian Tribes. Washington, 1855.

STRATTON, R. B. The Captivity of the Oatman Girls. New York, 1857.

BOURKE, J. G. Notes on the Cosmogony and Theogony of the Mojave Indians. (*Journal of American Folklore,* vol. II, pp. 169–189, 1889.)

CURTIS, E. S. The North American Indian, vol II.

KROEBER, A. L. Preliminary Sketch of the Mohave Indians. (*American Anthropologist,* N. S., vol. IV, pp. 276–285, 1902.)

Yuman Tribes of the Lower Colorado. (University of California Publications in American Archaeology and Ethnology. vol. XVI, pp. 475–485, 1920.)

Chapters L and LI, "The Mohave," of "The Indians of California," (in press as Bulletin of the Bureau of American Ethnology, Washington, D. C.).

Tepecanos

The Tepecanos were formerly a tribe of some importance, occupying considerable territory on the southern slopes of the Sierra Madre range in Western Mexico. Here they were found by the early Spanish conquerors who refer to them as Chichimec tribes. Their subsequent history is yet to be culled from prosy Mexican records. They probably fought valiantly against the white invaders but were defeated. As the country became settled and European blood introduced, the conservative members of the tribe continually retreated, until to-day they occupy but one village, Azqueltán, in the northern part of the state of Jalisco, and a few square miles of surrounding territory. Their numbers are reduced to a few hundred and many of these are mixed-bloods.

Physically the Tepecanos are closely akin to the other native tribes of western Mexico. The same may be said as regards their language, though in this respect the differences are greater. The Tepecano language is very closely related to the Tepehuane, Papago and Pima of northwestern Mexico and Arizona and more distantly related to Huichol, Cora, Aztec and Ute.

Little of a connected nature has been written on the Tepecano. The following list includes practically all the extant literature:

OROZCO Y BERRA, MANUEL. Geografía de las lenguas y carta etnográfica de México; México, 1864. pp. 49, 279, 282.

LUMHOLTZ, CARL. Unknown Mexico, vol. II, p. 123, New York, 1902.

HŘDLIČKA, ALEŠ. The Chichimecs and their Ancient Culture. (*American Anthropologist*, N. S., vol. III, 1903.)

    Physiological and Medical Observations. (Bulletin 34, Bureau of American Ethnology, Washington, 1908.)

LEÓN, NICOLÁS. Familias Lingüísticas de México, Mexico, 1902.

THOMAS, CYRUS, and SWANTON, JOHN R. Indian Languages of Mexico and Central America. (Bulletin 44, Bureau of American Ethnology, Washington, 1911.)

MASON, J. ALDEN. The Tepehuan Indians of Azqueltán. (Proceedings 18th International Congress of Americanists, London, 1912.)

    The Fiesta of the Pinole at Azqueltán. (*The Museum Journal*, III, University Museum, Philadelphia, 1912.)

    Tepecano, A Piman Language of Western Mexico. (Annals of the New York Academy of Science, vol. XXV, New York, 1917.)

    Tepecano Prayers. (*International Journal of American Linguistics*, vol. I, II, 1918.)

    Four Mexican Spanish Folk Tales from Azqueltán, Jalisco. (*Journal of American Folklore*, vol. XXV, 1912.)

    Folk Tales of the Tepecanos. (*Journal of American Folklore*, vol. XXVII, 1914.)

Aztecs

For general account and bibliography see Spinden, H. J. Ancient civilizations of Mexico and Central America. (American Museum of Natural History, Handbook series. No. 3. 1917.)

Mayas

I

The picture of life in the Old Maya Empire of Central America during the sixth century after Christ is reconstructed almost entirely from the archæological evidence. Unlike many of the indigenous cultures of our own country which have survived with all their wealth of legend, myth, rite and ceremonial, down to the present day, the Old Maya Empire had vanished centuries before the Discovery of America. The episode in the life of a boy who might have lived in those colorful times must necessarily be based upon what we may glean from the monuments, temples and palaces of the period, helped out here and there by some few ethnological facts about the New Maya Empire gathered a millenium later.

The term "True Man," *halach vinic,* was that given by the Maya only to their highest chiefs, their hereditary rulers, who would seem to have lived in a state not unlike feudalism, even discounting the indubitable feudalistic bias with which all the early Spanish chroniclers wrote. The rulers together with the priesthood would appear to have been nearly, if not quite absolute; succession to the supreme office passed by hereditary descent, though probably individual unfitness therefor could and did modify the operation of strict primogeniture; finally a system of vassalage, of lesser chieftains dependent upon an overlord, certainly obtained. Indeed, such are the extent and magnificence of the architectural and monumental remains of the Maya civilization that in order to have achieved them, it is necessary to postulate a highly centralized form of government, administered by a small, powerful caste.

II

Chichen Itza has had a long and varied history. Founded by the Mayas about 500 A. D. in their northern migrations from their original homes in Honduras and Guatemala, abandoned for four hundred years and settled again about the year 1000, Chichen was now to have two hundred years of growth and prosperity. Many of the older buildings still standing, date from this period. The famous League of Mayapan, Uxmal, and Chichen Itza, was a working alliance which resulted in all the cities of Yucatan making great strides forward in many of the arts. Several of the more famous structures at Chichen were erected in this epoch. Our story begins with the disruption of this League, when Mayapan brought in Mexican forces to prey upon the other cities of the peninsula. Peace gave way to many years of civil strife. The final destruction of Mayapan, about the middle of the fifteenth century, marked the end of the Maya civilization. The Spaniards found only the lingering remnants of the former splendor.

None of the ruined cities of Yucatan is more wonderful than Chichen Itza, stately and grand even now when many of its temples have fallen into decay, and others are buried in the depths of the forest. The sharp outlines of the Great Pyramid still rise above the level line of the trees of the jungle. The fine proportions of the pyramid, and the temple still standing on its top, mark it as perhaps the most complete and perfect building still extant in the whole Maya area. The substantial walls of the Ball Court remain as solid as when they were built. One of the stone rings still projects from the wall, a witness to the love of sport of the ancient people. The beautiful Temple of the Tigers, standing on the end of one of the walls, has been a prey to the devastating forces of man, of beast, and of nature. Vines and the roots of trees have gained a foothold on the roof, and many of the carved stones have fallen. Iguanas run in all directions when the chance visitor approaches. The frescoes of the inner chamber are but blurred remains of a former art.

And the Cenote of Sacrifice, that famous well, so vividly described by the early Christian priests, is now but a deserted shrine. Trailing vines, ferns, and palms almost cover the precipitous sides. The dark green waters are almost concealed by the slime of decaying vegetation. But the sight of the silent, sinister pool, surrounded by the unbroken forest, makes it easy, even now, to picture the scenes of sacrifice which it has witnessed.

The country is still peopled by the Mayas but their greatness is a thing of the past. The present-day native may well pause to wonder what the ruined buildings of his country were really for. He knows only what his white masters have told him. "They are the temples of your ancestors who have had a past unequaled in the early history of the New World, a past stretching back almost to the beginning of the Christian Era." He only shakes his head and murmurs in his adopted language, *"Quien sabe."*

The Maya civilization formerly embraced the whole peninsula of Yucatan, Chiapas and Tabasco, states of Mexico, the greater part of Guatemala, British Honduras, northern Honduras, and northern Salvador. This country is still occupied in general with peoples speaking various dialects of the Maya language.

The Mayas, both linguistically and culturally, are distinct from the Zapotecs in Oaxaca and the Nahua-Aztec peoples of Central Mexico. There is little doubt, however, that all the cultures of Mexico and Central America go back to a common origin. The Maya civilization is older than that of the Toltecs in Mexico which, in turn, preceded that of the Aztecs.

The Toltec culture greatly influenced the late Maya of northern Yucatan about 1200 A. D.

MAYA CHRONOLOGY (CHICHEN ITZA)

?–200 A. D.	Period of migrations.
200–600	duras flourished.
	Chichen Itza founded.
520	Chichen Itza abandoned.
640–960	Itzas at Chakanputun.
700–960	Chichen rebuilt. League of Mayapan.
960–1200	Old Empire. Great cities of Guatemala and Hon-
1200–1442	Toltec influence, especially at Chichen Itza.
1442	Fall of Mayapan and end of Maya civilization.

The historical accounts upon which parts of our story are based are:

MOLINA, J. Historia del discubrimiento y conquista de Yucatan, 1896, pp. 47–51
HERRERA, Historia General, 1601–1605.
PRESCOTT, Chapter III, after Herrera, Torquemada, etc.
LANDA (156), Brasseur de Bourbourg ed. 1864, pp. 344–346.
　　Relacion de Valladolid (1579) in Col. de Doc. Ineditos, 1898–1900, vol. XIII,
　　　　p. 25

Other historical and general references are:

History:

COGOLLUDO, D. L. Historia de Yucatan, 1688.
VILLAGUTIERRE, J. Historia de la conquista de la Provincia del Itza, 1701.
MEANS, P. A. A history of the Spanish conquest of Yucatan and of the Itzas, in
　　Papers of the Peabody Museum, vol. VII, 1917.

Chronology:

MORLEY, S. G. The correlation of Maya and Christian chronology. (*American
　　Journal of Archaeology,* 2nd series, vol. XIV, pp. 193–204.)
　　The historical value of the Books of Chilam Balam (*American Journal of
　　Archaeology,* 2nd series, vol. XV, pp. 195–214.)

Ruins:

STEPHENS, J. L. Incidents of travel in Yucatan, 1843.
　　Incidents of travel in Central America, Chiapas, and Yucatan, 1841.
MAUDSLAY, A. P. Biologia Centrali-Americana Archaeology, 1889–1902.
HOLMES, W. H. Archaeological Studies among the Ancient Cities of Mexico.
　　(*Field Columbian Museum, Anthropological Series,* vol I, 1895–1897.)
JOYCE, T. A. Mexican Archaeology. 1914.

SPINDEN, H. J.   A study of Maya art.   (Memoirs of the Peabody Museum, vol. VI, 1913.)

GORDON, G. B., THOMPSON, E. H., and TOZZER, A. M. in Memoirs of the Peabody Museum.

Hieroglyphic writing:

BOWDITCH, C. P.   The numeration, calendar systems and astronomical knowledge of the Mayas, 1910.

MORLEY, S. G.   An introduction to the study of the Maya hieroglyphs, (Bulletin 57, Bureau of American Ethnology, 1915.)

The inscriptions at Copan, (Carnegie Institution, 1920.)

Present population:

TOZZER, A. M.   A comparative study of the Mayas and the Lacandones, 1907.

Maya language:

TOZZER, A. M.   A Maya grammar with bibliography and appraisement of the works noted (*Papers of the Peabody Museum,* vol. IX, 1921.)

Relation with surrounding cultures:

SPINDEN, H. J.   Ancient civilizations of Mexico and Central America.   (Handbook Series, No. 3, American Museum of Natural History, 1917.)

The origin and distribution of agriculture in America.   (Proceedings of the 19th International Congress of Americanists, New York, 1917.)

TOZZER, A. M.   The domain of the Aztecs, (Holmes Anniversary Volume, 1916.)

The Shellmound People

The Shellmound people who lived on the shores of San Francisco Bay for perhaps three or four thousand years, down to early historic times, are regarded as having belonged towards the end to the Costanoan linguistic family. These Costanoans inhabited the portion of California extending from the Golden Gate south to Soledad, and from the Pacific Ocean east to the San Joaquin River. Although totalling more than 7000 square miles in extent, this territory was nevertheless largely occupied by mountains and marshes unsuitable for permanent habitation. The principle settlements were in consequence confined to the ocean shore, the bay shore, and the portion of the San Joaquin valley lying between the marsh and the Coast Range foothills. Seven Spanish missions were established in the territory during the latter part of the 18th century, and from the old records of these institutions Bancroft has extracted the names of some two hundred villages, several of which, however, were outside the Costanoan territorial limits. The estimated population may be placed conservatively at about 10,000.

One of the principal dialectic divisions of the Costanoan stock was known as the Mutsuns or Mutsunes; and for purposes of the story the Ahwashtee tribe, to which Wixi and his villagers of Akalan belonged, has been connected with this group. As a matter of fact, the Ahwashtees are definitely reported to have lived on the bay shore, though probably the Mutsunes did not.

There is next to no available historical data about the Shellmound people, as such, and very little archæological evidence in the shellmounds themselves that the Indians continued to inhabit them after the arrival of the white man. The principal references are:

BANCROFT, H. H. Native Races of the Pacific States of North America, vol. I, 1874.

MASON, J. A. The Mutsun Dialect of Costanoan. (University of California Publications in American Archaeology and Ethnology, vol. XI, No. 7. 1916.)

NELSON, N. C. Shellmounds of the San Francisco Bay Region. (University of California Publications in American Archaeology and Ethnology, vol. VII, No. 4. 1909.)

POWERS, STEPHEN. Tribes of California. (Contributions to North American Ethnology, vol. III. 1877.)

UHLE, MAX. The Emeryville Shellmound. (University of California Publications in American Archaeology and Ethnology, vol. VIII, No. 1. 1907.)

Yurok

The Yurok are one of half a dozen tribes in northwestern California who exhibit jointly a surprisingly complex way of living. Others of this highly cultured group are the Hupa, the Karok, the Tolowa, the Chilula, and the Wiyot. One element especially in the tribal life of the region, is the notion of aristocracy based upon wealth. This makes them rather grasping. Every injury, from slander to rape, demands its money price. The Yurok, accordingly, become adept at the art of taking offense. Quarrelsomeness is a religion, and wrangling for a price, a fine art. Some Yurok are born "stinkers" in money matters. The remainder have that quality thrust upon them by the pressure of tribal feeling. They speak an Algonkian language, live along the lower part of the Klamath River, subsist mostly on fish (though they eat a lot of acorns) and are nice folks when you know their ways (not until then, however). The principal works which describe the Yurok are:

POWERS, STEPHEN. Tribes of California (U. S. Interior Department, Contributions to North American Ethnology, vol. III.)

WATERMAN, T. T. Yurok Geography (University of California Publications in American Archaeology and Ethnology, vol. XVI.)

Notes on Yurok Culture (Museum of the American Indian, Heye Foundation, [in press]).

A book which has no title, except a dedication "To the American Indian," by a Yurok woman, privately printed at Eureka, California, in 1916.

GODDARD, P. E. Life and Culture of the Hupa, University of California Publications in American Archaeology and Ethnology, vol. I. (a very fine work, describing not the Yurok, but the neighboring Hupa, who follow the same mode of life.)

Nootka

The Nootka Indians, sometimes known as Aht, are a group of tribes occupying the west coast of Vancouver Island, from about Cape Cook south to Sooke Inlet, also the extreme northwest point, Cape Flattery, of Washington. The Indians of Cape Flattery, generally known as Makah, are sometimes considered distinct from the Nootka, but their speech is practically identical with that of the Nitinat, the southern group of Vancouver Island Nootka. The dividing line between the Nitinat and northern Nootka (Nootka proper) is a little south of Cape Beale. It is determined by linguistic considerations, the Nitinat dialects and those of the northern Nootka being mutually unintelligible groups. The dialectic differences within the groups are comparatively slight. Directly north of the northernmost Nootka are the Quatsino, one of the Kwakiutl tribes; south of the southernmost island Nitinat are the Sooke, a Coast Salish tribe of the Lkungen-Clallam group; while south of the Makah are the Quilleute, a Chimakuan tribe.

The total number of Nootkas in 1906 was about 2500, of which over 400 belonged to the Makah. The Nootkas in no sense form a political unit. They are merely a group of independent tribes, related by language, inter-tribal marriage, and close cultural inter-influences.

The Nootkas, using the term in its widest sense, are fairly remote linguistic relatives of the Kwakiutl (including Kwakiutl proper, Bella Bella, and Kitamat), who occupy the northernmost part of the island and adjoining parts of the mainland of British Columbia as well. Nootka and Kwakiutl are often combined by ethnographers into the "Wakashan" stock.

The Nootka tribes are culturally quite distinct from both the Kwakiutl and the Coast Salish tribes of the southeastern part of Vancouver Island, but have been much influenced, particularly in ceremonial respects, by both.

The chief works on the Nootka are:

BOAS F. The Nootka (Report of British Association for the Advancement of Science, Leeds meeting, 1890, pp. 582–604; reprinted, pp. 30–52, in Sixth Report on the Northwestern Tribes of Canada.)

The Nootka ([Religious Ceremonials] pp. 632–644 of The Social Organization and the Secret Societies of the Kwakiutl Indians, in Report of U. S. National Museum, 1895).

Sagen der Nutka (pp. 98–128 of *Indianische Sagen von der Nord-Pacifischen Küste Amerikas*, Berlin, 1895).

HUNT, GEORGE (collector). Myths of the Nootka (pp. 888–935 of Boas, F.: Tsimshian Mythology, 31st Annual Report of the Bureau of American Ethnology, 1909–10.)

JEWITT, JOHN R. (also JEWETT) Adventures and Sufferings of John R. Jewitt, only Survivor of the Crew of the Ship *Boston* during a captivity of nearly three years among the Indians of Nootka Sound (Middletown, 1815; Edinburgh, 1824; often reprinted, see edition of Robert Brown, London, 1896); also published as The Captive of Nootka, or the Adventures of John R. Jewett (Philadelphia, 1841).

SAPIR, E. A Flood Legend of the Nootka Indians of Vancouver Island (*Journal of American Folklore*, 1919, pp. 351–355).

A Girl's Puberty Ceremony among the Nootka Indians (Transactions of the Royal Society of Canada, 3rd series, vol. VII, 1913, pp. 67–80).

Some Aspects of Nootka Language and Culture (*American Anthropologist*, N. S., vol. XIII, 1911, pp. 15–28).

Vancouver Island, Indians of (in Hastings' Encyclopædia of Religion and Ethics; deals with Nootka religion).

SPROAT, G. M. Scenes and Studies of Savage Life (London, 1868).

SWAN, JAMES G. The Indians of Cape Flattery (Smithsonian Contributions to Knowledge, vol. XVI, part 8. pp. 1–106, Washington, 1870).

Chipewyan

A Northern Athabascan group extending over a considerable area in Canada, from the Churchill River to Lake Athabaska and the Great Slave Lake. They are sometimes mistaken for the Algonkian Chippewa (Ojibwa). Their number is set at nearly 1800.

BIBLIOGRAPHY

HEARNE, SAMUEL. Journey from Prince of Wales's Fort in Hudson's Bay, to the Northern Ocean. (London, 1795).

PETITOT, E. Traditions indiennes du Canada nord-ouest. (Alençon, 1887.)

RUSSELL, FRANK. Explorations in the Far North. (Des Moines, 1898.)

GODDARD, P. E. Chipewyan Texts. *(Anthropological Papars American Museum of Natural History,* vol. X, pp. 1–65.)

LOWIE, ROBERT H. Chipewyan Tales. *(ibid.,* vol. X, pp. 171–200.)

Ten'a

Anvik is a village on the Anvik River, a tributary of the Yukon River, about four hundred miles from its mouth and about one hundred and twenty-five miles from the coast.   The village is populated by the most northern of one of the Athabascan peoples, called Ingalik or Ingilik by the Russians, meaning Lousy, according to Jetté, an Eskimo name, or Tinneh or Ten'a, a native name.   The native name for Anvik is Gudrinethchax; it means Middle People, a place name, as are the other native names for the river villages.

The only published accounts of the Ten'a are those of the French missionary Jetté, stationed at Konkrines and the American missionary Chapman, stationed at Anvik.   At the American mission Mr. Reed was educated, and his opportunities to observe his own people have been in certain particulars limited.   In spite of his knowledge of English, and of American culture he is, however, unusually unsophisticated and he has been an acute and sympathetic observer of the life at Anvik, White and Indian. He is therefore what we frequently look for among school-taught Indians but rarely find—a qualified interpreter of native culture.   As the time available for working with him was quite limited, he was asked to present his information as if he were telling the story of an Anvik villager from birth to death.

BIBLIOGRAPHY

JETTÉ, J.   On the Medicine-Men of the Ten'a.   (*Journal of the Royal Anthropological Institute,* XXXVII [1907], 157–188.)

    On Ten'a Folklore (*ibid.* XXXVIII [1908], 298–367).

    On the Superstitions of the Ten'a Indians, (*Anthropos,* VI [1911], 95–108, 241–259, 602–615, 699–723).

    Riddles of the Ten'a Indians.   (*ibid.* VIII [1913], 181–201, 630–651.)

CHAPMAN, JOHN W.   Notes on the Tinneh Tribe of Anvik, Alaska.   (Congrès International des Américanistes, 15th Session, II, 7–38. Quebec, 1907.)

    Athabascan Traditions from the Lower Yukon.   (*Journal of American Folklore,* XVI [1903], 180–5.)

    Ten'a Texts and Tales.   (Pub. American Ethnological Society, VI, Leyden, 1914.)

Eskimos

The Eskimos occupy the whole Arctic coast from Behring Strait to Labrador and Greenland. They have also a few isolated villages on the extreme eastern point of Siberia. Notwithstanding a general uniformity of cultural life, there are marked differences between the Eskimo of the region west of the Mackenzie River and the eastern group. The Eskimo of Greenland are considerably modified by European contact. The group to which the tale refers are the Eskimo of Baffin Land, the large island extending from Hudson Strait northward and forming the west coast of Davis Strait and Baffin Bay, more particularly of the eastern shore of the island. The total number of individuals living in this area does not exceed 400.

Individuals belonging to these villages make extensive travels and come into contact with the natives of the northern coast of Hudson Bay and of the mainland northwest of Hudson Bay. Only Eskimo tribes are known to them.

The principal descriptions of these tribes are found in the following publications:

Boas, Franz. The Central Eskimo (6th Annual Report of the Bureau of Ethnology, Washington, 1888).

The Eskimo of Baffin Land and Hudson Bay (Bulletin, vol. XX, American Museum of Natural History, New York, 1901, 1907).

Other important publications may be found in the bibliographies attached to these volumes. The most important recent publication on the Eskimo of Greenland is:

Thalbitzer, William. The Ammassalik Eskimo; Meddelelser om Gronland, vol. XXXIX, Copenhagen, 1914.

ILLUSTRATOR'S NOTES

Takes-the-pipe, a Crow Warrior

The center, a pair of Crazy-Dog sashes. Also the figures connected with the warrior's visions—the moon, the buffalo, the bear. The stick used by the Hammer Stick Society; that used in counting "coup"; that planted in the ground by the aspirant for the rank of chief, as he leads in fight. At top, the moths the boy rubbed on his chest; Takes-the-pipe's moccasins; at bottom his captured horses. At sides, a skin ornament worn by Crow medicine men.

Smoking-star, a Blackfoot Shaman

A Blackfoot medicine man's tepee, by the shore of a lake, in the foothills. The border, typical beadwork pattern. At bottom, a medicine pipe, a medicine bundle, wand used by medicine man, and beavers.

Little-wolf Joins the Medicine Lodge

Center, a medicine lodge, roofed with sheets of birch-bark; the walls are upright sticks. At sides, otter-skin medicine bags. Below, a ceremonial drum of wood covered with stretched buckskin. A medicine pipe. The shells used in "shooting medicine," with their bead necklaces. At top, gourd medicine rattles. The patterns are from typical beadwork and the dyed mats used in lodges.

Thunder-cloud, a Winnebago Shaman, Relates and Prays

Center, the Beings invoked in the prayers, appearing in the smoke from a medicine pipe. Ornament, typical beadwork.

How Meskwaki Children Should Be Brought Up

Central background, typical beadwork.   Center, a warrior's neck ornament with bear claws; woman's necklace of bone and beads; crossed below, a war club and the stick used in the ball game.   At sides, the beaded cylinders are those through which a woman's hair passes; the long straps hang as ornaments.   Typical moccasins.

In Montagnais Country

An Indian calling moose with a birch-bark horn.   Across top a ceremonial carrying-strap.   Snowshoes.   At sides, knives, spearhead, fishhook.   At bottom, birch-bark baskets, wooden spoons, ceremonial pipe. The patterns, typical beadwork.

Hanging-flower, the Iroquois

Four masks used by the Society of False Faces.   A turtle-shell medicine rattle.   Tomahawks and war clubs.   A tall basket, and the wooden pestle used by the women for making corn meal.

The Thunder Power of Rumbling-wings

Rumbling-wings invoking the Thunder Bird.   At bottom, the little mask Rumbling-wings wears.   War clubs.

Tokulki of Tulsa

At top sides, beaded pouches.   Sides, cloth with beaded ornament.   At bottom, a ceremonial drum, of earthenware with buckskin stretched over it; ball-game sticks; balls; spoons; the head ornament of white deer hairs and feathers worn by the ball players.   Center, reference to the myth that the eclipse of the sun is caused by a giant toad.   At sides of center, gourd medicine rattles and a carved stone pipe.

Slender-maiden of the Apache

Upper center, the mask with its fan-like ornament, worn in the dance. A girl's buckskin shirt; below it the pendant ornament worn at her waist. An Apache basket.   At either side of shirt, ornaments of cloth and cut-out leather.   The other ornaments, typical beadwork.   The oak-leaf borders indicate the Apache use of acorns.

When John the Jeweler was Sick

The center is a part of one of the Navaho sand paintings made for curing ceremonial. The figures are supernaturals, the central objects represent growing corn; the bent rectangular figure, the rainbow. In the four corners are dance masks used in the same ceremony, and at the bottom is the rug, with the various ceremonial objects laid upon it, which is a feature of the ceremony.

Waiyautitsa of Zuñi, New Mexico

The figure is a conventionalization showing how the girls let the bang fall over the face in the dance; the painted flat board headdress worn by them in the harvest dance, and the tablet they carry in each hand. The jar, out of which the figure grows, is a typical Zuñi water jar. The bowl at top is a sacred meal bowl. The side borders are from altar paintings, showing animal spirits. Prayer sticks.

Zuñi Pictures

Background and borders, a paraphrase of the ceremonial blanket, of Hopi weave. At bottom, the box with notched stick on top, used in the sword-swallowing ceremony. Over it, the war-god image. The sticks with turkey feathers are the "swords" that are swallowed. Zuñi masks.

Havasupai Days

View in Cataract Cañon. Bow and skin quivers. Cooking bowls of earthenware. Horn ladles. A carrying-basket.

Earth-tongue, a Mohave

View of the Needles, on Colorado River. Above, Spiders, Scorpion, Ant, Serpent. The two Ravens. Below, bow, arrows, war clubs, pottery utensils.

The Chief Singer of the Tepecano

The landscape pictures the belief in the omnipresence of the sacred serpent in nature's manifestations: the storm cloud, rain, springs, rivers, wind. The hawk is a sacred bird. The ornament is typical of a rich variety of patterns; those used here are largely rain or water symbols. Ears of corn, and under the shield, the conventional representation of the steel for striking fire.

The Understudy of Tezcatlipoca

Background, a reconstitution of the vanished temple in Mexico City; the data for this are very meagre.   At top, the great stone Aztec calendar. At sides, the serpent motif.   Below, the carving or bowlder, still existing, which records the taking of Cuernavaca.

How Holon Chan Became the True Man of His People

From the existing remains of temples, and from various details of the same period, a reconstitution has here been made of the color and form that may have characterized the doorway in which Holon Chan stood at sunset.   His figure is arrived at in somewhat the same way: from the author's description and from the highly complicated and conventionalized detail of the sculptures.

The Toltec Architect of Chichen Itza

Center, the stone ring through which, in the ball game, the ball was thrown.   Background, a detail from the great colored frieze upon the interior walls of one of the temples.   Sides, stone columns, representing the Plumed Serpent, at either side of the doorway of the Ball Court Temple.   Above, two conventional plumed serpents.

Wixi of the Shellmound People

The landscape is the Ellis Island Mound in San Francisco Bay.   Below, shell pendants, necklaces, fishhooks, beads.

All Is Trouble Along the Klamath

A view of the Klamath.   Typical patterns.

Sayach'apis, a Nootka Trader

At sides, the human figures are wooden house posts.   At top, two masks; one at left represents a mythical bird; one at right, the wolf mask. Center, a Nootka drum, painted with symbols of Thunder Bird, Plumed Serpent and Whale.   The figures in background, conventionalized whales. At bottom, a mask representing a cuttlefish.   Behind it, Sayach'apis paddling his canoe.   At sides, painted canoe-paddles and clubs used to kill seals.

Cries-for-salmon, a Ten'a Woman

At top, two dance masks. At bottom wooden bowls. Center, a ceremonial figure representing Salmon. A woman's bag, made of fish skin, embroidered and painted. Bone awls. Two little ornaments at central sides are bobbins.

An Eskimo Winter

The arctic hare, the ptarmigan, the seal. Below, caribou, feeding. Above them a kayak. In borders, fish and seal spears, bows and arrows, skinning knives.